ISBN 978-90-04-75145-3

Full text of the General Course published in May 2025 in the *Recueil des cours*, Vol. 446.

Cover photograph: *The Kiss of Peace and Justice*, 1654. Laurent de La Hyre (French, 1606-1656). Oil on canvas; framed: 68.5 x 89 x 6.5 cm (26 15/16 x 35 1/16 x 2 9/16 in.); unframed: 54.9 x 76.2 cm (21 5/8 x 30 in.). The Cleveland Museum of Art, John L. Severance Fund 1971.102.

THE HAGUE ACADEMY OF INTERNATIONAL LAW

A collection of law lectures in pocketbook form

BRILL | NIJHOFF

2025

Natural Justice in Recognition and Enforcement of Foreign Judgments

Natural Justice in Recognition and Enforcement of Foreign Judgments

ANDREW DICKINSON

TABLE OF CONTENTS

ACKNOWLEDGEMENTS

I would like to thank The Hague Academy, and its director, Jean-Marc Thouvenin, for inviting me to deliver a special course of lectures on a topic that I have long found interesting. Members of staff at the Academy, in particular Sabine Amiel, Andrea Kramer and Anna Vasilyeva, have offered valuable guidance and support in preparation for the course.

The bulk of this work was completed during a period of research leave granted by the University of Oxford and by my College, St Catherine's. During this period, I was fortunate to have the opportunity to visit the University of Sydney Law School, Notre Dame Law School (as Global Visiting Professor), New York University School of Law (as Scholar in Residence) and the Max Planck Institute for Comparative and International Private Law in Hamburg, using their libraries and other facilities to advance my research. I would like to thank members of the faculty at these institutions for their kindness in welcoming me, for material support and for valuable discussions about my research topic. Vivienne Bath and Jeanne Huang (Sydney), Marcus Cole, Paul Miller and Monica Caro (Notre Dame), Franco Ferrari and Linda Silberman (NYU) and Ralf Michaels (MPI) were gracious and accommodating hosts.

In a project in which I have often found myself straying beyond my core expertise, and sometimes beyond my comfort zone, I have been able to rely on advice, assistance and insight from friends and colleagues in many institutions. In addition to those mentioned above, I am indebted to the following (with apologies to those whom I have troubled but omitted here through negligence): in Oxford, Thomas Adams, Roxana Banu,

Adrian Briggs, Timothy Endicott, Wolfgang Ernst, Brooke Marshall, Edwin Peel, Sophie Ryan, Johannes Ungerer; and in other places, Tobias Lutzi (Universität Augsburg); Maggie Gardner (Cornell Law School); John Cairns (University of Edinburgh); Mary Keyes (Griffith University); Dicky Tsang (City University of Hong Kong); Wouter Druwé, Geert van Calster (KU Leuven); Francisco Garcimartin (Universidad Autónoma de Madrid); Roger Alford, Samuel L. Bray, Christian Burset, Diane Desierto, Bruce Huber, Mary-Ellen O'Connell, Jeffrey Poganowski, Francisco J. Urbina (Notre Dame Law School); Peter B. Kutner (University of Oklahoma); Rick Verhagen (Radboud Universiteit and Clifford Chance); Samuel Fulli-Lemaire (University of Strasbourg); Luke Nottage (University of Sydney); Felix Berner (University of Tübingen).

Above all, I would like to thank my family – Ann Marie, Jonathan and Nell – for putting up with my absences of body and mind during the year. Without their support, the lectures and the publication that followed it would not have come to fruition.

CHAPTER I

FOREIGN JUDGMENTS IN THE CONFLICT OF LAWS

A. Introduction

1. Courts dispense justice. They resolve disputed questions of legal entitlement, matters of right or wrong.

2. The judges who perform this function within a political society exercise authority to adjudicate on its behalf and in its name. From the earliest times, this adjudicatory authority has been exercised not only in disputes between those who are members, in the fullest sense, of a given society but also those between members and outsiders and, to a more limited extent, between two or more outsiders[1]. It has also been exercised on occasions when the subject matter of the disputed legal entitlement is somehow extraneous to the political society whose court is called upon to decide the dispute[2].

---

[1] In Rome, the peregrine praetor oversaw the administration of justice in cases involving non-Roman citizens (Institutes of Gaius, 1.6; Digest 1.2.2.28 (Pomponius, *Enchiridion*); David Daube, "The Peregrine Praetor" (1951), 41 *Journal of Roman Studies* 66).

[2] In the courts of England and Wales, where the system of trying cases originally demanded that the jury be drawn from the town, parish or hamlet where the facts giving rise to the dispute were stated to have arisen, the law drew a distinction between "local actions" in which the claimant had to specify in his pleading the true venue and "transitory actions" in which the claimant could lay the venue in any county. For transitory actions, and local actions where the cause of action had arisen in England but some other relevant fact had occurred outside the realm, it became acceptable for the pleader to use a fiction, for example, that the relevant fact had occurred "in the parish of St Mary le Bow in the Ward

Courts today apply a wide variety of legal rules, gathered and discussed in textbooks under the heading "rules of jurisdiction", to decide which cases with an external aspect they can and will hear and which they cannot or will not.

3. Judgments are the vessels by which justice is dispensed. They are themselves laws, limited in their sphere of application according to the nature and the subject matter of the dispute[3]. Judgments produce a variety of legal effects, falling into the following categories.

Dispositive: a judgment may alter existing statuses, rights and obligations. For example, a judgment *in rem* may affect title to property and a judgment *in personam* may supersede and extinguish a pre-existing obligation.

---

of Cheap" (Sir William Holdsworth, *A History of English Law*, London: Sweet & Maxwell, 1924, Vol. 5, pp. 140-142; Moffatt Hancock, *Torts in the Conflict of Laws*, Ann Arbor: University of Michigan Press, 1942, pp. 1-5; *British South Africa Co* v. *Companhia de Moçambique* [1893] AC 602 (UKHL)).

This fiction, harmless when used in these ways to oil the wheels of justice, was later put to more contentious use in supporting the exercise of jurisdiction over persons locally present, however brief their sojourn and regardless of the degree of connection between the dispute and the forum (see *Burnham* v. *Superior Court of California, Marin County* (1990) 495 US 604, 610-612 (Scalia J.), but cf. *ibid.*, 633-635 (Brennan J.). See further below, [153]-[159] and [356]-[359].

3 "A *lex specialis*, ruling some particular relation", Carl Ludwig von Bar, *Das Internationale Privat- und Strafrecht*, Hannover: Hahn'sche hofbuchhandlung, 1862, Book 4, [125], p. 465, trans. George Robert Gillespie, *International Law: Private and Criminal*, Boston: Soule & Bugbee, 1883, p. 564. Von Bar gives a very detailed treatment to the subject of foreign judgments in his later work, *Theorie und Praxis des Internationalen Privatrechts*, Hannover: Hahn'sche Buchhandlung, 1889, Vol. 2, Book 11, [411]-[472], pp. 409-546, trans. George Robert Gillespie, *The Theory and Practice of Private International Law*, Edinburgh, William Green 1892, pp. 887-1005. See below, [250].

Preclusive: a judgment may prevent further disputation of a particular claim or issue.

Constitutive: a judgment may generate new rights and obligations, for example, an obligation to pay a sum by way of damages or to perform a contractually mandated act.

Facultative: a judgment may enliven powers vested in the court or another person to take steps to ensure that it is an effective means of resolving the parties' dispute, for example, through the seizure of a losing party's assets to satisfy an obligation to pay a sum of money or loss of liberty as a punishment for failure to comply with a court order.

4. As with other types of law, judgments frequently have, or purport to have, effects beyond the sphere of influence of the political society under whose authority they were issued. For example, property to which a judgment *in rem* relates may move across borders; one of the parties to the dispute, or a connected person, may initiate fresh proceedings elsewhere with the same or a related subject matter; the judgment may in terms require something to be done overseas; the measures available locally to render a judgment effective against the losing party or its assets may be inadequate, with other legal orders better placed to secure compliance.

5. In these circumstances, it is necessary to enquire whether a judgment issued by a court dispensing justice within the legal order of one political society (the "adjudicating order") can be recognised or enforced within another political society's legal order (the "receiving order"), and if so on what terms.

6. *Recognition* takes place when the receiving order adopts or carries across [4] at least some of the legal effects

[4] The language used here is deliberately imprecise to accommodate the range of legal theories that explain the transposition of the laws of one legal order to that of another. See Ralf Michaels, "Tertiary Rules", Chap. 16, in Nico Krisch

that the judgment had under the law of the adjudicating order. This most frequently applies to the *dispositive*, *preclusive* and *constitutive* effects of judgments. For example, (1) a court in the receiving order tasked with determining title to an item of tangible movable property may apply the adjudicating order's judgment *in rem* fixing proprietary entitlements to that thing (dispositive), (2) a court in the receiving order adjudicating upon a contractual dispute may adopt the conclusions reached by a court in the adjudicating order when the same or a similar dispute had previously been litigated before it on common questions of fact or law (preclusive), or (3) a court in the receiving order dealing with insolvency proceedings may accept that the debtor had been adjudged by a court in the adjudicating order to be indebted to the petitioning creditor (constitutive).

7. *Enforcement* takes place when the receiving order not only *recognises* the legal effects of another legal order's judgment in one or more of the ways described but also accords specific legal effects to that judgment to promote its effectiveness in resolving the underlying dispute. For example, (1) by ordering the delivery up of property to the person adjudged to be entitled to it by a judgment *in rem*, (2) by using its procedural powers to dismiss an attempt to re-run a contractual claim that had failed before a court in the adjudicating order or (3) by ordering seizure of the debtor's assets to satisfy a money judgment.

8. In these cases, the laws and legal institutions of the adjudicating order and the receiving order combine to promote the just resolution of disputes. This is advantageous to the political societies that they represent. Without effective mechanisms to bring legal disputes to an end, aggrieved parties may resort to contested

---

(ed.), *Entangled Legalities beyond the State*, Cambridge: Cambridge University Press, 2021.

measures of self-help or vengeance, feel resentment as the victim of an injustice or break off previously fruitful and mutually beneficial relations.

9. In the subject known as the conflict of laws, or private international law, questions of the recognition and enforcement of foreign judgments have often been treated as an appendage to more detailed treatment of questions of (adjudicatory) jurisdiction and choice of law in cases with a foreign element[5]. They are, however, a fascinating microcosm of the challenges that the subject presents – to address and resolve problems generated by the interconnected spheres of influence of two or more political societies through techniques that seek to rationalise and, where possible, co-ordinate their laws. Rules of recognition and enforcement operate at the interface between the adjudicatory authority of courts in distinct legal orders

10. The terms "political society"[6], "legal order"[7] and "sphere of influence" used here differ from those commonly used by judges and legal writers in this field.

---

[5] See, for example, Lord Collins of Mapesbury and Professor Jonathan Harris (eds.), *Dicey, Morris & Collins – The Conflict of Laws*, London: Sweet & Maxwell, 16th ed., 2022 [1–004].

[6] John Locke uses "political society" interchangeably with "civil society" to describe "persons who are united into one body and have a common established law and judicature to appeal to", Locke, *Two Treatises*, 2nd treatise, Chap. 7, [87], p. 324.

The term "civil society" is also used by English translators of the works of Samuel Pufendorf (from the original Latin, *civitas*) and Emer de Vattel (from the original French, *Société Civile*). Although evocative, its usage here would risk confusion with its deployment in other contexts to describe non-State forms of social cohesion, Craig Calhoun (ed.), *Dictionary of the Social Sciences*, Oxford: Oxford University Press, "civil society", pp. 69-70. For that reason, the term "political society" is used here.

[7] "Legal order" refers to the lawmaking and law-enforcing institutions of a particular society, including its legislature, government agencies and courts.

This is a deliberate choice, borne of a desire to avoid committing (at least at this early stage in our enquiry) to a "rulemaker centred" account of the subject, casting "legal sovereigns" as the lead actors and defined territorial areas as the theatres in which they act.

11. Rather than fixing our attention on rulemakers, we should at least countenance the possibility of pursuing a more holistic, anthrocentric approach to our subject, taking seriously the condition, needs and desires of the eight billion or so human beings who inhabit this planet and for whose mutual protection and advantage political societies supposedly exist. Framing the enquiry in this way allows us to see that "sovereignty" and "the State", and "territory" and "country", are abstract concepts. Although they have served and continue to serve useful purposes in legal reasoning, they are not self-evident truths and do not fully expose the reasons why foreign judgments are recognised and enforced.

12. The Supreme Court of Canada expressed this sentiment in the following way[8]:

> "Modern-day commercial transactions require prompt reactions and effective remedies. The advent of the Internet has heightened the need for appropriate tools. On the one hand, frontiers remain relevant to national identity and jurisdiction, but on the other hand, the globalization of commerce and mobility of both people and assets make them less so. The law and the justice system are servants of society, not the reverse."

This way of thinking will be familiar to students of ancient and modern accounts of the law of nature *(ius naturale)*. These envision law as but one means to a

---

[8] *Pro Swing Inc.* v. *Elta Golf Inc.* [2006] 2 SCR 612, [1] (Deschamps J.). See also *Gray* v. *Formosa* [1963] P 259, 271, ("rules of private international law are made for men and women - not the other way round").

common end, defined in terms of human flourishing or wellbeing[9].

13. Natural law accounts were influential in shaping legal science in the seventeenth, eighteenth and early nineteenth centuries. Writers of great learning and distinction sought to account for the existence of political societies and the legal institutions serving them, as well as their relationships with each other – the so-called law of nations, more vividly captured in the French, *droit des gens*. They laid the foundations and provided the construction materials for modern doctrines of public and private international law.

14. In the nineteenth and twentieth centuries, the influence of natural law accounts waned. No single reason can be given for this shift[10]. In the West, natural law approaches had been closely linked to theological explanations of human relations with God, but this connection became less influential as, first, the spheres of

---

[9] Writers on natural law use a variety of sources and techniques, reason in different ways and identify and pursue different ends. What they all have in common is a concern with advancement of the human condition and with the role played by political societies and by law in that process. See John Finnis, "Natural Law Theories", in Edward N. Zalta (ed.), *The Stanford Encyclopedia of Philosophy*, Summer 2020 ed., https://plato.stanford.edu/entries/natural-law-theories/, [3] ("Law, fit to take a directive place in practical reasoning towards morally sound judgment, is for the sake of human persons: all the members of the community regulated by that law and all other persons within that law's ambit").

[10] See, with particular reference to the United States' experience, Stuart Banner, *The Decline of Natural Law – How American Lawyers Once Used Natural Law and Why They Stopped*, Oxford: Oxford University Press, 2021. In Europe at least, the law of nature was closely associated with philosophical advocates of the revolution in France and greatly discredited by the horrifying events of *La Terreur* and the wars that followed Napoleon's rise to power (see below, [202]-[204]).

law and religion became separate[11] and, second, religious observance declined in many societies. A new age of scientific enquiry fuelled scepticism about scholarly theories that reasoned from first principles, rather than by deduction from observed and measured patterns of behaviour. Technological advances drove societal changes, leading legal rules to become at the same time both more complex and more widely accessible[12]. In many legal orders, unwritten civil law was replaced by written codifications[13].

15. In this period, the age of the "grand sovereign" reached its apogee. As the First World War approached, the British Empire held sway over almost 423 million people, almost a quarter of the world's population at the time[14]. Other nations (Belgium, France, Germany, Italy, Portugal and Russia) retained significant colonial power outside their municipal territories.

16. Legal positivist theories, narrowing the focus of enquiry to define law in terms of the particular expressions of the will of an abstract, authoritative figure, the "sovereign", came to the fore[15]. In the imperial age, it is unsurprising that legal scholars sought to place these supreme rulers, rather than the human beings whose obedience they demanded, at the centre of their accounts of the legal universe.

---

11 Banner (n. 10), Chap. 4.

12 *Ibid.*, Chap. 5.

13 Section III.F.

14 The 1911 census gave the total population of the Empire at 422,963,684, with an estimated land area of 13,318,000 square miles (c. 345 million square kilometres) (source: Canada Year Book 1934-1935, p. 165 (table)). The Population Division of the United Nations Secretariat estimates the world population in 1910 at 1.75 billion (United Nations Secretariat *The World at Six Billion* (UN Document ESA/P/WP154, 12 October 1999), p. 5 (table)).

15 John Austin, *The Province of Jurisprudence Determined*, London: John Murray, 1832, Lecture V. See Section III.E.3, 4 and 5.

17. Although the natural law tradition faded into the background in juristic reasoning, its rootstock remained embedded in the legal ordering. Indeed, it enjoyed something of a revival as the twentieth century progressed[16]. Three aspects of this reversal of fortune merit our attention. First, the renewed emphasis placed on fundamental human rights in the international legal order following the cataclysmic loss of life and destruction of human society in the First and Second World Wars[17]. Second, a strengthening belief in the principle of self-determination[18] accelerating the process of decolonisation, particularly in the post-war period[19]. Third, economic, political and technological drivers resulting in a rapid growth of commerce and human mobility, overcoming – or at least daring to overcome – physical barriers erected by a global order centred on theories of sovereignty and territoriality[20]. In more recent times, the reaction of our natural environment to the intensification of human manipulation of the

---

[16] Banner (n. 10), Chap. 9; also Louis Le Fur, "La théorie du droit naturel depuis le XVIIe siècle et la doctrine moderne" (1928) 18 *Recueil des cours* 259, 349-365; John M. Kelly, *A Short History of Western Legal Theory*, Oxford: Clarendon Press, 1992 pp. 418-425.

[17] Universal Declaration of Human Rights, adopted by the General Assembly of the United Nations on 10 December 1948; European Convention on Human Rights, opened for signature on 3 November 1950; Inter-American Convention on Human Rights, opened for signature in San José, 22 November 1969; African Charter of Human and Peoples' Rights, adopted by the Organisation of African Unity on 1 June 1981; Asian Human Rights Charter, declared in Kwanju on 17 May 1948. See Section III.H.

[18] United Nations Charter, signed in San Francisco on 26 June 1945, Article 1 (2).

[19] R. Iniyan Ilango, "The Colonial Legacy of the Right to Self-Determination", UNA-UK Magazine, 22 October 2018, https://una.org.uk/magazine/2018-1/colonial-legacy-right-self-determination.

[20] Section II.I.4.

Earth's resources has reinforced the fragility of these contrivances.

18. In some legal orders, a visible trace of the earlier influence of natural law reasoning survives. They retain the term "natural justice" to describe fundamental principles of procedural fairness to be observed by those exercising decision-making authority. In the English common law world, this terminology captures a range of circumstances in which serious defects in the adjudicating order's decision-making processes justify a refusal by the receiving order to recognise or enforce the decision. Although that historical marker has disappeared elsewhere, other legal orders control the recognition and enforcement of foreign judgments using rules that substantially correspond in their rationale, function and content to the common law's principles of natural justice[21].

19. This prompts the question whether principles of natural law not only operate as part of the set of reasons why a foreign judgment *may not be* recognised or enforced but can also help to explain why foreign judgments *should be* recognised and enforced. The argument in favour of that proposition can be briefly summarised – in order to promote the peaceful conditions that are essential for our species to flourish, it is necessary to establish mechanisms for the just resolution of disputes that are effective not only within but also across the political societies engaged in this common human enterprise.

B. *Outline*

20. With these introductory points in mind, this study of the principles governing the recognition and enforcement of foreign judgments will take the following path.

---

[21] Section IV.B.3 and 4.

First, we will examine how influential seventeenth and eighteenth century accounts of the law of nature drew upon the authors' appraisal of the human condition to explain the emergence and the authority of political societies and the role of judges in revolving disputes, as well as the relationships existing between distinct political societies.

Second, we will consider how writers and judges dealing with problems that we now identify as belonging to the conflict of laws adopted and utilised this natural law toolbox, as the rules that we apply today to regulate foreign judgments began to take shape.

Third, we will trace the development of foreign judgments law during the nineteenth and twentieth centuries, as the influence of natural law ideas ebbed and flowed, considering both national practice and the views of the some of most influential scholars of the period.

Fourth, we will examine the legacy of natural law reasoning in the common law world, in the form of the principles of "natural justice", as well as the counterparts of these principles in other legal systems and in international instruments.

The concluding section will put the case for "renaturalising" the law in this area, highlighting the utility and vitality of the natural law toolbox in this important facet of the conflict of laws (private international law).

21. The account given here will focus on judgments given in proceedings that are concerned with interpersonal obligations and that are contentious rather than collaborative. This is not to underestimate the importance of other kinds of judgments, including those relating to things *(in rem)* or personal status, or to deny that natural law ideas may contribute to our understanding of their effectiveness between legal orders.

By narrowing our enquiry in this way, we will be able to delve into some of the intricacies of the subject and, hopefully, to highlight the importance of these ideas for our understanding of the past, appreciation of the present and aspirations for the future. Key components of the natural law toolbox *(constrained natural liberty; equality; the promotion of peaceful relations; duties of humanity; the administration of justice)*, applied to individual relationships, to the relationships of individuals with the political societies to which they belong or with which they engage, and to the relationships of distinct political societies *inter se*, contribute to a framework that (in Chap. II) will frame an account of the earlier and later development of conflict of laws rules governing the recognition and enforcement of judgments (Chap. III), account for the modern legacy of "natural justice" principles in the common law world and their counterparts in other systems (Chap. IV) and inform our understanding of the current shape and possible future direction of the law in this area (Chap. V).

CHAPTER II

A NATURAL LAW TOOLBOX

A. Natural law and natural justice

22. "The doctrine of natural law is as old as philosophy."[22] For as long as humans have had the time

[22] Heinrich A. Rommen, *Die ewige Wiederkehr des Naturrechts*, Leibzig: Jacob Hedner, 1936, trans. Thomas R. Hanley, *The Natural Law – A Study in Legal and Social History and Philosophy*, St Louis, B. Herder, 1947, in the new edition, Indianapolis: Liberty Fund, 1998, p. 3.
In the first chapter of his work, Rommen (a refugee from Nazi Germany to the United States, where he taught at Georgetown University) gives a valuable account of early, Greek and Roman, writing before turning, in Chapter 2, to consider the "Age of Scholasticism", from the 11th century. Writers in this era – most prominently, Thomas Aquinas (1225-1274) – combined Christian theological doctrine with Aristotleian and Stoic accounts and Roman juristic commentary to develop detailed accounts of "the natural moral law", being "a judgment of reason which presents actions as commanded of forbidden by the Author of reason, because the light of reason shows them to be in agreement or disagreement with man's essential nature; and at the same time reason judges that God wills that which accords with nature: essential being ought to be realised" (*ibid.*, p. 57).
In keeping with this tradition, the judgment of the Court of Exchequer Chamber in *Calvin's* Case (1608) 7 Co Rep 1a defines the law of nature as "that which God at the time of creation of infused into his heart, for his preservation and direction; and this is *lex aeterna*, the moral law".
Later Scholastic scholars, notably Francisco de Vitoria and Francisco Suárez, fleshed out theories of a law of peoples *(ius gentium)* that laid the foundations of modern international law, see Peter Haggenmacher, "Sources in the Scholastic Legacy", Chap. 1 in Jean d'Aspremont and Samantha Besson, *The Oxford Handbook of the Sources of International Law*, Oxford: Oxford University Press, 2017.

and the inclination to think deeply, they have reflected on the nature of our species and its place in the world. In this tradition, recorded and passed down between generations, a central thread has been the ethical and political implications of the human condition, woven into normative accounts of interpersonal, societal and intersocietal relationships.

23. Accounts of natural law and natural justice[23], ancient and modern, remain valuable for legal scholars. The perspectives that they offer can nourish, test and refine our understanding of the ways that law develops and the role that it plays in our world. Today, the law of nature is no longer seen as a supreme legal ordering, sanctioned by divine providence, from which human laws cannot depart[24]. It is not necessary to commit ourselves here to a particular view on the jurisprudential question whether "natural law" qualifies as law in any meaningful sense or the surrounding framework as a legal system. We can proceed on the basis that the legal orders of political societies are constitutionally independent of natural law – the laws and judgments that they produce

---

See further Louis Le Fur, "La théorie" (n. 16), esp. 271-294; John Finnis, *Natural Law and Natural Rights*, Oxford: Clarendon Press, 1980, pp. 42-49 and 398-403.

[23] In this chapter, the term "natural justice" is used synonymously with the law of nature, or at least that part of the law of nature that concerns itself with questions of justice, whether distributive or compensatory (for the distinction, see Grotius, *Prize*, Chap. 2 (Prolegomena), [11a] (p. 37); also Finnis, *Natural Law and Natural Rights*, above, Chap. 7). A more specific meaning, still used today with respect to the reception of foreign judgments, will be examined and developed in later chapters (Chaps. IV and V).

[24] Richard H. Helmholz, *Natural Law in Court*, Cambridge: Harvard University Press, 2015, pp. 4-5. As this account of judicial practice in Europe, England and the United States reveals, tensions between natural law imperatives and positive rules of law were addressed principally by conforming statutory interpretation, *ibid.*, pp. 68-79, 112-121, 165-170.

may be systemically valid even if they conflict with a duty imposed by the law of nature[25].

24. Studying these texts can nonetheless strengthen our appreciation of legal history and allow us to trace patterns and flows in legal thought. Lawmakers have always sought inspiration, or reassurance, from accounts that set their localised activities against the backdrop of a wider, universal human endeavour. The insights to be gained from this enquiry may, in turn, prove valuable in assessing how our modern, positive rules of law can best be developed to promote the ethereal concept of the "common good" and to advance the common objectives of the political societies that represent and serve the planet's inhabitants. In this regard, we can agree with John Finnis' assertion that[26]:

> "A theory of natural law need not be undertaken primarily for the purpose of this providing a justified conceptual framework for descriptive social science. It may be undertaken . . . primarily to assist the practical reflections of those concerned to act, whether as judges or as statesmen or as citizens. But in either case, the undertaking cannot proceed securely without a knowledge of the whole range of human possibilities and opportunities, inclinations and capacities, a

---

[25] For discussion of these questions, see Finnis, *Natural Law and Natural Rights*, (n. 22) esp. Chaps. 1 and 12. Cf. Grotius, *War and Peace*, Book 2, Chap. 2, Title 5, p. 433 ("The civil law can enjoin nothing which the law of nature forbids, nor forbid any thing which that enjoins; yet it may restrain natural liberty, and prohibit what was naturally lawful. . ."). By the same reasoning, natural law is independent of civil law and does not depend on its approval or adoption by any political society.

[26] Finnis, *Natural Law and Natural Rights*, above, pp. 18-19. On the concept of the "common good", see Adrian Vermeule, *Common Good Constitutionalism*, Cambridge: Polity Press, 2022, Chap. 1; Finnis, *Natural Law and Natural Rights*, above, Chap. 6.

knowledge that requires the assistance of descriptive and analytical social science."

25. Within this vast body of knowledge, certain accounts are particularly deserving of our close attention. Alongside their historical and intellectual worth, they undoubtedly played a significant role in shaping the constitutional and legal frameworks that we study today, not least in the fields of public international law and the conflict of laws. The works in question date from the early seventeenth to mid-eighteenth century, a period associated not only with Enlightenment and Reason but also with War and Revolution[27]. In Europe, the Peace of Westphalia of 1648 brought an end to the calamitous Thirty Years War; the following year, the English King, Charles I, was executed after a bitterly fought civil war – a century of political turmoil was becalmed in 1689 by a peaceful invasion, bringing new rulers from the Netherlands and the declaration of a Bill of Rights; the War of the Spanish Succession, in which the battlefield extended beyond Europe to the colonies of the competing powers in North America, was brought to an end in 1713 by the Treaty of Utrecht; the Founding Fathers of the United States of America declared independence from Great Britain in 1776; the new nation, successful in its war against its former colonial power, adopted its Constitution in 1789, the same year that fermented the French Revolution and led to the fall of its monarchy and the creation of the First Republic three years later, followed by the Reign of Terror; as the eighteenth century closed, the French Revolutionary Wars and Napoleonic Wars drew in the major European powers. In China, in the seventeenth century, the transition between the Ming and Qing dynasties was only secured after a conflict

[27] For a valuable intellectual history of the period, see Anthony Pagden, *The Englightenment and Why It Still Matters*, Oxford: Oxford University Press, 2015.

lasting more than six decades and claiming an estimated twenty-five million human lives, the second most costly conflict in human history. As that conflict came to an end, war racked the Mughal Empire in India killing five million more.

26. A full study of the seminal natural legal texts of this period[28] is not possible within the framework of this study. This chapter will outline distinctive and important features of the accounts presented by authors whose works have been particularly influential. The account is thematic, identifying certain key tenets of these authors' accounts of the human condition, of the formation of political societies and the establishment of legal orders, and the relationships between those societies and between their legal orders. Particular attention will be paid to issues bearing upon the administration of justice and the resolution of disputes.

27. In opening with a brief biographical account of the authors whose works we will examine, note that, with the exception of Emer de Vattel (who was dogged by illness), all encountered significant difficulties in their lives by reason of their expression of political, theological or philosophical opinions[29]. The order follows the dates of publication of their principal works[30]. Cross-citations and detailed examination of particular arguments reveal that the earlier works influenced the later.

---

[28] For background, see Le Fur, "La théorie" (n. 16), esp. pp. 295-335.

[29] At this time, the three fields were closely intertwined.

[30] Where possible, the versions used here are readily available online, in print on demand versions or as student texts. When quoting from texts, *(a)* I have updated the language used in the English translation to improve accessibility, and *(b)* I have retained the author's original references to the masculine form of nouns and pronouns (e.g. man, men, mankind, he, his). In commentary, gender neutral terms have been used where possible.

28. Hugo de Groot (Grotius) (1583-1645), born in Delft, Holland[31]. Grotius, a child prodigy, was sentenced to life imprisonment in 1618 after finding himself on the wrong side of a politically contentious, theological dispute within the Dutch Republic. With the assistance of his wife, he escaped in 1621, spending time in Paris and (after a brief, but troubled, return to his home country) in Hamburg. In 1634, he was appointed Ambassador to France of the Kingdom of Sweden, a position that he held until 1644, a year before his death at Rostock.

29. Of Grotius' works, two are of particular interest to our enquiry. His commentary on the *Law of Prize and Booty (De Iure Praedae)*, completed in 1606 but not published in full until 1868[32], includes a specification by Grotius of the precepts of the law of nature. His three-volume work, *The Rights of War and Peace (De iure belli ac pacis)*[33], first published in 1625, contains a fuller account and ranks as one of the most influential works of scholarship in human history.

30. Thomas Hobbes (1588-1679), born in Malmsebury, England[34]. A scientist as well as a political philo-

[31] Source: John Miller, "Hugo Grotius", in Edward N. Zalta (ed.), *The Stanford Encyclopedia of Philosophy*, Spring 2021 ed., https://plato.stanford.edu/entries/grotius/.

[32] Grotius, *Prize*, see Introduction and Note on the Text, pp. xiii-xxiii.

[33] Grotius, *War and Peace*, see Book I, Introduction, pp. ix-xxiii. The edition principally used in this special course is the anonymous English translation (1738) based on the French translation (1724) by Jean Barbeyrac, Professor of Law at Groningen.
Barbeyrac (1674-1744), who also prepared French translations of Pufendorf's principal works (text to nn. 38 and 39), was a noted natural law scholar in his own right. See Tim Hochstrasser, "Conscience and Reason: The Natural Law Theory of Jean Barbeyrac" (1993) 36 *The Historical Journal* 289.

[34] Source: Stewart Duncan, "Thomas Hobbes", in Edward N. Zalta (ed.), *The Stanford Encyclopedia of Philosophy*, Summer 2022 ed., https://plato.stanford.edu/entries/hobbes/.

sopher, Hobbes spent the 1640s in exile in Paris, having been associated with the royalist cause in the English Civil War. There, he served as tutor to the future King Charles II. He returned in early 1652, following the publication of his best known work, *Leviathan*[35], but his influence at the royal court had waned, and he retired from public life, remaining intellectually active, in spite of deteriorating health, until his death. Alongside *Leviathan*, Hobbes' earlier work *On the Citizen (De Cive)* contains a clear and concise account of the precepts of natural law[36].

31. Samuel Pufendorf (1632-1694), born in Saxony during the Thirty Years War, the son of a Lutheran pastor[37]. Having studied at Leipzig, he travelled and worked in Denmark and Holland before taking up a professorship in philology and the law of nations in Heidelberg, moving in 1668 to take up a chair in the law of nature and nations and of ethics and philosophy at the University of Lund. It was there that he completed his best known work, *On the Law of Nature and Nations (De Jure Naturae et Gentium, Libro Octo)*[38], the content of which resulted in attempts by some of his colleagues to censor the work. The closure of the university as a result of Danish occupation during the Dutch War led Pufendorf to take up a position in the royal court in

[35] Hobbes, *Leviathan*, see Introduction and Note on the Text, pp. ix-xxxvii.

[36] Hobbes, *Citizen*, see Introduction, pp. viii-xxiii. This work was first published in 1642 during Hobbes' exile in Paris, with an unauthorised English translation in 1651, *ibid*, pp. xxxiv-xxxvii. The Latin edition used to prepare the translation referred to in this special course was published in Amsterdam in 1647.

[37] Principal source: Michael Seidler, "Pufendorf's Moral and Political Philosophy", in Edward N. Zalta (ed.), *The Stanford Encyclopedia of Philosophy*, Fall 2021 ed., https://plato.stanford.edu/entries/pufendorf-moral/.

[38] Pufendorf, *Nature and Nations*, see Introduction, pp. 11a-19a. The Latin edition used to prepare the translation referred to in this special course was published in Amsterdam in 1688.

Stockholm. This office took him to Berlin, where he died in 1694. Following the publication of his principal work in 1672, Pufendorf prepared a precis, *On the Duty of Man and Citizen according to the Law of Nature (De Officio Hominis et Civis Juxta Legem Naturalem)*, which appeared in print the following year[39].

32. John Locke (1632-1704), born in Somerset, England[40]. Locke studied and was elected a Student and Lecturer at Christ Church College, in the University of Oxford, where he trained as a physician and engaged in scientific and philosophical enquiry. His work in the field of medicine led to a meeting with Lord Ashley (later created 1st Earl of Shaftesbury) and a move to London where he found himself "at the very heart of English politics"[41], working in government and serving as Ashley's personal physician. Ashley's political demise and exile in the early 1680s put Locke in jeopardy resulting in his own flight to Holland in 1683. It was in this period that he completed his most important works, of which the most significant for our purposes is his *Two Treatises of Government*[42]. This work was published anonymously in 1689 (although the date given on the title page is 1690) and was not formally attributed to Locke in his lifetime, although its authorship was an open secret. In the same year, Locke had returned to England following the Glorious Revolution, returning to a role in government, which he held until his retirement in 1700.

---

39 Pufendorf, *Whole Duty*, see Introduction, pp. ix-xviii.

40 Source: William Uzgalis, "John Locke", in Edward N. Zalta (ed.), *The Stanford Encyclopedia of Philosophy*, Fall 2022 ed., https://plato.stanford.edu/entries/locke/.

41 *Ibid.*, [1.1].

42 Locke, *Two Treatises*. The edition used in this special course was prepared using a copy of the revised 1698 edition marked up by Locke and by his amanuensis, Pierre Coste, see Introduction, pp. 9-11 and Editorial Note, pp. 127-132.

33. Christian Wolff (1679-1754), born in Breslau[43]. Having studied in Jena and Leipzig, Wolff secured a position as Professor of Mathematics at the University of Halle, engaging also in philosophical enquiry. His writing on metaphysics led to a dispute with his colleagues, resulting in Wolff's removal from his post and banishment from Prussia in 1723. Welcomed in Marburg, in Hesse, he worked productively there before returning to Halle on the accession of Friedrich II. Less well known today than the other writers studied here, his work, *The Law of Nations Treated according to a Scientific Method*[44] is nonetheless deserving of attention for its detailed account of the law of nature as applied to the relations between nations. It was highly influential at the time and provided the springboard for the last of our sextet of natural law writers.

34. Emer de Vattel (1714-1763), born in Neuchâtel, the son of a Protestant clergyman[45]. Having studied in Geneva, under the tutelage of Jean-Jacques Burlamaqui, he took up a position in the court of the Elector of Saxony, working principally in his native Switzerland. Although struggling with ill-health and in straitened financial circumstances, Vattel was extremely productive and in 1757 published his most important work, *The Law of Nations (Le droit des gens)*[46], which improved

---

[43] Source: Matt Hettche and Corey Dyck, "Christian Wolff", in Edward N. Zalta (ed.), *The Stanford Encyclopedia of Philosophy*, Winter 2019 ed., https://plato.stanford.edu/entries/wolff-christian/.

[44] Wolff, *Nations*, see Introduction, pp. ix-xvi and Note on the Text, p. xxv.

[45] Source: "Vattel: Life and Works", Liberty Fund, https://oll.libertyfund.org/page/vattel-life-and-works.

[46] Vattel, *Nations*, see Introduction, pp. ix-xx and A Note on the Texts, pp. xxi-xxii.
An accessible version of the French text of the revised edition is available at https://gallica.bnf.fr/ark:/12148/bpt6k97657820 (vol 1) and https://gallica.bnf.fr/ark:/12148/bpt6k9765781k?rk=42918;4 (vol 2).

his personal position, although illness drove him to early retirement.

35. These writers, and others engaged in this field in the period, employ different tools and techniques of reasoning to reach their conclusions, which are equally divergent. For the most part, their reasoning is founded on propositions that they consider to be axiomatic, supplemented by their own and others' anthropological observations. They rely on a range of source materials – historical, philosophical, scientific and theological. Today, with the advantage of a more advanced state of scientific knowledge and a quarter of a millennium of empirical data, alongside immensely powerful research tools and a wealth of unquantifiable human experience, it is easy to yield to the temptation of critiquing the premises, evidence or paths of reasoning and to dismiss the conclusions as subjective, inconsistent or self-evident. Today's readers will recoil at some of the opinions expressed, which, although conforming to the political or social opinions and mores of the time, seem inconsiderate, prejudiced and in places inhumane.

36. Yet we should not lightly reject the notion that we, that is to say, the current occupants of this planet, share with these writers[47] the advantage of standing on the shoulders of giants. For just as they could not have pursued their endeavours with a blank slate, all of our computing power would avail us little[48], if it were not for the body of accumulated knowledge passed down to us, and the ever-present desire of a sufficient class of individuals in the preceding generations to learn,

---

[47] The concluding chapter (Sec. V.A) highlights the importance of considering and accounting for other perspectives bearing on the subject matter of this special course and on the conflict of laws more generally.

[48] If, that is, we allow ourselves the conceit that we would have this technology in the absence of centuries of scientific research.

to investigate, and to use their powers of reason to develop that body of knowledge as well their powers of communication to express their conclusions in a way that may prove useful to others [49]. Indeed, it is this thirst for and willingness to share knowledge and ideas, and not the ability to reason or use language in themselves, that distinguishes humankind from the other species with which we share our planet.

37. With that introduction, we can proceed to consider what insights these accounts offer us for our own enquiry, without treating them as infallible guides either to the human condition or to the science of law, in their own times or today. Natural law scholarship offers a toolbox of ideas, concepts and principles that remain valuable in framing and addressing the questions posed within the conflict of laws today.

B. Setting the scene

38. Writing towards the end of the eighteenth century, Immanuel Kant argued that "all men are entitled to present themselves in the society of others by virtue of their right to communal possession of the earth's surface" [50].

---

[49] Pufendorf, *Nature and Nations*, Book 2, Chap. 2, [2] (p. 155), "[N]ote all the things we now use in life and consider how difficult it would have been for any one to discover them all by his own powers, had not the guidance and labour of other men preceded him"; also Friedrich Carl von Savigny, *System des heutigen Römischen Rechts*, Berlin: Voet, Vol. 1, 1840, Preface, p. 1, "The individual work is as transient as the individual human being in his visible appearance; but imperishable is the thought that . . . every contribution of the individual, however small, finds its lasting life".

[50] Immanuel Kant, *Zum ewigen Frieden – Ein philosophischer Entwurf*, Königsberg, Friedrich Nicovius, 1795, trans. Hugh B. Nisbet, "Perpetual Peace", in Hans Reiss (ed.), *Kant – Political Writings*, Cambridge: Cambridge University Press, 2nd ed., 1991, pp. 93-130 (at p. 106); also Immanuel Kant,

He reasoned that[51]:

> "Since the earth is a globe they cannot disperse over an infinite area, but must necessarily tolerate one another's company. And no-one originally has any greater right than anyone else to occupy any particular portion of the earth."

39. Some basic set theory may help to develop this line of thought as the backdrop to our exploration of natural law ideas. Our universal set consists of all living humans, a number that reached 8 billion in November 2022 and is estimated to reach 9.7 billion by 2050[52]. Each of those human beings is a member of the set. If we then reimagine the globe as the rectangular area of a large sheet of paper or a screen[53] and locate each member of the set at a point that represents the individual's geographical position on the planet at a given point in time, we can achieve an approximate representation of the population distribution.

40. Of course, this map is and has always been constantly changing. If then we take out movements that are transitory, including travel for business or leisure, the map will now more closely represent the centres of individual lives – a more stable, but still constantly shifting, pattern of usual residence.

Metaphysische Anfangsgründe der Rechtslehre, Königsberg: Friedrich Nicovius, 1795, trans. (extract) Nisbet, "The Metaphysics of Morals", in Reiss (ed.), *Kant – Political Writings*, above, pp. 131-175 (at [62], pp. 172-173).

51 Kant, "Perpetual Peace", above, p. 106.

52 Source, United Nations, "Our Growing Population", https://www.un.org/en/global-issues/population#:~:text=Our%20growing%20population,and%202%20billion%20since%201998.

53 With apologies to those who debunked the conception that the Earth is flat.

41. In 1750, using the United Nations' population estimates[54], the mapping would have produced continental subsets shown in Figure 1 (population sizes in millions).

Figure 1

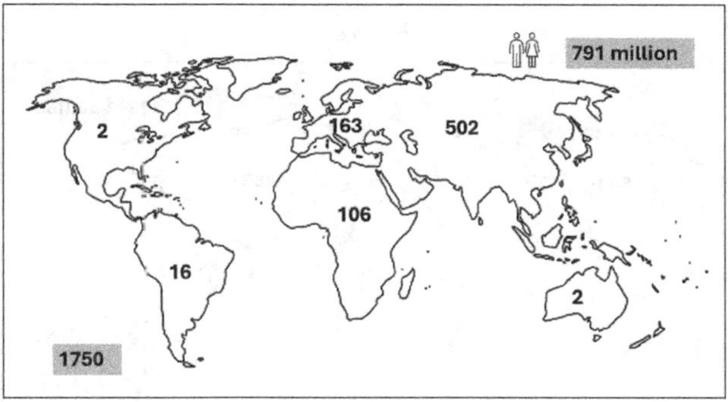

42. Updated to 2015, the projection shifts as shown in Figure 2 (population sizes in millions).

Figure 2

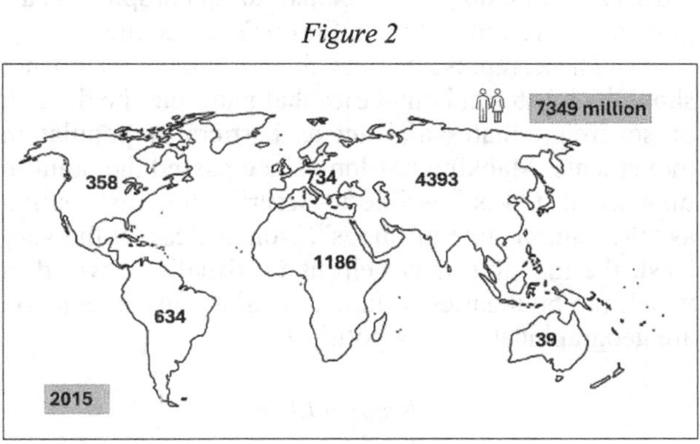

[54] Sources: *The World at Six Billion* (n. 14), p. 6; United Nations Department of Economic and Social Affairs, *UN World Population Prospects* (2015 revision), p. 1.

With a tenfold increase in the world's population in this quarter millennium, one may note, most strikingly, the increase in the population of the Americas from an estimate of less than twenty million to almost one billion.

43. The projection forward to 2100 (Fig. 3) shows changes that are just as striking.

Figure 3

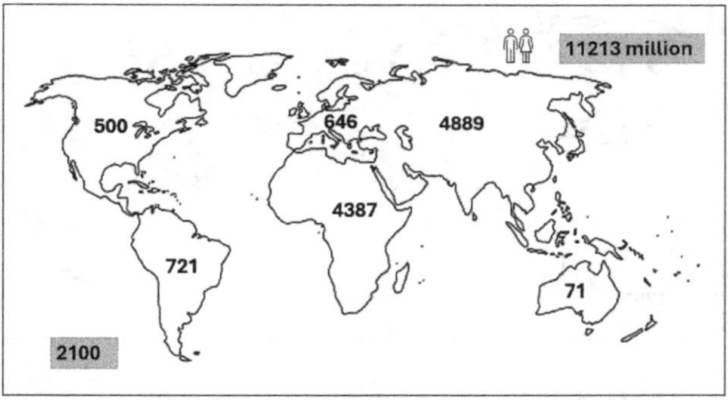

The world's population continues to grow, but while Africa's population is predicted to quadruple, Asia's population is stabilising and Europe's in decline.

44. These representations of the human set do not show the territorial boundaries that mark out the domain of sovereign States and act as barriers to population movements. Mankind has long since passed the point in time when it was possible to describe this distribution as "the natural state of things". Nonetheless, at the very least, the mapping may help us to visualise a world in which the boundaries to human activity and interaction are geographical and not political.

C. Natural liberty

45. This brings us to the first, and most important, of the concepts with which our authors engage, that of natural liberty. It is possible to conceive of this liberty

in one of two ways. First, as a human faculty to reason and to act in accordance with reason[55]. As a tool for developing a framework to regulate human relations, this is an unpromising starting point. All human beings are naturally different, with impediments to the exercise of human will (internal and external) varying according to individual situation. The second, and for our purposes more useful, conception is the normative freedom to act, or to choose not to act, in a particular way, marked out by the absence of a duty to any other person[56]. It was in this sense that the term "Liberty" was used by Hobbes and Pufendorf and those who followed them. There is, however, a remarkable difference between the accounts of these two writers.

46. For Hobbes, in *Leviathan*, "the right of nature . . . is the liberty each man has, to use his own power, as he will himself, for the preservation of his own nature . . . and consequently of doing any thing, which in his own judgement and reason, he shall conceive to be the aptest means to that end"[57]. He clarifies immediately that "liberty" means "the absence of external impediments" which "may take away part of a man's power to do what he would"[58]. Importantly, this liberty, as defined

---

[55] Aristotle, *Politics*, VI.ii ("a man should live as he likes"). Grotius cites this passage, *Prize*, Chap. 2 (Prolegomena), [10] (pp. 33-34), although his conception of "natural liberty" appears to straddle the factual and legal conceptions described in the text. See also Institutes of Justinian, 1.1.2.

[56] This conception of "natural liberty" can be more fully described using the labels favoured by Wesley Newcomb Hohfeld, "Some Fundamental Conceptions as Applied in Judicial Reasoning" (1913), 23 *Yale LJ* 16 and (1917) 26 *Yale LJ* 710, in terms of a privilege (denoting the absence of a duty correlative to the claim right of another) coupled with an immunity (denoting the absence of a liability correlative to the power of another to effect a change in the legal relationship).

[57] Hobbes, *Leviathan*, Chap. 14, [64], p. 91.

[58] *Ibid.*

by Hobbes, includes the power to judge what is to be done[59]. For Hobbes, because each individual was able to exercise his own judgment as to the measures to be taken for their own preservation, without being subject to the will of another, "it follows that in such a condition, every man has a right[60] to everything; even to another's body"[61]. Put more straightforwardly, "nature has given all things to all men"[62].

47. Pufendorf's starting point was the same as Hobbes' – for him, "the state of nature has come to be described as a natural liberty, since every man, antecedent to any act of man, is understood to be under his own right and power, and to be subject to the power of no other man"[63]. Accordingly, no unilateral human act could limit the natural liberty of another. For Pufendorf, however, it did not follow that this natural liberty was unconstrained, for it remained subject to "the rule of natural laws and right reason"[64]. Following Grotius, Pufendorf concluded that the liberty did not extend to acts which injure the person, or by extension[65], the property of another[66]. Pufendorf approvingly cites Cicero[67]:

---

59 Pufendorf, *Nature and Nations*, Book 2, Chap. 2, [3] (p. 158), "every man is by natural right a judge".

60 I.e. a "liberty" in the sense used here, see text to n. 56.

61 Hobbes, *Leviathan*, Chap. 14, [64], p. 91; also *Citizen*, Chap. 1, [8], p. 27.

62 Hobbes, *Citizen*, Chap. 1, [10], p. 28.

63 Pufendorf, *Nature and Nations*, Book 2, Chap. 2, [3], p. 158.

64 *Ibid.*, p. 159; also Book 7, Chap. 1, 7, p. 961, "That right against all men and to all things, which according to Hobbes accompanies the state of nature, is to be extended no further than sane reason admits. . .".

65 See Pufendorf, *Nature and Nations*, Book 3, Chap. 5, [3] (pp. 391-392); also Grotius, *Prize*, Chap. 2 (Prolegomena), [6], pp. 23-24.

66 Grotius, *Prize*, Chap. 2 (Prolegomena), [7], pp. 26-27; Pufendorf, *Nature and Nations*, Book 3, Chap. 1, [1], pp. 313-314; Pufendorf, *Whole Duty*, Book 1, Chap. 6, [2]-[3], pp. 95-96. See below, [50].

67 Cicero, *On Duties (De Officiis)*, [III.5].

> "For a man to take anything wrongfully from another, and to increase his own means of comfort by his fellow-man's discomfort, is more contrary to nature than death, than poverty, than pain, than anything else that can happen to one's body or his external condition. In the first place, it destroys human intercourse and society."

48. For Pufendorf, this imperative *(officium)* was "absolute" (i.e. universal and owed to all men)[68] and was "the most necessary, because without it human society cannot be preserved"[69]. Peaceful relations cannot be secured if human beings are not restrained from injuring one another, for such injury, or the threat of it, brings into play the natural liberty to defend oneself, by bodily force if necessary[70]. The law of nature does not, in Pufendorf's view, "allow one man a privilege above another, so that he can violate the laws against another, while the other is bound to keep the peace with him"[71]. Consequently, for Pufendorf, "an obligation *(obligatio)* lies upon both of them, and makes the exercise of the offices of peace a mutual duty"[72].

49. Pufendorf's conclusions as to the extent of the natural liberty of humankind are worth setting out in full[73]:

> "[First] men, constituted in a natural state, may use and enjoy everything that is open to them, and may secure and do everything that will lead to their

---

[68] Pufendorf, *Whole Duty*, Book 1, Chap. 6, [1], p. 95.

[69] *Ibid.*, Book 1, Chap. 7, [2], p. 96.

[70] *Ibid.*, Book 1, Chap. 5, [17] and [19] (pp. 85-86, 88); Pufendorf, *Nature and Nations*, Book 2, Chap. 5.

[71] Pufendorf, *Nature and Nations*, Book 2, Chap. 5, [1], pp. 264-265.

[72] *Ibid.*, p. 265.

[73] Pufendorf, *Nature and Nations*, Book 2, Chap. 2, [3], p. 158, emphasis added; also Book 7, Chap. 1, [7] (p. 961). See also Locke, *Two Treatises*, 2nd treatise, Chap. 2, [4]-[6].

> preservation, *insofar as no injury is done to the right of others*. And [second], that they may use their own judgment and decision, *provided, of course, that it is framed on this natural law*, just as they use their own strength, to secure their own defence and preservation."

As this quotation shows, Pufendorf's constrained natural liberty creates, for each human being, an exclusive zone of freedom from interference, at least with respect to what we describe today as a person's bodily integrity. No one can seek to justify taking a life or injuring another human being, unless that other human being has given him reason to act in self-defence[74]. Outside this exclusive zone, the natural liberty that a human being enjoys is common to all.

50. Hobbes and Pufendorf agree that an individual's natural liberty may be extended or restricted by voluntary human action. Each saw this, in slightly different ways, as the basis for human institutions of contract and property. This enabled Pufendorf to specify that the duty not to injure another encompassed "all institutions and conventions whereby anything is secured for men"[75], whether arising under the laws of nature or "by any human institution or compact"[76]. For Hobbes, these human institutions were the only way that one person's natural liberty could be limited, and another's restricted, in such a way as to generate enforceable legal duties between them[77].

---

[74] Pufendorf, *Nature and Nations*, Book 2, Chap. 5, [6] (p. 273) ("[S]ince we are obliged by nature to cultivate peace with others, it is assumed that every one will meet that obligation, unless he is shown by clear signs to be contrary minded, and unless it is clear that he will not obey sound reason. . ."). See also Locke, *Two Treatises*, 2nd treatise, Chap. 2, [6] (p. 271).

[75] Pufendorf, *Nature and Nations*, Book 3, Chap. 1, [1], p. 314.

[76] Pufendorf, *Whole Duty*, Book 1, Chap. 6, [2]-[3], pp. 95-96.

[77] Hobbes, *Citizen*, Chap. 2, [3]-[5] and Chap. 3, [4], p. 45; Hobbes, *Leviathan*, Chap. 14, [65]-[66], pp. 92-94 and

D. Equality and self-love in the natural order

51. The conception of natural liberty is tied to the proposition that all human beings are, in the natural order, equal. Ambitiously, Hobbes argues for a natural equality of human faculties of mind and body, reasoning that even "the weakest has strength enough to kill the strongest", by weapons, or covert plotting, or by joining forces with others [78]. This claim is not only fanciful [79] but of little value as an analytical tool.

52. Pufendorf advances a different, normative claim. In his view, the precept of natural law that "[e]very man should esteem and treat another man as his equal by nature" follows from the premise that "human nature belongs equally to all men, and no one can live a social life with a person by whom he is not rated as at least a fellow man" [80]. This equality, he emphasises, is not an equality of strength or of reasoning power, but of liberty [81]. "[H]owever much one man may excel others in mental and bodily gifts, he is none the less bound to exercise towards them the duties of natural right, and he

---

Chap. 15, [71]-[72], pp. 100-101. Compare Pufendorf, *Nature and Nations*, Book 3, Chap. 5, [2]-[5], pp. 390-393.

[78] Hobbes, *Leviathan*, Chap. 13, [60], p. 87.

[79] See Pufendorf, *Nature and Nations*, Book 3, Chap. 2, [2], pp. 330-332.

[80] Pufendorf, *Nature and Nations*, Book 3, Chap. 2, [1], p. 330; also text to n. 71.

[81] *Ibid.*, [2] (p. 332) ("all share equally in liberty, so however much one man may excel other in mental and bodily gifts, he is none the less bound to exercise toward them the duties of natural right, and he may expect the same of others as well"); also Pufendorf, *Whole Duty*, Book 1, Chap. 7, [1], pp. 100-101; Locke, *Two Treatises*, 2nd treatise, Chap. 2, [5] (p. 270); Vattel, *Nations*, Preliminaries, [18], p. 75. As Vattel puts it: "Power or weakness does not in this respect produce any difference. A dwarf is as much a man as a giant". See text to n. 260.

may expect the same of others as well."[82] Accordingly, "whatever one man can claim for or hope for from another, the same others can claim or hope for from him, other things being equal"[83].

53. There is, however, an important caveat. Recall that the natural liberty common to all, whatever view one may take of its scope, includes the power of each individual to judge the measures necessary for their own wellbeing[84]. In exercising that judgment within the sphere of their own liberty, an individual may choose to prioritise self-interest over the interests and wellbeing of others. For Hobbes, this is the only game in town – "whatever anyone wants seems good to him precisely because he wants it, and it may either contribute to his preservation or at least seem to do so"[85]. Grotius proceeds from the observation that "[a]ll things in nature are tenderly regardful of self, and seek their own happiness and security" to the proposition that "[i]n human affairs the first principle of a man's duty relates to himself"[86]. Pufendorf similarly drew attention to the self-love that humankind shares with all things conscious of their own existence, which may serve to justify not only acts of self-protection but also acts of self-aggrandisement[87]. Importantly, in his view, the priority given to self-love did not mean that "one should under all circumstances prefer only himself before all others or measure everything by his own advantage"[88]. Rather, the freedom to prefer one's own interests could

---

82 Pufendorf, *Nature and Nations*, Book 3, Chap. 2, [2], p. 332, adding that "nor, for all his gifts, is he allowed any greater licence to injure others".
83 *Ibid.*
84 Text to n. 57; see also below, [66].
85 Hobbes, *Citizen*, Chap. 1, [10], p. 28.
86 Grotius, *Prize*, Chap. 2 (Prolegomena), [5'a], pp. 21-22.
87 Pufendorf, *Nature and Nations*, Book 2, Chap. 3, [14], p. 205; Pufendorf, *Whole Duty*, Book 1, Chap. 3, [2], p. 53.
88 Pufendorf, *Nature and Nations*, Book 2, Chap. 3, [14], p. 207. See Finnis, *Natural Law and Natural Rights* (n. 22), pp. 107-108.

be justified because, first, it is in the nature of human beings that they think first of themselves and, second, this was where the responsibility for securing wellbeing fell naturally – "there is no one on whom the clear and special care of myself can more fittingly fall"[89]. More altruistically, those who take care of themselves may be better equipped to advance the interests of others[90].

54. In Pufendorf's view, this natural equality between all human beings had other consequences. Not least, "if a man wishes to avail himself of the assistance of other men for his own advantage, he must in his turn tend his own talents to their accommodation"[91]. For otherwise, they would be treated as inferiors. Equally, this natural equality would be disturbed if individuals were to apply different rules in judging their own entitlement and that of another in exactly similar cases – "[o]ne who enjoys no right peculiar to himself shall not claim more for himself than for others, but he shall permit others to enjoy the same right that he himself does"[92]. The same principle would apply whenever an individual had the task of adjudicating upon the rights of others – in principle, "he should treat them as equals and should favour no one above another"[93].

E. Of (private) war and peace

55. The difference between Hobbes and Pufendorf's accounts of natural liberty[94] is quite narrow[95], but

---

89 Pufendorf, *Nature and Nations*, Book 2, Chap. 3, [14], p. 207.
90 *Ibid.*, Book 2, Chap. 4, [1], p. 231.
91 Pufendorf, *Nature and Nations*, Book 3, Chap. 2, [4], p. 335; also *ibid.*, Book 3, Chap. 4, [8], p. 388; Pufendorf, *Whole Duty*, Book 1, Chap. 7, [3], p. 102.
92 Pufendorf, *Nature and Nations*, Book 3, Chap. 2, [4], p. 336.
93 *Ibid.*, [5] (p. 337), adding "except in so far as a particular right belongs to a man".
94 Section II.C.
95 The gap narrows further if we accept Hobbes' concession in his earlier work that a person may violate the law of nature if

nonetheless important. For Hobbes, the common right of every individual to every thing, or at least those things judged subjectively to be necessary for self-preservation, was of little value, being "almost the same as if there were no right at all"[96]. For, on Hobbes' view of the natural order of things, even the extinction of life (the ultimate interference with humankind's natural liberty) could be justified by reference to the killer's own natural liberty and the accompanying power to judge the measures necessary for their own preservation. Hobbes considered this perpetual conflict of liberties, heightened by the propensity of human beings to quarrel and cause each other harm[97], to warrant the conclusion that "for as long as every man holds this right, of doing anything he likes; so long are all men in the condition of war"[98]. In that state, every human being could invoke their own liberty to justify causing harm to others[99]. As both sides enjoy a privilege to act according to what in their judgment serves their essential interests, "nothing can be unjust" in the natural order[100].

56. For Pufendorf, this pessimistic view of the natural condition of humankind could not be tolerated. He challenged Hobbes' diagnosis of humankind's belligerent tendency[101]. More fundamentally, Pufendorf, unlike

---

he claims that something contributes to his self-preservation but does not believe that it does so (Hobbes, *Citizen*, Chap. 1, [10] (note) (p. 29) and Chap. 3, [27] (note), p. 54).

96 Hobbes, *Citizen*, Chap. 1, [11], p. 29.

97 Hobbes, *Leviathan*, Chap. 13, [60]-[62], pp. 87-88.

98 *Ibid.*, Chap. 14, [65] (p. 92); also Hobbes, *Citizen*, Chap. 1, [12] (p. 29): Hobbes, *Leviathan*, Chap. 13, [63] (p. 90) ("a war of every man against every man").

99 Hobbes, *Leviathan*, Chap. 14, [65], p. 92.

100 *Ibid.*, Chap. 13, [63], p. 90.

101 Pufendorf, *Nature and Nations*, Book 2, Chap. 2, [6]-[7] (pp. 166-170) and [9], p. 172.
Pufendorf reinforced this behavioural claim with the practical argument that "since those who are widely separated

Hobbes, considered that the risk of conflict was alleviated to a significant extent by what he considered to be universally recognised limits on the natural liberty of humankind, in particular the duty "not to harm one who is not injuring him"[102]. This led him to conclude that "[t] he natural state of men . . . is not one of war but one of peace"[103]. Locke reached the same conclusion, criticising Hobbes for confounding the state of nature with the state of war[104].

57. Notwithstanding these differences of opinion, a more harmonious view emerged on one important issue – the responsibility of all human beings to seek peace as a means of avoiding or terminating the state of war. The perpetual war that Hobbes saw as being inherent in the natural state was, in his view, "incompatible . . . with the preservation of the human race"[105]. Given that there could be no security for as long as the common natural liberty of every human being to all things persisted, all must exercise their own natural liberty to secure peace, so far is this end was in their judgment attainable[106]. In Hobbes' vision, an enduring peaceful state could only be secured through an agreement between a sufficient number for each to give up part of their natural liberty

---

cannot do mutual harm, so long as they do not come into contact with one another, there seems no good reason why such persons should not be reckoned as friends rather than enemies", *ibid.*, [8], p. 170. With the advance of technology, we now have reason to question Pufendorf's assumption here.

102 Pufendorf, *Nature and Nations*, Book 2, Chap. 2, [9], p. 172. See above, [47].

103 Pufendorf, *Nature and Nations*, Book 2, Chap. 2, [9], p. 172; also *ibid.*, Book 2, Chap. 5, [1], pp. 264-265; Book 8, Chap. 6, [2], p. 1292.

104 Locke, *Two Treatises*, 2nd treatise, Chap. 3, [19], p. 280; also Vattel, *Nations*, Book 4, Chap. 1, [1], pp. 651-652.

105 Hobbes, *Citizen*, Chap. 1, [13], p. 30.

106 *Ibid.*

in order to establish a political society for their mutual protection[107].

58. For Pufendorf, the maintenance of peace was the function of both natural and civil law[108]. In his view, "man was created to maintain peace with his fellows, and all the laws of nature which concern other men have, as their first concern, the establishment and maintenance of peace"[109]. This was, however, no easy task given that "so many transactions pass between men, and the way is opened to many controversies"[110]. Although Pufendorf considered human relations to be naturally peaceful[111], he accepted that human vices continuously threaten that peaceful order[112]. This led him to confess that "this natural peace is but a weak and untrustworthy thing" and "without other safeguards, but a poor custodian of man's safety"[113].

59. Pufendorf acknowledged that violence, as a means of self-defence, was justified in some circumstances. Indeed, "to forbid the use of force in self-defence, so far from conducing to peace, would mean the end of mankind"[114]. However, the authority of every individual to determine the means necessary for self-preservation was "moderated by the dictates of true reason and by the rules of the law of nature"[115]. Even when under the threat of injury, the individual must consider "more

---

107 Hobbes, *Leviathan*, Chap. 14, [64]-[65], pp. 91-92; Hobbes, *Citizen*, Chap. 2, [2]-[3], p. 34.
108 Pufendorf, *Nature and Nations*, Book 5, Chap. 3, [1], p. 524.
109 *Ibid.*, Book 2, Chap. 5, [1], p. 264.
110 *Ibid.*, Book 5, Chap. 3, [1], p. 524.
111 See above, [56].
112 Pufendorf, *Nature and Nations*, Book 2, Chap. 2, [12], Book 2, Chap. 5, [6], p. 273 and Book 7, Chap. 1, [4], p. 954.
113 *Ibid.*, Book 2, Chap. 2, [12], p. 176.
114 *Ibid.*, Book 2, Chap. 5, [1], p. 264; also Pufendorf, *Whole Duty*, Book 2, Chap. 5, [13], p. 183.
115 Pufendorf, *Whole Duty*, Book 2, Chap. 1, [8], p. 170.

harmless remedies"[116] and must be willing to put up with a slight wrong, if convenient to do so, rather than risking greater danger by using violent means against another[117]. Pufendorf counselled that a "wise man should try every means before arms"[118]. If a dispute could be resolved by peaceful means, whether by friendly discussion or by an agreement to be bound by the decision of a third party, then this course of action was to be preferred to a state of war[119].

60. Before moving on, note that our authors adopt the terminology of "war" and "peace" in their accounts of individual human relationships, treating this as a topic deserving, or demanding, of study in its own right before turning to examine the laws of war and peace in the relations between nations. Grotius devotes an entire chapter[120] to "the division of war into public and private", which he considers to be "the most general and the most necessary"[121]. Woolf, in turn, asserts that "the nature of public war is to be determined from that of private war" and that "in the law of nature and nations war is to be

---

[116] *Ibid.*, Book 1, Chap. 5, [14], p. 83. The examples given are keeping out the invader by cutting off their access, withdrawing into strong places and admonishing them to desist. See also Pufendorf, *Whole Duty*, Book 2, Chap. 1, [11], p. 173.

[117] Pufendorf, *Whole Duty*, Book 1, Chap. 5, [14], p. 83; also Pufendorf, *Nature and Nations*, Book 2, Chap. 5, [3], p. 267 and Book 5, Chap. 13, [3], p. 826.

[118] Pufendorf, *Whole Duty*, Book 1, Chap. 5, [14], p. 83.

[119] *Ibid.*, Book 2, Chap. 1, [11], pp. 173-174; Pufendorf, *Nature and Nations*, Book 2, Chap. 5, [3], pp. 267-268 and Book 5, Chap. 13, [3], pp. 826-827.
In the latter passage, Pufendorf cites Ovid (*Tristia*, Book V), "Unjustly the hard sword dispenses justice". See also Hobbes, *Citizen*, Chap. 3, [20], p. 51; Vattel, *Nations*, Book 4, Chap. 1, [1], p. 641 and below, [66].

[120] Grotius, *War and Peace*, Book 1, Chap. 3; also Grotius, *Prize*, Chap. 6.

[121] Grotius, *War and Peace*, Book 1, Chap. 3, [1], p. 240.

defined in such a way that the definition may be equally applicable to public and private war"[122].

F. Duties of humanity (mutual assistance)

61. For Grotius, sociability among human beings constituted "the fountain of right"[123]. He recognised the practical truth that self-defence alone would not preserve humankind. To achieve that end, it was necessary that each should have regard for the welfare of others[124]. The acceptance of this obligation was, Grotius suggested, a distinguishing characteristic of the species[125], allowing him to speak of a "brotherhood of man" and "world state" *(mundi civitas)*[126].

62. This state of interdependence, as well as the human propensity towards selfish and harmful conduct, were key factors in Pufendorf's opinion that human beings were under mutual obligations to be "sociable" towards

---

122 Wolff, *Nations*, Chap. 6, [608], pp. 447-448; also *ibid.*, [613], pp. 450-451.

123 Grotius, *War and Peace*, Book 1, Preliminary Discourse, [8], pp. 7-8.
As to the nature of Grotius' conception of sociability, see Stephen Darwall, *Modern Moral Philosophy – From Grotius to Kant*, Cambridge: Cambridge University Press, 2023, 22, 36-38 ("sociability the fountain of an order involving all persons that is mediated by universal 'General Principles' enshrining rights with which individual members take themselves to have standing to demand compliance").

124 Grotius, *Prize*, Chap. 2 (Prolegomena), [6'], p. 24, quoting Seneca ("You must needs live for others, if you would live for yourself" (*Epistles*, xlvii, 2-3)). See also *ibid.*, [7], p. 27, again quoting Seneca ("Security must be obtained by offering security in exchange", *On Mercy*, I.xix, [5]-[6]).

125 Grotius, *Prize*, Chap. 2 (Prolegomena), [6'], p. 26.

126 *Ibid.*, [7], p. 27, with reference to Cicero, *On Laws (De Legibus)*, [I.23]. As to Grotius' views on the human need and desire for society, more fully elaborated in War and Peace, see below, [74].

one another[127]. In his opinion, it was a fundamental law of nature that every individual with the capacity to do so "should cultivate and preserve toward others a sociable attitude, which is peaceful and agreeable at all times to the nature and end of the human race"[128].

63. No one was to be deprived of the advantages of this "general friendship" unless "monstrous iniquities have made him unworthy"[129]. Pufendorf nonetheless acknowledged that this social bond was relatively weak unless reinforced by a common legal framework – in a state of natural liberty, others may be looked on as friends but not freely trusted[130].

---

[127] Pufendorf, *Nature and Nations*, Book 2, Chap. 3, [15], pp. 207-208, Book 2, Chap. 2, [2], p. 155 and Book 2, Chap. 3, [16], pp. 212-213. See also Grotius, *War and Peace*, Book 1, Preliminary Discourse, [6]-[10], pp. 79-89 and Chap. 1, [3], point 1, p. 136, noting in both passages the annotations in the translation prepared by Jean Barbeyrac (n. 33); Pufendorf, *Whole Duty*, Book 1, Chap. 3, [7], pp. 55-56 and Book 1, Chap. 5, [5], p. 93.
On Pufendorf's duty of sociability, see generally Craig L. Carr and Michael J. Seidler, "Pufendorf, Sociability and the Modern State" (1996), 17 *History of Political Thought* 354; Darwell (n. 123), pp. 63-65, 70-72; also Stephen Darwell, "Valuing Humanity in 'Common Life': Grotius and Pufendorf on Equal 'Sociable Dignity'", Chap. 5 in Sara Buss and Nancy Theunissen, *Rethinking the Value of Humanity*, Oxford: Oxford University Press, 2023; Kari Saastamoinen, "Pufendorf on the Law of Sociality and the Law of Nations", Chap 5 in Simone Zurburchen (ed.), *The Law of Nations and Natural Law* 1625-1800, Leiden: Brill, 2019.

[128] Pufendorf, *Nature and Nations*, Book 2, Chap. 3, [15], p. 208. See also Pufendorf, *Whole Duty*, Book 1, Chap. 3, [9] (p. 56), expressing the same "fundamental law" in terms that "every man ought, as much as in him lies, to preserve and promote society, that is the welfare of mankind" and Book 1, Chap. 8, [1] (p. 104), requiring that "every man ought to promote the Good of another, so far as conveniently he may".

[129] Pufendorf, *Nature and Nations*, Book 2, Chap. 3, [18], p. 213.

[130] Pufendorf, *Whole Duty*, Book 2, Chap. 1, [10], pp. 171-172.

64. For Vattel, the mutual obligations flowing from the "natural society of men" – the "universal society of the human race"[131] – were conducive to the general happiness of humankind[132]. Every individual, regardless of their situation, was bound to cultivate this natural society and to discharge the offices of humanity associated with it[133].

65. Importantly, these duties of humanity are *mutual* and *imperfect*. Mutuality, as Pufendorf emphasises, is a by-product of the equality of humankind – it is repugnant to that natural equality that one should be bound to another, without the latter being likewise bound to the former[134]. An imperfect duty is one that cannot be enforced, either by bodily force or by appeal to a superior authority[135], the only "sanction" for non-

---

[131] In the French original, "la société universelle du genre-humain", Vattel, *Nations*, Preliminaries, [11], p. 72.

[132] Vattel, *Nations*, Preliminaries, [10]-[11], p. 72 and Book 2, Chap. 1, [3], [16], pp. 262, 268-269.

[133] *Ibid.*, Preliminaries, [11], p. 72 and Book 2, Chap. 1, [2]-[3], pp. 261-262, at p. 261: "The offices of humanity are those succours, those duties, which men owe to each other, as men, that is, as social beings formed to live in society, and standing in need of mutual assistance for their preservation and happiness, and to enable them to live in a manner conformable to their nature". See further below, [98].

[134] Pufendorf, *Nature and Nations*, Book 3, Chap. 4, [8], p. 388; Pufendorf, *Whole Duty*, Book 1, Chap. 7, [3], p. 102. See above, [54].

[135] Grotius, *War and Peace*, Book 2, Chap. 22, [16], pp. 1112-1113; also *ibid.*, Book 1, Preliminary Discourse, [42], p. 113 and Chap. 1, [8], pp. 142-143; Pufendorf, *Nature and Nations*, Book 2, Chap. 4, [6] and [9], pp. 386, 388; Pufendorf, *Whole Duty*, Book 1, Chap. 9, [4], p. 110; Vattel, *Nations*, Preliminaries, [17], pp. 74-75 and Book 1, Chap. 1, [10], p. 266.
See also Samuel von Pufendorf, *Two Books of the Elements of Universal Jurisprudence* (1660), translation by W. A. Oldfather in the edition edited by Thomas Behme for the *Natural Law and Enlightenment Classics* series, Indianapolis: Liberty Fund, 2009, Book 1, Definition VII,

conformity being disapproval[136] and withdrawal of reciprocal performance[137]. An individual who falls short in the offices of humanity may act dishonorably, but does not act unjustly[138].

G. Administering natural justice

66. The law of nature has no courts or other formal structures for the administration of justice[139] – each individual is the judge of both his or her own entitlement and of the measures (including the application of force) that are appropriate to protect or vindicate that entitlement[140]. In this state, the risk of conflict is high. As Hobbes points out, even if individuals strive to conform to the duties imposed on them, doubtful points and disputes will arise every day, and circumstances may readily occur in which both parties to a dispute consider themselves to be the injured party[141]. The risk of private war is, however, mitigated by the requirement to maintain peaceful relations, whenever practicable[142]. If no other just remedy was available, and efforts to reach

---

[1], pp. 87-88 and Definition VIII, [2] and [5], pp. 92-93. Cf. Pufendorf, *Whole Duty*, Book 1, Chap. 5, [5], p. 93, dealing with the case of extreme necessity.

136 Pufendorf, *Whole Duty*, Book 1, Chap. 9, [4], p. 110.

137 *Ibid.*, [2], p. 109.

138 *Ibid.*, Book 1, Chap. 2, [15], p. 51, Chap. 8, [8], pp. 107-108 and Chap. 9, [4], p. 110.

139 Grotius, *War and Peace*, Book 1, Chap. 3, [1], p. 240 ("Courts of Justice are not from nature"); Pufendorf, *Nature and Nations*, Book 5, Chap. 13, [2], p. 826 ("Now among those who live in natural liberty there is no judge who may by his authority settle and dispose of the disputes that arise"); also Hobbes, *Citizen*, Chap. 1, [9].

140 See above, [46]-[47], [53].

141 Hobbes, *Citizen*, Chap. 3, [20] (p. 51); also Hobbes, *Leviathan*, Chap. 15, [78], pp. 108-109; Grotius, *War and Peace*, Book 2, Chap. 1, [20], p. 393; Pufendorf, *Nature and Nations*, Book 5, Chap 3, [1], p. 524.

142 See above, [57]-[59].

a negotiated or mediated resolution had been exhausted, the duty to promote peaceful relations could still be satisfied if both parties were willing to consent to the settlement of their dispute by a third party "arbitrator" whose verdict they would bind themselves to respect[143].

67. The nature of ths appointment, and the fundamental requirement to maintain equality between the parties, dictate that the arbitrator must not be a party to the dispute[144], and should have no financial or personal interest in its outcome[145], or be bound by prior agreement to act otherwise than fairly between the parties[146]. In adjudicating on questions of fact, equal weight should be given to the parties' own testimony[147]. The arbitrator must show no more favour to one than to the other and

---

143 Hobbes, *Citizen*, Chap. 3, [20], p. 51, specifying as a precept of natural law that: "parties who have a dispute of right among them should both submit to the arbitration of a third party"; also Hobbes, *Leviathan*, Chap. 15, [78], pp. 108-109; Grotius, *War and Peace*, Book 1, Chap. 3, [1], pp. 240-241; Pufendorf, *Nature and Nations*, Book 5, Chap. 13, [3], pp. 826-827.

144 Hobbes, *Citizen*, Chap. 3, [21], p. 52; ("no one should be judge or arbitrator in his own case") Hobbes, *Leviathan*, Chap. 15, [78], p. 109.

145 Hobbes, *Citizen*, Chap. 3, [22], p. 52; Hobbes, *Leviathan*, Chap. 15, [78], p. 109; Pufendorf, *Nature and Nations*, Book 5, Chap. 13, [4], p. 827.

146 Hobbes, *Citizen*, Chap. 3, [24], p. 52; Pufendorf, *Nature and Nations*, Book 5, Chap. 13, [4], p. 827.

147 Hobbes, *Citizen*, Chap. 3, [23], p. 52; also Hobbes, *Leviathan*, Chap. 15, [78], p. 109; Pufendorf, *Nature and Nations*, Book 5, Chap. 13, [9], p. 832. Pufendorf, *Whole Duty*, Book 2, Chap. 1, [11], pp. 173-174.
In Hobbes' view, no weight should be given to contradictory evidence given by the parties, and the arbitrator should seek the testimony of witnesses who seem fair to both parties. Pufendorf also rejects the contradictory, unsworn assertions of the parties and suggests that it is safer not to admit the evidence of those with a particular affection for, or animus against, one party.

not base right upon affection[148]. Pufendorf adds that the agreement to submit to the arbitrator's decision cannot be subject to the condition that the decision is just, as this would nullify the purpose of the agreement – if one party were then to deny the justice of the award, then that question would need to be referred to a second arbitrator[149]. In this way, things would run on for ever, and the dispute would not be resolved. Nor can any appeal be lodged against the arbitrator's decision, as there is no superior judge that can review it[150].

68. By reason of the parties' mutual agreement to settle their dispute by these means, the law of nature imposes a *perfect obligation* to abide by the outcome. If the losing party does not willingly comply, the other may in a state of natural liberty resort to forceful means to recover the thing awarded or assets to the same value[151]. The arbitrator, by contrast, has in the law of nature no authority to force the parties to abide by the decision[152]. As Pufendorf notes, it may be tempting for one who has confidence in his own strength to ignore the award[153].

H. *The significance of the natural legal order*

69. These accounts of the natural legal order were open to the objection that they ignored both historical

---

148 Pufendorf, *Nature and Nations*, Book 5, Chap. 13, [4], pp. 827, 829. In the latter passage, Pufendorf observes that "[t]he statement that one has to abide by the decision of the arbitrator, whether it be just or not, must be taken with a grain of salt. . . . For whoever clearly leans to one side or the other is unfitted to pose as an arbitrator". See also Pufendorf, *Whole Duty*, Book 2, Chap. 1, [11], p. 173.

149 Pufendorf, *Nature and Nations*, Book 5, Chap. 13, [4], p. 828.

150 *Ibid.*, pp. 827-828.

151 *Ibid.*, Book 5, Chap. 13, [10], pp. 835-836.

152 *Ibid.*, Book 5, Chap. 1, [8], p. 963.

153 *Ibid.*, also Locke, *Two Treatises*, 2nd treatise, Chap. 9, [126], p. 351.

fact[154] and contemporary political reality, for human relations were and are regulated not by laws of nature but by laws made by human beings governing particular political societies.

70. Locke briefly addresses this objection[155]. His answer is twofold. First, the princes and rulers of all independent governments throughout the world *are* in a state of nature with each other. We will return to this point shortly[156]. Second, all human beings remain in a state of nature in their relations with each other unless they are part of the same political society. He gives the examples of contracts between two men on a desert island[157] or between a Swiss and a member of the indigenous population in the woods of America. Grotius gives further examples of a contract made on the high seas or by letter at a distance[158].

71. It is doubtful whether these examples carry forward to the twenty-first century, in which the habitable surface of the Earth has been fully charted and cross-border transactions are a routine incident of daily life for a large proportion of the global population[159]. Today, the relationship that naturally exists between human beings when they engage with one another co-exists with their relationships as members of, or participants, in the political societies that seek to regulate these transactions.

72. Significantly, our authors use their models of the natural legal order as a rhetorical and theoretical tool to

---

[154] See generally Fernanda Pirie, *The Rule of Laws: A 4000 Year Quest to Order the World*, London: Profile Books, 2021.

[155] Locke, *Two Treatises*, 2nd treatise, Chap. 2, [14]-[15], pp. 276-278.

[156] Section II.J.

[157] Taken from Garcilaso de la Vega, *Histoire des Incas, rois de Perou*, Paris: Prault fils, 1744.

[158] Grotius, *War and Peace*, Book 2, Chap. 11, [5], p. 709. For further discussion of this passage, see below, [87] and [154].

[159] See further text to n. 207.

account for the conditions under which, and the manner in which, human beings combine to form political societies for their own protection and the effects of that combination on legal regulation and the administration of justice. Although a full account is beyond the ambit of this study, certain features of this modelling are deserving of closer attention.

I. Political societies and the law of nature

1. The formation of political societies

73. At the beginning of his work, Vattel defines nations or States as[160]:

> ". . . bodies politic, societies of men united together for the purpose of promoting their mutual safety and advantage by the joint efforts of their combined strength".

74. Accounts of the nature, purpose and formation of political societies lie at the heart of these natural law accounts. A sketch of Grotius' narrative will serve as an illustration[161]. Patchy compliance with the precepts of the law of nature, and inefficient enforcement mechanisms, coupled with the growing global population, albeit widely distributed, encouraged family groups to combine in larger social units, which eventually settled in a single locality, offering the individuals concerned a more dependable means of protection and the sharing of resources and labour[162]. Over time, these social arrangements crystallised into more formalised patterns of collaboration for mutual advantage. In view of the common purpose, each collective can be described as a

---

160 Vattel, Nations, *Preliminaries*, [1], p. 67.

161 Grotius, *Prize*, Chap. 2 (Prolegomena), [10']-[12], pp. 35-43.

162 *Ibid.*, [10'], p. 35.

"commonwealth" *(Respublica)*[163] and can be conceived of as a unified and permanent body, a moral person, governed by its own legal order[164]. Its institutions administer justice between individuals by allocating resources and burdens, bestowing honours and imposing sanctions upon those who injure the community[165]. By this arrangement, the interests of individuals are subordinated to the common good of the whole group[166], through the operation of municipal law[167].

75. Of necessity, the commonwealth also assumes the function of resolving disputes within the society, for the discord that would result from each person being allowed to judge their own entitlement cannot be tolerated[168]. Judicial pronouncements, applying general legal rules to the facts of a particular case, crystallise the parties' entitlements[169]. As a corollary, in order to promote peaceful relations, the disputing parties are no longer authorised to use force as a means of asserting or defending their entitlement[170], save when it is not practicable to have recourse to the judicial procedure[171].

---

163 *Ibid.*, p. 36.
164 *Ibid.*, [10']-[11], pp. 36-37.
165 *Ibid.*, [11], p. 37.
166 *Ibid.*, [11a]-[11'], pp. 38-40; also text to n. 182.
167 *Ibid.*, [11'], pp. 40-41.
168 *Ibid.*, [11']-[11'a], pp. 41-42 (at p. 42: "Accordingly, even though the precepts of nature permitted every individual to pronounce judgement for himself and of himself, it is clear that all nations deemed it necessary to institute some orderly judicial system, and that individual citizens gave general consent to this project."). See H. L. A. (Herbert) Hart, *The Concept of Law*, Oxford: Oxford University Press, 3rd ed., 2012, pp. 96-98.
169 Grotius, *Prize*, Chap. 2 (Prolegomena), [11'a], p. 42.
170 *Ibid.*, [11'a]-[12] (pp. 42-43); also Grotius, *War and Peace*, Book 1, Chap. 3, [1], pp. 240-241.
171 Grotius, *Prize*, Chap. 2 (Prolegomena), [13']-[14] (p. 49) and Chap. 8, [37']-[38], pp. 130-132; Grotius, *War and Peace*, Book 1, Chap. 3, [2], pp. 241-242.

76. Although the details vary, other accounts follow a similar pattern[172]. Importantly, for present purposes, the writers are unanimous that the responsibility for adjudicating upon disputes involving the members of a political society is vested in the society's judicial organs[173] and that the natural liberty of individuals to use force in pursuit of their own cause is limited accordingly[174].

77. Vattel elegantly captures this idea[175]:

> "[O]ne of the principal duties of a nation relates to justice[176]. They ought to employ their utmost attention in causing it to prevail in the state, and to take proper measures for having it dispensed to everyone in the most certain, the most speedy, and the least burdensome manner. . . . The nation will therefore neglect her duty to herself, and deceive the individuals,

---

172 See Hobbes, *Citizen*, Chap. 5; Hobbes, *Leviathan*, Chaps. 17-18; Pufendorf, *Nature and Nations*, Book 7, Chaps. 1-2; Pufendorf, *Whole Duty*, Book 2, Chaps. 5-6; Locke, *Two Treatises*, 2nd treatise, Chaps. 8-9; Vattel, *Nations*, Preliminaries, [1]-[2], [4], Chap. 1, [1]-[2] and Chap. 2, [15]-[16].

173 Hobbes, *Leviathan*, Chap. 18, [8], p. 125; Pufendorf, *Nature and Nations*, Book 7, Chap. 4, [4], p. 101; Pufendorf, *Whole Duty*, Book 2, Chap. 5, [7], p. 190, Chap. 7, [4], p. 200 and Chap. 12, [2], p. 221; Locke, *Two Treatises*, 2nd treatise, Chap. 7, [88], pp. 324-325: Vattel, *Nations*, Book 1, Chap. 13, [158], p. 185.

174 Hobbes, *Citizen*, Chap. 6, [3], pp. 77-78; Pufendorf, *Nature and Nations*, Book 2, Chap. 5, [7], pp. 275-276 and Book 8, Chap. 6, [8], p. 1292; Pufendorf, *Whole Duty*, Book 2, Chap. 5, [16], [18], pp. 84, 87 and Chap. 12, [2], p. 221; Locke, *Two Treatises*, 2nd treatise, Chap. 7, [88], pp. 324-325; Vattel, *Nations*, Book 1, Chap. 13, [158], p. 185.

175 Vattel, *Nations*, Book 1, Chap. 13, [158], p. 185. The position is the same for foreigners residing or visiting a particular place, see Wolff, *Nations*, Chap. 3, [302], p. 219.

176 The passage begins with the words, "Next to the case of religion. . .", see Chap. 12. With the separation of church from State in many political societies, this sense of priorities no longer prevails today.

if she did not seriously endeavour to make the strictest justice prevail. Confusion, disorder, and despondency, will soon arise in a state, when the citizens are not sure of easily and speedily obtaining justice in all their disputes: without this, the civil virtues will become extinguished, and the society weakened."

78. For Vattel, securing justice is one of the ends of political society, a commitment undertaken to secure the preservation and perfection of that society[177]. The best and safest method for the resolution of disputes is to establish courts, with judges "distinguished by their integrity and knowledge"[178]. Although the justice system may allow for the possibility of an appeal to correct errors, the ultimate decision-maker must be given the authority to pronounce a definitive sentence – otherwise, Vattel observes, "the whole proceeding will be in vain, and the dispute can never be determined"[179].

2. *The elasticity of consent as a guiding principle*

79. These narratives posit that a political society assumes or exerts power over individuals as a result of a consensual divestment of part of their natural liberty[180].

---

177 Vattel, *Nations*, Book 1, Chap. 2, [14]-[15], p. 86, at p. 15: "The end or object of civil society is to procure for the citizens whatever they stand in need of, for the necessities, the conveniences, the accommodation of life, and, in general, whatever constitutes happiness, – with the peaceful possession of property, a method of obtaining justice with security, and, finally a mutual defence against all external violence".
See also Wolff, *Nations*, Chap. 1, [28]-[31], pp. 28-34.

178 Vattel, *Nations*, Book 1, Chap. 13, [163], p. 187 and [165], pp. 188-189.

179 *Ibid.*, [165], p. 188.

180 In addition to the following references to Grotius' account, see Hobbes, *Citizen*, Chap. 5; Hobbes, *Leviathan*, Chap. 17, [87]-[88], pp. 120-121 and Chap. 18, [88]-[89], pp. 121-

Accordingly, Grotius refers to a "social unit formed by a general agreement for the common good" and to the "will of individuals, manifested either in the formal acceptance of pacts . . . or in tacit indication of consent"[181]. Grotius asserts that the individual participants in a political society have consented to subordinate their own interests to the common good[182]. This foundation of civil laws is, in his view, "conformable to nature"[183]. More specifically, addressing the resolution of disputes within a political society, he states that individual citizens "gave general consent" to the institution of an orderly judicial system, for "it is quite commonly acknowledged, the very nature of jurisdiction renders it absolutely impossible for any jurisdiction to be established save by general consent"[184]. Vattel refers to a "social compact" under which individuals consent to divest themselves of a component of their natural liberty in order to attain security and more certain justice[185].

80. Our authors identify the facility of individuals to bind themselves by consent as one of the key precepts of the law of nature[186], accounting for expansion or

---

122; Pufendorf, *Nature and Nations*, Book 7, Chap. 2, [6]-[12], pp. 973-983; Pufendorf, *Whole Duty*, Book 2, Chap. 6; Locke, *Two Treatises*, 2nd treatise, Chap. 8.

181 Grotius, *Prize*, Chap. 2 (Prolegomena), [10'], p. 36.

182 *Ibid.*, [11], pp. 39-40.

183 Grotius, *War and Peace*, Book 1, Preliminary Discourse, [16], p. 93.

184 Grotius, *Prize*, Chap. 2 (Prolegomena), [11'a], p. 42.

185 Vattel, *Nations*, Book 1, Chap. 13, [158], p. 185.

186 Grotius, *Prize*, Chap. 2 (Prolegomena), [10]-[10'], pp. 34-35 (Rule III); Grotius, *War and Peace*, Book 2, Chaps. 11 and 12; Hobbes, *Citizen*, Chap. 2 and Chap. 3, [1]-[4], pp. 32-57; Hobbes, *Leviathan*, Chap. 14, [64]-[70], pp. 94-99; Pufendorf, *Nature and Nations*, Book 3, Chap. 5; Pufendorf, *Whole Duty*, Book 1, Chap. 9; Wolff, *Nations*, Prolegomena, [23], pp. 25-26; Vattel, *Nations*, Book 2, Chap. 12, [163], p. 142. See also Locke, *Two Treatises*, 1st treatise, Chap. 4, [43], pp. 170-171 and 2nd treatise, Chap. 7, [82], [85], pp. 321-322.

contraction of an individual's natural liberty, within certain limits[187], as well as the binding force of treaties in the law of nations[188]. It is, therefore, easy to see the allurement of the idea of a "social contract" as a means of explaining, and justifying, the creation and continuance of political authority[189].

81. We should not allow ourselves to take the metaphor too literally[190]. Sir William Blackstone, whose own highly influential *Commentaries on the Laws of England* began with an excursus on the "nature of laws"[191], lampoons the idea that there was a time when "individuals met together in a large plain, entered into an original contract, and chose the tallest man present to be their governor"[192]. In his view, it was humankind's sense of weakness and imperfection that demonstrated the necessity of union and provided the cement of society.

---

187 E.g. Locke, *Two Treatises*, 2nd treatise, Chap. 24, [23], p. 284 (slavery) and Chap. 9, [131] (common good).

188 Grotius, *Prize*, Chap. 2 (Prolegomena), [12']-[12'a], p. 45 (Rule VIII); Grotius, *War and Peace*, Book 2, Chap. 15; Pufendorf, *Nature and Nations*, Book 8, Chap. 9; Pufendorf, *Whole Duty*, Book 2, Chap. 16, [16]-[17], p. 244 and Chap. 8; Wolff, *Nations*, Prolegomena, [23], pp. 25-26 and Chap. 4; Vattel, *Nations*, Book 2, Chap. 2, [28], p. 276 and Chap. 12. See Section III.G.

189 Naomi Zack, *Democracy: A Very Short Introduction*, Oxford: Oxford University *Press*, 2023, Chap. 4; Ann Cudd and Seena Eftekhari, "Contractarianism", in Edward N. Zalta (ed.), *The Stanford Encyclopedia of Philosophy*, Winter 2021 ed., https://plato.stanford.edu/archives/win2021/entries/contractarianism/.

190 In addition to the references in the surrounding footnotes, see J. W. (John) Gough, *The Social Contract – A Critical Study of Its Development*, Oxford: Clarendon Press, 2nd ed., 1957; Hart, *The Concept of Law* (n. 168), Chap. 6, esp. pp. 116-117.

191 Sir William Blackstone, *Commentaries on the Laws of England*, Oxford, Clarendon Press, 4 vols., 1765-1769, in the edition edited by Wilfried Prest, Oxford: Oxford University Press, 2016, Book 1, Introduction, Section 2.

192 *Ibid.*, [47], p. 38.

The "original contract", as he saw it, "must always be understood and implied, in the very act of associating together"[193]. Nor did our authors take a formalistic or technical view as to the conditions for laws and judicial decisions to bind. All acknowledged the sufficiency of tacit indications of an individual's attachment to a particular political society[194].

82. Elsewhere, Grotius advances an argument, attributed to "natural equity", which offers a surer foundation for the binding force of human laws and judicial pronouncements than theories based on consensual submission[195]. Grotius' point is that "since we derive advantages from political society, . . . we should likewise suffer its disadvantages"[196]. The argument, captured by the Latin maxim *qui sentit commodum, sentire debet et*

---

193 *Ibid.*, [47]-[48], p. 39. See also the very full discussion of the "original contract" by Joseph Story, *Commentaries on the Constitution of the United States*, Boston: Hilliard, Gray and Co, 1834, Vol. 1, [325]-[338], pp. 293-306.
For trenchant criticism of the theory as well as of Blackstone's account of the nature of law more generally, see Jeremy Bentham, *A Fragment of Government*, London: T. Payne, 1776, in the edition edited by J. H. (James) Burns and H. L. A. (Herbert) Hart, Cambridge: Cambridge University Press, 1988, Chap. 1, esp. [36]-[47]; John Austin, *The Province of Jurisprudence Determined* (n. 15), Lecture VI, esp. pp. 248-281. See also Gertrude Himmelfarb, "Bentham versus Blackston" (1978), 47 *The American Scholar* 537.

194 Grotius, *Prize*, Chap. 2 (Prolegomena), [10], p. 34 and [10'], p. 36; Hobbes, *Leviathan*, Chap. 18, [90], pp. 123-124 and Review and Conclusion, [391], pp. 395-396; Pufendorf, *Nature and Nations*, Book 7, Chap. 2, [20], pp. 994-995; Locke, *Two Treatises*, 2nd treatise, Chap. 8, [119], pp. 347-348; Vattel, *Nations*, Book 1, Chap. 19, [212], pp. 217-218, [218], p. 220 and [220], p. 221.
See also Pufendorf, *Whole Duty*, Book 1, Chap. 9, [9], p. 111 ("Silence in some cases, and attended with some circumstances, passes for a sign expressing consent").

195 Grotius, *Prize*, Chap. 8, [48], p. 158.

196 *Ibid.*, also Pufendorf, Book 7, Chap. 2, [20], p. 994 ("all the more if he wishes to enjoy its advantages").

onus and the English idiom "one cannot have one's cake and eat it", is an attractive one[197].

3. Attachment to a political society

83. Whatever view one takes of the theoretical basis of the authority to regulate human conduct, the following question presents itself – which *indicia* of attachment suffice to connect an individual with a particular political society? Broadly speaking, those discussed in our texts fall into two categories, political and social.

84. With respect to the former, the exemplar is that of an individual who actively participates in the governance of a society[198]. As only a minority fall within this description, the texts focus principally on those who are formally identified as members of the society, the citizens *(cives)*. The status of citizenship may, depending on the society's own norms, be acquired by birth, succession or adoption[199].

85. For those who are not citizens, the qualifying social ties discussed in these accounts range from those who have established their home within the society,

---

197 See, for example, *International Shoe Co* v. *State of Washington* (1945) 326 US 310, 319-320 (Stone CJ); *Boissière & Co* v. *Brockner & Co* (1889), 6 TLR 85 (Cave J.); *Re Dulles Settlement* (No. 2) [1951] Ch 842, 847; Andrew Dickinson, "Foreign Submission" (2019), 135 *Law Quarterly Review* 294, 316-319. See below, [366] and [390].

198 Pufendorf, *Nature and Nations*, Book 7, Chap. 2, [20], p. 995, with reference to Aristotle, *Politics*, Book 3, Chap. 1 and [21] (both p. 995). As to the position of the founders of a political society, see *ibid.*, Book 7, Chap. 2, [20], p. 994.

199 Pufendorf, *Whole Duty*, Chap. 6, [13], p. 197; Vattel, *Nations*, Book 1, Chap. 19, [212], [214], [215], pp. 218-219. Vattel suggests that the status of children as citizens is subject to ratification upon attaining the age of majority when they "act as a citizen", Vattel, *Nations*, Book 1, Chap. 19, [220], p. 221.

through those who reside there temporarily, to those who merely own property (especially immovable property) within the locality or are visiting for a particular purpose[200]. For Pufendorf, a person who enters the territory controlled by a State, and in particular one who wishes to enjoy its advantages[201], "is held to have given up his natural liberty, and to have subjected himself to the sovereignty of the state, at least for so long a time as he desires to remain there"[202]. If it were otherwise, he suggests, the safety of the society would be imperilled[203]. Locke considers that not only an individual's physical presence but also the possession of land involve the enjoyment of privileges and protection under a country's laws and are sufficient to bind, without qualifying the individual as a full member of the commonwealth[204]. Wolff argues forcefully that "the right against foreigners

---

200 Vattel, *Nations*, Book 1, Chap. 19, [213], p. 218 and [218]-[219], p. 220.

201 See above, [82].

202 Pufendorf, *Nature and Nations*, Book 7, Chap. 2, [20], p. 994; also Grotius, *War and Peace*, Book 2, Chap. 1, [5], p. 709; Pufendorf, *Whole Duty*, Chap. 6, [13], p. 197; Wolff, *Nations*, Chap. 3, [303]-[304], pp. 219-221; Vattel, *Nations*, Book 1, Chap. 19, [213], p. 218 and Book 2, Chap. 8, [101], pp. 312-313; also Blackstone, *Commentaries* (n. 191), Vol. 1, [358], pp. 237-238.
See Laetitia Ramelet, "Pufendorf's Contract Theory of the State and the Distinction between Citizens and Foreigners", Chap. 4 in Peter Schröder (ed.), *Pufendorf's International Political and Legal Thought*, Oxford: Oxford University Press, 2024, at pp. 87-90.

203 Pufendorf, *Nature and Nations*, Book 7, Chap. 2, [20], p. 994; also Vattel, *Nations*, Book 2, Chap. 8, [101], p. 312.

204 Locke, *Two Treatises*, 2nd treatise, Chap. 8, [119]-[122], pp. 348-349, cf. Wolff, *Nations*, Chap. 3, [303]-[304], pp. 219-221, describing foreigners, while present, as "temporary citizens".
For discussion of the extent of adjudicatory authority over persons temporarily present in a particular place, see Sections III.C.5, IV.D and V.B.3.

is to be measured from the purpose for which they have associated themselves temporarily with citizens"[205].

4. Territoriality and the scope of "sovereign" authority

86. Before moving onwards, and in anticipation of what is to come, it may be useful to add the following coda.

87. There is, understandably, little discussion in the texts of the consequences of engagement with a political society, or with its members, at a distance, without entering its territory. As noted[206], Grotius expressed the view that a contract concluded by letter between parties in different places remained within the exclusive province of the law of nature. As a guide to the limits of lawmaking authority, the statement seems unduly cautious for its time and is untenable today. Communication and commerce fall within the sphere of influence of government of a political society when they affect its members[207]. Individuals residing in different political societies may use these channels purposefully in order to associate with each other, communicating with a view to commercial dealings or sending goods across the border. Potentially, both societies affected by this activity may assert the authority to regulate the activity and to resolve disputes that arise from it. In accordance with the view expressed by Wolff, the extent of that authority will depend on the circumstances of the case, having regard to the nature and purpose of the association and, in particular, to the element of the parties' relationship giving rise to the dispute[208].

---

205 Wolff, *Nations*, Chap. 3, [304], pp. 220-221.

206 Text to n. 158.

207 Vattel, *Nations*, Book 2, Chaps. 8 and 9; also Joseph Story, "Nations, Law of", pp. 141-149, in Francis Lieber (ed.), *Encyclopedia Americana*, Philadelphia: Lea & Blanchard, Vol. 9, 1835, at p. 145.

208 Text to n. 205. See e.g. *Koster* v. *Automark Industries*, 640 F 2d 77, 79, 7th Cir, 1981 (use of cross-border communication

88. This leads to a wider point about "territory" and "territoriality"[209]. Political societies are formed, and constantly sustained, by the actions of human beings. It is from those human actions that a political society's institutions derive their authority to exercise control over things, including land, rather than the other way round. States, embodying one or several political societies[210], are defined *inter alia* by their borders[211], and international law demands respect for the integrity of the territory within those borders[212], analogously to the respect that the law of nature demands for an individual's bodily integrity[213]. Political societies exercise exclusive authority[214] over what Wolff and Vattel describe as the

---

channels in contractual negotiations does not, of itself, satisfy jurisdictional requirements when a dispute arises upon the contract).

209 For other perspectives on this topic, see Alex Mills, "Justifying and Challenging Territoriality in Private International Law", Chap. 8, in Michael S. Green, Ralf Michaels and Roxana Banu (eds.), *Philosophical Foundations of Private International Law*, Oxford: Oxford University Press, 2024; Jean Gottmann, *The Significance of Territory*, Charlottesville: The University Press of Virginia, 1973; Christopher Rudolph, "Sovereignty and Territorial Borders in a Global Age" (2005), 7 *International Studies Review* 1; David Storey, "States, Territory and Sovereignty" (2017), 102 *Geography* 116.

210 In a union or federal State (such as Australia, Germany, United Kingdom or the United States), relations between the legal orders of the constituent political societies are governed by constitutional rules, written or unwritten.

211 For example, "a set of institutions that possesses a monopoly on rule-making and the legitimate use of force within a bounded territory", Calhoun (ed.), *Dictionary of the Social Sciences* (n. 6), "state", p. 462.

212 UN Charter (n. 18), Article 2 (4); Sir Michael Wood, "Territorial Integrity", in *The Princeton Encyclopedia of Self-Determination*, https://pesd.princeton.edu/node/686.

213 See above, [49] and below, [97].

214 Vattel, *Nations*, Book 1, Chap. 18, [203], p. 213 and Book 2, Chap. 7, [79], pp. 301-302; also Story, "Nations, Law of", in *Encyclopedia Americana*, Vol. 9 (n. 207), at p. 144.

"domain", qualifying in this respect the natural liberty that individuals would otherwise enjoy in respect of the things that lie there[215]. It is, however, a logical error to reason from these premises to the conclusion that the legislative or adjudicatory power of a political society is generally confined to persons and things that, at the relevant time, are *physically* situated within its geographical boundaries[216]. The governing principle is more accurately stated by Vattel – that a political society has the power to dispense justice in all places within its domain, authorising it "to take cognisance of . . . the differences that arise in the country"[217]. With every dispute having at least two parties, linked in some way by the circumstances giving rise to the contest, more than one political society may have a sufficient interest in the matter to warrant the exercise of this power to administer justice[218].

---

215 Wolff, *Nations*, Chap. 3, [281] and [305]-[307], pp. 206, 221-223; Vattel, *Nations*, Book 1, Chap. 18, [203]-[204], p. 213 and Chap. 20, [244], p. 232. As these extracts emphasise, a political society's authority with respect to its domain was originally derived from, and explained by reference to, the natural entitlement of its members to the land that they possessed.

216 An error of this kind was made by the US Supreme Court in *Pennoyer* v. *Neff* (1878), 95 US 714, but has since been corrected, see *International Shoe Co* v. *Washington* (n. 197). The English courts fell into the same trap, see Andrew Dickinson, "*Schibsby* v. *Westenholz and the Recognition and Enforcement of Judgments in England*" (2018), 134 *Law Quarterly Review* 426, esp. at 430-435 and Sections III.C.5 and IV.D.

217 Vattel, *Nations*, Book 2, Chap. 7, [84]-[85], pp. 303-305 and [103], p. 313. See Section III.D.2.

218 *Ibid.*, p. 304, see Sections IV.D and V.8.3.
George Rutherglen and James Y. Stern, "Sovereignty, Territoriality and the Enforcement of Judgments", Chap. 1, in Paul B. Stephen (ed.), *Foreign Court Judgments and the United States Legal System*, Leiden: Brill Nijhoff, 2014, suggest that the error of the US Supreme Court in *Pennoyer*

89. It will be obvious from these remarks that an individual may have overlapping attachments of different kinds, in different degrees to different political societies. Political societies are not hermetically sealed units – the intercourse between them occupies the attention of students of the conflict of laws. Returning to the (admittedly, imprecise) analogy with set theory[219], it is the intersection of legislative and adjudicative authority of different political societies that shapes the discipline.

Figure 4

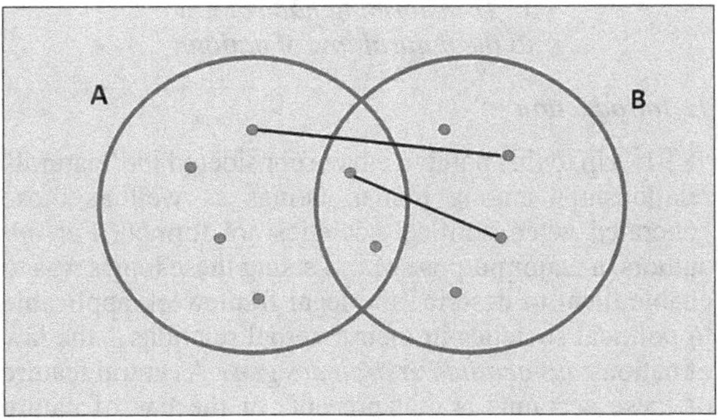

90. The diagram in Figure 4 represents, in simplified form, a tiny part of the universal set of humankind. Several members of that set (illustrated by dots) are distributed across two political societies, A and B. Some (dots appearing in the intersection) have political or social connections to both societies, for example, a person who

---

(above, n. 216) lay "in transposing the strict requirements of territorial presence for issues of execution at the end of the lawsuit to those of personal jurisdiction at the beginning". See also Andrew Dickinson, "Keeping Up Appearances: The Development of Adjudicatory Jurisdiction in the English Courts" (2016) 86 *British Yb Int L* 6, 10-16.

219 See above, [39].

is a citizen of A but lives for part of the year within B's domain. The lines show relationships between or among members of the two societies, involving activity crossing the line between their respective spheres of influence (such as the formation or performance of a contract). The objects appearing in the intersection illustrate the potential for the legislative or adjudicatory authority of the institutions of the two societies to overlap, creating the need for conflict of laws rules to reduce friction in the intercourse between them.

J. Transforming natural law to the natural law of nations

1. Introduction

91. Up to this point, we have considered the "natural" relationships among human beings as well as those generated when political societies are formed. For our authors, a major purpose of traversing these topics was to enable them to describe the legal framework applicable to political societies in their external relations – the law of nations, *ius gentium* or *droit des gens*. A central feature of these accounts is that precepts of the law of nature governing individual human relationships carry across to the relations between nations, as well as to the relations that each nation has with the members of other nations[220].

---

[220] Grotius, *War and Peace*, Book 1, Preliminary Discourse, [18], p. 94 and Chap. 1, [15], pp. 164-165, noting here the critical comment (fn. 3 on p. 165) taken from the translation prepared by Jean Barbeyrac (n. 33); Hobbes, *Citizen*, Chap. 14, [4], p. 156; Hobbes, *Leviathan*, Chap. 30, [185], p. 244, "the Law of Nations, and the Law of Nature, is the same thing"; Pufendorf, *Nations*, Book 2, Chap. 2, [4], p. 163 and [7], p. 168 and Chap. 3, [23], p. 226; Pufendorf, *Whole Duty*, Book 2, Chap. 1, [6], p. 168; Locke, *Two Treatises*, 2nd treatise, Chap. 12, [143], p. 164; Wolff, *Nations*, Prolegomena, [1]-[8], pp. 12-17 and [17], p. 22; Vattel, *Nations*, Preface, xiii, p. 14 and Preliminaries, [4]-

The rules governing war, peace and the resolution of disputes in the public sphere were originally derived from, and linked to, the treatment of those matters in the private sphere[221].

92. There are, of course, significant differences of theory and of detail in the connections drawn between the law of nations and the law of nature. Most notably, the authors differ as to the role played by natural law precepts in the system of the law of nations and their relationship to other sources of that law, in particular treaty and custom. These differences lay at the heart of the scholarly contest in the eighteenth and nineteenth centuries between "Grotians" and "naturalists" and between "rationalists" and "positivists" to capture the soul of the emerging discipline of public international law[222]. As we will see, the emerging discipline of

---

[28], pp. 68-79. See also Joseph Story, "Nations, Law of", in *Encyclopedia Americana*, Vol. 9 (n. 207), at pp. 141-142, 143.

221 Grotius, *War and Peace*, Book 1, Chap. 1, [1], p. 133 and Book 2, Chap. 1, [16], p. 416; Wolff, *Nations*, Chap. 6, [607]-[608], pp. 447-448, "the nature of public war is to be determined from that of private war". See above, [60].

222 Stephen C. Neff, *Justice among Nations*, Harvard: Harvard University Press, 2014, Chaps. 4-8; Alex Mills, *The Confluence of Public and Private International Law*, Cambridge: Cambridge University Press, 2009, pp. 40-44, 53-56; Marti Koskenniemi, *From Apology to Utopia – The Structure of International Legal Argument*, Helsinki: Lakimiesliiton Kustannus, 1989, pp. 83-127; Arthur Nussbaum, *A Concise History of the Law of Nations*, New York: Macmillan Co, 1953, pp. 147-185, 232-236.
See also Miloš Vec, "From the Congress of Vienna to the Paris Peace Treaties" and Marti Koskenniemi, "A History of International Law Histories", Chaps. 27 and 39, in Bardo Fassbender and Anne Peters (eds.), *The Oxford Handbook of the History of International Law*, Oxford: Oxford University Press, 2012, esp. at pp. 666-671, 948-958; Jean d'Aspremont, "International Legal Positivism and the European Quest for Scientificity", and Mary Ellen O'Connell, "The Role of Natural Law in the Rise and

private international law had its own version of this contest[223].

93. Although we will examine some of these issues in the next chapter in considering the writing of Ulrik Huber[224], it is not necessary here to adopt or defend a particular view as to the theoretical basis, or the content, of modern public international law[225]. Our primary interest here is to observe how a normative framework governing human relations can be transformed into one governing the external relations of political societies.

2. *From the law of nature to the natural law of nations*

94. Using Vattel's influential account of the law of nations[226], we can map the concepts discussed in the preceding sections within this chapter to a framework of rules and principles governing the relations of independent nations and their legal orders. This framework accounts for important features of the legal landscape within public and private international law today[227].

Decline of European International Law", Chap. 15 in Anne van Aaken, Pierre d'Argent, Lauri Mälksoo and Johann Justus Vasel (eds.), *The Oxford Handbook of International Law in Europe*, Oxford: Oxford University Press, https://academic.oup.com/edited-volume/46846.

223 Section III.E.3-5.

224 Section III.C.4.

225 The terms "law of nations" and "nation(s)" are used here, in preference to "(public) international law" and "state(s)", to distinguish this natural law framework from the system and rules that operate today in the international legal order.

226 Vattel, as he readily acknowledged, drew inspiration from the more detailed work of his contemporary, Wolff, see Vattel, *Nations*, Preface, xi-xii, pp. 12-13, although he rejected one of that author's key conclusions (see n. 242).

227 Joseph Story subdivided international law into the public and private law of nations, with the former regulating "the rights, intercourse and obligations of nations, as such, with each other" and the latter "the rights more immediately belonging to their respective subjects", Story, "Nations,

(a) *Personality*

95. We have noted Vattel's definition of a "nation" as a body politic, a union of human beings combined for mutual safety and advantage[228]. Every nation, by deliberating and making resolutions in respect of its own affairs and interest, is characterised as a moral person, distinguishable from its subjects[229] and capable of expressing its will and holding rights and obligations[230].

(b) *Natural legal order and liberty*

96. As a moral person, a nation comprises "so many free persons living together in a state of nature"[231]. As individual human beings are in a state of natural liberty in relation to one another[232], so too are nations "absolutely free and independent with respect to all other [humans[233]], all other nations, as long as it has not voluntarily submitted to them"[234]. This natural liberty, to be exercised principally, but not exclusively[235], within

---

Law of", in *Encyclopedia Americana*, Vol. 9 (n. 207), at p. 141.
As to terminology, see also Henry Wheaton, *Elements of International Law*, Philadelphia: Carey, Leach and Blanchard, 1836, p. 36, fn. 2.

228 Vattel, *Nations*, Preliminaries, [1], p. 67.

229 As to the personality of States in international law today, see *The Law Debenture Trust Corporation plc* v. *Ukraine* [2023] UKSC 11, [2024] AC 411, [18]-[19].

230 Vattel, *Nations*, Preliminaries, [2], p. 67.

231 *Ibid.*, [4], p. 68.

232 Section II.C.

233 Substituted here for "men".

234 Vattel, *Nations*, Preliminaries, [4].

235 Following the logic of the proposition that it is the embodiment of the persons who constituted it (see above, [95]), a nation assumes and may assert in its relations with other nations the natural liberty of its members, which although not boundless is not spatially limited to the nation's domain (see above, [38] and Section II.C).

each nation's domain[236], constitutes their "jurisdiction" in international law[237], although the use of this language in different senses in public and private international law has long been an unhappy source of confusion[238].

97. As with individuals, the law of nature imposes constraints upon the natural liberty of nations, with concomitant duties on them towards others, who in turn are able to protect themselves against unwarranted

---

In particular, the liberty to navigate and exploit the open sea is, by the law of nature, common to all, Vattel, *Nations*, Book 1, Chap. 23, [281], p. 250, and a nation that attempts to exclude seafarers from other nations from that area acts unlawfully, *ibid.*, [282]-[283], p. 251.

236 See above, [88].

237 *Ibid.*, Book 2, Chap. 7, [84], pp. 301-302. See *The Case of the SS Lotus* (1927) PCIJ Series A No. 10, 19 ("[A] wide measure of discretion which is only limited in certain cases by prescriptive rules; as regards other cases every State remains free to adopt the principles which it regards as best and most suitable").

238 The word "jurisdiction" has its root in the Latin *iuris* (genitive singular of *ius*, law or right) and *dictio* (nominative singular, a saying or pronouncement). In the conflict of laws, the term "jurisdiction" refers to the actual or potential exercise of legislative or adjudicative authority by a nation's institutions within their sphere of influence and not to the relationship existing between nations. This is a Hohfeldian power, whereas the term "jurisdiction" in public international law refers to a Hohfeldian liberty (see n. 56). In *The SS Lotus* (n. 237), the Turkish court exercised criminal jurisdiction in the conflict of laws sense with respect the French officer held partly responsible for the collision and the resulting deaths of eight Turkish nationals, Lieutenant Demons. The Permanent Court of International Jurisdiction held that this fell within the scope of the liberty afforded to Turkey as a matter of public international law to regulate its own affairs. Accordingly, Turkey was not under any duty to France to refrain from acting.
See Sophie Ryan, "Fundamental Legal Conceptions and the International Law of (Civil) Jurisdiction" (2025), 42 *Australian Yearbook Int L* 130.

interference with their own natural liberty[239]. This accounts for the principle of territorial integrity in international law[240] as well as the wider principle of non-intervention with the internal affairs of other nations[241].

(c) *Natural and political society and duties of humanity*

98. Society is necessary if humankind is to to survive and to thrive. In this natural society – Vattel's "universal society of the human race"[242] – "each individual should do for the others every thing which their necessities

---

[239] Vattel, *Nations*, Preliminaries, [5], p. 68; also *ibid.*, [7] (p. 70) and [15], p. 74, "[E]ach nation should be left in the peaceable enjoyment of that liberty which she inherits from nature".

[240] *The SS Lotus* (n. 237), 18-19; UN Charter (n. 18), Article 2 (4).

[241] Vattel, *Nations*, Preliminaries, [9], p. 71, Book 1, Chap. 4, [36]-[37], p. 97, Book 2, Chap. 4, [54], p. 289, Book 2, Chap. 7 and Book 3, Chap. 18, [296], pp. 648-649; also Wolff, *Nations*, Chap. 2, [255]-[257] and [269], pp. 188-190, 198.
See Sir Michael Wood, "Non-Intervention (Non-Interference in Domestic Affairs)", in *The Princeton Encyclopedia of Self-Determination*, https://pesd.princeton.edu/node/551, crediting Vattel as being the first to formulate this principle; also Maziar Jamnejad and Michael Wood, "The Principle of Non-Intervention" (2009), 22 *Leiden J Int L* 345.
Admittedly, the analogy with individual relationships takes us only so far, and it is necessary to consider the particular character and resources that nations possess, Vattel, *Nations*, Preliminaries, [6], p. 649; also Story, "Nations, Law of", in *Encyclopedia Americana* Vol. 9 (n. 207), at p. 144, noting that "their means are more extensive, and their authority more complete than those of individuals".

[242] Vattel rejects Wolff's conception of a natural, universal political society between nations, the *civitatis maximae*, Vattel, *Nations*, Preface, xiii-xv, pp. 14-15. Compare Kant, "Perpetual Peace" (n. 50), pp. 102-105; UN Charter (n. 18), Preamble (see below, [304]).

require, and which he can do without neglecting the duty that he owes to himself"[243]. Human beings "by their very nature and essence" are "obliged to unite their common efforts for the perfection of their own being and that of their condition"[244].

99. Membership of a political society[245] does not discharge this individual duty of humanity towards the rest of humankind[246]. However, as Vattel points out, the primary responsibility for fulfilling that duty now rests with the nation rather than with the individual[247]. Moreover, nations, as moral persons, owe a like duty to each other[248].

100. This leads Vattel to the following striking conclusion[249]:

> "Since the object of the natural society established between all mankind is that they should lend each other mutual assistance in order to attain perfection themselves and to render their condition as perfect as possible, and since nations, considered as so many free persons living together in a state of nature, are bound to cultivate human society with each other, the object of the great society established by nature between all nations is also the interchange of mutual assistance for their own improvement and that of their condition."

101. This overarching obligation of humanity, manifested in many ways[250], is nonetheless qualified in two

---

[243] Vattel, *Nations*, Preliminaries, [10], pp. 71-72; also Book 2, Chap. 1, [2]-[3], pp. 261-262. See above, [64].
[244] Vattel, *Nations*, Book 2, Chap. 1, [3], p. 262.
[245] See above, [83]-[85].
[246] Vattel, *Nations*, Preliminaries, [11], p. 72.
[247] *Ibid.*, pp. 72-73. See below, [107].
[248] Vattel, *Nations*, p. 73; also Book 2, Chap. 1, [3], p. 262.
[249] Vattel, *Nations*, Preliminaries, [12], p. 73. See UN Charter (n. 18), Article 1 (2)-(4).
[250] Vattel, *Nations*, Book 2, Chap. 1.

important respects. First, it is subject to the paramount duty of each nation to secure its own happiness and perfection[251], taking such steps as it is lawfully able to, consistently with principles of justice and honour[252]. Second, the duty imposed on each nation to provide mutual assistance to other nations is itself an imperfect duty[253]. Measures of support from another nation can be asked for but not demanded or compelled by the use of force[254].

102. Accordingly, although bound by a common duty of humanity to contribute to the perfection of other nations, each nation, exercising its natural liberty independently of others, is free to judge for itself how to strike the balance between its own interests and those of other nations[255]. Other nations, for their own part, can choose to strike this balance for themselves in the same or in different ways. A nation, dissatisfied with the way in which it or its subjects have been treated is at liberty to declare that it will respond in kind, by an act of *retorsion*[256]. By withdrawing co-operation, one nation may hope that the other will alter its stance[257].

---

[251] As to this concept, see Vattel, *Nations*, Preliminaries, [12], (p. 73), Book 1, Chap. 1, [15], p. 86 and [21]-[23], pp. 88-89 and Book 2, Chap. 1, [6], pp. 264-265 and [18], pp. 271-272. With respect to the administration of justice, see above, [78]. With specific reference to the recognition and enforcement of judgments, see Section III.E.2.

[252] Vattel, *Nations*, Preliminaries, [14], pp. 73-74.

[253] See above, [65].

[254] Vattel, *Nations*, Book 1, Preliminaries, [16]-[17], pp. 74-75 and Book 1, Chap. 1, [10], p. 266. A failure to provide assistance upon request is not a just cause of war (*ibid.*, Book 3, Chap. 3, [26], pp. 48-49).

[255] Vattel, *Nations*, Book 1, Preliminaries, [16], p. 74 and [20]-[21], pp. 75-76 and Book 2, Chap. 1, [9], p. 266.

[256] *Ibid.*, Book 3, Chap. 18, [341].

[257] See generally text to n. 270; also below, [229] and Sections III.F and V.B.5, on the requirement of reciprocity in the recognition and enforcement of foreign judgments.

(d) *Equality of nations*

103. All nations are naturally equal[258] in their relations with each other and have the same obligations and rights[259]. "A small republic is no less a sovereign state than the most powerful kingdom."[260] This natural equality, expressed in the maxim *par in parem non habet imperium*, grounds the fundamental principle of sovereign equality of States in international law[261], from which the doctrine of State immunity is derived[262].

(e) *The administration of justice between nations*

104. Vattel emphasised that nations are under "a strict obligation to cultivate justice towards each other"[263]. This requires them to respect the rights of other nations, by observing the limits that the law of nature imposes[264]. Although each may measure and prefer its own interest in performing the common duty of humanity[265], it must refrain from acts that exceed its lawful jurisdiction and that cause injury to another nation, by impairing their condition, perfection or progress[266].

---

258 Section II.D.

259 Vattel, *Nations*, Preliminaries, [18]-[19], p. 75 and [21], pp. 75-76. See UN Charter (n. 18), Article 2 (2); Le Fur, "La théorie" (n. 16), 425-429.

260 Vattel, *Nations*, Preliminaries, [18], p. 75.

261 UN Charter (n. 18), Article 2 (1).

262 *Jurisdictional Immunities of the State (Germany* v. *Italy)*, Judgment, *ICJ Reports 2012*, p. 99, [57].

263 Vattel, *Nations*, Book 2, Chap. 5, [64], p. 296; also Wolff, *Nations*, Chap. 2, [264]-[265], p. 195.

264 Vattel, *Nations*, Preliminaries, [5], p. 96 and Chap. 5, [63]-[64], p. 296.

265 See above, [101].

266 Vattel, *Nations*, Book 2, Chap. 1, [18], pp. 271-272 and Book 2, Chap. 18, [324], p. 448; also Wolff, *Nations*, Chap. 2, [173], [179], [255]-[257], [269], pp. 130-131, 134-135, 188-190, 198.

105. If a nation faced with an actual or threatened breach by another nation of an enforceable (that is to say, perfect[267]) obligation has not received just satisfaction of its complaint[268], it may resort to force[269] or lawful countermeasures[270] to ensure its security or to vindicate its rights[271].

106. The freedom to resort to such measures in self-defence must nonetheless be exercised cautiously, showing restraint in cases of doubt[272]. The law of nature generally requires the parties to an international dispute to exhaust peaceable means to resolve it, by an amicable accommodation, compromise, mediation or arbitration[273]. Countermeasures are lawful only if the injured party has demanded, but not received, justice[274]. An otherwise lawful basis for the use of force may become unlawful if the wrongdoer offers just satisfaction[275]. These features of the law of nations are founded on the fundamental

---

267 See above, [65].

268 Vattel, *Nations*, Book 2, Chap. 18, [324], p. 448.

269 *Ibid.*, Preliminaries, [22]-[23], pp. 76-77, Book 2, Chap. 4, [49]-[52], pp. 288-289 and Chap. 5, [65]-[70], pp. 296-297 and Book 3, Chap. 1, [3]-[5], pp. 469-471 and Chap. 3, [26]-[28], pp. 483-484.

270 *Ibid.*, Book 2, Chap. 18, [342]-[354], pp. 460-467 (reprisals). As to retorsion, in response to conduct that does not amount to a breach of duty, see text to n. 256. See also UN draft Articles on Responsibility of States for Internationally Wrongful Acts (2001) (A/RES/56/83), Part II, Chap. 3.

271 Vattel, *Nations*, Preliminaries, [22]-[23], pp. 76-77, Book 2, Chap. 4, [49]-[53], pp. 288-289 and Chap. 5, [65]-[70], pp. 296-297 and Book 3, Chap. 1, [5], p. 471.

272 *Ibid.*, Preliminaries, [21] and Book 2, Chap. 5, [70].

273 *Ibid.*, Book 2, Chap. 18, [326]-[334], pp. 450-456 and Book 2, Chap. 3, [38], p. 489. See also UN Charter (n. 18), Article 33 (1).

274 *Ibid.*, Book 2, Chap. 18, [343], pp. 460-461 and [350], p. 464.

275 *Ibid.*, Book 3, Chap. 3, [36], p. 488 and Chap. 4, [1], pp. 500-501 and Book 4, Chap. 1, [6], pp. 654-655.

obligation of all human beings[276], and by extension all nations, to cultivate peace and to avoid a state of war[277].

107. This framework also applies to the resolution of disputes between the members of different political societies. The maintenance of peace within, and among, nations would be jeopardised if private individuals could act as a judge in their own cause and resort to force or other self-help mechanisms to redress perceived wrongful conduct by the subject of another nation[278]. Instead, aggrieved parties must resort to the mechanisms available for the administration of justice within their own society or their opponent's society. Historically, this may have involved a direct appeal to the sovereign, but the primary means of redress today are provided by courts[279]. If a nation acts unjustly towards the subject of another nation, this may itself constitute an internationally wrongful act, with the consequences described above[280]. Again, however, Vattel urges caution – this conclusion is not one that is lightly to be reached[281]. Vattel emphasises that the injustice must be "manifest and palpable"[282].

K. Summary and conclusions

108. From this broad-ranging narrative, we can narrow our focus to questions concerning the recognition and

---

276 Section II.E.

277 Vattel, *Nations*, Book 4, Chap. 1, [1]-[4], pp. 651-654. See UN Charter (n. 18), Article 1 (1)-(2), Article 2 (3) and Chap. VI.

278 Vattel, *Nations*, Book 2, Chap. 18, [346], p. 462 (reprisals) and Book 3, Chap. 1, [4], pp. 470-471.

279 See Vattel, *Nations*, Book 2, Chap. 6, [77], pp. 300-301.

280 *Ibid.*, Book 2, Chap. 6, [77], pp. 300-301 and Book 3, Chap. 18, [350], p. 464; also Grotius, *War and Peace*, Book 3, Chap. 2, [5], point 1, pp. 1239-1240. See generally Edwin M. Borchard, *The Diplomatic Protection of Citizens Abroad*, New York: Banks Law Publishing, 1925, esp. Chap. 8.

281 Vattel, *Nations*, Book 2, Chap. 7, [84], p. 304.

282 *Ibid.*, Book 3, Chap. 18, [350], p. 464.

enforcement of judgments, with the following six general propositions in mind:

(1) When a dispute arises between two parties who belong to different political societies, it is in the interests of the parties and of the two societies concerned that the dispute be resolved by peaceful means. A state of war between them, or between their nations, is to be avoided if at all possible.

(2) The peaceful resolution of a dispute is unlikely if both parties act as the judges in their own cause. If the parties, seeking a peaceful settlement, choose a third party to adjudicate their dispute, they will be bound by the decision of this "common judge"[283]. By the nature of that appointment, the latter must act independently of, and impartially towards, the parties, treating them as equals.

(3) One of the main objects of every political society is the administration of justice, including by providing mechanisms for the peaceful resolution of disputes within the society, predominantly by an official appointed to serve as a common judge. These mechanisms override the parties' natural liberty to act as the judges in their own cause. Of necessity, to promote attainment of this object, the parties are bound by the final decision of the political society's judicial organs acting within the limits of their authority.

(4) The authority that every political society has to administer justice by adjudication is not limited to disputes between citizens or permanent residents but extends to other disputes that arise within its sphere of influence. The extent of its authority depends on the degree of connection that the parties and the subject

[283] This term was used by Locke to contrast the administration of justice in a state of nature with that within a political society, Locke, *Two Treatises*, 2nd treatise, Chap. 3, [19], p. 281.

matter of the dispute have to the society and to the domain over which it exercises control.

(5) Every nation as a moral person representing one or more political societies is subject to an imperfect duty, the common duty of humanity, to contribute to the perfection of other nations. This duty extends to the administration of justice. In judging how to perform this duty, each nation may legitimately choose to prefer its own essential interests (including the administration of justice within its own society) over those of other nations.

(6) If a nation acts in a way that is manifestly and palpably unjust towards the subjects of another nation, in particular by denying them equal access to justice, this may engage the former nation's international responsibility towards the latter. As injustice is an anathema to the perfection of a political society, no nation has a duty to perpetuate it.

109. For the avoidance of doubt, it is not necessary to hold an unshakeable belief that law's authority is tied to precepts of the law of nature in order to accept these propositions as meritorious. A pragmatist should be willing to countenance the social and economic benefits that will result for any society from the peaceful resolution of disputes by an independent and impartial adjudicator and to acknowledge the advantages that may result from collaboration with others to secure that end. Natural law provides a toolbox, which may aid the design and implementation of legal rules at the national level. Nevertheless, within the broad limits of the liberty recognised in (public) international law[284], every political society remains free to regulate its own mechanisms for the administration of justice, in line with its own priorities, acting unilaterally or in concert with

284 See above, [96]-[97].

others. This explains the wide variety of approaches to the recognition and enforcement of judgments across the world's legal orders.

CHAPTER III

NATURAL LAW AND THE RECOGNITION AND ENFORCEMENT OF JUDGMENTS

A. Fundamental questions

110. The natural law accounts considered here are alive to the difficulties created when a dispute of entitlement arises between members of different political societies. The questions are of three kinds. First, who has the authority to adjudicate? Second, what is the source of the rules of law that are to be applied in adjudicating upon the question of relative entitlement? Third, by what means is the adjudication to be made effective [285]? Every political society, exercising its liberty, can give its own answers to these questions, provided that it observes limits imposed by the law of nations. The most important of these limits is that it cannot secure the effectiveness of its judgments by the use of force within the territory of another nation or by violating the principle of non-intervention in another nation's internal affairs [286].

---

[285] These represent, of course, the issues of jurisdiction, choice of law (applicable law) and the effectiveness of judgments around which texts and courses on the conflict of laws/ private international law are still organised today.

[286] See above, [97].
The principle would be violated, for example, if the adjudicating order were to purport to direct a court in another legal order to take steps to ensure the effectiveness of a judgment. In *SAS Institute* v. *World Programming Ltd.* [2020] EWCA Civ. 599, the English Court of Appeal held that an order made by a United States court against a party to United States litigation requiring it to assign the debts of its United Kingdom customers and to turn over payments received from those customers infringed "generally accep-

B. *Grotius (reprise)*

111. Grotius' analysis of these questions, although meagre, illustrates the hurdles that need to be overcome if the just and peaceful resolution of a dispute of this kind is to be achieved. He considers that acts between private parties undertaken while both are present in a particular place are subject to the laws of that place[287], while acts undertaken at a distance remain subject to the law of nature[288]. Grotius approaches the question of adjudicatory jurisdiction with similar caution. In his earlier work on *Prize*, having acknowledged the customary practice of nations that disputes between the citizens of different nations[289] are to be resolved through

---

table principles of customary international law" (*ibid.*, [111]-[112]) (for criticism, see Andrew Dickinson, "The Interference Paradox" (2020), 136 *Law Quarterly Review* 569).

Courts in England and other common law jurisdictions are themselves willing, in certain circumstances, to grant injunctions to restrain the enforcement of a foreign judgment throughout the world, see *Bank of St Petersburg PJSC* v. *Arkhangelsky* [2014] EWCA Civ 593, [2014] 1 WLR 4360; *SAS Institute*, above, [92]-[99]; Tiog Min Yeo, "Foreign Judgments and Contracts: The Anti-Enforcement Injunctions", Chap. 10, in Andrew Dickinson and Edwin Peel (eds.), *A Conflict of Laws Companion*, Oxford: Oxford University Press, 2021. This practice seems more likely to cross a red line in international law than the order made by the US court in *SAS Institute*.

287 Grotius, *War and Peace*, Book 2, Chap. 11, [5], point 2 (p. 709).

288 *Ibid.*, point 3, pp. 709-710. See above, [87].

289 It may be that Grotius would have treated differently the case in which both parties are both present in a single place at the time that the proceedings are initiated, on the basis that a foreigner present in a particular locality should conform to its laws, Grotius, *War and Peace*, Book 2, Chap. 2, [5], p. 33, c 11, [5], point 2, p. 709 and Chap. 14, [8], p. 810. It is, however, doubtful whether these comments, directed to

a judicial procedure[290], he notes the possibility of a "disagreement as to which of two states should be the one to discharge this function"[291]. He suggests that "the most suitable" way of resolving this conundrum would be to give precedence to the courts of the defendant's citizenship, unless "the said state proves remiss in the discharge of its judicial duty", in which case the courts of the claimant's citizenship should adjudicate[292]. Tellingly, his reason for proffering this solution is that the judgment could most easily be executed by the defendant's court as that it where assets are likely to be found to ensure an equitable outcome[293].

112. Grotius does not discuss the consequence if those assets should prove inadequate to discharge the judgment debtor's obligation to the judgment creditor. He hints that a judgment in the *defendant's* favour given by the defendant's home court might bring an end to the matter, excluding further recourse by the claimant before their own courts, but only if the adjudicating court has discharged its judicial duty to act justly. Discussing a situation in which "a state stubbornly defends an injury inflicted by its citizens", Grotius argues that "the conduct of the trial passes by . . . natural law to the other party, namely the state that has complained of injury suffered either by itself or by one of its citizens"[294]. He continues[295]:

---

issues of substantive law, extend to the power to adjudicate, cf. Wolff, *Nations*, Chap. 3, [302], p. 219.
See Sections II.C.5 and IV.D.

290 Grotius, *Prize*, Chap. 2 (Prolegomena), [12']-[13], p. 47, Law XII.

291 *Ibid.*, [13], p. 47.

292 *Ibid.*, [13] (p. 47) (Rule IX); also *ibid.*, Chap. 8, [47'], p. 157 stating that this Rule demands a just judicial recourse for foreigners as well as citizens.

293 Grotius, *Prize*, Chap. 2 (Prolegomena), [13], p. 47.

294 *Ibid.*, [13'], p. 48.

295 *Ibid.*, [13'], p. 48 (emphasis added).

> "Accordingly, *in cases of this kind*, the mere passing of judgement in any form whatsoever will not suffice, *as it does when a judge lays down the law within a single state*."

113. Can one infer that, in a case in which the defendant's home court had conducted a fair trial of the dispute, Grotius would consider that its judgment should have the same effect as if both parties had shared the same citizenship, when both would be bound[296]? Without a clear statement to that effect, this would be a matter of speculation. It is, however, corroborated in the later and more famous of Grotius' works, *War and Peace*. In discussing the possibility of reprisals "where a right is denied"[297], the author gives two examples – *(a)* when a judgment cannot be obtained within a reasonable time and *(b)* a case that does not admit of any doubt. He suggests, however, that "in doubtful cases the presumption is in favour of the judges established by public authority" and proceeds to draw a distinction between the force of a judgment against "strangers" and against subjects. In his view, subjects are bound by the sentence of the court, even though it may be unjust. Although strangers retain the power to use unilateral, coercive measures[298], this cannot be exercised while "they may recover their right in a judicial way"[299]. Their liberty to defend themselves is constrained, so long as the interests of justice are being served.

---

296 *Ibid.*, [11'a], p. 42. Presumably, if justice had been denied to the defendant by their own courts, the latter would be entitled to raise an internal complaint but this would not directly concern the claimant or the nation of which the claimant was a citizen.

297 Grotius, *War and Peace*, Book 3, Chap. 2, [5], pp. 1239-1240.

298 Exercised through their own nation.

299 Grotius, *War and Peace*, Book 3, Chap. 2, [5], p. 1240.

C. Going Dutch – Paulus and Johannes Voet, and Ulrik Huber

1. Introduction

114. These questions received more detailed treatment in the major works of Paulus Voet (1619-1677), Ulrik Huber (1636-1694) and Johannes Voet (1647-1713). Huber has had a greater influence upon the conflict of laws in the common law world, while the Voets, father and son, have been held in higher esteem in civilian and Roman-Dutch systems[300].

[300] On Paulus and Johannes Voet, see Mathijs ten Wolde, "Voet, Paulus and Johannes", in Jürgen Basedow, Giesela Rühl, Franco Ferrari and Pedro de Miguel Asensio, *Encyclopedia of Private International Law*, Cheltenham: Edward Elgar, 2017, Vol. 2, pp. 1821-1824; A. B. (Basil) Edwards and D. M. (David) Kriel, "The Selective Paulus Voet", reproduced in (2007) 13 Fundamina: A Journal of Legal History 1, esp. at 1-25 (Chap. 1) and 310-516 (Chap. 4), https://journals.co.za/toc/funda/13/1; Johannes van Kralingen, "Paulus Voet", in Wim Decock and Janwillem Oosterhuis (eds.), *Great Christian Jurists in the Low Countries*, Cambridge: Cambridge University Press, 2021, Chap. 7.
On Ulrik Huber, see Mathijs ten Wolde, "Huber, Ulrich" in *Encyclopedia of Private International Law*, above, Vol. 1, pp. 876-880; Ernest G. Lorenzen, *"Huber's De Conflictu Legum"* (1919), 23 *Illinois L Rev.* 376; D. J. Llewelyn Davies, "The Influence of Huber's *De conflictu legum* on English Private International Law" (1937), 18 *British Yb Int L* 49; Edwards and Kriel, above, 397-405; Margaret Louise Hewett, *De Ratione Juris docendi et discendi diatribe*, Nijmegen: Gerart Noodt Institut, 2010, https://pure.uva.nl/ws/files/1513124/74250_thesis.pdf, pp. 79-83; Nikitas E. Hatzimihail, *Preclassical Conflict of Laws*, Cambridge: Cambridge University Press, 2021, esp. Chaps. 11-14; Atsuko Fukuoka, "Ulrik Huber", in *Great Christian Jurists in the Low Countries*, above.
As to the political setting for these works, written by scholars residing in the United Provinces of the Netherlands during the seventeenth century, see Hessel E. Yntema, "The Comity Doctrine" (1966), 65 *Michigan L Rev.* 9, 16-19; Hatzimihail, above, Chap. 12.

115. These authors, working in the United Dutch Provinces in the second half of the seventeenth century, approached the subject from a different standpoint. Although they were familiar with the contemporary writers on the law of nature, including Pufendorf and Hobbes[301], and frequently refer to the published work of their countryman, Grotius[302], they relied mainly on the classical texts of Roman law, as well as post-classical commentators upon the *corpus iuris civilis*. In addressing conflicts between the laws of different nations, their principal sources were "statutist" models developed by European writers, notably Bartolus of Saxony (1314-1357), Charles Dumoulin (1500-1566) and Bertrand d'Argentré (1519-1590)[303]. However, whereas these earlier texts, holding to the ideal of a *ius commune* shared by the inheritors of the Roman law tradition, had little of interest to say about our topic[304], the Dutch authors used the concept of comity to construct a new

---

301 See esp. Huber, *De Jure Civitatis libri tres*, Franeker: Johannes Gyselaar, 1684, Book 1, Chaps. 1-4 and *De Jure Civitatis libri tres* (Franeker: Apud Henricum Amama and Zachariam Taedema, 3rd ed., 1694), Book 1, Chaps. 1-5. See below, [131].
On Huber's perspective on the law of nature, see A. W. G. Raath and J. J. Henning, "Huber, Natural Law and the Reformational Basis of the *iurisprudentia universalis*" (2005), 30 *Journal for Juridical Science* 30.

302 Principally, but not exclusively, *War and Peace*, recalling here that the manuscript of *De Jure Praedae* was not published until much later (text to n. 32). See below, [117] and [128]-[148].

303 Pavel Kalenský, *Trends of Private International Law*, Prague: Academia, 1971, Chaps. 2 and 3; Edwards and Kriel (n. 300), 26-53, Chap. 2; Pietro Franzina, "Bartolus", in *Encyclopedia of Private International Law* (n. 300), Vol. 1, pp. 158-163; Hatzimihail (n. 300), Chaps. 7-10. See the materials collected in *Ius Commune, De Collisione Legum*, Frankfurt am Main: Vico Verlag, 2006.

304 Lorenzen, *"De Conflictu Legum"* (n. 300), 391.

bridge between the legal orders of distinct political communities[305].

2. Paulus Voet

116. The breakthrough[306] came in the elder Voet's work *De Statutis*, published in 1661[307]. His references, in various grammatical forms[308], to "comity"[309] as

[305] See Yntema, "The Comity Doctrine" (n. 300); Kurt H. Nadelmann, "The Comity Doctrine: Introduction" (1966), 65 *Michigan L Rev.* 1; Irina Getman-Pavlova, "The Concept of 'Comity' in Ulrik Huber's Conflict Doctrine", Higher School of Economics Research Paper WP BRP/LAW.2023, https://ssrn.com/abstract=2240233; Thomas Schultz and Jason Mitchenson, "The History of Comity" (2019), 4 *Jus Gentium – Journal of Legal History* 383, 398-407; also Joel R. Paul, "Comity in International Law" (1991), 32 *Harvard Int LJ* 1; Adrian Briggs, "The Principle of Comity in Private International Law" (2012), 354 *Recueil des cours* 65, esp. Chap. 4; Gilles Cuniberti, "Le fondement de l'effet des jugements étrangers" (2018), 394 *Recueil des cours* 93, Chap. 4.
For a valuable, broader account, see Timothy Endicott, "Comity among Authorities" (2015), 68 *Current Legal Problems* 1.

[306] For detailed treatment, with citations from Paulus Voet's published works, see Edwards and Kriel (n. 300), esp. at 333-347 and 379-380; also Yntema (n. 300), 22-23. Edwards and Kriel conclude (at 343) that Paulus Voet's conception of *comitas* "was a highly original one".

[307] *De Statutis Eorumque Concursu*, Amsterdam: Johannes van Waesberge, 1661 (Paulus Voet, *De Statutis*). The bracketed page number references in the following footnotes are to the Latin text (first reference) and English translation (second reference) in Edwards and Kriel (n. 300), pp. 55-309.

[308] Paulus Voet, *De Statutis*, s. 4, Chap. 2, (in the list of contents) [17] *(ex comitate)* and (in the main text), [17] *(comiter)*; s. 4, Chap. 3, 15 *(ex comitate)*, [17] *(comiter)*; s. 10, Chap. 4 *(comiter)*, s. 11, Chap. 1, [5] *(ex comitate)*.

[309] From *comes* (companion, associate) and *comis* (courteous; obliging; friendly). See also n. 335, considering the terminology used by Ulrik Huber.

a reason for the legal order of one political society to support or follow another's laws are typically combined with references to *aequitas* (equality or fairness)[310] and *humanitas* (humanity or human nature)[311]. Paulus Voet uses the latter term alone in discussing the execution of judicial sentences. Distinguishing the fragmented legal landscape of his time from the unified *imperium* of the Roman Empire, Voet observes that "in terms of our customs judges of a particular territory usually order a sentence given elsewhere to be executed *ex humanitate*, following letters of request, although they are not obliged to do this"[312]. Accordingly, as the commentary accompanying a recent translation explains, comity in Paulus Voet's work is "the expression of the desire to regulate legal relationships involving a foreign element in such a way that full expression may be given to the demands of *aequitas* and *humanitas*"[313].

---

310 From *aequus* (equal; fair; equitable; impartial). See Paulus Voet, *De Statutis*, s. 4, Chap. 2, [17], pp. 71, 72; s. 10, Chap. 1, [4] (comment), pp. 224, 225; s. 11, Chap. 2, [4], pp. 274, 275 (where *aequitas* alone – *ex aequitate* – is used to describe an act of judicial assistance in remitting assets).

311 Human nature; humanity; the qualities, feelings and inclinations of mankind. See Paulus Voet, *De Statutis*, s. 4, Chap. 3, [17] (comment), pp. 132, 133, counselling "deference to humanity *(humanitate)*, when a people out of comity *(ex comitate)* respect the decrees of a neighbouring people in order to avoid the confusion of many".

312 Paulus Voet, *De Statutis*, s. 10, Chap. 1, [14], pp. 238, 239. Voet adds that the people of Gelderland refuse to action such requests and that a judge will be far less likely to allow such execution against goods situated locally "if that statute was passed in conflict with a statute of his own territory" *(ibid.)*.

313 Edwards and Kriel (n. 300), p. 380, supporting the conclusion drawn by Roland Kollewijn, *Geschiedenis van de Nederlandsche wet van het international privaatrecht tot 1880*, Amsterdam: Noord-Hollandsche Uitg, 1937, pp. 90-91, and referring also to Ellison Kahn, "The Territorial and Comity School of the Conflict of Laws", in *Huldingbundel Daniel Pont*, Cape Town: Juta & Co, 1970, p. 232.

3. Johannes Voet

117. Johannes Voet built upon the foundations laid by his father in the first book of his commentary on the Pandects, published in 1698[314]. He begins with an account of the nature of justice and law. Voet takes issue with the views expressed by both Grotius and Pufendorf on the foundation of natural law, holding it to be an ordinance of God rather than a dictate of right reason (Grotius) or deduction from the social character of mankind (Pufendorf)[315]. Notwithstanding this difference in starting point, Johannes Voet's reasoning follows a similar path, concluding that the human condition demands the cultivation of a broader society and community of life with others[316] and that this common purpose would be frustrated without some constraint upon liberty of action and the existence of reciprocal offices of humanity[317].

118. These passages resonate in Voet's description of the role played by comity in the reception of foreign laws and judicial decrees[318]. Having noted that an individual's failure to render mutual services to others will make their life in society a miserable one, even if no duty would

---

314 *Commentarius ad Pandectas* (Leiden: Johannes Verbessel, Vol. 1, 1698; The Hague: Abraham de Hondt, Vol. 2, 1704) (Johannes Voet, *Commentarius*). The references in the following footnotes to "Gane" are to the English translation by Percival Gane, *The Selective Voet, Being the Commentary on the Pandects* (Paris edition of 1829), Durban: Butterworth & Co (Africa) Ltd., Vol. 1, 1955; Vol. 6, 1957.
See Edwards and Kriel (n. 300), 382-386.

315 Johannes Voet, *Commentarius*, Book 1, Title 1, [15], Gane (n. 314), Vol. 1, p. 18.
See H. J. Erasmus, "Natural Law: Voet's Criticism of De Groot" (2016), 22 *Fundamina* 40.

316 Johannes Voet, *Commentarius*, Book 1, Title 1, [15], Gane, above, Vol. 1, p. 18.

317 *Ibid.*, Vol. 1, p. 20 *(reciprocando humanitatis officia)*.

318 Cf. Hatzimihail (n. 300), p. 486, suggesting that the arguments deployed here by Voet are "pragmatic".

thereby be violated, Voet carries this reasoning across to relations between independent legal orders – a failure by lawmakers[319] to mitigate the rigour of their own laws and, "by mutual comity" (*mutua comitate*[320]), to approve and uphold the commands of others will not only "confound, upset and annul the good acts, decrees and enactments" of those others but also suffer their own laws and judgments to be confounded through "retaliation and strict law"[321]. Voet notes the possibility for special agreements or established customary practices between neighbours to mitigate the risk that "the exercise of comity and of assisting offices should be vague, uncertain and often not mutual", giving several examples[322].

119. In a separate discussion of the mechanisms for enforcement of foreign judgments, Voet recognises that "it is a matter of [mere[323]] comity, and in no way matter of [necessity[324]]"[325] if a judge in one legal order asks a judge in another, independent legal order to take steps to render a judicial decision effective[326]. He emphasises,

---

319 Magistrates, including those exercising judicial as well as legislative authority.

320 Johannes Voet, *Commentarius*, Book 1, Title 4, Appendix, [12], Gane (n. 314), Vol.1, p. 111. See also *ibid.*, *Summaria* (*comiter*; *ex comitate*; *mutua comitate*), [11] (*ex comitate*, twice), [12] (*ex comitate*, twice), [14] *(beneficio et comitate)*, [16] *(comitate)*, [17] *(comitatis, ex comitate)*.

321 Johannes Voet, *Commentarius*, Book 1, Title 4, Appendix, [12], Gane, above, Vol. 1, p. 111.

322 *Ibid.*, [17], Vol. 1, p. 115.

323 Substituted here for Gane's "sheer".

324 Substituted here for Gane's "need".

325 *Merae comitatis est, haud quaquàm necessitatis*. As his father had done, Johannes Voet contrasts this form of mutual assistance to the mandatory force of judgments within the former Roman Empire, citing Digest 42.1.15.1, Ulpian on the *Duties of Consul*, Book 3 and 5.1.45.1, Papinian, *Opinions*, Book 3.

326 Johannes Voet, *Commentarius*, Book 42, Title 1, [41], Gane (n. 314), Vol. 6, p. 340, giving the same example as his father (n. 312) regarding practice in the province of

however, the limited role of the receiving order's judge when comity *is* in play[327]:

Gelderland (see also *ibid.*, Book 1, Title 4, Appendix, [7]). He also expresses *(ibid.)*, the view that this assistance can be provided only upon a letter of request on the basis that "it is unfair for a judge who has had no cognizance of the cause to thrust himself into a suit judicially decided by another, so long as he is not invited through a request made by him who gave his decision to fill as it were the role of him that makes the request, and to act in his request", Gane, above Vol. 6, p. 341.

See also Simon à Groenewegen van der Made, *Tractatus de Legibus Abrogatis et Inusitatis in Hollandia Vicinisque Regionibus*, Leiden: Apud Franciscum Moyardum et Davidem Lopez de Haro, 1649, trans. Ben-Zion Beinart, *A treatise on the laws Abrogated and No Longer in Use in Holland and Neighbouring Regions*, Johannesburg: Lex-Patria, 1974-1984, comment on Digest 5.1.75, [6], Vol 2, pp. 51-52.

327 Johannes Voet, *Commentarius*, Book 42, Title 1, [41], Gane (n. 314), Vol. 6, p. 341.

Voet cites two authorities for this proposition, Digest 5.1.75, Julian, *Digest*, Book 36 and an opinion given in the work, *Consultatien, advysen en advertissementen, gegeven ende geschreven by verscheyden treffelijcke Rechts-geleerden in Hollandt*, Rotterdam: Johannes Naeranus, Vol. 2, 1645, Part 2, consultation 234.

The Digest text concerns the enforcement of default judgments, given after due citation of the proceedings to the defendant, and offers possible exceptions (fraud, extenuating circumstances) to the general rule that the enforcing judge cannot reopen the merits of the case.

The opinion (given in 1645 and apparently constituting advice to the Council of State of the United Provinces) relates to the enforcement of a judgment given by the municipal court of Tongeren, and affirmed on appeal, against assets held by the judgment debtor's son. With reference to sources including Code 9.3.2 and Digest 42.1.15.1, the authors opine that the sentence of one judge must be executed elsewhere, on account of the fact that one jurisdiction must help another. The opinion emphasises, with reference to sources including Code 7.50.3 and Code 7.53.2, 6, 8, that the proper role of the receiving order is to execute the judgment, using its own force and arms. *Res*

"[A]s a general rule the judge to whom the request is directed does not inquire into the justice of the judgment delivered by the other judge, nor subject it afresh to a rather searching examination, but presumes in favour of its justice and equity."[328]

120. Voet adds that enforcement may be refused if the foreign judgment would be incompatible with a local statute or if it is manifestly without legal effect[329].

4. Ulrik Huber

121. Ulrik Huber's treatment of conflict of laws issues appeared in three works first published between 1684 and 1689[330]. Huber's mark of distinction lies in

---

judicata must be respected. Cf. Code 7.52.1, allowing for an exception in the case of fraud.

328 *Sed pro justitiâ ejus ac aequitate praesumat.*

329 Johannes Voet, *Commentarius*, Book 42, Title 1, [41], Gane (n. 314), Vol. 6, p. 341, referring to Groenewegen (n. 326), Vol. 2, p. 52, [7] (comment on Digest 5.1.75).

330 Huber, *De Jure Civitatis libri tres* (Franeker: Johannes Gyselaar, 1684), Book 3, Chap. 10 (entitled *"De Conflictu Legum in diversis Imperiis"*); *Heedendaegse Rechtsgeleertheyt, soo elders als in Frieslandt gebruikelijk*, Leeuwarden: Hero Nauta, 1686, Book 1, Chap. 3 (entitled *"Van 'tgebruik der Friesche rechten in andere landen, en die van andere landen in Friesland"*); *Praelectionum Juris Romani et Hodierni, Pars II, Quae est ad Libros undeviginti priores Pandectarum*, Franeker: Apud Henricum Amama and Zachariam Taedema, 1689, Book 1, Title 3, Appendix (entitled *"De Conflictu Legum Diversarum in Diversiis Imperiis"*).
English translations of the relevant section in the second volume of Huber's *Praelectionum*, using later editions, have been prepared by Ernest Lorenzen (n. 300), 401-418 and by D. J. (David) Llewelyn Davies (n. 300), 64-78. A translation of a later edition of *Heedendaegse Rechts* (*Contemporary Jurisprudence*) appears in Percival Gane, *The Jurisprudence of My Time*, Durban: Butterworth & Co Africa Ltd., 1939, with the relevant section in Vol. 1, pp. 11-18.

his identification of what he described as "fundamental rules"[331] for structuring the subject, consisting of three axioms – statements considered by Huber to be so well-established or self-evident as to require no proof[332]. This device enabled him to offer an account of the subject that moved away from the statutist models favoured by other writers, including Paulus and Johannes Voet[333].

122. Huber's three axioms, in their final iteration in the second volume of his *Praelectionum*, are as follows[334]:

A French translation of this section in the *Praelectionum* has more recently been prepared by Bertrand Ancel and Horatia Muir Watt, reproduced in B. Ancel, *Eléments d'histoire du droit international privé*, Paris: ed. Panthéon-Assas, 2017, pp. 340-351.

References in the following footnotes to "Huber, *De Conflictu Legum*", including page numbers, are to Llewelyn Davies (n. 300), whose work uses the Appendix to Title 3 of Book 1 of the second volume of Huber's *Praelectionum* as reproduced in the 1707 edition combining all three volumes (text to n. 422). The Latin text appears alongside the English translation.

For a very thorough examination of Huber's approach to the conflict of laws, see Hatzimihail (n. 300), esp. Chaps. 11-14.

331 Huber, *De Conflictu Legum*, [1] (p. 65).

332 *Ibid.*, "For the purpose of unfolding the difficulty of this particularly intricate subject, we shall formulate three maxims, which being accepted, as undoubtedly it appears they should be, seem to clear the way for us for the solution of the remaining questions".

333 See Edwards and Kriel (n. 300), 396-400; Hatzimihail (n. 300), pp. 427-434, 464.

Although Huber and Johannes Voet were contemporaries, neither makes reference to the work of the other, although it should not be attributed to a personal or geographical rivalry, Hatzimihail (n. 300), p. 340, fn. 40. Huber died in 1694, four years before the publication of the first volume of Johannes Voet's *Commentarius*.

334 Huber, *De Conflictu Legum*, [2], p. 65, using Llewelyn Davies' translation (but cf. below, [125]-[126]. Certain Latin terms in the third axiom have been added here as an aid to understanding.

"(1) The laws of every sovereign authority have force within the boundaries *[terminos]* of its state and bind all subject to it, but not beyond.

(2) Those are held to be subject to a sovereign authority who are to be found within its boundaries, whether they are there permanently or temporarily.

(3) Those who exercise sovereign authority *[rectores imperiorum]* so act from comity *[id comiter agunt*[335]*]* that the laws of each nation *[populi]* having been applied within its own boundaries should retain their effect everywhere so far as they do not prejudice the power or rights of another state *[imperantis]* or his subjects *[civium]*."

123. Although the first two axioms represent Huber's view of the limits of the lawmaking authority of a given political society[336], he attributes the third

---

335 Although the axioms appear also in Huber's earlier works, *De Jure Civitatis* (n. 330), Book 3, Chap. 10, [8]-[10] (below, [132]-[137]) and *Heedendaegse Rechts* (n. 330), Book 1, Chap. 3, [4]-[6]), Huber uses different words to describe the rationale that leads to exercises of sovereign authority (*imperium*) having effect elsewhere – in *De Jure Civitatis*: *indulgent sibi mutuo* (mutually grant to each other); in *Heedendaegse Recht*: *bieden elkander de handt* (offer each other hands).
As "comity" is merely a useful label for this rationale, describing the motive for action *(id comiter agunt)*, the underlying reasons for which need to be more closely examined, this shifting terminology is of no great consequence. Huber's uses the term *comiter* adverbially. Paulus and Johannes Voet also used ablative and genitive forms of the noun, *comitas (comitate, comitatis)* (see nn. 308 and 320). The modern noun form, "comity", is used in this and later chapters.

336 See the observations on the position of foreigners in Huber, *De Conflictu Legum*, [2], citing Grotius, *War and Peace*, Book 2, Chap. 11, [5], pp. 709-710. But cf. the criticism of Grotius' opinion above, at [87], and the discussion of Huber's approach to jurisdictional questions in Hatzimihail

to "the convenience and tacit consent of nations"[337], for[338]:

> ". . . nothing could be more inconvenient[339] to the commerce and general [usage[340]] of nations than that which is valid by the law of one place should be rendered [of no effect[341]] elsewhere owing to a difference in the law".

124. These much discussed observations require close attention, for they can be read[342] as expressions of opinion by Huber either (1) that comity is merely a matter of convenience or utility or (2) that comity is part of what Grotius termed the (voluntary) law of nations *(ius gentium)*, in contradistinction to the law of nature *(ius naturale)*[343]. For contrasting reasons, both represent challenges to an approach to the conflict of laws that draws on the natural law toolbox. On the one hand, the "convenience" of a single nation or the community of nations seems both too imprecise to found a general

---

(n. 30), pp. 453-454. The first two axioms are more closely examined at Section III.V.C.

337 *Commodis et tacito populorum consensu.*

338 Huber, *De Conflictu Legum*, [2], p. 66.

339 Or "disadvantageous", see below, [126].

340 *Usu gentium*. Llewelyn translates this as "intercourse of nations", but Lorenzen's translation has been preferred here, Lorenzen, "Huber's *De Conflictu Legum*" (n. 300), 403.

341 *Infirmaerentur*, from *infirmo*. Llewelyn translates this as "invalid", but Lorenzen's translation, has again been preferred here, Lorenzen, above, 403.

342 See e.g. Getman-Pavlova (n. 305), 5-6, 10. On the second point, see also Yntema (n. 300), 22-24; Rodolfo De Nova, "Historical and Comparative Introduction to Conflict of Laws" (1966), 118 *Recueil des cours* 435, 449-450; Edwards and Kriel (n. 300), 399-400.

343 Grotius, *War and Peace*, Book 1, Preliminary Discourse, [18], (p. 94), [41], pp. 111-112 and Chap. 1, [13]-[14], pp. 162-163, noting here the critical comment (fn. 3 on p. 163) taken from the translation prepared by Jean Barbeyrac (see n. 33 and below, [128]).

principle, and also too weak, given that the natural liberty enjoyed by all nations allows them to judge what is, and what is not, convenient[344]. If foreign laws have effect only because the lawmaker considers that the balance of convenience favours this and not because of a sense of obligation towards others, this would make it the exclusive preserve of civil law *(ius civile)*, which Huber denies[345]. On the other, if comity has binding force only if and because nations consent to it, and not because the law of nature otherwise demands it, then the enquiry called for will be a very different one from that undertaken so far. It would be necessary to examine the evidence of customary practice over time and to specify the nature and content of the rule of international law thereby created[346], as well as its current standing. By contrast with the examples of special agreements or customary practices to which Johannes Voet referred[347], Huber's third axiom is expressed in terms that would give it universal effect regardless of special agreement or custom.

125. Accordingly, *if* references in translation to "the convenience and [the] tacit consent of nations"[348] fully and accurately state the reasons why laws and judgments are effective outside the legal order that created them, this is problematic both because "convenience" sets the

---

[344] See above, [101]-[102].

[345] Huber, *De Conflictu Legum*, [1], [2], pp. 65-66. See below, [127].

[346] For a summary of the requirements to demonstrate a rule of customary international law today, see *Benkharbouche* v. *Secretary of State for Foreign and Commonwealth Affairs* [2017] UKSC 62, [2019] AC 777, [31], Lord Sumption.

[347] Text to n. 322.

[348] Llewelyn Davies (n. 300), 66; Lorenzen, *"De Conflictu Legum"* (n. 300), 227. The additional word in parentheses appears in the latter translation. Cf. Hatzimihail (n. 300), pp. 363, 482 ("the common weal and the tacit consent of the nations").

bar too low and because "tacit consent" sets the bar too high. Let us examine each proposition more closely.

126. The first point (as to convenience) can be disposed of without undue difficulty, if "advantage" (or "common advantage"[349]) is taken more aptly to capture the meaning of Huber's noun, *commodum*, than "convenience". If we then ask ourselves what this supposed common benefit of nations might be, Huber supplies the answer. Without acts of comity, laws and judgments may be rendered ineffective[350]. Comity is required to give more perfect effect to the expressions of will of those governing political societies for the benefit of persons under their protection. Furthermore, whatever particular meaning we may choose, the adverb *comiter*[351] gives the clear sense of the motivation for an act that is not self-interested but virtuous. This is reinforced by Huber's use elsewhere in the same work of the term *humanitas*[352] to explain acts of judicial assistance between independent legal orders[353]. So, comity is more than mere convenience or personal advantage. Although it motivates acts that form part of the *ius civile* in particular places, it does not derive its authority from the civil law.

127. The second point (as to tacit consent) is more challenging. Huber's texts are lightly particularised and not easy to reconcile[354]. As they are built upon the

---

349 Hatzimihail (n. 300), pp. 363, 482 ("common weal").

350 See above, [123]; also *De Jure Civitatis* (n. 330), Book 3, Chap. 10, [2].

351 See e.g. Adam Littleton, *A Latin Dictionary in Four Parts*, London: T. Bassett, J. Wright and R. Chiswell, 1684, *comiter*: gently, courteously, kindly, civilly.

352 For Paulus Voet's use of the same term, see above, [116].

353 *Praelectionum Juris Romani et Hodierni, Pars II* (n. 330), Book 5, Title 1, [57] (extradition); *Praelectionum Juris Romani, Pars III* (Franeker: Apud Henricum Amama and Zachariam Taedema, 1690), Book 42, Title 1, [52] (execution of judicial decisions).

354 Readers who wish to bypass the following detailed textual analysis will find the conclusions below, [147]-[148].

foundations of Roman law, it is instructive to remind ourselves as to how the relevant terms are defined in the *Corpus Iuris Civilis*. The civil law *(ius civile)* is the law which each community *(civitas)* establishes for itself[355]. The *ius gentium* is that which natural reason *(naturalis ratio)* establishes between all human beings and is equally maintained by all communities[356]. The law of nature (*ius naturale*) is defined in at least two different ways, as that which nature teaches to all animals, not being peculiar to the human race[357], and as the natural laws commonly observed by all nations and established by divine wisdom[358].

128. Grotius opens his preliminary discourse in *War and Peace* by distinguishing the civil law of particular societies from the law that governs among many peoples or rulers of peoples, whether derived from nature or instituted by divine commands or introduced by custom and tacit consent[359]. He expresses the view that civil laws are "conformable to nature" because derived from tacit promises made upon forming political societies[360]. Grotius then defines natural law as "the dictate of right reason *[recta ratio]*, indicating that any act, from its agreement or disagreement with the rational [and social] nature of man has in it a moral turpitude or a moral necessity"[361]. He rejects the Roman usage that fixes on the

---

355 Institutes, 1.2.1, following Gaius, *Institutes*, 1.1 (Digest [1.9.1]).
356 *Ibid.*
357 Institutes 1.2.pr, based on Digest 1.1.3 (Ulpian, *Institutes*, Book 1).
358 Institutes 1.2.11.
359 Grotius, *War and Peace*, Book 1, Preliminary Discourse (*Prolegomena*), [1] (p. 75).
360 *Ibid.*, [16] (p. 93). See Section II.I.1.
361 Grotius, *War and Peace*, Book 1, Chap. 1, [10], point 1, pp. 150-151.
The translation used here is that of William Whewell in *De jure belli et pacis, liber tres*, London: John W. Parker, 1853, Vol. 1, p. 10. As Whewell notes, Barbeyrac inserted the

common nature of human beings and other creatures as "of little or no use"[362] and distinguishes the law of nature from the voluntary law *(ius voluntarium)* arising from either human or divine will[363]. Civil law, resulting from the exercise of power within a *civitas*, is distinguished from less extensive and more extensive types of human law[364]. The former covers family relationships, as well as those between a master and servant. The latter is the law of nations *(ius gentium)*, which, in Grotius' view, "derives its authority from the will of all, or at least of many, nations"[365]. The law of nations is to be proved,

---

words *ac sociali* ("and social") after "rational" in the text of his Latin edition, assuming it to have been a transcriber's or printer's error as Grotius subsequently uses this composite phrase *(natura rationali ac sociali)* in describing the ways in which the law of nature may be proved (see Grotius, *War and Peace*, Book 1, Chap. 1, [12], p. 159).

362 Grotius, *War and Peace*, Book 1, Chap. 1, [11], p. 157, with reference to Cicero, On Laws, *De Officiis*, [I.50]. Cicero's text, addressing "The principles of human society", states:

"But it seems we must trace back to their ultimate the principles of fellowship and society that Nature has established among men. The first principle is that which is found in the connection subsisting between all the members of the human race; and that bond of connection is reason and speech, which by the processes of teaching and learning, of communicating, discussing, and reasoning associate men together and unite them in a sort of natural fraternity. In no other particular are we farther removed from the nature of beasts; for we admit that they may have courage (horses and lions, for example); but we do not admit that they have justice, equity, and goodness; for they are not endowed with reason or speech." (trans. Walter Miller in the edition prepared for the *Loeb Classical Library*, Cambridge, MA: Harvard University Press, 1913, pp. 53, 55).

See further text to n. 375.

363 Grotius, *War and Peace*, Book 1, Chap. 1, [13], p. 162.

364 *Ibid.*, [14], pp. 162-163.

365 *Ibid.*, p. 163.

in the same way as the unwritten (customary) civil law, by continual use *(usu continuo)* and the testimony of experts[366].

129. Huber wrote several commentaries addressing the Roman law texts on the relationship between *ius civile, ius gentium* and *ius naturale*. A valuable starting point[367] is the account in his *Positiones Juris*, which may have begun as lectures given in his capacity as a professor at the University of Franeker. First published in 1682, the fourth edition was printed in 1685[368].

130. In this work, Huber first distinguishes natural from positive law, dividing the latter into divine or human positive law[369] and further subdividing human law into the law of nations and civil law[370]. He addresses these concepts in the following Title, with reference to the Roman law sources. Like Grotius, he rejects as improper the notion that the law of nature is that which nature has taught all animals[371]. Instead, Huber defines the law of nature as "nothing other than the highest reason innate in nature, which commands what must be done and prohibits the contrary"[372]. Having recited the Institutional definition of the law of nations *(ius gentium)* as "that which natural reason has established among humans"[373], and divided this into primary *(primaevum)*

---

366 Grotius, *War and Peace*, Book 1, Chap. 1, [14], p. 163.

367 On Huber's approach to sources of law more generally, see Hatzimihail (n. 300), pp. 396-407, with particular reference to the account in *Heedendaegse Rechts* (n. 330).

368 Huber, *Positiones Juris secundum Institutiones et Pandecta*, Franeker: Apud Johannem Gyselaar, 4th ed., 1685.

369 *Positiones Juris*, above, Book 1, Title 1, [19]-[20].

370 *Ibid.*, [25].

371 *Ibid.*, Book 1, Title 2, [1]; also *ibid.*, [6] ("natural law does not apply to beasts because law is reason *(jus est ratio)* and a general precept, which brutes do not use").

372 *Ibid.*, Book 1, Title 2, [6].

373 *Ibid.*, [2].

and secondary *(secundarium)*[374], Huber cites Grotius[375] to support a slightly different definition, that the law of nations is that which receives its obligatory force by the will of the people using right reason[376]. This insight allows Huber to align the law of nature with the primary (primordial) law of nations[377] and the law of nations in the narrower sense favoured by Huber with the secondary[378]. Finally, for Huber, civil law is what each free people establishes for itself[379].

131. Huber offers a much more detailed account of these matters in *De Jure Civitatis*. The edition of this work published in 1684, in which his commentary on the conflict of laws first appears, includes separate chapters on the law of nature, on Hobbes' views on the law of nature and on the law of nations[380]. In the last of these chapters, he refers to "another common law of the human race" which concerns things that "conform to natural reason, not however immediately from its command but deduced by a degree of judgment, as the exigencies and needs of humanity require"[381]. This, Huber asserts, is the

374 *Ibid.*, [3] (see text to nn. 384 and 458).

375 The reference is to *War and Peace*, Book 1, Chap. 1, [11], where Grotius rejects the distinction in Roman law, between the law of nature, "in a strict sense" (that common to humans with animals) and the law peculiar to humans, which they (i.e. Roman jurists) "often style the law of nations".

376 Huber, *Positiones Juris* (n. 368), [8] *(ex voluntate populorum recta ratione utentium vim obligandi accepit)*.

377 *Modus gentium*.

378 Huber, *Positiones Juris* (n. 365), [9].

379 *Ibid.*, [10].

380 Huber, *De Jure Civitatis* (n. 330), Book 1, Chaps. 2-4. The third edition, published in 1694 (n. 301), includes additionally a chapter (Chap. 4) addressing the views of Baruch Spinoza (1632-1677), with the treatment of the law of nations following in Chap. 5.

381 Huber, *De Jure Civitatis* (n. 330), Book 1, Chap. 4, [2] *(in super aliud commune jus generis humani traditur, quod circa ea vertatur, que convenienter quidem rationi naturali, non tamen immediate ex ejus dictamine, sed per modum*

law of nations to which Grotius refers, being established by the consent of all or at least most civilised nations[382]. The law of nature is innate and engraved upon human beings, whereas the law of nations must be discovered and reasoned out[383]. Having repeated his criticisms of the Institutional sources[384], Huber turns his attention to the arguments, advanced by Hobbes and Pufendorf, among others, that there is no law of nations distinct from the law of nature[385]. Huber, defending Grotius' position, argues for the third category, reasoning by analogy with the law of nature[386] to explain the reason for its authority (consent[387]) and the mechanisms for its enforcement. He argues that there are many human institutions, which flourish among the majority of peoples, and which could not have force without an act of human will[388]. Therefore, Huber deduces, those things cannot be considered natural, that is inherent in the human condition[389]. Nor, as they are not founded on the authority of a specific people, can they be called civil law[390]. Accordingly, a third category, the law of nations, becomes necessary to account for these institutions[391]. Huber suggests that, although the

---

arbitramenti, usu ita exigenti et humanis necessitatibus, inde deducta sunt).

382 Huber, *De Jure Civitatis*, above, [4], citing Grotius, *War and Peace*, Book 1, Chap. 1, [14], p. 162.

383 *Ibid.*, [5]-[6] *(quod hoc fit innatum homine ac inscultum, illud repertum et excogitamum).*

384 *Ibid.*, [9]-[13], repeating analysis in *Positiones Juris* (n. 368) of the concepts of the primary (primordial) and secondary law and nations (see text to nn. 374 and 458).

385 Pufendorf, *Nature and Nations*, Book 2, Chap. 3, [23], pp. 226-229, setting out also Hobbes' position, Hobbes, *Citizen*, Chap. 14, [4]-[5], pp. 156-157.

386 *Analogia juris naturae.*

387 See Grotius, *War and Peace*, Book 1, Preliminary Discourse, [16], p. 93.

388 Huber, *De Jure Civitatis*, Book 1, Chap. 4, [23].

389 *Ibid.*, [24].

390 *Ibid.*, [25].

391 *Ibid.*, [26].

law of nations should accord with natural reason, it may in a hypothetical case conflict with it[392].

132. These background materials illuminate Huber's commentary on the conflict of laws, in Chapter 10 of the third book of *De Jure Civitatis*[393]. Although translators and commentators have focused on the version of this commentary appearing in the second volume of Huber's later work, *Praelectionum Juris Romani et Hodierni*[394], it is instructive to see both the development of the author's thinking and the connections to his earlier discussion of the links between the different categories of law.

133. The preceding chapter, Chapter 9, within the third book of *De Jure Civitatis*, addresses "the things that foreigners owe each other"[395]. Citing Grotius, Huber examines the things that are owed to neighbouring nations and their human populations in cases of necessity, such as famine and the protection of refugees[396]. The subject matter is evidently part of the law of nature[397],

---

392 *Ibid.*, [29].

393 (n. 330.)

394 *Praelectionum Juris Romani et Hodierni, Pars II* (n. 330).

395 Huber, *De Jure Civitatis* (n. 330), Book 1, Chap. 9 *(De his quae exteri fibi invicem debent)*.

396 *Ibid.*, [4]. The reference is to Grotius, *War and Peace*, Book 2. For the particular examples, see *ibid.*, Book 2, Chap. 2, [18]-[19], pp. 449-450 and Chap. 21, [5]-[6], pp. 1067-1076.

397 In situations of famine, Grotius explains that to impede the acquisition of things that another nation needs for the subsistence its people would be contrary to to the "nature of human society", Grotius, *War and Peace*, Book 2, Chap. 2, [18], pp. 449-450.
In an intriguing passage, Huber observes that although judges have not been appointed in disputes arising between foreigners (*quamvis exteri in exterorum causis nullo modo judices constituti sint*), the law of nature nonetheless permits, indeed commands, that assistance be provided to those who suffer from the application of lawful force *(vim justam)* by others, provided that the injury is manifest, not requiring protracted enquiry and that appropriate assistance can be

being cases that later writers consider in their more detailed accounts of duties of humanity and necessity[398]. Chapter 9 concludes with what may appear to be a rather bland statement, that whatever natural law, divine law, and the usage of nations dictate or prohibit, the various peoples and rulers are bound to each other in this[399]. This last paragraph is a stepping stone to the next topic, the conflict of laws.

134. Huber's commentary in Chapter 10 of *De Jure Civitatis* begins with the statement that, among the things that foreigners owe each other, the observance of the laws of other legal nations beyond their territories is "rightly emphasised"[400]. For, he adds, even if the nations concerned are not bound by a pact, or the necessity of subordination, the general usage of peoples based on reason demands mutual indulgence[401]. The first part of the opening paragraph in this chapter alludes to the preceding chapter (Chap. 9), without building upon its foundations. The second part, although using different terminology, fits with Huber's specification of the (secondary) law of nations, linking the practice of nations in their relations with each other to the exercise of reason.

135. Whichever formulation one fixes on[402], Huber's conception of the *ius gentium* is a curious hybrid,

---

provided, Huber, *De Jure Civitatis*, Book 3, Chap. 9, [22]. Although speculative Huber may have had in mind acts of humanitarian assistance during warfare. The following texts concern the treatment of captives.

398 Vattel, *Nations*, Book 2, Chap. 1, [5], [9] (famine), pp. 263-264, 266 and Book I, Chap. 19 [229]-[233], pp. 226-228 (treatment of those in exile); Wolff, *Nations*, Chap. 1, [145]-[150], [152] (treatment of those in exile and suppliants) and Chap. 3, [340], p. 251 (famine).

399 Huber, *De Jure Civitatis* (n. 330), Book 3, Chap. 9, [27].

400 *Ibid.*, Book 3, Chap. 10, [1].

401 *Ibid., (promiscuous usus ratio inter gentes mutuam hac in parte flagitat)*.

402 See text to n. 376 *(Positiones)*, n. 381 (*De Jure Civitatis*, Book 1) and n. 401 (*De Jure Civitatis*, Book 3).

combining elements of Grotius' law of nature and his (voluntary) law of nations. In his *Positiones Juris*, Huber uses the same words that lie at the heart of Grotius' definition of the law of nature, *recta ratio*[403], in tandem with the expression of will that Grotius considers to be characteristic of the *ius gentium* as a distinct body of law[404]. Moreover, while Huber places great emphasis on the proposition that the (secondary) law of nations depends upon acts of human will, whereas the law of nature does not[405], Grotius had recognised that it was appropriate, in cases of uncertainty, to prove precepts of the law of nature through an external *(a posteriori)* method of reasoning by searching for a general opinion among nations[406]. Huber's *ius gentium* is closer to that of Gaius[407] than that of Grotius – it is that which right reason has established among humans, with the dictate of natural reason being demonstrated by reference to the practice of nations in their relations with each other.

136. Next, Huber identifies the adverse consequences if his rule were not followed and one nation were to refuse to recognise or give force to the laws of another – infinite acts and contracts would every day be rendered ineffective, and commerce on land and sea could not be sustained[408]. He complains that the Roman sources are of little value in an account in addressing this topic, for the jurists never had to grapple with the modern diversity

---

403 Text to nn. 361 and 376.
404 Text to nn. 365 and 376.
405 Text to nn. 378 and 382.
406 *Ibid.*, [12] (p. 159). Note that Huber himself suggests that "no one hitherto seems to have entertained any doubt" regarding his third axiom, Huber, *De Conflictu Legum*, Book 1, Title 3, Appendix, [2], p. 66.
407 Gaius, *Institutes*, 1.1 ("that which natural reason *(naturalis ratio)* establishes between all men is equally maintained by all communities, and is called the law of nations *(ius gentium)*" (see n. 355).
408 Huber, *De Jure Civitatis* (n. 330), Book 3, Chap. 10, [2].

of laws[409]. Huber then makes what appears to be a significant claim[410]:

> "It is apparent that this question must be decided according to the reasoning of the law of nations *[ex ratio juris gentium]*, because different peoples do not use civil law, and therefore I would like this example to be observed as the most evident argument, to prove that the law of nations is truly distinct from the law of nature, to which this question cannot in any way be referred."

137. However, in the following passages, Huber does not seriously advance a claim that the law of nature is redundant in this area of law. He suggests that discussions of this topic by "the most learned jurists" (i.e. the statutists) have made the subject "more involved and more perplexing"[411]. He proposes to treat of the matter "as easily and briefly as possible" on the basis of three fundamental propositions[412]. Huber then lays down, for the first time, his three axioms[413]. Having emphasised that the matter is essentially one of public, not private, law and summarised the interaction of his rules[414], Huber

---

409 *Ibid.*, [3]-[5].

410 *Ibid.*, [6].

411 *Ibid.*, [7].

412 *Ibid.*, [7].

413 *Ibid.*, [8]-[10].
The axioms, as they appear here, may be translated as follows:

> "The first is that the laws of each Republic hold and bind all those subject to the same authority, and no further. The second is that those are considered subjects who are found in the territory of any *Civitas*, as long as they reside there . . . The third is that the holders of supreme power in every Republic mutually grant that the rights and laws of others may have effect in other territories, as far as it can be done without prejudice to the grantor."

414 Huber, *De Jure Civitatis* (n. 330), Book 3, Chap. 10, [11]-[12], referring in the latter passage to the "mutual advantage of nations" *(mutua . . . utilitas gentium)* to describe the ratio-

proceeds to illustrate this by examples concerning the validity of a will, sale of goods, marriage, succession, the transfer of movable and immovable property and personal status[415]. He proclaims the application of his axioms to be a matter of universal public law[416]. He then addresses cases involving acts of a foreign legal order detrimental to the receiving order or its people, or inconsistent with its specific laws, which may justify a refusal to recognise their effect[417]. The concluding paragraph[418], with its acknowledgement that the adjudicating court can apply its own laws if it wishes and its reference to "reciprocal advantage" as the basis of the rule of the *ius gentium* relied upon[419], does not seem so far removed from the thinking of Paulus and, subsequently, Johannes Voet on the subject.

138. In 1678, Huber had published a commentary on Justinian's Institutes, entitled *Praelectiones ad Institutiones Justinianeas*[420]. In 1687, a new edition of that work was published under the title, *Praelectionum Juris Civilis Pars Prior*[421], to which Huber's commentaries on

---

nale for his third axiom. See also ibid. [18] ("it is received among peoples", *inter populus receptum est*) and [19] ("it is settled among us ", *convenitur apud nos*).

415 *Ibid.*, [13]-[15] (wills), [19]-[21] (sale), [23]-[25] (marriage), [27]-[32] (succession), [33]-[34] (property), [35]-[42] (personal status).

416 *Ibid.*, [16] *(juris publici universalis)*.

417 *Ibid.*, [22], [24], [41], [43], [44]; also *ibid.*, [26], [28], [31]-[33] on the protected status of immovable property (but cf. *ibid.*, [30]).

418 *De Jure Civitatis* (n. 330), Book 3, Chap. 10, [45].

419 *Sed ob recipocam utilitatem in disciplinam juris gentium abiit.*

420 See Robert Feenstra, Margreet Ahsmann and T. J. Veen, *Bibliografi van hoogleraren in de rechten aan de Franeker Universiteit tot 1811*, Amsterdam: Koninklijke Nederlandse Akademie van Wetenschappen, 2003, pp. 62-63.

421 Ulrik Huber, *Praelectionum Juris Civilis, Pars Prior, Quae est secundum Institutiones Justinaeas*, Franeker: Apud Henricum Amama and Zachariah Tedama, 1687.

the Digest would later be added. A notable element of this work, as the title page makes clear, is that it includes extracts from the Scholia by Christian Thomasius (1655-1728) providing a commentary upon Huber's *Positiones*[422], as well as Huber's responses[423]. The work begins with a discussion by Huber of the relationship between the law of nature and nations and civil law[424]. To avoid repetition, selected highlights are offered here.

139. In the first Title of Book 1 of this work (on Justice and Law), Huber responds to an objection raised by Thomasius to his classification of the law of nations as positive, human law distinct from the law of nature. Thomasius cites Pufendorf, contrasting the views of Grotius and Rachel[425]. In his response, Huber refers to "Book 5, Chapter 9" of *Digressiones*, which is to be understood as a reference to Chapter 9 in the first book of the second part of his own work under that title, published

---

[422] Christian Thomasius (compiler), *Ulrici Huberi Positiones sive lectiones juris contractae secundum et Institutiones et Pandectas* (Leipzig and Frankfurt: Mauritii Georgii Weidmanni, 1685?). Huber had noted the existence of this work (giving the date as 1684) in the Preface to his own (4th) edition of the *Positiones* (n. 368) but records that he had not yet seen it. He undertook to his readers that he would adapt his lectures to provide explanations and correct any errors on his part. The work discussed here delivers on that promise.
A later edition, comprising all three volumes of Huber's *Praelectionum*, includes additional notes by Thomasius, in rejoinder to Huber, *Praelectionum Juris Civilis Tomis Tres, Secundundum Institiones et Digesta Justiniani, Editio Nova*, Leipzig: Jo. Friderici Gledischii, 1707. Thomasius' preface to the latter work contains a tribute to Huber, as well as explaining his own interactions with the work.

[423] These are marked in the text as "Scholium" and "Responsio".

[424] *Praelectionum Juris Civilis, Pars Prior* (n. 421), Book 1, Title 1, [9], with the Scholium and Responsio immediately following (*ibid.*, p. 10) and Book 1, Title 2.

[425] Samuel Rachel (1628-1691).

the following year[426]. We will consider its significance shortly. Huber's reference to it here, as he explains, was designed to support his counterargument that there are examples of rules of the law of nations that cannot easily be referred to the law of nature "such as when a matter adjudicated elsewhere has effect in foreign territories [427], or when a contract or will validly executed in one place is recognised elsewhere". Huber adds that the common advantage of nations has introduced this, being "far removed" from the law of nature[428].

140. In the second title of Book 1 of this work, Huber offers the Institutional definition of *ius gentium* as that which natural reason establishes among all humans[429]. He observes that Grotius defines the concept differently[430]. However, the definition apparently attributed to Grotius[431] is not taken from *War and Peace*, either from the passage cited[432], which discusses Ulpian's zoocentric view of natural law[433], or from any other part of that work. It is instead Huber's definition from

---

426 Ulrik Huber, *Digressiones Justinianae, In Partes Duas* (Franeker: Apud Johannem Gysellar, Henricum Amama and Zachariam Taedama, 1688). Although the first part of the work had first been published in 1670, *Digessiones Justinianea, Quibus varia et praesertim humaniora Juris continentur*, Franeker: Johannes Wellens, the earlier editions contained only four books. A second part, presumably ready for publication at the time that Huber wrote this response, was added to the 1688 edition, with its own book and chapter numbers.

427 *Res alibi judicata in alienis territoriis effectum habent.*

428 *Praelectionum Juris Civilis, Pars Prior*, Book 1, Title 1, [9], with Scholium and Responsio on p. 10 *(utilitas communis gentium introduxit, penitus vamen à jure naturali remotum effe videtur)*.

429 *Ibid.*, Book 1, Title 2, [2].

430 *Ibid.*

431 *Jus gentium, quod ex voluntate populorum recta ratione utentium vim obligandi accepit.*

432 *War and Peace*, Book 1, Chap. 1, [11].

433 Text to nn. 356 and 362.

his *Positiones Juris*[434], with the reappearance of the idea of right reason *(recta ratio)* characteristic of Grotius' account of the law of nature[435].

141. Huber offers the same definition in a later passage[436]. He suggests that Justinian has conflated the law of nature with the law of nations[437], but the same charge could be levelled in his direction[438].

In this passage, Huber's definition of *ius gentium* is followed immediately by an objection from Thomasius[439]:

> "But these peoples never declared this will *[voluntatem]*; they could not oblige themselves by way of law *[legis]* above this, because they are equals among one another *[quia inter se pares sunt]*."

Huber responds to this objection in the following manner[440]:

> "The declaration [of will] is sufficiently clear from the practices *[ex institutis]* instituted among most civilised peoples . . .[441] But there is a difficulty in the binding force *[obligatione]* of the law of nations, which does not seem to be distinct from the precept to maintain peace[[442]], which is [a precept] of the law

434 Text to n. 376.

435 Text to n. 361.

436 *Praelectionum Juris Civilis, Pars Prior* (n. 421), Book I, Title 2, [4].

437 *Ibid.*, referring to Institutes 1.2.11.

438 See above, [135].

439 *Praelectionum Juris Civilis, Pars Prior* (n. 421), Book I, Title 2, [4], Scholium, p. 12.

440 *Praelectionum Juris Civilis, Pars Prior* (n. 421), Book I, Title 2, [4], Responsio, p. 12. In the 1707 edition (n. 422), Thomasius complains, p. 9, that Huber did not present his Scholium in full and gives further detail.

441 Huber refers here to a passage in his *Digressiones* (n. 426), Part 2, Book 1, Chap. 9, [8], discussed below, [144].

442 See e.g. *De Jure Civitatis*, Book 1, Chap. 3, [35]. This specific argument is addressed below, [144]-[145].

of nature, for mutual utility *[mutua utilitas]* cannot add coercive force. Therefore, the matter comes back to what is recorded in the text. The law of nature arises either from the immediate command of reason *[dictamine rationis immediato]*, such as the distinction between the honourable and dishonourable, or consequentially, such as dominium, sovereignty, the rights of war and other matters previously mentioned. Those of the former *[prioris]* kind are said to be the law of nature; those of the latter kind *[posterioris]*, the law of nations. Indeed, examples of the former and latter kind differ so clearly from each other, such that the former correctly claim the name of the genus and the latter deserve to be distinguished by a particular designation, so that both are rightly attributed to a broad understanding of the law of nature *[juri nature late sumpto]*."

Huber retrenches his position in order to defend himself from Thomasius' objection. In this reformulated argument, the practice of nations is identified as a means of deducing precepts of the law of nature that merit separate nomenclature and examination but do not stand apart from it. If sustained, this addresses the point here under discussion. For Huber, comity belongs both to the law of nations and the law of nature.

142. A final insight gleened from this work is that, in describing custom as a source of law arising from long usage, Huber attributes its force to the tacit consent of the people, using the same words as he uses in the second part to explain his third axiom[443]. This is noteworthy but does not seem particularly significant for the matter under discussion.

143. The new edition of Huber's *Digressiones*, to which reference has already been made, was published

---

[443] *Praelectionum Juris Civilis, Pars Prior* (n. 421), Book I, Title 2, [11] *(tacito populi consensu vim obligandi accepit)*.

in 1688. In the second part, Chapter 9 of Book 1[444] is concerned with philosophical and juristic discussion of the law of nations and of the question whether it is distinct from the law of nature[445]. On this occasion[446], in opening, Huber accurately quotes Grotius' definition of the law of nations as gaining its force from the will of all or many nations[447]. He then cites the contrary opinions of Hobbes and Pufendorf to the effect that there is no law of nations distinct from the law of nature and civil law[448]. Huber wonders whether he should dissent from this and still dare to support the Grotian position[449]. In search for inspiration, he turns again to the Institutional texts[450]. Ulpian's definition of the law of nature is quickly rejected[451] in favour of the definition of the law of nations *(ius gentium)* given by Justinian (following Gaius)[452]. Here, Huber observes[453]:

> "It is truly this. By the law of nations, Justinian understands the same thing that we in the preceding

444 The heading "Cap. XI" in the 1688 edition (p. 483) is a typographical error.
445 Huber, *Digressiones* (n. 426), Part 2, Book 1, Chap. 9, [1].
446 Cf. above, [140].
447 Huber, *Digressiones* (n. 426), Part 2, Book 1, Chap. 9, [1] (*quod gentium omnium aut multaru voluntate vim obligandi accepit*), citing Grotius, *War and Peace*, Book 1, Chap. 1, [14].
448 Huber, *Digressiones*, above, Part 2, Book 1, Chap. 9, [2] (see text to n. 385).
449 Huber, *Digressiones*, above, Part 2, Book 1, Chap. 9, [3].
450 *Ibid.*, [3]-[5].
451 *Ibid.*, [4].
452 Text to n. 355.
453 Huber, *Digressiones* (n. 426), Part 2, Book 1, Chap. 9, [5], quoting from Institutes 1.2.1 and referring also to Institutes 1.2.11 and Digest 41.1.1.pr, Gaius, *Res Cottidianae*, Book 2. Huber concedes that there is a measure of agreement between the ancient jurists and Hobbes on this point.

chapters[454] have shown to be the law of nature. For what else is this than what 'natural reason has established among all humans', as the Emperor says."

144. Having made this concession to Hobbes and Pufendorf, Huber stakes his claim that the law of nations, coinciding with the law of nature in this sense[455], is not of the same species[456]. "For", he adds, "some things are suggested directly by natural reason while others are deduced by the mode of judgment and drawing from it, as required 'by the demands of use and human necessities'"[457]. He links this to the distinction drawn between the primary *(primaevum)* and secondary *(secundarium)* law of nations[458], the former containing the congenital and immediate dictates of nature and the latter, revealed within human institutions by reason, yet introduced by the consent of peoples[459]. Huber continues[460]:

---

454 Huber, *Digressiones* (n. 426), Part 2, Book 1, Chaps. 7 and 8. Chapter 8 contains a forceful critique of Hobbes' view of the state of natural liberty. See Section II.C.

455 I.e. as being attributable to natural reason.

456 Huber, *Digressiones* (n. 426), Part 2, Book 1, Chap. 9, [6].

457 *Ibid.*, quoting from Institutes 1.2.2 and giving examples with reference to Digest 1.1.5, Hermogenianus, *Epitomes of Law*, Book 1.

458 Although Huber does not specify his source, he may have had in mind the writing of Fernando Vázquez de Menchaca (1512-1569), see Gustavo Gozzi, *Rights and Civilizations: A History and Philosophy of International Law*, Cambridge: CUP, 2019, p. 20, referring to Vázquez's work *Controversiarum illustrium aliamruque usu frequenium libri tres*, Venice: Rampazetus, 1564. Note also Grotius, *Prize*, Chap. 2 (Prolegomena), [6'] (p. 25) and [12'], p. 45, with reference to Vázquez.

459 Huber, *Digressiones* (n. 426), Part 2, Book 1, Chap. 9, [7] *(consensu populurum introducta)*.

460 *Ibid.*, [7]. The remainder of the passage notes the opinion of Pufendorf on the question as to what can, and what cannot, be attributed to the law of nature, Pufendorf, *Nature and Nations*, Book 2, Chap. 3, [22], pp. 225-226.

"Truly these institutions are either such that they are necessary for the peace of the human race, or likely at least advantageous *[utilia saltem et probabilia]*. If necessary, then without doubt they pertain to the law of nature and can be referred to it; if otherwise, they are more likely to be seen as part of civil law, because they derive their force from the power of legislators who are concerned with public affairs and who come together for the sake of institutional advantage in confirming that agreement *[qui ob utilitatem instituti in eo consensu confirmandi conspiraverint]*."

145. In the following passage, Huber restates Grotius' position that the law of nations is part of the voluntary law, but expresses doubt, at least in the absence of a treaty or relationship of subordination[461]. If, at this point in the discussion Huber seems to be turning in a circle, he now seeks to make a decisive break. His argument is as follows – (first) things attributed to the (secondary) law of nations require voluntary human acts[462]; (second) at the same time, natural reason has clearly dictated that peace cannot be attained otherwise than by those things being established for mutual benefit[463]; and (third) if such voluntary acts cause those things to be of the law of nations, the same reason seems to claim them for the law of nature[464]. On this view, hinted at in his earlier work[465], it is the universal obligation to take steps to maintain peace that underpins the force of these human institutions within the law of nature. This is an obligation

---

461 *Ibid.*, [8], referring to Grotius, *War and Peace*, Book 1, Chap. 1, [13]-[14], pp. 162-163.

462 Huber, *Digressiones* (n. 426), Part 2, Book 1, Chap. 9, [9] *(actus humanae voluntatis)*.

463 *Ibid. (Naturalem rationem satis evidenter dictasse, pacem aliter haberi non posse, quam illis rebus commodo mutuo constitutis)*.

464 *Ibid. (rationis eadem Juri naturae vindicare videatur)*.

465 Text to n. 442.

that Huber explicitly recognises in the preceding chapter as "necessarily understood by the dictates of reason"[466].

146. Having summarised the preceding material[467], Huber concludes his discussion, as follows[468]:

> "Nor are there lacking institutions of the law of nations *[ius gentium]*, which deviate further from the simplicity of nature *[naturae simplicitate]*, than may be ascribed to the law of nature. Among which are the things that we have placed in the third book of *De Jure Civitatis* regarding the effect of the jurisdiction of each people beyond their territories. For example so that matters judged in one *civitas [res in una civitate judicatae]* have effect in other domains *[imperiis]*, the mutual advantage of nations *[utilitas promiscua gentium]* has made it so that it is held as law everywhere . . .[469] Therefore, there still appears to be no reason why we should not label and employ the laws of nature and nations distinctly, as we have been accustomed to."

Read in its context, this statement does not support the creation of a third (tertiary) category of the law of nations, which lies *beyond* the boundaries of the law of nature[470]. Rather, it offers a further

---

466 Huber, *Digressiones* (n. 426), Part 2, Book 1, Chap. 8, [6] *(necessario rationis dictamine cognovisse)*.

467 *Ibid.*, Part 2, Book 1, Chap. 9, [10], from *"Denique sic . . ."* to *". . . Jure civili dominatur"*.

468 *Ibid.*, from *"Neque vero desunt. . ."* to the end of the paragraph.

469 Huber here gives a further example concerning contracts entered into according to the customs of a particular place.

470 A similar passage, in a later work, distinguishes the rules applicable in these conflict of laws situations from practices received and established within the law of nations that are *contrary to* the law of nature, such as acts of violence against those who have not provided a just cause for war, Ulrik Huber and Zacharias Huber (eds.), *Eunomia Romana sive Centura Censurae Juris Justinianaei*, Franeker: Apud

example[471] of a human institution that, in Huber's view, is appropriately recognised and labelled as a species of law distinct from, although part of the same genus as, the precepts of natural law that are deducible by reason alone.

147. We return to our starting point, the commentary on the conflict of laws in the second volume of Huber's *Praelectionum*, published in 1689. Overall, the evidence strongly suggests that Huber considered his third axiom to belong to law of nature, as well as the law of nations, being deduced by reference to the institutional acts of legal orders when they give effect to each other's laws *accompanied* by the insight that such recognition is necessary to ensure that laws are not rendered ineffective, to the detriment of the persons and the societies that they concern. These two elements combine, neither being sufficient alone to establish the force of the rule. In this way, common advantage *(commodum*[472]*)* is paired with the tacit consent of nations *(tacito populorum consensu)*[473]. On Huber's terms, we can agree wholeheartedly with him that the subject of the conflict of laws "pertains more to the law of nations than to the civil law, since that which different nations should observe among themselves clearly pertains to the law

---

Leonardum Strickium, 1700, *"Ulpian d Lib 1 Inst"*, [2], p. 12.
Eunomia Romana was a collection of academic disputations over which Huber presided in the period 1692-1694, which were gathered and revised for publication posthumously by his son, Zacharias. Huber makes several references to these disputations in the 1694 edition of *De Jure Civitatis*. See Feenstra, Ahsmann and Veen (n. 420), pp. 94-95.

471 Not among those given by Hermogenius (n. 457).

472 See above, [126].

473 Huber, *De Conflictu Legum*, [3], p. 66, "yet nothing could be more [disadvantageous] to the commerce and general intercourse of nations" *(ita commerciis et usu gentium promiscuo nihil foret magis incommodum)*.

of nations"[474]. This does not compel us to treat Huber's comity as having nothing to do with the law of nature.

148. Moreover, as Huber's formulation of the third axiom indicates, the obligation that comity imposes is imperfect[475], of the kind that Grotius recognised as attendant in the exercise of beneficial virtues such as "liberality, mercy and prudent administration of government"[476]. Huber's use elsewhere of the language

---

474 Huber, *De Conflictu Legum*, [1], p. 65.

475 Thomas Schultz and Jason Mitchenson, "The History of Comity" (n. 305), 402-405.
Cf. Alan Watson, *Joseph Story and the Comity of Errors*, Athens: University of Georgia Press 1992, p. 21 and "The Failure of Scottish Legal Education in the Seventeenth Century, and the American Civil War", in *Authority of Law; and Law*, Stockholm: Institutet för rättshistorisk forskning, 2003, Lecture 7, at p. 159. Here, Watson uses Pothier's definition of "imperfect obligation", corresponding to what Vattel calls "internal", Vattel, *Nations*, Preliminaries, [17], p. 74, i.e. not owed to any specific person. Cf. Vattel, *Nations*, Book 1, Chap. 1, [10], p. 266.
In his submission that Huber's third axiom contemplates a perfect obligation, enforceable in court, Watson does not appear sufficiently to distinguish between the end-product of a legal order's decision to follow the dictate of comity in determining the parties' rights and obligations and the legal consequences of a failure to do so in its relations with other nations.
If comity were a rule of international law, in the modern sense, and if it imposed a perfect, enforceable duty, it would not be possible to justify non-compliance by reference to a conflicting rule of municipal law or the public policy of the receiving order (see (1929) 29 *Am J Int L* 1029).

476 Grotius, *War and Peace*, Book 1, Chap. 1, [8] (p. 142); also *ibid.*, Book 1, Preliminary Discourse, [42] (p. 113), distinguishing "things belonging to right properly and strictly so called" from cases in which "acting otherwise is repugnant to some other dictate of right reason" (i.e. an "imperfect right" in Grotius' classification).
See also Jörn Axel Kämmerer, "Comity", in Anne Peters and Rudiger Wolfrum (eds.), *Max Planck Encylopedia of*

of humanity *(humanitas*[477]*)* supports that assessment, foreshadowing the use of that term by Wolff and Vattel to describe the duties of mutual assistance owed among nations. As with other duties of this kind, each nation is the ultimate judge in balancing its own interests with the interest of other nations in securing the effectiveness of their laws and judgments[478].

This ends discussion of the second point[479].

149. Huber's specific treatment of the subject of foreign judgments in his *Praelectionum*[480] sheds relatively little light on the topic, save to emphasise the qualification to the third axiom when the receiving order acts for its own protection or that of its subjects[481].

5. *The scope of adjudicatory jurisdiction: Huber's first two axioms*

150. Commentators have justifiably focused on Huber's third axiom, and in particular on the role

---

Public International Law, Oxford University Press, 2008, https://opil.ouplaw.com/home/mpil, [3].

477 Text to n. 352.

478 See above, [101]-[102].

479 For the avoidance of doubt, if the best interpretation of Huber's texts is that his third axiom gives rise to a perfect, enforceable obligation that is part of the law of nations, but not the law of nature, the contrary opinion of Johannes Voet (see above, [119]- [120]) is to be preferred.

480 Huber, *De Conflictu Legum*, [6], pp. 68-70, dealing with judgments in both criminal and civil matters; also *Praelectionum Juris Romani, Pars III* (n. 353), Book 42, Title 1, [52]; *Heedendaegse Rechts* (n. 330), Book 1, Chap. 3, [24]-[26].

481 In a particular example, Huber supports the view that a court in Holland had been justified on public interest grounds in refusing to enforce a default judgment given by a court in Friesland against one of its citizens, even though the defendant had agreed by a contract to resolve disputes in that court. Huber criticises a contradictory decision of a Frisian court. This example is discussed by Hatzimihail (n. 330), p. 417 and is examined below, [159].

played by comity. The first two axioms also deserve our attention. On first reading, they seem rather mundane in comparison[482]. One issue that immediately presents itself is whether the word *terminos*, which appears in all three axioms[483], should be taken to refer to the physical limits of the area over which the State exercises authority (its domain)[484] or the figurative, legal limits of that authority (its jurisdiction)[485]. Although the cited Digest texts point in different directions[486], Huber's commentary makes clear that, in formulating rules to determine the legal effects of an act or transaction with a foreign element, his first instinct was to think geographically. Huber repeatedly refers to the place (or *locus*) of a specific person or the parties to a specific transaction to connect a given situation to a particular legal order[487].

151. In places, Huber's approach is more refined, for example, when he acknowledges the possibility that the parties' intentions at the time of contracting may determine the law applicable to their relationship[488]. This subtlety can be seen to good effect in his discussion of questions of adjudicatory jurisdiction, principally

---

482 "(1) The laws of every sovereign authority have force within the boundaries *[terminos]* of its state and bind all subject to it, but not beyond. (2) Those are held to be subject to a sovereign authority who are to be found within its boundaries, whether they are there permanently or temporarily. . .". See above, [122].

483 Translated by Llewelyn Davies as "boundaries" and by Lorenzen as "limits".

484 See above, [88].

485 See above, [96].

486 Digest 2.1.20, Paul, *On the Edict*, Book 1, cited in support of the first axiom, supports reading *terminos* in its figurative sense, whereas Digest 48.22.7.10ff, Ulpian, *On the Duties of Proconsul*, Book 2, suggests the physical sense.

487 See, for example, the discussion of cases concerning the validity of a will, Huber, *De Conflictu Legum*, [4], in which the status of the testator as a citizen or temporary visitor makes no difference to the outcome.

488 Huber, *De Conflictu Legum*, [9].

contained in the second volume of his *Praelectionum*[489]. Huber emphasises that the primary rule for determining the competent forum is that the claimant must sue in the defendant's place of domicile[490]. The reason for this, according to Huber, is not that the defendant is more favoured than the claimant[491], but "because the necessity of summoning and compelling another to fair justice *[jus aequum]* can only proceed from a higher authority, and the higher authority for each is not someone else's ruler but their own"[492]. Although judgments involve the use of a power to compel, the competence of a forum does not rest solely on physical power over the individual as a matter of fact[493] but is recognised only if the "subject matter and equity" *(res et aequitas)* allow[494]. For Huber, fair justice is to be secured primarily at the place of the defendant's domicile, and additionally in the place where the thing in dispute is located, and (within certain limits[495]) where the act giving rise to the claim was

---

489 *Praelectionum Juris Romani et Hodierni, Pars II* (n. 330), Book 5, Title 1, [38]-[58]. As to prorogation of jurisdiction by agreement or appearance, see below, [157]-[159].

490 *Praelectionum Juris Romani et Hodierni, Pars II* (n. 330), Book 5, Title 1, [38].

491 Cf. Digest 50.17.125, Gaius, *On the Provincial Edict*, Book 5, to which Huber refers.

492 *Praelectionum Juris Romani et Hodierni, Pars II* (n. 330), Book 5, Title 1, [38].

493 Cf. *McDonald* v. *Mabee* (1917) 234 US 90, 91 (Holmes J.); Arthur Taylor von Mehren, "Recognition and Enforcement of Foreign Judgments – General Theory and the Role of Jurisdictional Requirements" (1980), 167 *Recueil des cours* 13, 52-53.

494 *Praelectionum Juris Romani et Hodierni, Pars II* (n. 330), Book 5, Title 1, [38] (*sine coactione Judicia forent elusoria; nec alibi Forum lege stabilitur, quam ubi illa cogendi facultas adhiberi potest; non tamen ut ubicunque illa valet, sit forum, sed ubi res et aequitas patitur*).

495 See below, [156].

done[496]. The Latin captures the scheme beautifully – *domicilii, rei sita, rei gesta*[497].

152. Huber explains his second axiom in the following way, disagreeing with those who deny that foreigners are subject to the laws of the place in which they act[498]:

> "[T]he proposition that all persons who act within the limits of a state are to be deemed subject thereto is absolutely certain, for it is in accordance both with the nature of the state, and the practice of subjecting all persons found therein to its authority, and with that which is accepted by almost all nations in regard to personal arrest."

Huber notes Grotius' view that a person who contracts in particular place counts as a "temporary subject"[499] and

---

[496] *Praelectionum Juris Romani et Hodierni, Pars II* (n. 330), Book 5, Title 1, [38]. Huber proceeds to consider the application of the rule based on the defendant's domicile (*ibid.*, [39]-[47]) before turning to consider jurisdiction based on the location of the thing in dispute (*ibid.*, [48]-[52]) and based on the location of the act, for contract (*ibid.*, [53]-[56]) and delict (*ibid.*, [57]-[58]).
In the case of claims based on a contract, Huber emphasises the need to look not at the place where the instrument was written but instead at where the business was actually transacted and disposed of or in which the parties have bound themselves to perform, *Heedendaegse Rechts* (n. 330), Book 4, Chap. 24, [1]; *Praelectionum Juris Romani et Hodierni, Pars II*, above, Book 5, Title 1, [53]. The rationale, it seems, is that the defendant, by voluntarily assuming the obligation in a particular place, has tacitly undertaken to answer for it there (see *ibid.*, [53], [54] and Digest 5.1.36.1, Callistratus, *Inquiries*, Book 1; also Digest 5.1.19.2, Ulpian, *On the Edict*, Book 60, stating that the parties may agree otherwise.

[497] *Praelectionum Juris Romani et Hodierni, Pars II*, above, Book 5, Title 1, [38]. See also *Heedendaegse Rechts* (n. 330), Book 4, Chaps. 22-24, dealing with each basis of jurisdiction in turn.

[498] Huber, *De Conflictu Legum*, [2].

[499] Grotius, *War and Peace*, Book 2, Chap. 11, [5], point 2 (p. 709) (see text to n. 287).

argues that the second axiom explains the requirement for foreigners "to submit to mesne arrest"[500].

153. This passage has had a remarkable afterlife, having played no small part in shaping the rules of adjudicatory jurisdiction of United States' courts in the nineteenth and twentieth centuries[501]. In that setting, Huber's second axiom was understood to support the proposition that a court has jurisdiction to adjudicate upon a claim made against a defendant present, even temporarily, within its domain[502], whether or not the dispute has any connection to the defendant's presence there, and provided only that the defendant is served with originating process before they depart[503]. The defendant's temporary presence when served with the document instituting proceedings has also been understood, at least in England and in other legal orders following her lead, to be a *sufficient* basis to recognise the authority of a foreign court for the purposes of recognising and enforcing its judgment, again without requiring that the dispute be in any way connected to the adjudicating order[504]. Various justifications have been offered for this

---

500 See below, [154].

501 *Burnham* v. *Superior Court of California* (n. 2), 611-616 (Scalia J.); James Weinstein, "The Dutch Influence on the Conception of Judicial Jurisdiction in Nineteenth Century America" (1990), 38 *Am J. Comp L* 73, 85-92.

502 I.e. that of the nation to which it belongs or (in the case of a nation comprising multiple legal orders) the area in respect of which its legal order exercises jurisdiction.

503 So-called "tag" jurisdiction. See *Burnham* v. *Superior Court of California* (n. 2), esp. 612-614 (at 612 (Scalia J.)): "Decisions in the courts of many States in the nineteenth and early twentieth centuries held that personal service upon a physically present defendant sufficed to confer jurisdiction, without regard to whether the defendant was only briefly in the State or whether the cause of action was related to his activities there"); Weinstein (n. 501), 86-92.

504 England and Wales: *Carrick* v. *Hancock* (1895) 12 TLR 59 (QBD); *Adams* v. *Cape Industries plc* [1990] Ch 433 (EWCA).

remarkable (and unattractive) proposition, including that the defendant owes "allegiance" to the nation to which the court belongs[505], that the defendant must accept the burden as well as the benefit of the nation's laws[506] and that the defendant has tacitly consented to be bound[507]. These ideas, familiar from examination of the lawmaking

---

Australia: *Herman* v. *Meallin* (1891) 8 WN (NSW) 38; *Close* v. *Arnot*, unreported, 21 November 1997 (NSWSC). South Africa: *Reiss Engineering Co Ltd.* v. *Isamcor (Pty) Ltd.*, 1883 (1) SA 1033 (W); *Richman* v. *Ben-Tovim* 2007 (2) SA 283.

In Canada, although it is unclear whether the presence rule has been subsumed within the modern "real and substantial connection" test (below, [363]), the balance of authority supports the sufficiency of presence as a basis for the exercise of adjudicatory jurisdiction – see *Teja* v. *Rai*, 2002 BCCA 16, 97 BCLR (3d) 44, [21]-[24] (Huddart J. A.); *Beals* v. *Saldahna* [2003] 3 SCR 416, 2003 SCC 72, [37] (Major J.), [209] (Le Bel J.); *UniNet Technologies Inc.* v. *Communication Services Inc.*, 2005 BCCA 114, 38 BCLR (4th) 366, [20]-[21]; *Club Resorts Ltd.* v. *Van Breda* [2012] 1 SCR 572, 2012 SCC 17, [79]; *Chevron Corp* v. *Yaiguaje*, 2015 SCC 42, [2015] 3 SCR 69; also Stephen G. A. Pitel and Cheryl D. Dusten, "Lost in Transition – Answering the Questions Raised by the Supreme Court of Canada's New Approach to Jurisdiction" (2006), 85 *La Revue Du Barreau Canadien* 61, 63-70.

See Peter Kutner, "Recognition and Enforcement of Foreign Judgments – The Common Law's Jurisdictional Requirements" (2019) 83 *RabelsZ* 1, 9-25.

For criticism of the presence rule as it applies in New Zealand and in Commonwealth African nations, see Maria Hook and Jack Wass, *The Conflict of Laws in New Zealand*, Wellington: LexisNexis NZ, 2020, [5.108]; Richard Frimpong Oppong, *Private International Law in Commonwealth Africa*, Cambridge: Cambridge University Press, 2013, pp. 326-327.

505 *Carrick* v. *Hancock*, above, 60 (Lord Russell of Killowen CJ), but cf. *Adams* v. *Cape Industries*, above, 518-519 and 553.

506 *Adams* v. *Cape Industries*, above, 518-519.

507 *Ibid.*, 555. For a critical view of the English decisions, see Dickinson, "*Schibsby* v. *Westenholz*" (n. 216), 430-437. See

authority of the institutions of a political society in the preceding chapter[508], will need be examined more closely when we return to the topic of adjudicatory jurisdiction in later chapters[509].

154. At this point, note that Huber's second axiom does not support the assertion that a nation enjoys *unqualified* legislative and adjudicatory jurisdiction over all persons present within its boundaries for as long as they remain there. Although Huber does endorse Grotius' idea that a person present in a particular place is temporarily subject to the laws of that place[510], there is no suggestion that this subjection is unlimited. Indeed, Grotius' example points in the opposite direction—the scope of legislative authority is defined by reference to a specific act, the making of a local bargain, and does not extend (for example) to a contract that the same parties made the previous month while on the high seas[511].

155. Nor does Huber's reference in the passage quoted to mesne arrest – i.e. depriving the defendant of his liberty as a means of forcing an appearance in court – or the specific example that he gives involving a default judgment given against an absent defendant[512] support the

---

also Blackstone, *Commentaries* (n. 191), Book 3, Chap. 9, [159]-[160], pp. 107-108.

508 Section II.I.

509 Section IV.D and Section V.B.3.

510 Huber, *De Conflictu Legum*, [2], p. 65 *(Qui in loco aliquo contrahit tanquam subditus temporarius legibus loci subjicitur).*

511 Grotius, *War and Peace*, Book 2, Chap. 11, [5], points 2 and 3, pp. 709-710. Huber makes a similar point in considering the law applicable to contracts, with the example of an authentic instrument, Huber, *De Conflictu Legum*, [7], pp. 70-71. He concludes that the law applicable to the validity of an instrument will not necessarily regulate the mechanism for its enforcement as the latter "constitutes almost a contract by itself and a separate matter" *(quae per se quasi contractum separatumque negotium constituit).*

512 (n. 481.)

claim that the mere fact of service of originating process on a person locally present suffices to establish the court's adjudicatory jurisdiction[513]. It is necessary to distinguish, as Huber does in his own account of the mechanisms for the adjudication of disputes[514], between the threshold question whether a court is a competent forum *(foro competente)* to determine a particular dispute and the distinct procedures adopted in particular legal orders (1) to use forceful means to compel a defendant to appear in court and to submit to its jurisdiction *(arrest)*, (2) to notify a defendant of the claim *(summons)*[515] and (3) to sanction a defendant who has been lawfully summoned and who does not appear *(judgment in default)*[516].

156. Huber identifies the defendant's presence as a basis of adjudicatory jurisdiction only in combination with the location of the place of the act giving rise to the claim[517]. He even qualifies this basis of jurisdiction, on grounds of equity, in circumstances where the

[513] Cf. Weinstein (n. 501), 79-92; Hatzimihail (n. 300), pp. 407-419.

[514] *Praelectionum Juris Romani et Hodierni, Pars II* (n. 330), Book 2, Title 5, [4]-[5]; also *Heedendaegse Rechts* (n. 330), Book 4, Chap. 32.

[515] *Ibid.*, Book 2, Title 4.

[516] *Ibid.*, Book 2, Title 6.

[517] See above, [151]; also *Heedendaegse Rechts* (n. 330), Book 4, Chap. 22, [6].
A very similar account, also based on Roman law sources, is given by the Scots judge and natural law scholar, Lord Kames (Henry Home) in his work *Historical Law Tracts*, Edinburgh: A. Kincaid and J. Bell, 1758, Vol. 1, pp. 352-373. According to Kames, pp. 353, 355, "[t]he inhabitants only are subjected to a territorial judge, and not every person who may be found occasionally within the territory", whereas in the case (for example) of a contractual dispute, "it is natural to apply for redress to the judge of that territory where the failure happens, provided that the party who fails be found there".

defendant's presence in a particular place was transient[518]. The justification for this, according to Huber, lies in considerations of equity, having regard to the hardship that the defendant would face in being required to travel to defend the cause[519]. Accordingly, the defendant's presence, although linked to the fair resolution of the dispute, is not a sufficient ground for adjudicatory jurisdiction to exist.

157. As Huber's description of mesne arrest makes clear[520], this process secured the court's adjudicatory power only indirectly, by coercing the defendant to make a formal appearance in court and thereby to submit to the court's jurisdiction[521]. Although

---

518 *Praelectionum Juris Romani et Hodierni, Pars II* (n. 330), Book 5, Title 1, [55]; also *Heedendaegse Rechts* (n. 330), Book 4, Chap. 24, [2].

519 *Heedendaegse Rechts* (n. 330), Book 4, Chap. 24, [2]; *Praelectionum Juris Romani et Hodierni, Pars II* (n. 330), Book 5, Title 1, [55], with reference to Digest 5.1.19.2, Ulpian, *On the Edict*, Book 60. It is otherwise if citation of the defendant is approved by the magistrate in the place of domicile, *Heedendaegse Rechts* (n. 330), Book 4, Chap. 24, [2].

520 *Praelectionum Juris Romani et Hodierni, Pars II* (n. 330), Book 2, Title 5, [5]; also *Heedendaegse Rechts* (n. 330), Book 4, Chap. 31, [3].

521 As to submission by appearance, see *Praelectionum Juris Romani et Hodierni, Pars II* (n. 330), Book 2, Title 1, [12]; *Heedendaegse Rechts* (n. 330), Book 4, Chap. 2, [32]. See also Johannes Voet, *Commentarius*, Book 2, Title 1, [20] (pp. 220-221).
The common law process of arrest by *capias ad respondendum* worked in a very similar way, securing jurisdiction by the defendant's physical appearance as a prisoner or formal appearance through an attorney, see Dickinson, "Keeping Up Appearances" (n. 218), 10-17. It is an error to treat the act of depriving the defendant of his liberty, or the physical capacity of the organs of State to perform that act, as the basis of the court's jurisdiction in such cases – Dickinson, above, 14-15. Cf. *McDonald* v. *Mabee* (n. 493),

indefensible today[522], the process was widely used at this time in neighbouring provinces and nations, as Huber acknowledges[523]. However, the legal order of Huber's Frisia[524] resisted the practice, deploying it only by retorsion to arrest the citizens of nations and provinces that had employed it in cases involving Frisian citizens[525]. Huber strongly criticises the practice[526]. The important point to note here is that, in cases in which the process was used, a judgment given against a defendant arrested and thereby compelled to participate in court proceedings was *not* a judgment given in default of appearance against an absent defendant, who had been served with process[527].

91; *Michigan Trust Co* v. *Ferry* (1913) 228 US 345, 353 (both Holmes J.).

522 See International Covenant on Civil and Political Rights (1966), Article 11; European Convention on Human Rights, Protocol No. 4 (1968), Article 1.
The writ of *capias ad respondendum* was finally abolished in England by s. 23 and Sch. 1, para. 1 of the Crown Proceedings Act 1947, although it had ceased to be used as a form of originating process in 1838 (Judgments Act 1838, ss. 1-2 (see Dickinson, above, 23-24; Bruce Kercher "The Transformation of Imprisonment for Debt" (1984) 2 Aust J L and Society 60).

523 *Praelectionum Juris Romani et Hodierni, Pars II* (n. 330), Book 2, Title 5, [4]; *Heedendaegse Rechts* (n. 330), Book 4, Chap. 31, [3], [7].

524 With the sole exception of the town of Leeuwarden, *Praelectionum Juris Romani et Hodierni, Pars II* (n. 330), Book 2, Title 5, [4]; *Heedendaegse Rechts* (n. 330), Book 4, Chap. 31, [5].

525 *Praelectionum Juris Romani et Hodierni, Pars II* (n. 330), Book 2, Title 5, [4]; *Heedendaegse Rechts* (n. 330), Book 4, Chap. 31, [6].

526 *Praelectionum Juris Romani et Hodierni, Pars II* (n. 330), Book 2, Title 5, [5].

527 In addition to the references in n. 521, see *Picquet* v. *Swan* (1828) 5 Mason 35, 44; 19 F Cas 609, 612-613 (Story J). Cf. *Pennoyer* v. *Neff* (n. 216), 733; *International Shoe Co* v. *Washington* (n. 216), 316.

158. Huber's analysis of the default judgment scenario in *De Conflictu Legum* is best understood by keeping in mind two rules of adjudicatory jurisdiction applied in his home province, Frisia. The first is that prorogation of jurisdiction by private agreement was considered to be contrary to the public interest and of no legal effect unless accompanied either by a summons or citation effective in the place where the defendant was physically present[528] or by the defendant's formal appearance. Huber considers such an agreement to be a mere pact, and to be opposed to the constitutional principle that adjudicatory jurisdiction and *res judicata* can be conferred only by a supreme power[529]. The second, already noted, is that the court of the place of contracting was considered a competent forum, but this was limited to cases in which the defendant was actually present in that place when proceedings were brought, or had assets within the forum, or a successful application had been made to the judge of the defendant's domicile to authorise his citation there[530].

159. In Huber's example[531], parties from the provinces of Holland and Groningen had agreed in their contract to submit disputes to the courts of Groningen.

---

[528] Note that this place may either be the forum or in the place in which the defendant resides but in the latter case only with the authorisation of a local judge, *Praelectionum Juris Romani et Hodierni, Pars II* (n. 330), Book 2, Title 1, [12].

[529] *Ibid.*, [9], [12]; *Heedendaegse Rechts* (n. 330), Book 4, Chap. 31, [25]-[32]. Cf. Digest 5.1.1-2, Ulpian, *On the Edict*, Books 2 and 3; Johannes Voet, *Commentarius*, Book 2, Title 1, [14], [26], pp. 215, 226-227.

[530] *Praelectionum Juris Romani et Hodierni, Pars II* (n. 330), Book 5, Title 1, [54]-[55]; *Heedendaegse Rechts* (n. 330), Book 4, Chap. 24, [2]-[4]. In the case where jurisdiction was founded on the presence of assets, execution of a judgment would be against those assets only.

[531] Huber, *De Conflictu Legum*, [6]. At the end of the passage, Huber refers approvingly to a decision given by a court in Amsterdam, refusing to enforce a Frisian judgment given

The latter summoned the former, who did not respond. The Groningen court then exhausted its procedures for citing an absent defendant and entered judgment in default, for contumacy. The claimant sought to enforce that judgment in Frisia, with evident success. Huber summarises the reasons given by the Frisian judges for this decision but dissents on the basis that "if a defendant cannot be found in the territory of the judge to whom he had submitted, he cannot by reason of the submission be proceeded against for contumacy . . . [532] nor can effect be given to such judgments without detriment to our own jurisdiction and prejudice to our own citizens"[533]. Huber's predominant objection is not that the judgment had been given against a defendant who was not present in Groningen when cited but rather that the court in Groningen had purported to assume jurisdiction on a basis that Huber considered to be incompatible with the principles governing adjudicatory jurisdiction within the Frisian legal order[534]. If, however, the defendant had been present in Groningen when summoned, the pact to submit would have been effective in these circumstances to prevent the defendant from raising any objection to jurisdiction[535]. Moreover, for contractual and delictual claims, the defendant's presence on a more than temporary basis would have allowed the exercise of jurisdiction

in the same circumstances. See also *Heedendaegse Rechts* (n. 330), Book 1, Chap. 3, [26].

532 Huber adds "as we shall see elsewhere", a reference to his discussion in Book 2, Title 1 of the question of prorogation by private act (see text to nn. 528-529).

533 Huber, *De Conflictu Legum*, [6].

534 See n. 529; also *Praelectionum Juris Romani, Pars III* (n. 353), Book 42, Title 1, [52], which refers back to this case.

535 *Praelectionum Juris Romani et Hodierni, Pars II* (n. 330), Book 2, Title 1, [12]; *Heedendaegse Rechts* (n. 330), Book 2, Chap. 14, [30]. See also Johannes Voet, *Commentarius*, Book 2, Title 1, [26] (pp. 226-227).

on the basis of the location of the act[536]. This explains why Huber distinguished a case in which the defendant was locally present when proceedings were brought, but this does not advance the theory that presence *alone* is capable of founding personal jurisdiction. As Huber makes clear, his reasoning in this passage rests upon this third axiom and not his second[537].

6. *Comity as a bridge between legal orders*

160. Although Huber's approach to the subject is more tightly structured, and presents a sharper and more intense formulation of comity than that of Paulus and Johannes Voet[538], all three accounts share common features and are underpinned by natural law thinking. The problem that all three authors were seeking to tackle[539] arises from the (natural) equality of independent nations and the recognition of their broad, and overlapping, (natural) liberty to regulate their own affairs. The solution that they all advocate involves recognising an imperative that each nation provide mutual legal assistance to others to ensure that legitimate, binding exercises of lawmaking powers are not rendered ineffective[540]. Comity, a mutual duty (or office[541]) of humanity, draws its vigour from the (natural) community that exists among human beings, as

---

536 See above, [151], [156].

537 Huber, *De Conflictu Legum*, [6], in approving the decision of a court in Amsterdam to refuse execution of a Frisian default judgment in a like case (see n. 531).

538 Compare Watson, *Joseph Story and the Comity of Errors* (n. 475), esp. at pp. 15-16 and "The Failure of Scottish Legal Education" (n. 475), esp. at pp. 145-146, contending that Huber's approach is fundamentally different from that of other Dutch jurists. Watson's view has been considered in an earlier footnote (n. 475).

539 Reflected, albeit imperfectly, in Huber's first two axioms (above, [150]).

540 Grotius, *War and Peace*, Book 1, Chap. 3, [7], p. 259.

541 Text to n. 317.

well as the nations representing them. The commitments thereby generated bind each nation as a moral person, as a standard by reference to which their laws and conduct may be evaluated. They are imperfect obligations, being matters for individual judgment, and give rise to no right enforceable between nations, although an aggrieved nation may demonstrate its disapproval of a failure to provide requested assistance by withdrawing its own support. The bond of comity may be overridden by measures taken to protect the receiving order or its members and does not demand obedience in any case if injustice would result.

161. In its application, more specifically, to judicial decisions, comity (humanity) demands that nations recognise and enforce each other's legitimate exercises of adjudicatory authority over persons (and things) subject to their authority, to promote the effective and just resolution of disputes. In accordance with that directive, they may not re-examine the merits of the case, although they may refuse to offer support if the judgment is manifestly unjust or incompatible with measures taken by the receiving order to protect itself or its members. Every nation is entitled to expect that others will provide mutual assistance of this kind and may indicate its disapproval by refusing to recognise or enforce the judgments of a non-conforming national legal order.

D. Reception and development in the eighteenth century

1. Reception into the common law

(a) *Reception in Scotland (Part I)*

162. At the turn of the eighteenth century, these ideas found an ideal receptor and transmitter in the legal system of Scotland. Its "common law" had developed distinctly from that of its neighbour, England, with diverse influences, most notably in the form of civilian

doctrine brought home by students travelling to France and, latterly, the Netherlands for their legal education[542]. Some of these students, no doubt, studied under Johannes Voet in Utrecht or Leiden or Ulrik Huber in Franeker[543]. Natural law principles formed part of this instruction, with Grotius and Pufendorf's works as the principal sources of instruction[544]. A chair in Public Law and the Law of Nature and Nations was established at the University of Edinburgh in 1707, followed shortly afterwards, in 1710, by a chair in Civil Law. As the current holder of the Professorship of Civil Law explains, generally speaking,

---

542 Brian Clark and Gerald Keegan, *Scottish Legal System*, Dundee: Dundee University Press, 3rd ed., 2012, pp. 1-4. As to the Dutch influence, see Robert Feenstra, "Scottish-Dutch Legal Relations in the Seventeenth and Eighteenth Centuries", in T. Christopher Smout (ed.), *Scotland and Europe 1200-1850*, Edinburgh: John Donald, 1986; Alan Watson, "The Failure of Scottish Legal Education" (n. 475), 147-149; Esther Mijers, "Scottish Students in the Netherlands 1680-1730", Chap. 10 in Alexia Grosjean and Steve Murdoch (eds.), *Scottish Communities Abroad in the Early Modern Period*, Boston: Brill, 2005, esp. at pp. 310-311, 328-330; John W. Cairns, "Importing Our Lawyers from Holland: Netherlands Influences on Scots Law and Lawyers in the Eighteenth Century", Chap. 8 in *Law, Lawyers and Humanism*, Edinburgh: Edinburgh University Press, Vol. 1, 2015.

543 These, together with Groningen, were the principal destinations for Scots seeking legal training (Mijers, above). Cairns ("Importing Our Lawyers", above, pp. 223-224) records that Sir John Clerk, who was appointed as a judge in Scotland shortly after the Act of Union with England, travelled to Leiden in 1694 and studied under Johannes Voet. James Craig, appointed Professor of Civil Law at the University of Edinburgh in 1710, had enrolled in Franeker shortly after Huber's death and defended his thesis before Huber's son, Zacharias (see John Cairns, "James Craig, Professor of Civil Law, 1710-1732", The Edinburgh Legal History Blog, 28 May 2013, https://www.elhblog.law.ed.ac.uk/2013/05/28/james-craig-professor-of-civil-law-1710-1732/).

544 Cairns, "Importing our Lawyers" (n. 542), p. 234.

"Scots who studied law in the Netherlands would have learned it as a polite, enlightened science, related to the study of philosophy, philology and history"[545]. As Scots legal education began to burgeon in this period, "natural law theory had become central to Scottish ethical thought"[546].

163. The period was also of enormous political significance for Scotland, with the conclusion in 1707 of the Act of Union with England, creating a unified kingdom with a single Parliament[547]. Importantly, the Union preserved the independence of the legal systems of the two nations so far as matters of private law were concerned[548]. But an important link between the two was soon recognised, in the form of a right of litigants to petition the upper chamber of Parliament, the House of Lords, to reverse judgments of lower courts in Scotland[549].

164. Soon after the Union, in *Goddart* v. *Swinton*, a claim was brought in the Court of Session to enforce a judgment obtained in England against an English subject, Sir John Swinton, following a successful maritime venture. Swinton denied that he was liable. The pursuer's advocate relied on Huber's *De Conflictu Legum*

---

545 *Ibid.*

546 *Ibid.*, p. 236, with reference to Roger L. Emerson, "Science and Moral Philosophy in the Scottish Enlightenment", pp. 11-36, in Michael A. Stewart (ed.), *Studies in Philosophy in the Scottish Enlightenment*, Oxford: Oxford University Press, 1990.

547 Union with Scotland Act 1706 (England), Articles 1 and 3; Union with England Act 1707 (Scotland), ss. 1 and 3.

548 Union with Scotland Act, above, Articles 18 and 19; Union with England Act, above, ss. 18 and 19.

549 David Lewis Jones, "The Judicial Role of the House of Lords before 1870", in Louis Blom-Cooper (ed.), *The Judicial House of Lords 1876-2009*, Oxford: Oxford University Press, 2009, at pp. 7-8; A. J. MacLean, "The 1707 Union: Scots Law and the House of Lords" (1984), 4 *Journal of Legal History* 50.

to support a rule that the courts of one nation cannot inquire into the decrees of another[550]. This was said to be "founded on great necessity and expediency, for the facilitating of trade and commerce, and for keeping up a good correspondence amongst independent nations"[551]. Otherwise, "the justest decrees . . . may be frustrated and eluded"[552]. The pursuer relied on the facts that the parties to the litigation and the contract were English subjects, engaged in trade in England and in dispute about the proceeds of the trade received in England, submitting that, in combination, these were "equivalent as if Sir John had given his obligation to pay"[553].

165. The defender's advocate argued, in reply, that Huber's comity required the courts of one nation to treat foreign judgments "with respect and civility but not as excluding review"[554]. He suggested two restrictions on Huber's principle, that the decrees must accord with principles of the law of nations, and that they must not be contrary to the particular laws of the receiving legal order[555]. Doubt was also cast on the finality of the English judgment and on the authority that decrees of the Scots courts had before English courts[556]. The

---

550 *Goddart* v. *Swinton* (1711) 4 Brown's Supplement to Morison's Dictionary of Decisions (Bro Supp) 848, 848; also *sub. nom. Goddart* v. *Swynton* (1713) Morison's Dictionary of Decisions (Mor) 4533, 4534.
An earlier hearing in the case is reported at (1709) Mor 6445, with a reference ((1709) Mor 6445, 6446) to Voet's *De Statutis*. The decision at that hearing, that the defender had ratified the judgment, was subsequently set aside.

551 (1711) 4 Bro Sup 848, 848; also (1713) Mor 4533, 4534.

552 (1711) 4 Bro Sup 848, 848-849; also (1713) Mor 4533, 4534.

553 (1711) 4 Bro Sup 848, 849; also (1713) Mor 4533, 4534, referring to "judiciary contracts".

554 (1711) 4 Bro Sup 848, 850; also (1713) Mor 4533, 4534.

555 (1711) 4 Bro Sup 848, 850; (1713) Mor 4533, 4535.

556 (1711) 4 Bro Sup 848, 850; (1713) Mor 4533, 4534.

defender argued that comity demanded reciprocity of treatment[557].

166. The Court of Session appeared hesitant, ruling in the pursuer's favour but on terms that suggested a willingness to enquire into the merits[558]. The pursuer appealed unsuccessfully to the House of Lords[559].

167. The same question arose a few years later in *Edwards* v. *Prescot*, in which the pursuer had secured an English judgment for damages caused by a fire that had started in the defender's lodgings. When Mrs Prescot fled to Scotland, the pursuer brought an action on the judgment in the Court of Session. Although the argument proceeded upon similar lines to the earlier case, on this occasion, the influence of Voet's work in particular is evident from the arguments reported by a young advocate, Henry Home (a name to remember)[560].

168. Again, the argument is more illuminating than the Court's decision, allowing execution to pass "unless

[557] (1713) Mor 4533, 4534, "[W]here the sentences of Sovereign Courts are put to execution in any other country, it is *ex comitate* not *ex necessitate*; so with us, the decrees of the Sovereign Courts in England cannot have the effect of *res judicata*, unless the decrees of Session be received as *res judicata* there"; also (1711) Bro Sup 848, 850.

[558] (1713) Mor 4533 ("The Lords sustained the decree of the Court of Queen's Bench, the pursuer instructing that his father was a partner, and that the defender was cashier or intromitter, to make the defender liable to the pursuer. . ."). As is common for the period in Scotland, the report contains no account of the reasons for the Court's decision.

[559] *Goddart* v. *Swinton* (1715) 1 Robertson's Scotch Appeal Cases 162. See A. E. (Alexander) Anton, "The Introduction into English Practice of Continental Theories on the Conflict of Laws" (1956), 5 *International and Comparative Law Quarterly* 534, 538.

[560] *Edwards* v. *Prescot*, reported in Henry Home, *Remarkable Decisions of the Court of Session from 1716 to 1728*, Edinburgh: Thomas Rudimann, 1728, Rem Dec, Vol. 1, No. 21, pp. 59-69; (1720) Mor 4535.

something competent in law or equity be objected against it"[561].

(b) *A look across the border: Early practice in England*

169. By the end of the seventeenth century, English courts had expressed a willingness to give effect to judgments of foreign admiralty and ecclesiastical courts[562]. These decisions rested on the understanding that these courts were part of a network across the European continent applying a common framework of rules and are of limited value to our enquiry[563]. Cases that rely upon these authorities to support the effectiveness of a foreign judgment in other circumstances must, for this reason, be treated with caution[564].

---

[561] (1720) Rem Dec, Vol. 1, No. 21, 59, 69; (1713) Mor 4535, 4542. The death of one of the parties shortly afterwards brought an end to the action. See also *Meres* v. *Company of Undertakers* (1628) Mor 8290, 8291.

[562] *Wier's case* (1607) 1 Rolle's Abridgement 530; *Cottington's* case (1678), noted 2 Swanston 326; *Hughes* v. *Cornelius* (1681) 2 Shower KB 232 (also reported (1681) Skinner 52); *Beake* v. *Tirrell* (1689) Comberbach 120; also *Jurado* v. *Gregory* (1669) 1 Ventris 32; *Newland* v. *Horseman* (1681) 1 *Vernon's Cases in Chancery* 21; *Green* v. *Waller* (1703) 2 Lord Raymond 891; *Roach* v. *Garvan* (1748) 1 Vesey Senior 157; *Bernardi* v. *Motteux* (1781) 2 Douglas 575; *Geyer* v. *Aguilar* (1798) 7 Term Rep 681, 695-696 (Lord Kenyon CJ); *The City of Mecca* (1879) 5 PD 28, 30-33 (Sir Robert Phillimore).
On the early use of "faith and credit" language in this context, see Kurt H. Nadelmann, "Full Faith and Credit to Judgments and Public Acts" (1957), 56 *Michigan L Rev.* 33, 44-45.

[563] *Jurado* v. *Gregory* (n. 562), 32 ("all the Courts of Admiralty in Europe are governed by the civil law, and are to be assistant one to another"); also *Dupleix* v. *Roven* (1705), 2 *Vernon's Cases in Chancery* 540.

[564] For example, *Burrows* v. *Jemineau* (1726) Select Cases Temp King 69, 70.

170. As the English courts began to grapple with questions of the effectiveness of foreign judgments more generally, they faced three distinct, but interrelated, challenges. First, constitutional issues as to the effect in England of judgments of courts acting under a distinct sovereign authority[565]. Second, identification of the form that an action founded upon a foreign judgment should take, at a time when taking the wrong club out of the legal bag would doom the claim to fail regardless of its merits[566]. Third, to determine the conditions under which a foreign judgment would be given effect in England and the extent to which it would be reviewable by the English court.

171. In 1744, the Lord Chancellor, Lord Hardwicke, addressed the constitutional question in the following way[567]:

> "[E]very sentence, having its authority from the sovereign in whose dominions it is given, cannot bind the jurisdiction of foreign courts, who own not the same authority, and have a different sovereign, and

---

565 The position was more complex for legal orders, including Scotland, sharing the same head of State as England, albeit under different constitutional arrangements. The detail need not trouble us here, for judgments of Scots and Irish courts were eventually treated by the common law in the same way as judgments of the courts of other States (see *Otway* v. *Ramsay* (1737) 2 Strange 1090; *Harris* v. *Saunders* (1825) 4 Barnewell & Cresswell 411, but cf. *Collins* v. *Matthew* (1804) 5 East 463).

566 Sir William Holdsworth, *A History of English Law*, London: Methuen & Co Ltd., 3rd ed., 1944, Vol. 9, p. 248. As to the forms of action, and their abolition, see Frederic William Maitland, *The Forms of Action at Common Law: A Course of Lectures*, Cambridge: Cambridge University Press, 1936, Lecture 1, pp. 1-11.

567 *Gage* v. *Bulkeley* (1744) Ridgeway Temp Hardwicke 263, 264. See also *Gage* v. *Buckley* (1744) Vesey Senior Supplement 409 (note); *Gage* v. *Lady Stafford* (1754) 2 Vesey Senior 556.

are only bound by judicial sentences given under the same sovereign power as they themselves act."

He explained, however, that although a foreign judgment could not be pleaded as a matter of record, it could be put in evidence in support of an action – although "it does not bind the court as a judgment, yet it may and does the justice of the case between the parties themselves"[568].

172. What was lacking at this point in the law's development was an explanation as to why a judgment that emanated from a different constitutional order should be taken to bind "the justice of the case" in such a way as to found a cause of action in England[569].

(c) *Reception in Scotland (Part 2)*

173. The law in Scotland, already at a more advanced state of development, continued to evolve. In *Wilson* v. *Brunton*[570], the Court of Session refused to enforce an English judgment for costs awarded to the pursuer, a customs collector, who had been successful in defending a tort claim brought by the defenders. Although formal reasons for judgment were not given, the report of Lord Kames (also known as Henry Home), by this time one of the judges of the Court of Session, endorses the objection raised by the defenders that execution should not be issued "upon a foreign decree which is materially unjust

568 *Gage* v. *Bulkeley*, above, 264, identifying the appropriate form of action as one of "assumpsit in nature of debt upon a simple contract". For early recognition that the action of *indebitatus assumpsit* would lie on a foreign judgment, see *Dupleix* v. *Roven* (n. 563).

569 See also *Crawford* v. *Witten* (1773) Lofft 154, *sub nom Crawford* v. *Whittal* (1773) 1 Doug 3 (note).

570 (1756) Mor 4549; (1756) Mor 4551; also – v. – (1756) 5 Bro Sup 841.

or contrary to equity"[571]. The defenders accepted that "[i]t is highly proper, that a certain *comitas* be observed by the Judges of different countries", while contending that "the only effect of a *comitas* is to presume in favour of a foreign decree, that it was just until the contrary is shown" and that "judges ought not to interpose their authority to legitimate injustice done to private parties"[572]. Both parties relied on Johannes Voet[573], with the defender citing *Edwards* v. *Prescot*[574].

174. The House of Lords reversed the decision, following a hearing at which only the pursuer's advocate appeared. Lord Kames reports, second hand, that the reversal by the House of Lords was on the ground that "in England the decrees of sovereign courts abroad are put in execution . . . without admitting any objection against them"[575].

---

571 (1756) Mor 4551, 4554.
The abbreviated report of James Burnett, later Lord Monboddo [(1756) 5 Bro Sup 841] suggests that Lord Kames, along with the Lord President of the Court (Lord Craigie), had supported a distinction between a judgment absolving the defendant and one condemning him, denying that comity demanded the enforcement of condemnatory judgments, in particular in the absence of reciprocity from the adjudicating order.
Although Kames would later support a distinction of this nature extrajudicially (see below, [177]), the reliability of Burnett's report seems open to doubt, given its brevity and inconsistencies with Kames' own report. Kames' practice was to take down instantly in writing the opinions of his fellow judges as well as his own observations.Lord Kames, *Select Decisions of the Court of Session from the Year 1752 to the Year 1768* (Edinburgh: Bell & Bradfute, 2nd ed, 1794), iv.

572 (1756) Mor 4549, 4551.

573 *Ibid.*, 4550, 4551.

574 *Ibid.*, 4551 (see above, [167]-[168]). Reference was also made to the treatise of Groenewegen (n. 326).

575 *Ibid.*, 4554; also (1756) 5 Bro Sup 841. See below, [178].

(d) *Lord Kames and Lord Mansfield*

175. Lord Kames was a central figure in the Scottish Enlightenment. Described as "a man of extraordinary energy and intellectual range"[576], he considered law to be a rational discipline, underpinned by natural law but expressed in different ways at different times and in different places[577]. His position as a judge of the Court of Session and (later) of the High Court of Justiciary did not quell his scholarly efforts[578].

176. In 1760, Kames produced the first edition of *Principles of Equity*. Its closing chapter contains an account of the effect given to foreign statutes and decrees in Scotland[579]. Kames identifies the governing principle as being that[580]:

---

576 James A Harris, "Introduction", p. x, in Henry Home (Lord Kames), *Historical Law Tracts*, Edinburgh: A Kincaid, 1758, reproduced as part of the *Natural Law and Enlightenment Classics* series, Indianapolis: Liberty Fund, 2019. For detailed accounts of Kames' work and influence, see William C Lehman and Henry Home, *Lord Kames and the Scottish Enlightenment*, Leiden: Martinus Nijhoff, 1971 and Ian Simpson Ross, *Lord Kames and the Scotland of His Day*, Oxford: Oxford University Press, 1972.

577 Harris, above, pp. x-xi. See Henry Home (Lord Kames), *Essays on the Principles of Morality and Natural Religion*, Edinburgh: R. Fleming, 1751, Essay 2, esp. Chaps. 7-9: also Henry Home (Lord Kames), *Principles of Equity*, Edinburgh: A. Kincaid and J. Bell, 2nd ed., 1767, Preliminary Discourse and Introduction, pp. 1-54.

578 Kames' account of the limits of adjudicatory jurisdiction in his 1758 work, *Historical Law Tracts*, which followed closely that of Huber, has been briefly considered above (n. 517).

579 Henry Home (Lord Kames), *Principles of Equity*, Edinburgh: A. Kincaid, 1760, Book 3, Chap. 8, Section VI, esp. pp. 288-289.

580 *Ibid*., p. 289. See Digest, 44.2.6, Paul, *On the Edict*, Book 70. In the 3rd edition of his work, Edinburgh: J. Bell and W. Creech, 1778, Kames expresses this idea more succinctly

"Public utility, regarding the safety and quiet of individuals, requires that there be some means for putting a final issue to every controversy that can be brought before a court; for otherwise law suits would be perpetual."

177. Kames supported a distinction between a foreign judgment supporting the claim, condemning the defendant, and one dismissing the claim and absolving[581]. Although the former has no extraterritorial coercive authority, the injustice that would result to the claimant if required to bring a fresh action against the judgment debtor had, in his view, "established a rule among all civilised nations, that a foreign decree shall be put in execution, unless some exception be opposed to it in law or equity"[582]. The decree is presumed to be just until the contrary is proved. By contrast, Kames suggested that no enquiry would be allowed into a foreign decree dismissing the claim. The reason that he gives for supporting this distinction is that, even if the dismissal of the claim is unjust, the court of the receiving order is not required actively to "support and promote injustice", as it would if awarding execution without enquiry[583]. Rather, at most, in upholding the dismissal, the court "forbears to interpose itself in behalf of justice"[584]. Although this reasoning is unconvincing, the idea that a judgment had greater potency when used defensively had some currency, until dispelled by Joseph Story[585].

– "There is nothing more hurtful to society, than that law-suits be perpetual" (p. 367).

581 Kames, *Principles of Equity* (n. 579), p. 288.

582 *Ibid.*

583 *Ibid.*, p. 289.

584 *Ibid.*

585 Joseph Story, *Commentaries on the Conflict of Laws, Foreign and Domestic*, Boston: Hilliard, Gray and Co, 1834, [598]-[602], pp. 503-504, discussed below, [228].

178. In the second edition of his *Principles*, published in 1767, Kames supplemented his analysis of the effects of foreign decrees with an extended note on *Wilson* v. *Brunton*[586]. He criticised the House of Lords in that case as acting "blindly to authorise execution upon a foreign degree, without admitting any objection against it", at the risk of injustice[587].

179. Kames dedicated the second edition to his fellow Scot, William Murray, Lord Mansfield, by that time a judge of the Court of King's Bench in England[588]. The two had corresponded following the publication of the first edition, with Mansfield expressing admiration for Kames' work[589]. Although Lord Mansfield's education and practice had taken him away from his native Scotland, he had retained close connections with its legal system, acting as counsel in Scots appeals to the House of Lords[590]. His familiarity with the works of Huber and Voet cannot be doubted.

180. In 1760, Lord Mansfield presided in *Robinson* v. *Bland*, an action to enforce contracts concluded between British subjects advancing money for the purposes of gambling in France. After hearing the parties' initial

[586] Lord Kames (Henry Home), *Principles of Equity*, 2nd ed. (n. 577), pp. 369-374. The report, omitting the criticism of the House of Lords (see the following text), was later published in Kames' *Select Decisions of the Court of Session from the Year 1752 to the Year 1768* (n. 571), 129.

[587] Kames, *Principles of Equity*, 2nd ed. (n. 577), pp. 373-374.

[588] Kames *Principles of Equity*, 2nd ed. (n. 577), "Letter to Lord Mansfield", dated April 1766, immediately following the title page.

[589] Michael Lobben, "Editor's Introduction", pp. xxiii-xxvi in the *Natural Law and Enlightenment Classics* edition of the work, Lord Kames (Henry Home), *Principles of Equity*, Edinburgh: J. Bell and W. Creech, 3rd ed., 1778, reproduced Indianapolis: Liberty Fund, 2014, https://oll-resources.s3.us-east-2.amazonaws.com/oll3/store/titles/2644/Kames_1635_LFeBk.pdf.

[590] Anton (n. 560), 538.

submissions, he indicated that he would "desire to hear another argument" and offered "a few hints"[591]. Following the adjournment, counsel addressed their submissions to questions of the conflict of laws, citing Grotius, Voet and Huber, among others[592]. In judgment, Lord Mansfield applied Huber's analysis to fix the law applicable to the contract[593]. This was the first occasion on which his work had been cited by an English court. Although *Robinson* did not open the floodgates to the widespread reception of Huber's axioms or continental scholarship more generally, it signalled a receptiveness within the English judiciary to new ways of thinking[594].

(e) *Reception in Scotland (Part 3)*

181. In the following years, two further decisions crystallised the Scots law on the enforcement of foreign judgments.

182. In *Laycock* v. *Clark*, the Court of Session enforced an order for costs made by an English court against an unsuccessful litigant[595]. The reasoning emphasises the need to presume the justice of the foreign decision, as well as the fact that the judgment debtor had chosen the English forum[596]. According to one report, Lord Kames expressed the opinion that[597]:

> "From the time of Mrs Prescot's case it is established in this country that, *ex comitate*, there is a presumption in favour of the foreign decree."

---

591 (1760) 1 Blackstone W 234, 246.
592 (1760) 1 Blackstone W 256, 257.
593 *Ibid.*, 258-259.
594 Anton (n. 560), 539-540.
595 *Laycock* v. *Clark* (1767) Mor 4554; (1767) Hailes 188.
596 (1767) Hailes 188, 189. The reporter, Lord Hailes, was a member of the Court.
597 *Ibid.* The reference is to *Edwards* v. *Prescot* (n. 560).

183. In the following year, in *Sinclair* v. *Fraser*[598], the Court of Session declined to apply the same presumption to a money judgment made by the Supreme Court of Jamaica against a defendant who asserted that her attorney had appeared without her authority. The Court upheld an order requiring the pursuer to produce evidence of the underlying debt. The pursuer, who had cited both Huber and Voet in support of the submission that "decrees of foreign courts of justice were everywhere put in execution *ex comitate*", appealed successfully to the House of Lords[599], which overturned the evidential order, declaring that "the judgment of the Supreme Court of Jamaica ought to be received as evidence *prima facie*, of the debt; and that it lies upon the defendant to impeach the justice thereof, or to show the same to have been irregularly obtained"[600].

(f) *Reception in England*

184. Across the border, in England, Lord Mansfield moved to centre stage. In *Robinson* v. *Bland*, he had observed, in passing, that "there are many cases, wherein foreign sentences are final, as with regard to the validity of marriages; many, where they are only a ground of evidence *prima facie*"[601]. Taken out of context, this remark may seem to give little credit to foreign judgments within the second category, opening

---

598 (1768) Mor 4542.

599 (1771) Mor 4543; (1771) 2 Paton 253. Lord Mansfield was, at the time, a member of the House of Lords and, according to one source, its "presiding spirit" in disposing of Scottish appeals (*Hilton* v. *Guyot* (1895) 159 US 113, 174).

600 (1771) Mor 4543, 4543-4544; (1771) 2 Paton 253, 254. The word "judgment" in this passage carries a double meaning, referring both to the documentary record, admitted in evidence, and the judicial act constituting the judgment debt.

601 *Robinson* v. *Bland* (n. 591), 259.

them up to the possibility of substantive review. But the specific example he gives, of a judgment relating to the validity of marriages, suggests a more subtle distinction, between a case in which the judgment would be immune from review[602] and one in which the English court had the authority to adjudicate on the question whether the judgment should be received or not.

185. In *Walker* v. *Witter*[603], decided in 1778, the claimants brought an action upon a judgment of the Supreme Court of Jamaica. The defendants denied that they were indebted and pleaded that there was no formal record of the debt. Ruling in the claimants' favour, Lord Mansfield stated as follows[604]:

> "The difficulty in the case had arisen from not fixing accurately what a Court of Record is in the eye of the law. That description is confined properly[[605]] to certain Courts in England, and their judgments cannot be controverted. Foreign Courts . . . have not that privilege . . . but the doctrine in the case of *Sinclair* v. *Fraser* was unquestionable. Foreign judgments are a ground of action every where, but they are examinable."

186. The reference to *Sinclair* is doubly significant. It demonstrates Lord Mansfield's wish to bring the law of England into line with Scots law. Moreover, it emphasises that what is "examinable" is the justice or regularity of

602 See n. 605.

603 (1778) 1 Doug 1. See also *Hall* v. *Odber* (1890) 11 East 118, 124 (Lord Ellenborough), 125 (Le Blanc J).

604 (1778) 1 Doug 1, 5-6.

605 As Lord Mansfield's judgment in *Bernardi* v. *Motteux* [(1781) 2 Douglas 575, 581] confirms, it extends at least to admiralty courts outside England. His dictum in *Robinson* v. *Bland* (text to n. 601) suggests that he would have extended it also to the decisions of ecclesiastical courts upon the validity of marriage. See above, [169].

the judgment itself and not the validity or otherwise of the underlying cause of action[606].

187. *Walker* v. *Witter* should have opened the way for the English courts to address their minds to the circumstances in which the presumption in favour of the justice of a foreign decision would arise and those in which it could be rebutted. Unfortunately, comity was lost in translation. Ironically, the force of Lord Mansfield's reasoning was diluted by judges who wished to emphasise the effectiveness of foreign judgments. In *Galbraith* v. *Neville*, Lord Kenyon expressed "very serious doubts" about *Walker*, which he considered to be a decision "that foreign judgments are not binding on the parties"[607]. Buller J, a member of the court in *Walker*, defended the decision, stating that "the foreign judgment shall be *prima facie* evidence of the debt, and conclusive till it be impeached by the other party"[608]. Subsequently, Lord Kenyon's view was characterised as the more expansive, pro-enforcement position, with that of Buller J. (and Lord Mansfield) seen as being more conservative and protective of the interests of the receiving order[609]. Some judges saw *Walker* as warranting an examination of the merits of the underlying dispute[610]. The muddle

---

606 See also *Crawford* v. *Witten* (n. 569), in which Lord Mansfield is reported to have ruled out investigating the merits of the underlying claim.

607 (1789) 1 Doug 5 (note).

608 *Ibid*., adding that the foreign judgment has "no more credit than is given to every species of written agreement, viz that it shall be considered as good till it is impeached". See also *Phillips* v. *Hunter* (1795) 2 Blackstone (H) 402, 410 (Eyre L. C. J.), distinguishing the vulnerability of a foreign judgment to review in enforcement proceedings from its supposed conclusiveness in other circumstances.

609 *Martin* v. *Nicolls* (1830) 3 Simons 458, 461-464 (Sir Lancelot Shadwell); *Houlditch* v. *Donegall* (1834) 2 Clark & Finnelly 471, 478-479 (Lord Brougham L. C.).

610 *Houlditch* v. *Donegall*, above, is the clearest example of this. See also *Frankland* v. *McGusty* (1830) 1 Knapp

took almost a century to resolve and (as we will see) left English law bereft of a guiding principle[611].

(g) *Reception in the United States*

188. *Walker* v. *Witter* was also influential in the United States, which had declared independence from Great Britain in 1776. It reflected the common law received by the former colonies[612] and was cited as an authority for the proposition that foreign judgments were only *prima facie* evidence of indebtedness and could be examined in enforcement proceedings[613]. That was the position adopted by US courts, although they (mostly[614]) did not get themselves as bogged down as their English counterparts in questions of substantive review[615]. As in Scotland with Lord Kames, American practitioners and judges were fortunate to have access to works of outstanding merit by individuals who combined judicial and academic careers, notably James Kent and Joseph Story. In consequence, the law of the United States

274; *Reimers* v. *Druce* (1857) 23 Beavan 135 (England); *Southgate* v. *Montgomerie* (1837) 15 S 507 (Scotland). But compare *Novelli* v. *Rossi* (1831) 2 Barnewell and Adolphus 757; *Henderson* v. *Henderson* (1844) 6 QB 288; *Bank of Australasia* v. *Nias* (1851) 18 QB 717.

611 Section III.F.6.

612 Ford W. Hall, "The Common Law: An Account of Its Reception in the United States" (1951) 4 *Vandebilt L Rev.* 791, 798-805.

613 Nadelmann, "Full Faith and Credit" (n. 562), 49-50.

614 Cf. *King* v. *Van Gilder* (1797) 1 D. Chipman's Vermont Reports 59, 61-62 (Chipman CJ), citing *Walker* v. *Witter*.

615 *Taylor* v. *Briden* (1811) 8 Johns 175, 176 (Kent C.); *Bissell* v. *Briggs* (1813) 9 Mass 462; *Bryant* v. *Ela* (1815) Smith (N. H.) 396, 404 (Smith J.); also *Hilton* v. *Guyot* (n. 599), 185-195; James Kent, *Commentaries on American Law*, New York: O. Halsted, 2nd ed., Vol. 2, 1832; New York: W. Kent, Vol. 2, 1858, Lecture 27, pp. 120-121, 2nd ed.; Story, *Commentaries on the Conflict of Laws* (n. 585), [608] and the other authorities there referred to.

emerged from the nineteenth century in a much more satisfactory state[616].

2. European evolution

189. Before considering later development of the law in England and the United States, we return to continental Europe to consider two significant accounts of the law relating to foreign judgments in the latter part of the eighteenth century.

(a) *Vattel*

190. Vattel's *Law of Nations* was published in 1758. We have noted Vattel's endorsement of duties of humanity requiring independent nations to provide mutual assistance to secure the perfection of each other's societies, subject to their own overriding interests[617]. Although Vattel does not cite their works or use the same terminology, his account is perfectly consistent with Johannes Voet's explanation of comity[618] and with the formulation of Huber's third axiom[619].

191. Among the matters within the ambit of Vattel's humanitarian duty was the administration of justice[620]. For Vattel, justice is "the basis of all society, the sure bond of all commerce" and demanded that all nations cultivate justice towards one another[621]. Each nation

616 See Sections III.E.6 and III.F.6.

617 Vattel, *Nations*, Preliminaries, [12]-[14], [16], pp. 72-74, and Book 2, Chap. 1, [1]-[3], pp. 259-262, Section II.J.2 *(c)*.

618 See above, [118].

619 See above, [122].

620 Vattel, *Nations*, Book 2, Chap. 1, [6], p. 264.

621 *Ibid.*, Book 2, Chap. 5, [64] (p. 296). A note by Vattel, included in the posthumous (1773) edition of his work asks, rhetorically, whether this may extend to the execution of foreign judgments, referring to a Dutch opinion addressing the question of reciprocity (see Emer de Vattel, *Le droit des gens ou Principes de loi naturelle, Nouvelle edition augmentée*, Neuchâtel: La Société Typographique, 1773, Book 2, Chap. 5, [64], note (*), p. 281).

ought to respect the entitlement of another to exercise justice in the places under her jurisdiction with respect to disputes arising there[622]. In Vattel's opinion[623]:

> "[T]he administration of justice necessarily requires that every definitive sentence, regularly pronounced, be esteemed just, and executed as such, – when once a cause in which foreigners are interested, has been decided in form, the sovereign of the defendants cannot hear their complaints. To undertake to examine the justice of a definitive sentence, is an attack on the jurisdiction of him who has passed it . . ."

Consequently, Vattel asserts[624]:

> ". . . the decisions made by the judge of the place within the extent of his power, ought to be respected, and to take effect even in foreign countries . . ."

192. Two interconnected propositions are in play here. According to Vattel, the administration of justice requires that a "definitive sentence", that is to say, a final judgment of another nation's court, is, first, "esteemed just" and, second, "executed as such". The first proposition demands restraint from the receiving legal order if it is asked to examine the justice of the foreign adjudication, to avoid interference with the administration of justice elsewhere; the second proposition brings into play the humanitarian duty of every nation to support the administration of justice by taking steps to carry a foreign judgment into effect.

193. In a later chapter, Vattel elucidates his thinking in the following way[625]:

---

[622] Vattel, *Nations*, Book 2, Chap. 7, [84], pp. 303-304. As to the limits of adjudicatory jurisdiction, see *ibid.*, Book 2, Chap. 8, [103], p. 313, with reference to Swiss practice.

[623] *Ibid.*, Book 2, Chap. 7, [84], p. 304.

[624] *Ibid.*, Book 2, Chap 7, [85], p. 304, followed by examples, pp. 304-305.

[625] *Ibid.*, Book 2, Chap. 18, [350], p. 464 (emphasis added).

"The law of nations directs that states should reciprocally pay that kind of deference to each other's jurisdiction, for the same reason as the civil law ordains within the state that every definitive sentence, passed in due form, shall be esteemed just. Between nation and nation, the obligation is neither so express nor so extensive: but it cannot be denied, *that it is highly conducive to their peace, and conformable to their duties towards human society,* to oblige their subjects, in all doubtful cases, and unless where there is a manifest wrong done to them, to submit to the sentences of the foreign tribunals before which their causes have been tried."

194. Accordingly, a nation need not stand back and allow its subjects to suffer injustice; indeed, it had a perfect entitlement to resist this[626]. Vattel recognises an exception to the requirement to exercise restraint in respect of the administration of justice in other legal orders, authorising a nation to intervene on behalf of its subjects "in cases where justice is refused, or palpable and evident injustice done, or rules and forms openly violated, or, finally, an odious distinction made to the prejudice of his subjects, or of foreigners in general"[627]. As the object of the duties of humanity is to aid other nations in attaining a state of perfection in their societies, the duty to aid the administration of justice obviously cannot require a nation, acting through its courts, to serve the cause of injustice. Furthermore, although Vattel does not reiterate the point here, it is clear from his earlier discussion of duties of humanity that a nation may refuse

[626] *Ibid.*, Book 2, Chap. 5, [65], pp. 296-297; also *ibid.*, [66]-[69], p. 297, concerning the entitlement to use force as a means of vindication and Book 2, Chap. 18, [350] on reprisals.

[627] *Ibid.*, Book 2, Chap. 7, [84], p. 304; also Book 2, Chap. 18, [350], p. 464.

assistance in aid of a foreign judgment when it considers it necessary to protect its own vital interests[628].

195. For Vattel, the framework governing the recognition and enforcement of foreign judgments belonged to that part of the law of nations derived from the law of nature. Judgments, as exercises of authority to adjudicate upon a particular dispute, as well as the rules that prescribe the legal effects of judgments and the measures available to secure their effectiveness, are institutions of the civil law, associated with a particular legal order. Unless it has bound itself by treaty, every legal order is (in a strict sense) at liberty to formulate rules governing the legal effect of foreign judgments, as well as the powers of its courts and enforcement agencies to adopt measures to secure their execution – a nation will not violate any enforceable duty towards another nation if it chooses to place limits upon the reception of foreign judgments or to exclude them entirely[629]. However, for Vattel, in formulating and applying those rules, a nation must heed the duty that it owes to other nations to provide mutual assistance in the administration of justice[630]. It must also exercise restraint in examining the justice of a decision, to avoid inferference with the exclusive liberty of each nation to administer justice within its own domain.

(b) *Louis Boullenois (1680-1762)*

196. The second contribution of note is the commentary by the distinguished French advocate, Louis Boullenois, published posthumously in 1766[631]. Boullenois' treatise builds on the work of his

---

[628] *Ibid.*, Preliminaries, [14], [16], pp. 73-74 and Book 2, Chap. 1, [9], p. 266.

[629] *Ibid.*, Book 2, Chap. 1, [18], p. 272.

[630] *Ibid.*, Preliminaries, [28], p. 79.

[631] Louis Boullenois, *Traité de la personnalité et de la réalité des lois, coutumes ou statuts, par formes d'observations*, Paris: Guillaume Desprez, 1766, in 2 volumes. A short

countrymen, Dumoulin and d'Argentré[632], as well as the Dutch jurist, Christian Rodenburg (1608-1668), In his opening remarks, he comments on the relationship between the law of nature and civil laws, acknowledging that this varies widely according to the character and circumstances of particular societies[633]. He suggests that, although what is just does not change, nevertheless justice may establish practices that vary according to time and location[634]. His realist approach nonetheless has a streak of idealism. While human beings may not be equally kind or perfect, nonetheless they form a whole of surprising economy and marvellous beauty[635]. Notwithstanding the variety of laws, each nation supports this entity in its own way, including by the provision of mutual support and service[636].

---

biographical account of Boullenois' life is to be found at pp. xv-xxiii of the work.
The American writer, Samuel Livermore, described Boullenois' work as "the most complete work which has been written on the subject", containing "a mine of learning" and displaying "great vigour and clearness of intellect", Samuel Livermore, *Dissertation on the Questions Which arise from the Contrariety of the Positive Law of Different States and Nations*, New Orleans: Benjamin Levy, 1828, [24], p. 11. He is much less complimentary about Huber (see *ibid.*, [26], pp. 12-13).
Joseph Story, who did not disguise the influence of Huber on his own work (Section III.E.6) cited from the preface of Boullenois' work on the title page of his *Commentaries on the Conflict of Laws* (n. 585) ("Il régnera donc toujours entre les nations une contrariété perpétuelle de loix; peut-être régnera-t-elle perpétuellement entre nous sur bien des objets. Delà la nécessité de s'instruire des règles, et des principes, qui peuvent nous conduire dans la décision des questions, que cette variété peut faire naître").

632 See above, [115]; Kalenský (n. 303), pp. 64-70.

633 Boullenois, *Traité* (n. 631), Vol. 1, Preface, pp. VI-XII.

634 *Ibid.*, p. XII.

635 *Ibid.*, "ils forment un tout d'une économie surprenante & d'une merveilleuse beauté".

636 *Ibid.*, pp. XII-XIII.

197. Boullenois' analysis of the recognition and enforcement of judgments focuses on questions of adjudicatory jurisdiction[637]. With respect to judgments in personal actions, he takes a conservative approach, admitting jurisdiction in proceedings between subjects of the adjudicating legal order and those brought by a foreigner against a subject. He justifies the former on the ground of the exclusive authority of the adjudicating order to regulate the affairs of the parties[638] and the latter on the ground of reciprocity and the need for judgments to be final[639]. In other cases, where the defendant is a foreigner (whether the claimant is a subject or foreigner), Boullenois recognises the competence of a judge in the place where a contract was formed or to be performed but only if the defendant has appeared to contest the case[640]. If, however, the judgment has been given against a foreigner by default, against a defendant who has not appeared or who has contested the exercise of jurisdiction, Boullenois opposes recognition on the ground that there has not been a contested adjudication between parties who accept the court's jurisdiction[641]. Finally, a judgment given between foreigners who have not transacted within the jurisdiction should, in Boullenois' view, have only the force of an arbitral award, being entitled to provisional execution[642].

(c) *Vattel's legacy*

198. Vattel's work transformed the law of nations, inspiring other authors to write similar works. Several followed Vattel in considering the adjudication of

637 *Ibid.*, Vol. 1, Observation XXV, pp. 601-650.
638 *Ibid.*, p. 605.
639 *Ibid.*, pp. 609-610.
640 *Ibid.*, pp. 607, 610.
641 *Ibid.*, p. 610.
642 *Ibid.*, pp. 608-609.

disputes involving foreigners and the reception of foreign judgments. In a remarkable work of comparative scholarship, published in 1843, the French jurist, Jean-Jacques Gaspard Foelix (1791-1853) recorded that[643]:

> "Among the authors who have written on the modern law of nations (droit des gens moderne) in Europe, Vattel[644], Martens[645], Klüber[646], Schmalz[647], de Kamptz[648] and Pinheiro-Ferreira[649], maintain that

---

643 Jean-Jacques Gaspard Foelix, *De l'Effet ou de l'exécution des jugements dans les pays étrangers*, Paris: Joubert, 1843, [201], p. 9.
Foelix's work was based on articles that he had published between 1842 and 1843 in the *Revue étrangère et française de législation, de jurisprudence et d'économie politique*, Vol. 9 (at 292, 380, 541, 720, 809, 885, 968) and Vol. 10 (at 100, 398). In the same year, he published his *Traité du droit international privé ou du conflit des lois de différentes nations en matière de droit privé*, Paris: Joubert, 1843, dealing with foreign judgments in Chap. 1 of Title 7, pp. 360-446. His comparative survey is examined in further detail below, Section III.F.

644 Vattel, *Nations*, Book 2, Chap. 7, [84]-[85], p. 304.

645 George Friedrich von Martens, *Précis du droit des gens moderne de l'Europe fondé sur les traités et l'usage*, Göttingen: Dieterich, 3rd ed., 1821, Book 3, Chap. 3, [94]-[95], pp. 175-178; also *ibid.*, [92]-[93], pp. 173-173 on adjudicatory authority and [96], p. 175 on denial of justice. For coverage of these topics in the first edition of Martens work, see *Précis du droit des gens moderne de l'Europe fondé sur les traités et l'usage*, Göttingen: Dieterich, 1789, Vol. 1, Book 3, Chap. 3, [81], pp. 117-122.

646 Johann Ludwig Klüber, *Europäisches Völkerrecht*, Stuttgart: J. G. Cotta'schen, 1821, Vol. 1, [59], pp. 102-104.

647 Theodor Anton Heinrich Schmalz, Léopold de Bohm (trans), *Le droit des gens européen*, Paris: N Maze, 1823, p. 155.

648 Karl Albert von Kamptz, *Beiträge zum Staats- und Völkerrecht*, Berlin: Nicolai, Vol. 1, 1815, Part 5, pp. 113-116.

649 Silvestre Pinheiro Ferreira, who contributed Notes to new editions of Marten's *Précis* (n. 645) and Vattel's *Le droit des gens* (n. 46), published in 1831 and 1838 respectively (Paris: J. P. Aillaud). The commentary on enforcement of

with the meeting of the conditions indicated below, the judgment rendered in one State must irrevocably make law and *res judicata* between the parties, and must be executed under the authority of the tribunals of a foreign state, as if the judgment had been rendered by the tribunals of the latter state."

199. Foelix took from the work of the German jurist and diplomat, George Friedrich von Martens (1756-1821), the conditions for reception of a foreign judgment, which were (1) that the court had jurisdiction according to the nature of the dispute or express or tacit conventions existing between the two States, (2) that the foreign litigant had been heard in the manner prescribed by the law of the adjudicating State as the equal of a subject in terms of access to appellate procedures and (3) that the case had been judged according to the laws of that State and was final[650].

200. In the first edition of his work (published in 1789), Martens had expressed the view that, absent a constitutional or treaty relationship between the two States, foreign judgments would *often* be executed for reasons of "mutual friendship and utility"[651], assuming reciprocity[652]. In the later edition (published in 1821), this statement had been watered down, noting that judgments were *sometimes* executed, reciprocally, between States not in a treaty relationship "for motives of friendship, neighbourhood or reciprocal convenience"[653] but adding that it was far from the case that this practice could be

foreign judgments is to be found at Vol. 1, Book 3, Chap. 3, [95], pp. 267-270 of that edition.

650 Martens, *Précis* (1821) (n. 645), [94], pp. 175-176.

651 "L'amitié & l'utilité réciproque."

652 Martens, *Précis* (1789) (n. 645), [81], pp. 120-121.

653 "Les motifs d'amitié, de voisinage, ou de convenance réciproque", Martens cites Vattel here, but the reference to Book 4, Chap. 2, on treaties of peace, does not assist.

said to be customary[654]. This could be seen as an early sign of the waning influence of natural law two decades into the new century.

E. The nineteenth century: Revolution and evolution[655]

1. Introduction

201. The direct influence of natural law theories on lawmakers had attained its zenith in the late eighteenth century. The American Declaration on Independence and French Declaration of the Rights of Man and the Citizen are a testament to this, borrowing heavily from the natural law lexicon. In 1776, representatives of the American Colonies declared their independence from the British Crown, asserting "the separate and equal station to which the Laws of Nature and of Nature's God entitle them" and the inalienable rights of "Life, Liberty and the pursuit of Happiness"[656]. There is no doubt that some of the Founding Fathers had read, and were influenced, by the works of Grotius, Pufendorf, Locke and Vattel[657]. They were recommended reading for lawyers of the time.

202. The Declaration of Independence and more detailed specifications adopted by the newly independent American States influenced, in turn, the Declaration of

---

654 Martens, *Précis* (1821) (n. 645), [95], pp. 177-178.

655 For an outstanding account of the development of private international law in this period, see Roxana Banu, *Nineteenth-Century Perspectives on Private International Law*, Oxford: Oxford University Press, 2018. See below, [385]

656 Declaration of Independence, Congress, Philadelphia, 4 July 1776.

657 Jesse S. Reeves, "The Influence of the Law of Nature upon International Law in the United States" (1909), 3 *Am J Int L* 547, 549-554; Brian Richardson, "The Use of Vattel in the American Law of Nations" (2012), 106 *Am J Int L* 547, 548-550.

the Rights of Man and of the Citizen adopted in 1789 by the National Constituent Assembly charged with the task of preparing a new Constitution for France[658]. This instrument proclaimed that "men are born free and equal" and that "the aim of every political association is the preservation of the natural and imprescriptible rights of Man"[659]. Liberty was defined as "being able to do anything that does not harm others", with the only permitted restraints being "to ensure to the other members of society the enjoyment of these same rights".

203. There were already strong dissenting voices. As the end of the century approached, the English lawyer, Jeremy Bentham, who had already published a fierce critique[660] of the portion of William Blackstone's *Commentaries on the Laws of England* discussing the origins of political society and government[661],

---

658 Georg Jellinek, *The Declaration of the Rights of Man and of Citizens: A Contribution to Modern Constitutional History*, New York: Henry Holt & Co, 1895.
Jellinek suggested (Chap. 3 and Chap. 4) that the Marquis de Lafayette, who had fought in the Revolutionary War, and advanced the motion to enact the Declaration, was particularly influenced by the Virginia Declaration of Rights of 12 June 1776. He rejected (Chap. 2) the widely assumed influence of the work of Jean-Jacques Rousseau. Although the American influence cannot be doubted, Jellinek's theory has been contested (see Michel Troper, "Jefferson et L'Interprétation de la Déclaration des Droits de l'Homme de 1789" (1999), 9 *Revue française d'histoire des idées politiques* 3; Iain McLean, "Thomas Jefferson, John Adams and the Déclaration des droits de l'homme et du citoyen", Chap. 1, in Robert Fatton Jr and Ruhi Ramazani (eds.), *The Future of Liberal Democracy: Thomas Jefferson and the Contemporary World*, New York: Palgrave Macmillan, 2004).

659 Declaration of the Rights of Man and of the Citizen *(Déclaration des droits de l'homme et du citoyen)*, Paris, 26 August 1789, Articles 1 and 2.

660 Bentham, *A Fragment on Government* (n. 193).

661 Blackstone, *Commentaries* (n. 191), Book 1, Introduction, Section 2, [38]-[62], pp. 33-47, considered above, [81].

and contributed to a work attacking the United States' Declaration of Independence[662], wrote a damning commentary on the French Declaration. Bentham's work, first published in French in 1816[663], described laws of nature as "imaginary laws . . . fancied and invented by poets, rhetoricians, and dealers in moral and intellectual poisons"[664]. Bentham's passion at the time was understandable. An honorary French citizen[665], he had close ties with France and had held out hope for peace even after the start of the Terror and the French Revolutionary War[666]. However, by 1795, that hope had evidently faded and Bentham had identified a scapegoat.

---

662 "A Short Review of the Declaration", in John Lind, *Answer to the Declaration of the American Congress*, London: T. Cadell, 1776, pp. 119-131. H. L. A. Hart describes this as "the first shot . . . of a long sceptical campaign conducted against the doctrine of natural and unalienable rights of man" (H. L. A. (Herbert) Hart, "Bentham and the United States of America" (1976), 10 *Journal of Economics and Law*, 547, 547, 555-556).

663 Jeremy Bentham and Etienne Dumont (trans), "Sophismes anarchiques", in *Traités des sophismes politiques et des sophismes anarchiques extraits des manuscrits de Jérémie Bentham*, Geneva, J. J. Paschoud, 1816, Vol. 2, pp. 269-392, with the original English manuscript (1795) reproduced in John Bowring (ed.), *The Works of Jeremy Bentham*, Edinburgh: William Tait, Vol. 2, 1843, pp. 489-534.

664 *The Works of Jeremy Bentham* (n. 663), p. 523. Bentham described the "natural rights" proclaimed in the Declaration as "nonsense on stilts" (*ibid.*, p. 501) and "a bastard brood of monsters . . . anti-legal rights, the mortal enemies of law, the subverters of government, and the assassins of security" (*ibid.*, p. 523). See Hugo Adam Bedau, "'Anarchical Fallacies': Bentham's Attack on Human Rights" (2000), 22 *Human Rights Quarterly* 261.

665 James Henderson Burns, "Bentham and the French Revolution" (1966), 16 *Transactions of the Royal Historical Society* 95, 109.

666 Emmanuelle de Champs, *Enlightenment and Utility*, Cambridge: Cambridge University Press, 2015, Chaps. 7-8.

2. *Natural law reasoning in early nineteenth century English case law*

204. The ongoing war with France, and the ensuing political instability in continental Europe, did not deter senior English judges from explicitly adopting natural law reasoning, and invoking comity, to support the recognition and enforcement of foreign judgments.

205. In 1802, Lord Eldon agreed with the proposition that "natural law requires the Courts of this country to give credit to those of another for the inclination and power to do justice"[667]. In 1807, in *Buchanan* v. *Rucker*, Lord Ellenborough assented to the submission that "[t] he presumption was in favour of a foreign judgment, as well as of a judgment obtained in one of the Courts of this country", provided that "the judgment appears on the face of it consistent with reason and justice"[668]. The same judge, in 1814, acknowledged that "[b]y the *comitas gentium*, the Courts of different countries will recognise and enforce the judgments of each other"[669] and, the following year, that "by the comity which is paid by us to the judgment of other Courts abroad of competent jurisdiction we give a full and binding effect to such judgments, as far as they profess to bind the persons and property immediately before them in judgment, and to which their adjudications properly relate"[670]. In 1826, Sir William Best, the Chief Justice of the Common Pleas stated that the rule established in *Sinclair* v. *Fraser*[671] "is founded on a plain and obvious principle of natural

---

[667] *Wright* v. *Simpson* (1802) 6 Ves Jun 714, 730 (". . . but not, if that presumption is proved to be ill founded in that transaction").

[668] *Buchanan* v. *Rucker* (1807), 1 *Campbell* 63, 66; also (1808) 9 East 192. See below, [330] and [360].

[669] *Alves* v. *Bunbury* (1814), 4 *Campbell* 28, 30. The issue in that case concerned the mode of proof of the judgment.

[670] *Power* v. *Whitmore* (1815), 4 *Maule and Selwyn* 141, 150.

[671] See above, [183]

justice"[672]. Although no authority was cited for these propositions, the judges were evidently familiar with the leading works on the law of nature and nations[673]. For a short period, natural law reasoning appeared to have gained a foothold in this corner of the conflict of laws.

3. *The incoming positivist tide*

206. The conflict with France had nonetheless brought about a significant change in the international legal order. As the victorious powers took it upon themselves to take responsibility for securing peace in Europe, following the Congress of Vienna[674], and the United States began to find its feet on the international

---

672 *Arnott* v. *Redfern* (1826) 3 Bingham 353, 357 (continuing, *ibid.*, 357-358, ". . . To whatever country a debtor flies, justice requires the courts of that country to compel him, if he can, to pay his debts. It will often be impossible to prove debts in a foreign state by the testimony of witnesses. The only way in which they can be established is by the judgment of the courts of that country in which the parties and their witnesses resided when such debts were contracted").

673 Lord Ellenborough had referred to Vattel's work in a Parliamentary debate in 1804 (Hansard, HL Deb, 27 March 1804, col 1028). The work of several writers, including Grotius, Pufendorf and Vattel, was cited in argument in a case before his Lordship in 1813 addressing questions of neutrality, *Hagedorn* v. *Bell* (1830), 1 *Maule & Selwyn* 450. His judgment in *Viveash* v. *Becker* (1814), 3 *Maule and Selwyn* 284, on consular immunities, refers extensively to Vattel's work. See also *Wolff* v. *Oxenholm* (1817), 6 *Maule and Selwyn* 92.
Lord Eldon's correspondence shows his familiarity with Vattel's work and points to his ownership of a copy of the *Law of Nations* (Letter to Sir William Scott (fragment), reproduced in Horace Twiss, *The Public and Private Life of Lord Chancellor Eldon*, London: John Murray, 1844, Vol. 2, references at pp. 273, 279).

674 Karol Wolfke, *Great and Small Powers in International Law from 1814 to 1920*, Wroclaw: Zakład Narodowy im Ossolińskich, 1961, Chap. 1.

stage[675], the vision of a universal legal order based on reason gave way to one dominated by a relatively small number of nations with close geographical or historical ties and centred on the manifestation of sovereign will[676]. As the century progressed, what Vattel termed the necessary law of nations[677], the application of the law of nature to international relations gave way to the voluntary law of nations[678] consisting of treaties and customary practices[679]. Accounts of the discipline for which Bentham had coined the term "international law"[680] took a predominantly positivist hue. Natural law reasoning was not eliminated entirely in this field[681], but it was pushed to the margins.

207. With the application of this positivist solvent, the bonds between the legal orders of independent nations were also loosened. If law was an expression of sovereign will, and the sovereign could not be subject to any external obligation without its express or tacit consent, then the rules governing the reception of foreign laws and judgments would (in the absence of any relevant treaty or customary rule[682]) become wholly internalised, judged by reference to the national interest, and not with regard to any obligation, even imperfect, perceived as

675 Notably, by the assertion in 1823 of the Monroe Doctrine, Jay Sexton, "The Monroe Doctrine in the Nineteenth Century", Chap. 1, in Andrew Preston and Doug Rossinow (eds.), *Outside In: The Transnational Circuitry of US History*, Oxford: Oxford University Press, 2016.

676 Mills, *Confluence* (n. 222), pp. 39-40; Neff (n. 222), pp. 221-226.

677 Vattel, *Nations*, Preliminaries, [7], p. 70.

678 Vattel, *Nations*, Preliminaries, [21], pp. 75-76.

679 See the materials referred to at n. 222.

680 Jeremy Bentham, *An Introduction to the Principles of Morals and Legislation*, London: T. Payne, 1789, pp. cccxxiv.

681 Mills, *Confluence* (n. 222), pp. 55-56; Vec (n. 222), pp. 670-671.

682 Mills, *Confluence* (n. 222), pp. 23-24.

being owed to the legal orders of other nations or to their subjects.

208. We have already drawn attention to other reasons why the influence of natural law ideas waned at this time[683]. Of particular importance, especially in countries following the civilian tradition, is the adoption of written constitutional instruments[684] and the replacement of unwritten law with written codifications[685].

4. *Wächter and Westlake*

209. The German jurist, Carl Georg von Wächter (1797-1880)[686], and the Englishman, John Westlake (1828-1913), offered State-centric, positivist accounts of private international law[687].

(a) *Carl Georg von Wächter*

210. Wächter's essay, *On the Collision of Private Laws of Different States*, was published in four

---

683 See above, [14]-[16].

684 Banner (n. 10), Chap. 3; Henry Bertram Hill, "The Constitutions of Continental Europe: 1789-1813" (1936), 8 *Journal of Modern History* 82.

685 Kalenský (n. 303), 78 gives the following list, up to the end of the nineteenth century: Prussia (1794), France (1804), Belgium (1807), Austria (1811), Haiti (1825), the Netherlands (1828), Peru (1852), Greece (1856), Italy (1865), Portugal (1867), Uruguay (1868), Argentina (1869), Columbia (1873), Costa Rica (1887), Spain (1888), Germany (1896), Japan (1898).

686 Kurt H. Nadelmann, "Wächter's Essay on the Collision of Private Laws of Different States" (1964), 13 *Am J Comp L* 414.

687 James Leslie Brierly, "John Westlake", in H. W. C. (Henry) Davies and J. R. H. (John) Weaver (eds.), *Dictionary of National Biography, 1912-1921*, London: Humphrey Milord, for Oxford University Press, 1927, p. 569; Lassa Oppenheim (ed.), *The Collected Papers of John Westlake on Public International Law*, Cambridge: Cambridge University Press, 1914, pp. 5-12; Mills, *Confluence* (n. 222), pp. 50-52.

instalments between 1841 and 1842[688]. Described as "the demolisher of the theory of the statutists"[689], Wächter's fundamental premise was that a judge can only apply the positive law of their own State, either in its express direction or according to its meaning and spirit[690]. He thought it legitimate for a legislator, in framing a rule, to consider, alongside the interests of its own legal system, "the international relations which come into play and require recognition of the alien's legal capacity as much as that of the citizen and which also make desirable on some points concessions to the foreign legislation"[691]. However, in Wächter's view, "even if considerations of utility, equity, amity, toleration

---

[688] Carl Georg von Wächter, "Über die Kollision der Privatgesetze verschiedener Staaten" (1841), 24 *Archiv fur die Civilistische Praxis* 230; (1842) 25 *Archiv fur die Civilistische Praxis* 1, 161 and 361.
Nadelmann, "Wächter's Essay" (n. 686) appends a translation of Wächter's "Guiding Principles" (*ibid.*, 417-428), and references to this work appear in the following foonotes alongside references to the original text in German.
See Nadelmann, "Wächter's Essay", above, 414-415; von Bar, *Theorie und Praxis* (n. 3), Vol. 1, [24], pp. 72-74, Gillespie, *Theory and Practice* (n. 3), pp. 52-54; Gerhard Kegel, "Story and Savigny" (1989), 37 *Am J Comp L* 39, 52-54.
Both von Bar, above, [23], pp. 67-68, Gillespie, *Theory and Practice*, above, pp. 49-50 and Kegel, above, 54-56, refer also to the work of Wilhelm Schaeffner, *Entwicklung des internationalen Privatrechts* (Frankfurt am Main: Sauerländer, 1841). Schaeffner was a critic of both the statutist theory and the principle of comity.

[689] Nadelmann, "Wächter's Essay" (n. 686), 415.

[690] Wächter (n. 688), [2], [9], [10] [(1841), 24 *Archiv* 230, 236-240, 261-270; (1961), 13 *Am J Comp L* 417, 417-423]. Although Wächter's focus is on written law, he necessarily acknowledged the potential for customary rules to play a part, De Nova (n. 342), 453-455.

[691] *Ibid.*, [2] [(1841), 24 *Archiv* 230, 240; (1961), 13 *Am J Comp L* 417, 418].

(connivens[692]*)* [or] natural law . . . may guide the legislator, and, indeed, should guide him to a certain degree", these were not matters to be taken into account by a judge whose sole duty is "to investigate what his legislator decided about the issue"[693]. Foreign laws and their effects were to be considered only to the extent that the judge's own law requires it[694]. In case of doubt, the judge should apply domestic law[695].

211. Whatever the consequences of the application of foreign law more generally[696], one would expect Wächter to conclude that foreign judgments are to be recognised and enforced only insofar as there is a written or unwritten rule that demands or authorises this. Surprisingly, without further explanation or reference to the letter or spirit of any law, and based on a single

---

692 Nadelmann observes [(1961), 13 *Am J Comp L* 417, 418] that this term is suggested by a passage from Johan Nikolaus Hertius' *Dissertatio de Collisione Legum* (Giessen: Christoph Hermannus Kargerus, 1688), s. 4, [3] (pp. 23-24), in which Hertius rejects Huber's concept of comity ("if we say that it relies solely on the connivance of the peoples, what effectiveness will it have as a law"). Accordingly, the term is not to be understood in a pejorative sense.
Wächter touches on comity only briefly in his essay [(1841), 25 *Archiv* 1, 13, fn. 192], observing that Huber's third axiom is "correct as a legislative principle", referring back to the passage quoted here but criticising Huber's application of the principle to judicial decisions.

693 Wächter (n. 688), [2] [(1841), 24 *Archiv* 230, 240; (1961), 13 *Am J Comp L* 417, 418; also *ibid.*, [10] [(1841), 24 *Archiv* 230, 267; (1961), 13 *Am J Comp L* 417, 421] ("[T]hey must hold to the interpretation of these sources, and not to a principle which lies outside of these, be it justice of equity or the interests of commercial intercourse, and so forth").

694 *Ibid.*, [10] [(1841), 24 *Archiv* 230, 265-266; (1961), 13 *Am J Comp L* 417, 421].

695 *Ibid.*

696 See e.g. Wächter's discussion in relation to obligations (*ibid.*, [28] [(1842) 25 *Archiv* 361, 389-397; (1961), 13 *Am J Comp L* 417, 423-427]).

contemporary source, he accepts that the *res judicata* effects of foreign decisions should be recognised[697]. Wächter's treatment of questions of enforcement is more nuanced[698]. There is, he suggests, no legal necessity to enforce a foreign judgment[699]. One nation cannot be bound by what another nation recognises as law nor be obliged to "offer its hand"[700] for the unconditional enforcement of a judgment that may be grossly unjust[701]. However, the international relationship and the interest of its own subject compel every nation not to insist strictly on its own law but to make concessions[702]. In deciding what concessions, if any, to make, Wächter urges that (first) a nation should establish the principle of reciprocity, to preserve its dignity and promote its own interests, (second) the competence of the foreign judge should be governed according to local standards as if the foreign legal order were part of the forum's legal order and (third) the judgment must not contradict the mandatory laws of the forum[703].

---

697 Wächter (n. 686), [32] [(1842) 25 *Archiv* 361, 417], with reference to Friedrich Wilhelm Tittmann, *De Competentia Legum Externarum et Domesticarum*, Halle: Typographia Gebaueriana, 1822, [5], p. 6. Tittmann's approach, above, [5]-[6], p. 6 supports the recognition of rights acquired under foreign law as a matter of private right and not by mutual indulgence between nations. There is no obvious synergy with Wächter's theory.

698 He defers to the treatment in specialist texts, with particular reference to an article by Mittermaier in the same journal ("Über das qualifizirte Geständniß" (1823) 16 *Archiv fur die Civilistische Praxis* 84).

699 Wächter (n. 688), [32] [(1842), 25 *Archiv* 361, 417].

700 This may be an allusion to Huber's concept of comity as expressed in *Heedendaegse Rechts* (nn. 335 and 725).

701 Wächter (n. 688), [32] [(1842), 25 *Archiv* 361, 417].

702 *Ibid.*

703 *Ibid.*, [32] [(1825), 25 *Archiv* 361, 417-419]. Wächter notes that some German States, including Württemberg, have adopted only the first two restrictions.

(b) *John Westlake*

212. The first edition of Westlake's work, *Private International Law*, was published in 1858[704].

213. In his general account of the subject, Westlake denies that Huber's third axiom explains what Westlake calls "the international obligation of law", giving the reason that "the doctrine that foreign laws are only to be admitted by a comity, limited by the rights and authority of the admitting state and its members, tells us indeed nothing, since it is just these rights and this authority of which the extent is in question"[705]. Westlake suggests that "the free reception of a foreign law does not infringe the principle of territorial sovereignty, since it is simply by the authority of the territorial sovereign that it is received"[706]. Westlake's explanation for this eliptical statement is that the sovereign "must be taken as cognisant of that general understanding, by which his own and all other judges enforce foreign laws in accordance with the principles of private international jurisprudence"[707]. By "principles of private international jurisprudence", he had in mind those put forward in the earlier statutist accounts[708].

214. For Westlake, the judge's principal task is to interpret the meaning of the text of his local code, using the principles established for that purpose[709], and

---

[704] John Westlake, *A Treatise on Private International Law, or the Conflict of Laws*, London: W. Maxwell, 1858. Westlake produced five editions of the work in his lifetime (the 5th edition in 1912). The first edition, being the first work of its kind published in England, is used here.

[705] Westlake, *Treatise*, above, [144] (p. 127); also *ibid.*, [160], p. 149.

[706] *Ibid.*, [144], p. 126.

[707] *Ibid.*, [145], p. 128.

[708] *Ibid.*, ("the old distinctions of real, personal, and mixed statutes").

[709] *Ibid.* The source of these principles, according to Westlake, is "that science of law to the ideas of which no legislator

to follow explicit conflict of laws rules[710]. If the code is silent, Westlake suggests that his supposed private international law principles must be taken to have been tacitly adopted by the local legislator, as "the principle of independent sovereignty did not destroy this branch of jurisprudence"[711]. At this point, Westlake's problems pile up. He admits immediately that "many questions arose" in working out his supposed principles[712] and that the continental approach has not been received within the English common law[713]. He is left scrabbling for answers, with sketchy references to "a national persuasion or conscience of that which is jurally right"[714] and to "the conception of private rights as created by a territorial authority external to the conscience of the person whom it binds"[715].

215. Westlake turns to consider "various modern theories"[716], beginning with Grotius' theory of the terri-

---

intends to run counter". This may be an oblique reference to natural law, although this may be to give the author too much credit. His reasoning is, at best, opaque. See further below, [215].

710 Westlake, *Treatise* (n. 704), [145], p. 128.

711 *Ibid.*

712 *Ibid.* The following discussion of personal and mixed statutes (*ibid.*, [146]-[148] (pp. 128-131) serves only to evidence these difficulties.

713 *Ibid.*, [149], pp. 131-132.

714 *Ibid.*, [150], pp. 133-135. The following paragraphs (*ibid.*, [151]-[155]) consider questions of particular significance for the British Empire in the mid-nineteenth century. Westlake's reasoning here (also below, [215]) has strong echoes of Savigny's Volksgeist (below, [236]). See below, [215].

715 *Ibid.*, [156], p. 143. This is subject to a qualification that "none of the territorial laws which it considers differs so widely from the others of them, as to shock the conscience of any of the nations to whose members the system may cause it to be applied" (*ibid.*, [156], pp. 143-144).

716 Westlake, *Treatise* (n. 704) [159], p. 147.

torial application of law[717]. Westlake opposes this approach as being potentially in conflict with the solution that might be reached according to a "common jural sense of mankind" and as incomplete, leaving transactions between parties in different places to a "vague law natural"[718]. He grapples, unproductively, with the approach of his German contemporary Savigny[719].

216. Having dismissed comity at the outset, Westlake is driven eventually back into its arms in his conclusion that[720]:

> "We must always look at the time when the duty correlative to every right arose, and to the territorial law to which at that time the party on whom the duty is imposed was subject. Then the principle applies that *rights which have once well accrued by the appropriate law are*, by comity if you please, though it is a comity almost demanded by a sentiment of justice, treated as valid everywhere."

217. Westlake opens his discussion of foreign judgments with the observation that a judgment can only be carried into execution in a particular place by a local sanction, which may take the form either of a declaration

---

717 Section II.B. See Oppenheim (ed.), *Collected Papers* (n. 687), pp. 286-288, 296-297.

718 Westlake, *Treatise* (n. 704), [160], pp. 148-149.

719 *Ibid.*, [160]-[164], pp. 149-154. See Section III.E.6 *(b)*.

720 Westlake, *Treatise* (n. 704), [165], p. 154 (emphasis in original).
See Oppenheim (ed.), *Collected Papers* (n. 687), p. 305 ("a right, which by the appropriate positive law has once arisen, shall thenceforward be respected and enforced by all tribunals which by the recognised rules of jurisdiction may have cognisance of the matter. And is not this the idea of modern international intercourse, commercial or social? It is not a vague comity, but the force of reason, which bids us recognise foreign laws and the rights which they originate"). Westlake considers this "system" to have a "similar basis" to "the received law of nations" (*ibid.*, p. 306).

of *exequatur* or a new judgment pronounced on the basis of the original[721], before turning to examine the English case law[722]. We can focus here on his specification of the reason why foreign judgments are carried into effect, being that[723]:

> ". . . on the person against whom the decree was made a duty was imposed by lawful authority to obey it, so that another court, *in lending its aid to the right correlative to that duty*, does but follow out of the principle of recognising internationally rights which have once well accrued. The competence then of the court, that is, the lawfulness of the authority which imposed the duty, is the foundation of all faith given to the *res judicata* of a foreign tribunal . . .".

218. This picks up on his earlier conclusion as to the reason for applying foreign law more generally. Although Westlake does not say so here, we may presume from his earlier conclusion on the general issue[724] that he would accept "comity", or "comity almost demanded by a sentiment of justice", as the reason why one court "lends its aid"[725] to another.

5. *The legal positivist conundrum*

219. These accounts are instructive, not only because they give a sense of the mood music in the middle of the nineteenth century but also because they demons-

[721] Westlake, *Treatise* (n. 704), [374], pp. 361-362. Westlake notes that the former approach is used in most parts of continental Europe, with the latter predominantly used in the British Isles and her present and former colonies.
[722] *Ibid.*, [375]-[395], pp. 362-378. See Sections III.D.1 *(f)* and III.E.2.
[723] Westlake, *Treatise* (n. 704), [378], p. 366 (emphasis added).
[724] See above, [216].
[725] This may itself be an allusion to Huber's concept of comity as expressed in *Heedendaegse Rechts* (nn. 335 and 700).

trate some of the difficulties in accommodating the recognition and enforcement of judgments within an account of the relationship between legal orders such as that favoured by Wächter or Westlake. The monistic and reductivistic nature of these "imperatival" accounts[726] struggles to handle the complexity of a world in which a multitude of legal orders, taking different forms, pursue similar objectives according to their own traditions and prescriptions. Foreign judgments raise the conflict of laws challenge in an acute form as the alternative to recognising the judgment is to leave the dispute unresolved. By contrast, for example, with questions as to the law applicable to a contract, there is usually[727] no corresponding rule of domestic municipal law that can be applied if the foreign judgment is not given effect.

220. The legal positivist's point of departure is clear and principled – that the obligation or power to give effect to a foreign law or judgment must emanate from a rule recognised[728] as belonging to the legal order that the judge serves[729]. So, if that legal order's civil code or a statute lays down constitutionally valid, unambiguous rules favouring or opposing the reception of foreign judgments of the kind in question, the judge must apply those rules. In promulgating such rules, as Wächter acknowledges[730], the legislative body may, again within

---

726 Leslie Green and Thomas Adams, "Legal Positivism", in Edward N. Zalta (ed.), *The Stanford Encyclopedia of Philosophy* (Winter 2019 ed.), https://plato.stanford.edu/archives/win2019/entries/legal-positivism/, [2].

727 Compare the case in which there is a pre-existing, or even supervening, judgment of the receiving legal order, engaging its *res judicata* rule.

728 Hart, *The Concept of Law* (n. 168), pp. 94-95, 100-110.

729 Albert Venn Dicey, *A Digest on the Law of England with Reference to the Conflict of Laws*, London: Stephens and Sons, 1896, pp. 2-6, 15-22, contrasting the "positive method" with the "theoretical method".

730 Text to n. 691.

any limits prescribed by its constitutional order[731], take account of any and all considerations that it considers appropriate, whether internal or external to its legal order. Nonetheless, as these two accounts demonstrate, greater challenges await once we move beyond this paradigm. What if the rule relied on is not unambiguous? What if there is no written rule that instructs the judge to receive, or not to receive, the foreign judgment? If, like Wächter or Westlake, one seeks to deploy a crude rule of recognition, such as the "will of the legislator" or the "authority of the sovereign", to bolt down every single detail as to how the receiving order relates to others, then this will likely lead either to isolation (Wächter[732]) or to artifice (Westlake[733]).

221. Faced with these practical difficulties, a degree of subtlety in reasoning is required to ensure the smooth administration of justice between legal orders. It is in this context that principles drawn from the natural law tradition, including but not limited to comity (humanity), are a valuable tool. They can be accommodated within a positivist framework, not as rules of positive law in their own right but as factors that inform the formulation and interpretation of such rules, written or unwritten. Both Wächter and Westlake made compromises of this kind

---

[731] For example, allowing a challenge to the *vires* of a rule on the basis that specific matters have improperly been taken into account.

[732] Wächter's proposition that, in case of doubt as to the legislator's will, the judge must apply domestic law (text to n. 695).

[733] Westlake's theory of the tacit adoption of statutist principles (text to nn. 711-715). Attempts to use private law concepts, such as contract, to offer a general theory as to why foreign judgments are enforced encounter similar difficulties (see below, [358] and [396]; also Westlake, *Treatise* (n. 704), [378] (p. 365); Dickinson, "*Schibsby* v. *Westenholz*" (n. 216), 435-437).

in their treatment of foreign judgments[734]. One does not have to forswear reliance on natural law principles to be accredited as a positivist[735].

6. Story and Savigny

222. The works of Joseph Story (1779-1845)[736] and Friedrich Carl von Savigny (1779-1861)[737] justly lay claim to be the two most influential works of the nineteenth century on the conflict of laws[738]. They are

734 In Wächter's case, his willingness to accept Tittmann's views on the recognition of judgments and his *ad hoc* principles for enforcement (above, [211]). In Westlake's case, his begrudging endorsement of comity as a reason for giving effect to foreign laws and judgments (above, [217]-[218]).

735 Green and Adams (n. 726), [1], [3] ("It is of the nature of justice that it properly bears on certain controversies. In legal decisions, especially important ones, moral and political considerations are present of their own authority; they do not need sources to propel them into action").

736 Ralf Michaels, "Story, Joseph", in *Encyclopedia of Private International Law* (n. 300), Vol. 2, pp. 1659-1667; also Luis Kutner, "Savigny: German Lawgiver (1972) 55 *Marquette L Rev* 250.

737 Michael Sonnentag, "Savigny, Friedrich Carl Von", in *Encyclopedia of Private International Law* (n. 300), Vol. 2, pp. 1609-1615.

738 Joseph Story, *Commentaries on the Conflict of Laws, Foreign and Domestic* (n. 585), first published in 1834. A revised and enlarged edition was published in 1841 (Boston: Charles C. Little and James Brown, 2nd ed., 1841) with a third published shortly after Story's death and incorporating his later annotations (Boston: Charles C. Little and James Brown, 3rd ed., 1846). References in the following footnotes to "Story, *Commentaries* (1834)" are to the 1st edition, to "Story, *Commentaries* (1841)" are to the 2nd edition and to "Story, *Commentaries* (1846)" are to the 3rd edition.
Friedrich Carl von Savigny, *System des heutigen Römischen Rechts* (Berlin: Veit, Vol. 8, 1849) (Savigny, *System*). Savigny's work was published in eight volumes between

essential reading for any scholar seeking to understand the subject's history and development, as well as the ideas underpinning it[739].

(a) *Joseph Story*

223. Story's *Commentaries on the Conflict of Laws* appeared in print in 1834. Having introduced the subject matter of his work, Story devotes his second chapter to what he describes as "general maxims of international jurisprudence"[740]. The influence of Huber's work here is evident. Story's first maxim is that "every nation possesses an exclusive sovereignty and jurisdiction within its own territory"[741]. This is undeniable, both as a matter of contemporary rules of (public) international law

---

1840 and 1849 (Savigny, *System*). Volume 1 (Berlin: Veit, 1840), Volume 5 (Berlin: Veit, 1841) and Volume 6 (Berlin: Veit, 1847) are also of interest for our enquiry. An accessible version of the German texts is available at https://www.deutschestextarchiv.de/book/show/savigny_system08_1849.

An English translation of Volume 8, by William Guthrie, was published in 1869 under the title *Private International Law, A Treatise on the Conflict of Laws and the Limits of Their Operation in respect of Place and Time*, Edinburgh: T & T Clark, 1869. An English translation of part of Volume 1, by William Holloway, was published in 1867 under the title, *System of the Modern Roman Law,* Madras: J. Higginbotham, 1867.

739 Ernest G. Lorenzen, "Story's Commentaries on the Conflict of Laws – One Hundred Years After" (1934), 48 *Harvard L Rev* 15; Kurt H. Nadelmann, "Joseph Story's Contribution to American Conflicts Law: A Comment" (1961), 5 *Am J Legal History* 230 and "Bicentennial Observations on the Second Edition of Joseph Story's *Commentaries on the Conflict of Laws*" (1988), 28 *Am J Comp L* 67; Kegel, "Story and Savigny" (n. 688); Roxana Banu, *Nineteenth-Century Perspectives* (n. 655), esp. pp. 29-41, 70-76, 183-201.

740 Story, *Commentaries* (1834), [17]-[38], pp. 19-38.

741 *Ibid.*, [18], p. 19; also *ibid.*, [8], pp. 8-9 (emphasis added).

and according to natural accounts of the law of nations[742]. Story's second maxim suggests that the exclusivity of each nation's authority extends to all persons (resident) and things (physically located) within her domain[743]. This partitioning of legislative (and adjudicatory) jurisdiction is really quite problematic, as Story seems to acknowledge[744], but need not detain us here[745].

224. It is Story's third maxim that captures the attention – "whatever force and obligation the laws of one country have in another depends solely upon the laws, and municipal regulations of the latter"[746]. Story describes this as "the natural principle flowing from the equality and independence of nations"[747]. He explains that a State may

---

742 See above, [97].

743 Story, *Commentaries* (1834), [20], p. 21. In Story's view *(ibid.)*, "it would be wholly incompatible with the equality and exclusiveness of the sovereignty of any nation, that other nations should be at liberty to regulate either persons or things within its territories". There are also hints (*ibid.*, [8], p. 9, and [18], p. 19) that he would extend this exclusivity to contractual or other rights arising there.

744 Story, *Commentaries* (1834), [21]-[22], pp. 22-24, addressing the case of a subject of one nation resident in another. Just as, if not more, problematic for Story's strong formulation of the exclusivity principle (n. 743) would be a resident of one nation concluding a contract or other transaction in another or residents of different nations concluding a contract or other transaction at a distance. See above, [87].

745 See Ernest G. Lorenzen, "Territoriality, Public Policy and the Conflict of Laws" (1924) 33 *Yale LJ* 736; Walter Wheeler Cook, "The Jurisdiction of Sovereign States and the Conflict of Laws" (1931) 31 *Columbia L Rev* 368.

746 Story, *Commentaries* (1834), [23], p. 24; also *ibid.*, [7], referring to Boullenois, *Traité* (n. 631), Vol. 1, p. 4 ("Of strict right, all the laws made by a sovereign have no force or authority except within the limits of his domains. But the necessity of the public and general welfare has introduced some exceptions in regard to civil commerce").

747 *Ibid.*, [8] (p. 8); also *ibid.*, [20], p. 21 and [32], p. 33, invoking the same principle.

exclude foreign laws entirely, or admit some and prohibit others, and it may even enlarge the rights to which foreign laws give rise[748]. Positive rules of law on this subject, written or unwritten, are to be followed[749]. Moreover, in Story's view, "[n]o nation can be justly required to yield up its own fundamental policy and institutions in favour of those of another nation" or "sacrifice its interests in favour of another"[750]. Pushing this principle of self-determination to its limit, he asserts that[751]:

> "The laws of one nation may be founded on a narrow selfishness, exclusively adapted to promote the personality or proprietary interests of its own subjects, to the injury or even ruin of the subjects of all other countries. A nation may refuse all reciprocity of commerce, rights and remedies to others."

225. Story appraises the work of continental writers of the statutist tradition[752]. He examines Huber's axioms, noting unfavourable assessments of them by other writers[753]. This leads into Story's discussion and endorsement of comity as the basis for the reception of foreign laws. The influence of Vattel and of Huber on

748 *Ibid.*, [23], p. 24.
749 *Ibid.*
750 *Ibid.*, [25], p. 26.
751 *Ibid.*; also *ibid.*, [32], p. 33.
752 Story quotes approvingly ("great truth") the criticisms of statutist models by Porter J., sitting in the Supreme Court of Louisiana, in *Saul* v. *His Creditors* (1827), 17 Martin R 569, 595-596 (Story, *Commentaries* (1834), [28], p. 26). Cf. Livermore's robust reaction to that decision in *Dissertation* (n. 631), Dissertation 1, [31]-[32], pp. 15-17.
753 Story, *Commentaries* (1834), [29]-[31], pp. 30-32, noting (at [30]) the arguments of Hertius (n. 692). Story's reference (at [31]) to unsuccessful attempts to undervalue the authority of Huber is likely a reference to the more recent account by Livermore, above. Story notes also (at [31]) Boullenois' approval of Huber's third axiom (Boullenois, *Traité* (n. 631), Vol. 1, p. 155).

Story's thinking is evident[754]. Indeed, his account is a synthesis of the two authors' works[755], countenancing an "imperfect obligation, like that of beneficence, humanity and charity"[756], to support other nations in the administration of justice[757], while empowering each nation to be the final judge of "the nature and extent of the duty" and "the occasions on which its exercise may be justly demanded"[758].

---

754 See, in particular, Story, *Commentaries* (1834), [8], [37] (Vattel) and [23], [29], [31], [38] (Huber), pp. 9-10, 24, 30, 32, 36-37.

755 Two years earlier, in his article on the law of nations in the *Encylopedia Americana*, Vol. 9 (n. 207), at p. 144, Story had foreshadowed this approach with the assertion that all nations "are bound to do justice, to perform the offices of humanity, and to render mutual assistance to each other, in the same manner, and upon the same principles, that bind individuals to like duties".

756 Story, *Commentaries* (1834), [33] (p. 33).
Story had addressed the distinction between perfect and imperfect obligations (at pp. 151-152) in an article written for the *Encyclopedia Americana* ("Natural Law", pp. 150-158, in *Enyclopedia Americana*, Vol. 9 (n. 207)).

757 Story, *Commentaries* (1834), [34], p. 34.
Story refers explicitly to "natural law" in denying that any nation has a "right . . . to insist" that its own positive laws shall prevail (Story, *Commentaries* (1834), [33], pp. 33-34). This is to deny an absolute duty, not an imperfect one (see text to n. 756).
Story's natural law credentials are undeniable. He was, as noted above (n. 756), the author of the *Encylopedia Americana* entry on natural law. One writer has described him as "possibly the most learned and influential defender of the natural law tradition" among American lawyers and judges" (James MacClennan, "Joseph Story's Natural Law Philosophy" (1993) 5 Benchmark 85). See also Bruce Wardhaugh, "From Natural Law to Legal Realism: Legal Philosophy, Legal Theory and the Development of American Conflicts of Law since 1830" (1989), 41 *Maine L Rev* 301, 308-319.

758 Story, *Commentaries* (1834), [33], p. 33; also *ibid.*, [34], p. 34 ("every nation must judge for itself, what is its true duty in the administration of justice").

For Story[759]:

> "The true foundation, on which the administration of international law must rest, is, that the rules, which are to govern, are those, which arise from mutual interest and utility, from a sense of the inconveniences, which would result from a contrary doctrine, and from a sort of moral necessity to do justice, in order that justice may be done to us in return."

This, he emphasises, is "a matter of the comity of nations, and not of absolute paramount obligation, superseding all discretion on the subject"[760].

226. Story still needed to "land the plane" by reconciling this qualified (moral) obligation towards other nations with his third maxim, which suggests that the force and obligation of foreign laws depend on the "express or tacit consent" of each legal order[761]. The landing is, admittedly, not an entirely smooth one. Although Story's starting point is that each legal order is entitled to decide for itself, in places he elides this with the collective customary practice of nations[762]. His conclusion nonetheless re-emphasises the individual autonomy that every nation enjoys. "Comity", he says, is "the most appropriate phrase to express the true foundation and extent of the obligation of the laws of one nation within the territories of another"[763]. The obligatory force of foreign law within a particular legal order derives from its own consent, and this is something that

759 *Ibid.*, [35] (p. 34), citing the work of Rodenburg and Jean Bouhier (1673-1746).

760 *Ibid.*, [36], p. 36.

761 *Ibid.*, [23], p. 24, referring to Huber, *De Conflictu Legum*, [2].

762 For references to the latter, see e.g. Story, *Commentaries* (1834), [30], p. 32 ("the practice of nations, as a solid proof of the acknowledged law of nations") and [36], p. 36 ("the doctrine owes its origin and authority to the voluntary adoption and consent of nations").

763 Story, *Commentaries* (1834), [38], p. 37.

courts (at least in common law jurisdictions) are entitled to infer if other municipal laws are silent and the foreign law is not repugnant to the policy or interests of the receiving order[764]. Although Westlake would later reach a similar conclusion[765], Story's account benefits from his willingness to acknowledge the natural law undercurrent and his embrace of comity. In Story's opinion, Huber's doctrine "would seem to stand upon just principles; and though from its generality, it leaves behind many grave questions as to its application, it has much to commend it, in point of truth, as well as of simplicity"[766].

227. In his chapter on foreign judgments[767], Story approvingly cites Vattel for the general proposition that the decisions of judges acting with authority ought to be respected and to take effect even in foreign countries[768]. Although Story acknowledged that this proposition had not been universally accepted, he suggested that

---

764 *Ibid.*, [38] (p. 37). By the time of the 2nd edition in 1841 (n. 738), Story was able to note the US Supreme Court's endorsement of this proposition (*Bank of Augusta* v. *Earle* (1839) 38 US (13 Peters) 519, 589 (Taney C. J.)).

765 Text to n. 711.

766 Story, *Commentaries* (1834), [38], p. 37.

767 Story, *Commentaries* (1834), Chap. 15. In the preceding chapter (Chap. 14), he had considered questions of jurisdiction, with extensive reference to Huber's account (see esp, ibid., [532]-[537], pp. 445-449) as well as to common law authorities concerned with the enforcement of foreign judgments (see *ibid.*, [547]-[549], discussing the decisions of the English courts in *Buchanan* v. *Rucker* (1808) 9 East 192 and *Douglas* v. *Forrest* (1828) 4 Bingham New Case 686 and referring in the footnotes to several other cases of this kind). See below, [360].
As Story makes clear at the beginning of Chap. 15, it is necessary to demonstrate that the adjudicating court acts with authority over the parties and the subject matter (*ibid.*, [584] and [586], pp. 491, 492). See Sections IV.D and V.B.3.

768 Story, *Commentaries* (1834), [585], p. 492, with reference to Vattel, *Nations*, Book 2, Chap. 7, [84]-[85], pp. 303-305. See above, [191]-[192].

it had been received more favourably in common law jurisdictions than in continental Europe[769].

228. With respect to judgments *in personam*[770], Story considers two unresolved issues. First, whether judgments relied on defensively (by the equivalent of the *exceptio rei judicatae* in Roman law) should be received on more favourable principles than judgments calling for some positive action to secure their effectiveness. Here, two similar lines of argument had been deployed by the common law courts and commentators to support such a distinction. The first was that nothing more needed to be done when the successful party pleaded a judgment in bar, because the judgment had conferred on him an immunity from further suit[771], whereas a successful party who invoked the judgment to secure a remedy from another legal order was actively seeking assistance to carry the judgment into effect[772]. The second, advanced by Lord Kames[773], was that greater injustice would be done by a positive act of enforcing an unjust judgment than by a mere forbearance to interfere with it and that in the latter case the policy of bringing an end to litigation

---

769 *Ibid.*, [586], p. 492.

770 Story considers first the treatment of judgments *in rem* and on questions of personal status (*ibid.*, [591]-[597], pp. 494-499).

771 John Erskine, *An Institute on the Law of Scotland in Four Books*, Edinburgh: John Bell, 2nd ed., 1785, Vol. 2, Book 4, Title 3, [4], p. 735.

772 Story, *Commentaries* (1834), [598]-[599], pp. 499-501, with reference to Kent's *Commentaries*, Vol. 2 (n. 615), pp. 119-120, 2nd ed. and English and American cases, including the judgment of Eyre L. C. J. in *Phillips* v. *Hunter* (1795) 2 Blacktsone (H) 402, 410. See also the cases referred to in *MacDonald* v. *Grand Trunk Ry Co* (1902) 71 NH 448.

773 See above, [177]. Story cites the 3rd edition of Kames' *Principles of Equity* (n. 589), pp. 365-368.
See also von Bar, *Theorie und Praxis* (n. 3), Vol. 2, Book 11, [414]-[415], pp. 419-421 and [436], pp. 461-464 (Gillespie, *Theory and Practice* (n. 3), pp. 899-901, 940-942).

should prevail[774]. In refuting the second argument, Story also fatally undermines the first (to which, on the face of things, he seems better disposed[775]). There is, he points out, "quite as much reason that a defendant should be protected against a new litigation, after there has been a final sentence in his favour, as there is, that a plaintiff should be protected in the enjoyment of any right, which is established by the sentence in his favour"[776]. That protection is sought, in each case, from the justice system of receiving order, which – according to Story's general theory – decides for itself the terms on which assistance is offered or refused[777].

229. Story turns to the question whether a foreign judgment is to be deemed conclusive, or whether the defendant is at liberty to go into the original merits, and if so to what extent[778]. Although Story notes the "fluctuation of opinion" in the English courts on this subject[779], he avoids the error of thinking that *Sinclair* v. *Fraser* had sanctioned a re-examination of the underlying cause of action. Story observes, quite correctly, that *Sinclair* "does not go to the extent of establishing the doctrine that the merits . . . are reexaminable *de novo*; but only that its justice may be impeached, or its irregularity or fraud shown"[780]. With acuity, he points out the practical difficulties that may arise if the matter were to be re-

774 Story, *Commentaries* (1834), [600]-[601], pp. 501-503.
775 *Ibid.*, [598] (p. 500) ("This distinction has been very generally recognised as having a foundation in international justice").
776 *Ibid.*, [602] (p. 502); also Westlake, *Treatise* (n. 704), [393], p. 376.
777 See above, [224].
778 Story, *Commentaries* (1834), [603], p. 504.
779 *Ibid.*, followed by a review of the authorities, at [604]-[606], pp. 504-506. He notes also (*ibid.*, [608], p. 508) that the question had yet to be settled under the law of the United States. See above, [187]-[188].
780 Story, *Commentaries* (1834), [605], pp. 505-506. See above, [183].

examined in its entirely – "showing the judgment to be merely *prima facie* evidence for the plaintiff would be a mere delusion"[781]. Story accepts that "a defendant can impeach the original justice of the judgment" in certain circumstances[782] and that "[t]o such an extent the doctrine is intelligible and practicable"[783].

230. In the final part of his chapter, Story examines continental jurisprudence[784], canvassing the opinions of Vattel[785], Huber[786], D'Argentré[787], Gaill[788] and Boullenois[789]. He examines the law prevailing in France, accepting the view of Charles Toullier that no foreign judgment can be executed, or recognised, in France without a review of the merits[790]. Story has only limited

---

781 Story, *Commentaries* (1834), [607], pp. 506-507. A similar argument had been advanced by the English lawyer, Jabez Henry, a decade earlier (*A Treatise on the Difference between Personal and Real Statutes and Its Effect on Foreign Judgments, Contracts, Marriages and Wills*, London: S. Sweet, 1823, p. 75). Story cites Henry's work on almost seventy occasions (see esp. Story, *Commentaries* (1834), pp. 510, fn. 1, 6, 8 and p. 515, fn. 2).

782 Those suggested by Story are as follows – (1) the adjudicating court had no jurisdiction, (2) the defendant never had notice of the suit, (3) the judgment was procured by fraud, (4) on its face, the judgment is founded in mistake or (5) the judgment was irregular and bad by the local *rei judicatae*.

783 Story, *Commentaries* (1834), [607], pp. 506-507.

784 *Ibid.*, [611]-[614], pp. 509-512.

785 Section III.D.2 *(a)*.

786 Section III.C.4.

787 Text to n. 303.

788 Andreas Gaill (von Gail) (1526-1587). The reference (Story, *Commentaries* (1841), [612], p. 868) is to Gaill, *Practicarum Observationum tam ad Processum Iudiciarium* (Cologne: Apud Ioannem Gymnicum, 1578), Book 1, Observation 113, [11]. Story's page reference (p. 201) suggests that he was using a later, posthumous edition of Gaill's work (Cologne: Apud Antonium Hierat, 1616).

789 Section III.D.2 *(b)*.

790 Story, *Commentaries* (1834), [617], pp. 514-515, with reference to Charles-Bonaventure-Marie Toullier, *Le droit*

information about the practice in other nations, but records his understanding of Dutch practice as giving foreign judgments the same force as local judgments, subject to the condition of reciprocal treatment. In his final words on the subject, Story approves of this principle of reciprocity, opining that[791]:

> "This is certainly a very reasonable rule; and may, perhaps, hereafter work itself firmly into the structure of international jurisprudence."

In fact, as we will see, this approach had already established itself in many European legal orders, although not in France. Story overlooked the fact that French law had been imposed on the Netherlands since 1811 and had continued in force after the new kingdom was established in 1813[792]. That legal framework, in turn, influenced the treatment of foreign judgments in the new Dutch code of civil procedure, adopted four years after Story's *Commentaries* first appeared in print[793]. Even if Story had become aware of these facts before his death, this passage was preserved in later editions[794]. He

---

civil français, Paris: Warée, Vol. 10, 1822, [76], pp. 93-94, 121. Story also refers (*ibid.*, [616], p. 513) to the work of Baltazard Emérignon, *Traité des assurances et des contrats à la grosse*, Marseille, Jean Mossy, 1783.

791 Story, *Commentaries* (1834), [618], p. 515. See Jacob B. van de Velden, *Finality of Litigation*, Groningen: Ulrich Huber Institute, 2014, p. 232, noting Story's reliance on the work of Jabez Henry (n. 791) and disregard of contemporary Dutch law and practice.

792 Van de Velden, *Finality*, above, pp. 266-271.

793 *Wetboek van Burgerlijke Rechtsvordering* (1838), Article 431. See van de Velden, *Finality*, above, pp. 272-276.

794 Story, *Commentaries* (1846), [618], pp. 1011-1012. The surrounding circumstances are worth noting. Story had corresponded with Foelix and had written an article on the legal system of the United States for the journal that Foelix had founded, William W. Story (ed.), *Life and Letters of Joseph Story*, Boston: Charles C. Little and James Brown, 1851, Vol. 2, pp. 169-170; (1835) 3 *Revue étrangère et*

could not have imagined how significant this misleading statement would turn out to be[795].

(b) *Friedrich Carl von Savigny*

231. Savigny possessed a copy of the first and second editions of Story's work. He privately acknowledged the latter, which seems to have been sent to him on Story's initiative, as a "precious work in an even more

---

française de législation, de jurisprudence et d'économie politique 65 *bis*. Foelix, in turn, had reviewed the first edition of Story's work in the journal, Michaels, "Story, Joseph" (n. 736), 1665, referring to (1834) 1 *Revue étrangère* 758 and to the summary of Foelix's review in (1835) 13 *American Jurist and Law Magazine* 237.
Story received a copy of Vol. 7 of the *Revue étrangère* containing the first part of Foelix's commentaries on the conflict of laws while the 2nd edition of his own work was at the proof stage and added numerous references to it, see Story, *Commentaries* (1841), p. 57, fn. 5; Nadelmann, "Bicentennial Observations" (n. 739), 68, 71-72. He praised the work in his foreword (*ibid.*, pp. iv-v). Foelix's account of the law relating to foreign judgments did not appear until 1842 and 1843 in Vols. 9 and 10 of the Revue étrangère (n. 643). If Story subsequently received copies of these works, he did not have the opportunity to take account of them in the annotations that were included in the 3rd edition, published posthumously.
No further references to Foelix's work had been added to the 8th edition, published in 1883, Joseph Story and Melvyn Bigelow (ed.), *Commentaries on the Conflict of Laws, Foreign and Domestic*, Boston: Little, Brown and Co, 8th ed., 1883. The passage referred to above, [230] had survived intact (*ibid.*, p. 839). By the time of the 7th edition, Boston: Little, Brown and Co, 1872, the then editor, Edmund Hatch Bennett, had added four pages of notes, opening with the despairing statement quoted in the final chapter (below, [403]). These notes were removed by Bigelow in the 8th edition.

795 See below, [282].

perfect form"[796]. In the preface to the eighth, and final, volume of his *System of Contemporary Roman Law*, Savigny lauded the "remarkable picture of this perfect but hopeful state of things" in Story's work, describing it as "extremely useful, as a rich collection of materials, for every enquirer"[797].

232. To refer at all to Savigny in this account may seem incongruous, given that he did not directly address questions as to the effect to be given in one legal order to the judgments of other legal orders. His account of local limits of the authority of the rules of law over legal relations[798] principally addresses questions of choice of law and of adjudicatory jurisdiction[799]. Savigny's extensive discussion in the sixth volume of his work[800] of the effects of legal process[801] and judgments focuses on domestic law and practice.

233. Savigny is nonetheless a hugely significant figure not only because of his pre-eminence as a scholar of the conflict of laws but also by virtue of his position as a founder and the ideological leader of the

796 Savigny's letter of acknowledgement, written to the American diplomat, Theodore S. Fay, is reproduced in W. Story (ed.), *Life and Letters* (n. 793), p. 378.

797 Savigny, *System*, Vol. 8, p. iv, Guthrie (n. 738), p. 2.

798 Herrschaft der Rechtsregeln über die Rechtsverhältnisse.

799 Savigny declares that questions of adjudicatory jurisdiction and civil procedure fall outside the scope of his System, Savigny, *System*, Book 5, [204], pp. 1-2; also *ibid.*, Book 1, [1], point 4, p. 3, Holloway (n. 738), pp. 2-3. He nonetheless provides a detailed discussion of the former topic in his discussion of origin and domicile, Savigny, *System*, Book 8, [355], pp. 72-75 and [358], pp. 92-93, Guthrie (n. 738), pp. 67-69, 80 and of obligations (*ibid.*, [369]-[371], pp. 203-246, Guthrie, above, pp. 150-174).
See also Savigny's comment on the relation between applicable law and jurisdiction (*ibid.*, [360], pp. 109-110, Guthrie, above, p. 89).

800 (n. 738).

801 More specifically, *litis contestatio* and notification of the proceedings (below, [249]).

historical school of jurisprudence[802]. The founders of this school contrasted their legal theory with that of the "philosophical" or "non-historical" school. In their view, the positive laws adopted by every nation could only be accounted by examining the nation's history and spirit; so too, the place of individual human beings within this ordering[803]. As a Professor at the University of Berlin, Savigny banished natural law scholarship from the curriculum[804]. Yet, as a young scholar, he had been attracted by its ideas[805].

234. These events in Savigny's life were in the rear view mirror by the time that he produced the first volume of his *System* in 1840. Although Savigny does not subscribe to natural law theory, his account uses a number of its tools and ideas[806]. Savigny is not opposed

802 Frederick C. Beiser, "Savigny and the Historical School of Law", Chap. 5 in *The German Historicist Tradition*, Oxford: Oxford University Press, 2011; Thomas Rüfner, "Historical School", in Jürgen Basedow, Klaus J. Hopt, Reinhard Zimmermann and Andreas Stier (eds.), *Max Planck Encyclopedia of European Private Law*, Oxford: Oxford University Press, 2012, pp. 830-834, https://max-eup2012.mpipriv.de/index.php/Historical_School.

803 Beiser (n. 802), pp. 214-215; Rüfner (n. 802), pp. 830-832.

804 Beiser, above, pp. 216-217. The author examines the reasons for Savigny's changed mindset, not least his opposition to Kant's moral and political philosophy, *ibid.*, pp. 224-227.

805 *Ibid.*, pp. 220-223. For the re-emergence of natural law idea's in Savigny's *System*, see *ibid.* pp. 246-252.

806 Mills, *Confluence* (n. 222), p. 56 ("Savigny . . . drew heavily on natural law processes of reasoning"; "imbued with the spirit of a natural law approach"); Beiser (n. 802), pp. 250-252.

In addition to the elements of the work discussed in this section, see Savigny's description of the central concept in his account of private law, the Rechtsverhältnisse (imperfectly translated as legal or jural relation) as an interpersonal relationship, determined by a rule of law, which consists in the assignment to the individual will of a province in which it to rule independently of every foreign will, Savigny, *System*, Vol. 1, Book 2, Chap. 1, [52] (p. 333),

to theory *per se*; indeed, in his view, danger arises when theory and practice become disconnected[807]. He is strongly critical of those who have "set an inordinate value upon the origination of new views, in comparison with the true vivid cultivation and satisfactory exposition of those already discovered"[808]. The "complete theorist", in Savigny's view, is one who engages in "the complete thorough contemplation of the entire practice of law", with all moral, religious, political and economic relations in mind[809].

235. Savigny sets his task as being to identify the system of modern Roman law applied by European nations, focusing on private, substantive law (as opposed to public or procedural law)[810],

---

Holloway (n. 738), p. 270. In explaining this idea, Savigny accepts a distinction between "original rights", concerned with inviolability of the person, and "acquired rights", which extend the power of the entitled person outwards beyond the natural limits of their being, *ibid.*, pp. 335-340, Holloway, above, pp. 272-276. See also Savigny, *System*, Vol. 8, Book 3, Chap. 1, [345], p. 10 (Guthrie (n. 738), p. 13) ("Every right presents itself in its primary aspect as a power belonging to a person").

Although Savigny distinguishes his approach from that of earlier writers (*ibid.*, pp. 332-333, Holloway, above, p. 270), his reliance on the concept of liberty in the natural law toolbox is evident (see Sec. II.C). As Beiser, above, submits (at p. 252), "though Savigny shuns the name Naturrecht, some of his later discussions of the universal aspects of law read like nothing more than an old natural law doctrine".

807 Savigny, *System*, Vol. 1, Preface (pp. xx, xxv), Holloway, above, pp. vii, xi.

808 *Ibid.*, p. xxiii, Holloway, above, p. x.

809 *Ibid.*, p. xxi, Holloway, above, p. ix.

810 *Ibid.*, Book 1, Chap. 1, [1], points 2-4, pp. 1-3, Holloway, above, pp. 1-3. Helpfully, Savigny gives judicial decisions as an example. The form and conditions as well as the execution of a judgment fall within the province of procedure, whereas the *res judicata* effects are within the scope of Savigny's *System*. See below, [249].

and acknowledging differences between legal orders[811].

236. For Savigny, positive law has its origin in the spirit of a people (Volksgeist) living and working in all individuals[812]. This invisible spirit is not documented and must be proved by other means. First, in the general, uniform recognition of positive law and its binding force[813]. Second, having regard to other characteristics of a people with an equally invisible, undocumented origin, for example, the custom of social life and above all speech[814]. Although this echoes natural law reasoning, Savigny immediately stakes out his theoretical boundary – the law lives in the common consciousness of the people not as abstract rules but as the living conception of the law's institutions in their organic connection, shaping rules through human interaction[815]. Over time, this primitive law evolves and is replaced by more sophisticated institutions, legislation and jurisprudence[816].

237. In Savigny's view, the general essence of law, stripped of its detail, is the regulated existence of a multitude of human beings[817]. History demonstrates that whenever people live together, they stand in a spiritual community that expresses itself and evolves through the use of speech[818]. In this "natural whole"[819] lies the seat of development of law[820]. It is not always easy to define

---

811 Savigny, *System*, Vol. 1, Book 1, Chap. 1, [3], p. 6, Holloway, above, p. 5.

812 *Ibid.*, Book 1, Chap. 1, [7], p. 14, Holloway, above, p. 12.

813 *Ibid.*, p. 15, Holloway, above, pp. 12-13.

814 *Ibid.*, p. 15, Holloway, above, p. 13.

815 *Ibid.*

816 *Ibid.*, pp. 17-18, Holloway, above, p. 14.

817 *Ibid.*, Book 1, Chap. 1, [8], p. 18, Holloway, above, p. 15.

818 *Ibid.*, p. 19, Holloway, above, p. 15.

819 Naturganzen.

820 Savigny, *System*, Vol. 1, Book 1, Chap. 1, [8], p. 19, Holloway (n. 738), p. 15.

these matters along territorial lines, as the boundaries of individual communities are indefinite and wavering[821]. Nevertheless, the "natural unity"[822] of a people is continuous, uniting the present with the past and the future, with law as a constantly present phenomenon[823].

238. In an important passage, Savigny relates his own account to natural law scholarship. He acknowledges that his view, that individual peoples are regarded as the creators and subjects of positive law, may seem too narrow to those who ascribe that generation to the universal spirit of humanity[824]. He sees, however, no conflict between the two views for "what works in an individual people is merely the general human spirit which reveals itself in that people in a particular manner"[825].

239. Savigny turns to consider the formation of the State, as the visible and organic manifestation of the invisible unity[826]. It originates in a higher necessity, being created by a force generated within the people[827]. In the State, the people first obtains true personality and the ability to act[828]. Before this point, the congruent feelings, thoughts and customs of its members have

---

821 *Ibid.*, p. 19, Holloway, above, pp. 15-16.

822 Natürliche Einheit.

823 Savigny, *System*, Vol. 1, Book 1, Chap. 1, [8], p. 20, Holloway (n. 738), p. 16.

824 *Ibid.*, p. 20, Holloway, above, p. 17.

825 *Ibid.*, pp. 20-21, Holloway, above, p. 17.

826 Savigny, *System*, Vol. 1, Book 1, Chap. 1, [9], pp. 21-22, Holloway, above, p. 17.
See Ralf Michaels, "Globalising Savigny? The State in Savigny's Private International Law and the Challenge from Europeanisation and Globalization", pp. 119-144 in Michael Stolleis and Wolfgang Streeck (eds.), *Aktuelle Fragen zu politischer und rechtlicher Steuerung im Kontext der Globalisierung*, Baden-Baden: Nomos, 2007, esp. at pp. 126-130.

827 Savigny, *System*, Vol. 1, Book 1, Chap. 1, [9], Holloway, above, p. 18.

828 *Ibid.*, p. 23, Holloway, above, p. 19.

only an invisible existence[829]. Savigny conceives of this imperfect "state of nature" as a theoretical concept only, for every people as soon as it appears will manifest itself as a State[830]. The State arises spontaneously and naturally, in a people, through the people and for the people[831]. Savigny rejects as pernicious the widely held opinion that States came into being by a contract, through the will of individuals[832]. This theory, in Savigny's submission, overlooks the natural unity preserved in the people as well as the inner necessity of formation of a State[833]. It is only through the State that injustice can be consistently eradicated[834] – its first task is to make the idea of law dominant in the visible world, protecting the individual against injurious invasion of their entitlement[835].

240. This brings Savigny, under the heading "Völkerrecht", to the relationship of neighbouring peoples. He suggests that this relation will appear at first similar to the relation of individuals brought together accidentally and not connected by a national

---

829 *Ibid.*

830 *Ibid.*

831 *Ibid.*, Book 1, Chap. 1, [10], p. 29, Holloway (n. 738), p. 23.

832 *Ibid.*, see Section II.I.2.

833 Savigny, *System*, Vol. 1, Book 1, Chap. 1, [10], p. 30, Holloway (n. 738), p. 24.
Savigny attributes the erroroneous line of argument to two factors. First, the perception of a wide variety of historical and institutional practice among States. Second, the constant and often interconscious interchangeability of different senses of the term "people", *ibid.*, pp. 29-31, Holloway, above, pp. 24-25. He acknowledges also that the formation and boundaries of a State may be impacted by external factors, such as conquest and fragmentation, *ibid.*, pp. 31-32, Holloway, above, pp. 25-26.

834 Savigny, *System*, Vol. 1, Book 1, Chap. 1, [9], p. 24, Holloway, above, pp. 19-20.

835 *Ibid.*, pp. 25-26, Holloway, above, p. 21. Savigny recognises also the need to defend the public interest through institutions of the criminal law.

community[836]. With the application of reason, each will apply to the accidental relationship the consciousness of justice that inheres from earlier relations, by a process of imitation and translation[837]. So, too, several independent States may voluntarily apply each other's law "so far as it is suitable and as they find it convenient", but no right arises in this way[838]. Savigny's theoretical approach and his conception of the Volksgeist enables him to supplement this – among peoples sharing tribal kinship and those sharing religious convictions, a similar community of legal consciousness can arise among different peoples, so as to create positive law in each people[839]. For Savigny, this "intellectual communion" is the basis of the law of nations existing particularly among the Christian States of Europe[840]. In his submission, this is positive law, although incompletely formed, lacking both certain content and the institutional structures of the State[841].

241. Savigny observes that the law originally established in the common consciousness of a people comprises two elements – an individual one belonging to each people in particular and a general one based on the human nature common to all[842]. Each element is rooted in legal history and philosophy[843]. Savigny criticises

[836] Savigny, *System*, Vol. 1, Book 1, Chap. 1, [10], p. 32, Holloway, above, p. 26.

[837] *Ibid.*, pp. 32-33, Holloway, above, p. 26.

[838] *Ibid.*, p. 33, Holloway, above, p. 26.

[839] Savigny, *System*, Vol. 1, Book 1, Chap. 1, [11], p. 33, Holloway, above, pp. 26-27.

[840] *Ibid.*, p. 33, Holloway, above, p. 27.

[841] *Ibid.* Savigny adds that Christian morality leads each people belonging to this communion of nations to apply this positive law analogically to peoples who neither share this mode of thinking nor reciprocate, *ibid.*, pp. 33-34, Holloway, above, p. 27.

[842] Savigny, *System*, Vol. 1, Book 1, Chap. 1, [15], p. 52, Holloway, above, p. 42.

[843] *Ibid.*

both writers on the law of nature, whom he considers to have taken too abstract a view of theory, and those who have purported to follow a more practical focus and who have neglected one or the other of these two elements[844]. The general problem that it is the enduring task of each people to solve, in its own way, is referable to the moral determination of human nature which, for Savigny, exhibits itself in the Christian view of life[845].

242. Savigny's true antipathy is towards accounts of law that are deficient, whether because they are ahistorical, or atheoretical, or lacking in practical insight or for some other reason. Natural law principles and ideas have a place within his *System*. He acknowledges that the considerations that bear on all human relationships cannot be overlooked when studying the rules governing relations within, or between, communities, while placing a greater emphasis on considerations that are specific to, or shared by, particular communities.

243. This account of Savigny's legal theory enables us to frame his treatment of conflict of laws issues in his eighth and final volume, published almost a decade later[846]. Savigny's starting point is that for every case

[844] *Ibid.* See Beiser (n. 802), p. 251 ("These passages are surprising because they give the concept of natural law a clear and firm place in Savigny's system. Having been banished from the public entrance to the temple of right, natural law makes a furtive re-entry through the backdoor").

[845] *Ibid.*, p. 53, Holloway (n. 738), p. 43. Savigny denies that it is necessary to supplement this ethical principle with a concept of the public good, in the pursuit of the State's economic interests, as the latter serve to enhance and refine the moral ends of human nature, *ibid.*, p. 54, Holloway, above, p. 43.

[846] In the Preface, Savigny confesses to a sense of inadequacy in seeking to master the difficulties presented by the materials in this subject area, Savigny, *System*, Book 8, p. iii, Guthrie (n. 738), p. 1.
A list of authors at the beginning of the first chapter indicates that he had consulted, among others, works by Paulus Voet,

the legal rule to be applied is defined and limited first and foremost by the subjection of the entitled person to a particular legal domain[847]. This prompts him to consider at length whether national origin (nationality) or territorial connection should determine the association of a person with a particular legal domain[848]. He recognises nonetheless that diverse and important qualifications to this proposition can occur through the relationship that certain things, acts or circumstances of life have to another legal domain[849].

244. In Savigny's opinion, territoriality had supplanted nationality as the key criterion for determining the scope of legal rules, which explains his preferred terminology of "local limits" to describe the sphere of application of laws[850] and his preference of domicile over nationality as a connecting factor[851]. Savigny accepts Huber and Story's propositions that every State can insist that only its law applies within its borders, and that no State can

---

Huber, Johannes Voet, Boullenois, Story, Wächter and Foelix, *ibid.*, Book 8, Chap. 1, [345], pp. 8-10, Guthrie, above, pp. 11-12.

847 Rechtsgebiet.

848 Savigny, *System*, Vol. 8, Book 3, Chap. 1, [346], pp. 14-18 and [350]-[357], pp. 39-106, Guthrie (n. 738), pp. 15-18, 42-88.

849 *Ibid.*, [345], p. 13, Guthrie, above, p. 14.

850 *Ibid.*, [346], pp. 17-18, Guthrie, above, p. 17.

851 *Ibid.*, [360], pp. 95-106, Guthrie, above, pp. 81-88. See Michaels, "Globalising Savigny" (n. 826), pp. 133-137. As Michaels notes, p. 136, nationality as a connecting factor enjoyed a resurgence in the latter part of the nineteenth century under the influence of the Italian, Pasquale Stanislao Mancini (1817-1888), see Yuko Nishitani, "Mancini, Pasquale Stanislao", in *Encyclopedia of Private International Law* (n. 300), Vol. 2, esp. pp. 1196-1197. Notwithstanding Savigny's influence in the field, nationality and not domicile was adopted in Germany as the connecting factor for questions of personal status, see *Einführungsgesetz zum Bürgerlichen Gesetzbuche*, 18 August 1896, Articles 7 and 29.

require the recognition of its law beyond its borders, but considers these to be of little value in themselves[852]. He also accepts Wächter's proposition that positive laws that direct how the case is to be resolved must be applied, while denying that an exhaustive set of such rules is to be found anywhere[853]. Savigny concedes that a State could require its judges to decide all cases in accordance with local rules of law, regardless of connections to other legal domains[854]. For Savigny, this was a theoretical possibility only, for in his opinion[855]:

> "The more multifarious and active the intercourse between different nations, the more [one will have to

---

[852] Savigny, *System*, Vol. 8, Book 3, Chap. 1, [348], pp. 24-25, Guthrie, above, p. 26.

[853] *Ibid.*, pp. 25-26, Guthrie, above, p. 26.

[854] *Ibid.*, p. 26, Guthrie, above, pp. 26-27.

[855] *Ibid.*, pp. 26-27, Guthrie, above, p. 27, using Guthrie's translation here, with adjustments indicated by square brackets. See also Kegel (n. 688), 56-59.
The original German text is as follows:

> "Je mannichfaltiger und lebhafter der Verkehr unter den verschiedenen Völkern wird, desto mehr wird man sich überzeugen müssen, daß es räthlich ist, jenen strengen Grundsatz nicht festzuhalten, sondern vielmehr mit einem entgegengesetzten Grundsatz zu vertauschen. Dahin führt die wünschenswerte Gegenseitigkeit in der Behandlung der Rechtsverhältnisse, und die daraus hervorgehende Gleichheit in der Beurteilung der Einheimischen und Fremden, die im Ganzen und Großen durch den gemeinsamen Vorteil der Völker und der Einzelnen geboten wird. Denn diese Gleichheit muß in vollständiger Ausbildung dahin führen, daß nicht bloß in jedem einzelnen Staate der Fremde gegen den Einheimischen nicht zurückgesetzt werde (worin die gleiche Behandlung der Personen besteht), sondern daß auch die Rechtsverhältnisse, in Fällen einer Kollision der Gesetze, dieselbe Beurteilung zu erwarten haben, ohne Unterschied, ob in diesem oder jenem Staate das Urteil gesprochen werde."

(source: https://www.deutschestextarchiv.de/book/view/savigny_system08_1849?p=48).

convince oneself that it is advisable not[856]] to adhere to such a stringent rule, but rather to substitute for it the opposite principle. This has resulted from that reciprocity in dealing with cases which is so desirable, and the consequent equality in judging between natives and foreigners, which on the whole [and by and large[857]] is [provided[858]] by the common interest of nations and of individuals. For it is the necessary consequence of this equality, in its full development, not only that in each particular State the foreigner is not postponed to the native (in which equality in the treatment of persons consists), but also that, in cases of conflict of laws, the same legal relations have to expect the same decision, whether the judgment be pronounced in this State or that."

245. For Savigny, this principle of equality is part of the shared consciousness of a community of nations interacting with one another[859], which had obtained wider recognition through the influence of a common Christian morality, and the resulting real advantage for all parties[860]. In his view, it follows that essentially

---

856 Substituted here for Guthrie's "the more men will be persuaded that it is not expedient".

857 Added to Guthrie's translation.

858 Substituted here for Guthrie's "dictated".

859 I.e. Völkerrecht in the strict sense, above, [240].

860 Savigny, *System*, Vol. 8, Book 3, Chap. 1, [348], p. 27, Guthrie (n. 738), p. 27. The original German text is as follows:

> "Der Standpunkt, auf den wir durch diese Erwägung geführt werden, ist der einer völkerrechtlichen Gemeinschaft der miteinander verkehrenden Nationen, und dieser Standpunkt hat im Fortschritt der Zeit immer allgemeinere Anerkennung gefunden, unter dem Einfluss teils der gemeinsamen christlichen Gesittung, teils des wahren Vorteils, der daraus für alle Teile hervorgeht."

(source: https://www.deutschestextarchiv.de/book/view/savigny_system08_1849?p=49).

the same approach is to be adopted for questions involving the conflict of laws of different States as applies to questions of rule conflict within a legal order[861].

246. The influence of Huber and Johannes Voet on this remarkable passage is clear. If the formulation left any room for doubt on this point, Savigny soon clears it up by citing both writers, observing that this principle, of equality, "may be described as a friendly accommodation among sovereign states, in accepting originally foreign laws among the sources from which domestic courts have to draw in assessing certain legal relationships"[862]. Strikingly, Savigny adds to his list of authorities a reference to Story's treatment of the subject[863]. His following

---

[861] Savigny, *System*, Vol. 8, Book 3, Chap. 1, [348], p. 27, Guthrie, above, p. 27 with a cross-reference to the preceding discussion of the latter question (*ibid.*, [347], pp. 19-33 (Guthrie, above, pp. 22-25); also *ibid.*, [348], p. 29, Guthrie, above, pp. 28-29, pointing out that it is a necessary consequence of the independence of the legal orders that there can be no overriding common rule that can resolve the conflict.

[862] Savigny, *System*, Vol. 8, Book 3, Chap. 1, [348], p. 28, Guthrie, above, p. 28. Savigny refers (in footnote *(f)*) to Johannes Voet, *Commentarius*, Book 1, Title 4, Appendix, [1], [2], [17] (Gane, *The Selective Voet* (n. 314), Vol. 1, pp. 97-99, 115) and Huber, *De Conflictu Legum*, [2] (see above, [118] and [122]-[123]).
The original German text is as follows:

> "Man kann diese Gleichstellung, im Gegensatz des oben erwähnten strengen Rechts, als freundliche Zulassung unter souveränen Staaten bezeichnen, nämlich als Zulassung ursprünglich fremder Gesetze unter die Quellen, aus welchen die einheimischen Gerichte die Beurteilung mancher Rechtsverhältnisse zu schöpfen haben."

(source: https://www.deutschestextarchiv.de/book/view/savigny_system08_1849?p=50).

[863] Savigny, *System*, Vol. 8, Book 3, Chap. 1, [348], fn. *(f)*, p. 28, Guthrie (n. 738), p. 28.

comment, denying that this friendly accommodation is "an expression of magnanimity or arbitrary will"[864], is a criticism not of Huber, Voet or Story, but of Wächter's hermetic sealing of the judicial function to exclude considerations of comity[865].

247. Savigny posits that this shared consciousness of a community of nations, although not recognised by more recent writers, forms the essential basis of the general customary law so frequently invoked by them in this inquiry[866]. Disagreements about its content are unsurprising and do not detract from the general principle – "the common assumption of its existence and the common search for its content" are, in Savigny's view, decisive here[867]. He concludes by noting that the

---

[864] Savigny, *System*, Vol. 8, Book 3, Chap. 1, [348], p. 28, Guthrie, above, p. 28. The original German text is as follows:

> "Nur darf diese Zulassung nicht gedacht werden als Ausfluß bloßer Großmuth oder Willkür, die zugleich als zufällig wechselnd und vorübergehend zu denken wäre."

(source: https://www.deutschestextarchiv.de/book/view/savigny_system08_1849?p=50).

[865] Savigny, *System*, Vol. 8, Book 3, Chap. 1, [348], fn. *(g)*, p. 28, Guthrie, above, p. 28, with reference to Wächter (n. 688), [2] and [16] [(1841) 24 *Archiv* 230, 240; (1842) 25 *Archiv* 1, 12-15] (see above, [210]).

[866] Savigny, *System*, Vol. 8, Book 3, Chap. 1, [348], p. 29, Guthrie, above, p. 29, with reference to Wächter (n. 688) [(1841) 24 *Archiv* 230, 255-261; (1842) 25 *Archiv* 151, 175-177; (1842) 25 *Archiv* 361, 371]; see also Savigny, *System*, Book 8, Chap. 1, [261], pp. 101, raising further objections to Wächter's theory.
For Wächter's response, published after the death of both men, see Carl Georg van Wächter and Oscar van Wächter (ed.), *Pankdekten*, Leipzig: Breitkopf and Härtel, 1880, [31], pp. 146-147, translated by Nadelmann (1964) 13 *Am J Comp L* 417, 427-428.

[867] Savigny, *System*, Vol. 8, Book 3, Chap. 1, [348], p. 30, Guthrie, above, p. 29.

advantages to which the principle leads are increasingly being secured by treaties[868].

248. For present purposes, it is not necessary to examine in detail how Savigny goes about the task that he sets himself of ascertaining, for every legal relation[869], the law area to which it belongs or is subject according to its peculiar nature[870]. As is well known, his general answer to that question lies in seeking to discover the "seat" of each legal relation[871]. Under Savigny's principle, judges must apply the law to which the disputed relation belongs, without distinction as to whether it is local or foreign law[872]. Savigny accepts, however, that this obligation is restricted for "certain types of laws whose special nature is contrary to such free treatment of the legal community between different States" and that this leads to the exclusive application of the judge's own law[873]. Savigny identifies and discusses two types of law that are prioritised for this reason, being (a) laws of a strictly positive, compulsory nature and (b) legal institutions of a foreign State whose existence is not recognised locally and which have no claim to protection[874].

(c) *Savigny on the recognition and enforcement of foreign judgments (reverie)*

249. Savigny's equality principle, taken together with his treatment of disputes and judgments in the fifth and

868 *Ibid.*, pp. 30-31, Guthrie, above, p. 30, giving examples from recent Prussian practice.

869 (n. 806).

870 Savigny, *System*, Vol. 8, Book 3, Chap. 1, [348], pp. 27-28, Guthrie (n. 738), p. 27.

871 *Ibid.*, [360], p. 108 and [361], p. 118, Guthrie, above, pp. 89, 94. See Sonnentag (n. 737), at pp. 1610-1611; Banu, *Nineteenth Century Perspectives* (n. 655), pp. 76-78.

872 Savigny, *System*, Vol. 8, Book 3, Chap. 1, [349], p. 32, Guthrie, above, p. 33.

873 *Ibid.*, p. 32, Guthrie, above, p. 34.

874 *Ibid.*, pp. 33-39, Guthrie, above, pp. 34-38.

sixth books of his *System*[875], allows us to imagine how (if he had written on the subject) Savigny would have addressed the topic of the recognition and enforcement of judgments. The earlier books give three insights as to Savigny's thinking on the subject of dispute resolution. First, the violation of a right gives rise to a new relationship between the parties involved, entitling the injured party to demand that their opponent take steps to remove the violation and giving that party the authority to bring a legal action[876]. Second, in Savigny's view[877], at the moment when the action is notified to the defendant, both parties come under an obligation to abide by the future judgment as if it had been delivered at that moment, avoiding any prejudice by reason of procedural delay[878]. Savigny characterises this obligation of obedience to the judgment as quasi-contractual. It does not depend on the parties' consent but arises from the "indispensable provisions of procedural law"[879]. Third, for Savigny, the *res judicata* effect of a judgment, resolving the parties' conflict, is one of the most important in the legal system[880]. In an enlightening discussion, he identifies the need for a legal order to strike a balance between "two

---

875 (n. 738).

876 Savigny, *System*, Vol. 5, Book 2, Chap. 4, [204]-[205], pp. 1-6. Savigny explains that this development is the "germ of an obligation", *ibid.*, p. 5.

877 In this regard, Savigny departs both from the position in classical Roman law and the view of some other commentators which attributed this effect to an act on the part of the defendant contesting the action *(litis contestatio)*, Savigny, *System*, Vol. 6, Book 2, Chap. 4, [278]-[279], pp. 237-247.

878 Savigny, *System*, Vol. 6, Book 2, Chap. 4, [258], pp. 34-35 and [279], pp. 246-247.

879 *Ibid.*, [258], pp. 31-32 ("unabweislichen Vorſchriften des Prozeßrechts").
Cf. Ernest G. Lorenzen, "The Enforcement of American Judgments Abroad" (1919) 29 *Yale LJ* 188, 190.

880 *Ibid.*, [280], pp. 257-258.

very serious dangers of opposite nature"[881], of upholding an erroneous judgment or of truly endless uncertainty of the legal situation[882]. He adopts the position that the judgment operates as an unchallengeable fiction as to the parties' true legal rights[883]. This is important and beneficial due to the inherent instability of many legal relationships[884]. Decisiveness is desirable for all parties[885].

250. Savigny's equality principle, as we have noted, is founded on the proposition that it is desirable that disputed legal relations should expect the same decision wherever litigated[886]. Equipped with this insight, there seems little doubt that Savigny would incline strongly towards the mutual recognition and enforcement of judgments within, and possibly beyond, a community of nations, irrespective of whether the disputed relation had its seat in the legal domain of the adjudicating court[887]. Two further conditions suggest themselves. First, the court delivering the judgment must have had

---

881 *Ibid.*, p. 260.
882 *Ibid.*, pp. 259-260.
883 *Ibid.*, p. 261. See Digest 50.17.207, Ulpian, *On the* Lex Julia *and* Papia, Book 1 *(res judicata pro Veritate accipitur).*
884 *Ibid.*, pp. 263-264.
885 *Ibid.*, p. 264.
886 Text to n. 855.
887 Compare the theory advanced by von Bar in *Internationale Privat- und Strafrecht* (n. 3), [125], pp. 465-466, Gillespie, *International Law* (n. 3), pp. 564-566 and *Theorie und Praxis* (n. 3), Vol. 2, Book 11, [412], pp. 413-414, Gillespie, *Theory and Practice* (n. 3), p. 895 and supported by Wharton, *A Treatise on the Conflict of Laws*, Philadelphia: Kay and Brother, 1873, [801], p. 524, based on the idea that a judgment is a *lex specialis* that falls to be applied, or not applied, to determine the parties' relative entitlement in the same way as the conflict of laws determines the application, or not, of any law.
This theory does not sufficiently distinguish the particular dispute that is the subject matter of the judgment, and the proceedings leading to it, from the parties' underlying legal relationship (see text to n. 876).

adjudicatory jurisdiction according to the standards of the nation called upon to recognise or enforce it[888]. Second, Savigny's formulation of his equality principle, and the object of that principle of ensuring consistency of outcome in adjudication, suggest that he would favour a condition or at least an aspiration of reciprocity between the two nations involved[889].

(d) *Story and Savigny: Contrast and commonality*

251. The approaches of these two titans are sometimes placed in sharp opposition. Ralf Michaels describes

---

Von Bar's theory may have a more limited sphere of application with respect to a judgment emanating from a legal order that considers its judgments, or the matter of contested litigation, not merely to operate as a procedural bar to further claims but also to negate or otherwise affect the underlying claim. The existence of such a rule would then raise a question of the substantive (dispositive) effects of the judgment, similar to that raised by judgments *in rem* or discharge of indebtedness by bankruptcy proceedings, to be answered by reference to the law governing the underlying claim.
However, the English common law and other legal orders that followed it did not consider that a foreign judgment had this effect (*Hall* v. *Odber* (1809) 11 East 118, 123-124 (Lord Ellenborough); *Bank of Australasia* v. *Harding* (1850) 9 CB 661, 686-687 (Wilde C. J.), 688 (Cresswell J.)), building on the proposition that a foreign judgment is not a matter of record (see text to n. 604); also *Wood* v. *Gamble* (1853) 65 Massachusetts Reports 8. For further authorities, and criticism, see Horace Emerson Read, *Recognition and Enforcement of Foreign Judgments in the Common Law Units of the British Commonwealth*, Cambridge: Harvard University Press, 1938, pp. 116-121; Albert A. Ehrenzweig, *A Treatise on the Conflict of Laws*, St Paul: West Publishing, 1962, pp. 217-218, cf. Civil Jurisdiction and Judgments Act 1982 (UK), s. 34.

888 Savigny affirms this requirement, Savigny, *System*, Vol. 5, Book 2, Chap. 4, [204], pp. 1-2, and gives detailed consideration to questions of adjudicatory jurisdiction in his final book (see n. 799).

889 See below, [260]-[261], [282]-[284], [291]-[292].

"the fundamental shift in the nature of the concept [of comity] as espoused by Joseph Story and by Friedrich Carl von Savigny"[890]. He contrasts Story's focus on relations between sovereign nations, as a department of public law[891], with Savigny's use of the idea of a "community of nations"(völkerrechtlichen Gemeinschaft[892]) to solve problems of private law[893]. Both have been said to depart from Huber's doctrine of comity with different trajectories, Story by weakening its obligatory force or dissolving it entirely[894] and Savigny of supplanting it with positive law in the form of Völkerrecht[895].

252. It is hardly surprising that Story, the common lawyer, and Savigny, the civilian, approach the subject in different ways. There are, nevertheless, points of commonality and connection. They were born in the same year (1779), had combined political[896] and judicial[897] appointments with their academic

---

[890] Ralf Michaels, "Public and Private International Law: German Views on Global Issues" (2008), 4 *J Priv Int L* 121, 126-127.

[891] Story, *Commentaries* (1834), [8], p. 8.

[892] See above, [240].

[893] Michaels, "Public and Private International Law" (n. 890), 127; also Kegel (n. 688), 59.

[894] Watson, *Comity of Errors* (n. 475), Chap. 2; Watson, "The Failure of Scottish Legal Education" (n. 475); Th. M. de Boer, "Living Apart Together: The Relationship between Public and Private International Law" (2010) 57 *Neth Int L Rev* 183, 189.

[895] De Nova (n. 342), 459-461; Mills, *Confluence* (n. 222), p. 57.

[896] In Story's case, as a representative in the Massachusetts legislature and, briefly, the US House of Representatives; in Savigny's case, in various roles within the Prussian Government, culminating in his appointment as Großkanzler, with responsibility for the justice system, from 1842-1848.

[897] Story was an associate justice of the US Supreme Court from 1812 until his death in 1845. Savigny served on the

roles[898] and were wrestling with the conflict of laws at a late stage in their varied careers.

253. The obvious difference in their conceptions of law's domain and authority may be partly attributable to the contrasting circumstances in which they were writing. Story, a citizen of an expanding and increasingly influential new nation, was content to rely on political fact, the will of a majority of the voting population, coupled with the means and power to make that will effectual[899]. Savigny, completing his project at a time when constitutional orders in Germany and elsewhere in Europe were being reshaped by revolution, rested on the more abstract and aspirational Volksgeist. These differences, top-down versus bottom-up, seeped into their understanding of the relations between distinct nations, peoples and legal orders.

254. Both were influenced by Huber's work[900], and Savigny in turn was influenced by Story's *Commentaries*[901]. Consequently, there are obvious similarities of form and function between Story's vision of comity[902] and Savigny's equality principle[903]. Both are underpinned by ideas of common interest and reciprocity and of moral rectitude[904]. Both accept that the obligatory force of the

Courts of Appeal and Cassation in Prussia from 1819-1841.

898 Savigny was a full professor at the University of Berlin from 1810 to 1842. Story was appointed to the Dane Professorship at Harvard University in 1829.

899 Story, *Commentaries on the Constitution* (n. 193), [330], pp. 299-300. Story discards the idea of the "original contract", describing it as "visionary" but unrealistic (*ibid.*, [326]-[327], pp. 294-297). Cf. Story, "Natural Law", in *Encyclopedia Americana*, Vol. 9 (n. 207), at pp. 153-154.

900 See above, [225]-[226] and [246].

901 See above, [231].

902 See above, [225].

903 See above, [244].

904 If Savigny had been alive and writing today, how would he express his principle? Would he identify any community of

principle is imperfect, that individual lawmakers must determine the extent to which foreign law is applicable within the limits of their own constitutional ordering and that it can, even if engaged, be overridden by local rules[905].

255. The most significant difference lies in the authors' conception of the function of their co-ordinating principle. For Story, comity serves the interests of justice by promoting the effectiveness of laws and judgments beyond the territory of a nation exercising sovereign authority – it softens what he considers to be a fundamental principle arising from the equality of the sovereignty of independent nations that every nation may judge for itself what force and obligation to accord to the laws of other nations[906]. Savigny's equality principle serves the interests of justice in a different way by ensuring that individuals, whether natives or foreigners, can expect the same decision wherever a dispute is adjudicated[907]. Although natural equality is central in both accounts, Story's comity tempers its application to relations between independent nations[908], whereas Savigny's principle promotes its application in relations between individuals[909].

---

nations outside those who have close ties of co-operation (most obviously, the Member States of the European Union)? What, if anything, would supplant Christian morality?

905 See above, [225] and [224].

906 See above, [224]-[226].

907 See above, [244] and [250]. Story was not blind to this concern (see Story, *Commentaries* (1834), [5], p. 6 ("unless some uniform rules are adopted . . . the grossest inequalities will arise in the administration of justice between the subjects of the different countries"); Banu, *Nineteenth-Century Perspectives* (n. 655), p. 40).

908 See above, [225].

909 See above, [244]-[245].

F. The contours of State practice

256. Foelix's comparative survey, published in 1843[910], shows that by the middle of the nineteenth century, the law on this subject was developing rapidly, through legislation, case law and international treaties.

257. Foelix's own views on the subject closely resemble those of Story[911]. The authority of *res judicata* draws its force from the civil law of the adjudicating nation, but that civil law cannot communicate its effects from one nation to another. Accordingly, in principle, judgments lose their civil force at the frontier. However, relations of good friendship *(comitas)* and considerations of utility and mutual convenience *(ob reciprocam utiliatem)* have resulted in the admission of numerous exceptions to this principle[912]. This rationale leads Foelix to support a requirement of reciprocity, in addition to the three conditions laid down by Martens[913].

258. In a survey focused almost exclusively on the practice of European nations[914], Foelix subdivided the legal orders studied into three groups. First, the nations (in Foelix's view, a majority of those surveyed[915]) giving effect to foreign judgments on a reciprocal basis without any review of the merits[916]. Austria and the States of the German Federation were among those following this approach. Second, those not giving effect to foreign

---

910 Section III.E.6 *(a)*.

911 For an account of dealings between the two, see n. 794.

912 Foelix, *De l'Effet ou de l'exécution des jugements* (n. 643), [196], pp. 4-5.

913 *Ibid.*, [202], pp. 10-11. See above, [199].

914 He deals briefly with the law of Haiti, Foelix, *De l'Effet ou de l'exécution des jugements*, above, [326], p. 147 and the United States, *ibid.* [335], pp. 157-158.

915 *Ibid.*, p. 11, noting the errata following p. 181. Foelix lists within this group the members of the German Confederation, Swiss cantons (excluding Geneva), the Papal States, Sardinia, Denmark and Schleswig-Holstein.

916 Révision du fond de la contestation, *ibid.*, [200], p. 9.

judgments, absent a treaty, without undertaking such a review, consisting of France and the nations who followed her legislative approach[917], including the Kingdom of the Netherlands, and a handful of others – Sweden and Norway, Russia, Spain and Portugal[918]. Third, the common law jurisdictions, England and the United States, which had adopted an intermediate position[919].

259. For present purposes, taking Foelix's survey as the point of departure and setting international treaties to one side[920], let us take as a (hopefully, representative) sample the laws of Austria, Germany, France, the Netherlands, Sweden, Great Britain and the United States, and Italy. Although not comprehensive, this selection allows us to contrast the different models for judgment enforcement which evolved at this time, and which have generally speaking been carried forward, with modifications, into the modern law[921].

---

917 Foelix lists Belgium, the Kingdom of the two Sicilies, the Netherlands, Tuscany, the Canton of Geneva, Greece and Haiti.

918 Foelix, *De l'Effet ou de l'exécution des jugements* (n. 643), [202], pp. 11-12, noting the errata following p. 181. Foelix lists Sweden, Norway, Russia, Spain and Portugal. As to the later development of Russian law, see *Hilton* v. *Guyot* (n. 599), 221-222.

919 *Ibid.*, p. 12.

920 Section III.G.

921 For a detailed comparative account in the early part of the nineteenth century, see Ernest G. Lorenzen, "The Enforcement of American Judgments Abroad" (1919) 29 *Yale LJ* 188 (1st part) and (1920) 29 *Yale LJ* 268 (2nd part), with translated extracts and summaries of the law of more than fifty countries (2nd part, 283-302). See Section III.F.8. For a survey of almost thirty jurisdictions carried out towards the end of that century, see Dennis Campbell (ed.), *Enforcement of Foreign Judgments*, London: LLP Limited, 1997. See, recently, Standing International Forum of Commercial Courts, *Multilateral Memorandum on Enforcement of Commercial Judgments for Money*, 2nd ed., 2021, containing thirty-three reports with a

1. Reciprocity (I) – Austria

260. At the beginning of the nineteenth century, Austian legislation[922] had imposed four conditions for the execution of a foreign judgment – (1) uncontested reciprocity in the adjudicating order's treatment of judgments rendered in favour of Austrian subjects, (2) competence of the foreign court under its own law, (3) observance of legal process requirements of the adjudicating order and (4) the judgment's status as *res judicata*[923]. The first and second requirements were to be attested by a superior court of the adjudicating order[924]. The request for execution must come from the judgment creditor[925]. Similar requirements continue to apply under Austrian law today[926].

2. Reciprocity (II) – Germany

261. Following unification in 1871, Germany took a similar approach in its new Civil Procedure Law (Zivilprozessordnung)[927]. The Law expressly provided that decision to grant enforcement of a foreign judgment must be issued without examining the legality of the decision[928]. Following earlier Prussian prac-

---

broad geographical distribution, https://sifocc.org/sifocc_documents/sifocc-memorandum-on-enforcement-2nd-with-international-working-group-commentary/.

922 Decrees of 18 May 1792, 18 January 1799 and 15 February 1805.

923 Foelix, *De l'Effet ou de l'exécution des jugements* (n. 643), [206], pp. 16-17.

924 *Ibid.*

925 *Ibid.*, pp. 17-18.

926 Exekutionsordnung (EO), Part 4, esp. ss. 406-408. As to reciprocity, see n. 1066.

927 Zivilprozessordnung (1877), ss. 660-662, https://deutschestextarchiv.de/book/show/unknown_civilprozessordnung_1877.

928 *Ibid.*, s. 661.

tice[929], the conditions for enforcement included a requirement that reciprocity be guaranteed[930]. These core elements have been carried over into the rules currently applied by German courts[931].

---

929 Arthur Lenhoff, "Reciprocity and the Law of Foreign Judgments: A Historical-Critical Analysis" (1956), 3 *Louisiana L Rev* 465, 480, suggesting that a majority favoured retaining the requirement in order to uphold the honor and dignity of the new German nation.

930 Zivilprozessordnung (ZPO) (1877), s. 661 (5). The first four grounds for opposing enforcement were that (1) the judgment lacks the status of *res judicata* or the force of law, (2) the judgment requires performance of an act that cannot be enforced under German law, (3) the foreign court has no jurisdiction under German law and (4) in the case of default judgments against a German debtor, the summons had not been served in person or with the assistance of German authorities.
This provision was followed by Japan in adopting its own Code of Civil Procedure in 1890, see Takao Sawaki, "Recognition and Enforcement of Foreign Judgments in Japan" (1989), 23 *International Lawyer* 29. Modern Japanese law retains a reciprocity requirement, Code of Civil Procedure (Act No. 109 of 26 June 1996), Article 118. When the ZPO was revised in 1898, ss. 660-662 were replaced by ss. 328 and 722-723. For a translation of these provisions in their original form, see Lorenzen, "Enforcement" (n. 921), 2nd part, 289.

931 ZPO (5 December 2005), ss. 328 and ss. 722-723, https://www.gesetze-im-internet.de/zpo/index.html, with English translation at https://www.gesetze-im-internet.de/englisch_zpo/englisch_zpo.html.
The latter provision, in its current form (adopted in 1986), contains the prohibition on reviewing the legality of a judgment and the requirement of finality. In addition to the reciprocity requirement (s. 328 (5)), the other grounds for opposing recognition and enforcement are that (1) the foreign court has no jurisdiction under German law, (2) a defendant who has not entered an appearance was not served with the document instituting the proceedings properly or in sufficient time to defend, (3) the judgment is irreconcileable with local or an earlier, recognised foreign judgment, (4) recognition would be manifestly

3. *Substantive review (I) – France*

262. Foelix disagreed strongly with the dominant opinion in France in the middle of the eighteenth century that foreign judgments lacked the status of *res judicata* and that French courts must enquire as to the merits[932]. The dispute centred on the interaction of four legislative provisions, the earliest of which dated back to 1629[933]. In Foelix's view, these provisions mandated a substantive review only when the interests of a French subject were at stake, and otherwise precluded the effectiveness of a foreign judgment contrary to the sovereignty of the French nation, to public law or public morality[934]. However, in 1819, the Cour de Cassation had held in the case of *Holker* v. *Parker* that a substantive review *(révision au fond)* was necessary in every case[935]. As Foelix notes,

---

incompatible with fundamental principles of German law, including fundamental rights. Under s. 328 (2) ZPO, the reciprocity requirement does not apply to a judgment upon a non-pecuniary claim if no German court had jurisdiction. See Dieter Martiny, "Recognition and Enforcement of Foreign Money Judgments in the Federal Republic of Germany" (1987) 35 *Am J Comp L* 721.

932 Foelix makes his view clear in the first paragraph of his detailed account of French law, arguing that this opinion is opposed to the literal meaning of the relevant legislative positions and finds its basis neither in commentary on those laws nor "in the sound appreciation of the relations that exist between the various nations", Foelix, *De l'Effet ou de l'exécution des jugements* (n. 643). [281], p. 84.

933 Ordinance of 15 January 1629 (Code Michaud), Article 121; Code civil (1804), Articles 2123, 2128; Code de procédure civile (1806), Article 546. The text of these laws is given by Foelix, *ibid.*, [281], pp. 84-85 and [283], pp. 88-89.

934 Foelix, *De l'Effet ou de l'exécution des jugements* (n. 643), [285]-[286], pp. 90-103.

935 *Ibid.*, [287], pp. 104-105, with reference to Cour de Cassation (Civil Chamber), 19 April 1819, Sirey Jurisprudence, I.28, https://www.doctrine.fr/d/CASS/1819/DE18 19041901, *Holker* v. *Parker*. For the background, see Kurt H. Nadelmann, "Non-Recognition of Amercan Money

this distinctive French position had led to measures of retorsion by other nations, which had refused to enforce French judgments to the detriment of French subjects[936].

263. Although controversial, this approach prevailed in France until the second half of the twentieth century[937]. The Cour de Cassation then moved away from its former position, holding that it was not within the supervisory power of a French judge asked to authorise execution to enquire into the merits of the decision, provided that the following requirements were satisfied – (1) the foreign tribunal had adjudicatory jurisdiction[938], (2) the foreign court had complied with its procedural rules, (3) the foreign court had applied the law designated by French conflict rules, (4) the judgment was compatible with *ordre public international*, consisting of "the principles of universal justice considered in French opinion to have absolute international value"[939], and (5)

Judgments Abroad and What to Do About It" (1957), 42 *Iowa L Rev* 236, 242-243; also *Hilton* v. *Guyot* (n. 599), 215-217.

Foelix is critical of the reasoning, *ibid.*, pp. 106-108. He relies on a decision of the Royal Court of Paris, 13 May 1820, supporting his own view, *ibid.*, [290], pp. 110-111.

936 Foelix, *De l'Effet ou de l'exécution des jugements* (n. 643), [293], p. 113. In his analysis of the Austrian law, Foelix had already referred to a legislative decree, passed in 1809, denying effect to French judgments for this reason, *ibid.*, [206], pp. 17-18. See also *Hilton* v. *Guyot*, above, 224.

937 James C. Regan, "The Enforcement of Foreign Judgments in France under the *Nouveau Code de Procédure Civil*" (1981), 4 *Boston College Int & Comp L Rev* 149, 159-160.

938 An autonomous, objective standard is applied (n. 1258).

939 Cour de Cassation (Civil Chamber), 25 May 1948 *(Lautour)* [1949] *Rev Crit DIP* 89 ("les principes de justice universelle

the absence of any fraud[940]. The second[941] and third[942] of these requirements have since been retired[943] and the requirements held to apply to judgments against French subjects and foreigners alike[944].

---

considérés dans l'opinion française comme dotés de valeur international absolue").

940 Cour de Cassation (1st Civil Chamber), 7 January 1964 *(Munzer)*, [1964] JCP II No. 13590, Jurisprudence, (https://www.legifrance.gouv.fr/juri/id/JURITEXT000006963473. See Kurt H. Nadelmann, "French Courts Recognize Foreign Money-Judgments: One Down and More to Go" (1964), 13 *Am J Comp L* 72.
This decision had been foreshadowed by an earlier decision of the Cour d'Appel de Paris (1st Chamber), 21 October 1955 *(Charr)*, [1956] *Recueils Dalloz et Sirey*, Jurisprudence 61. See Kurt H. Nadelmann, "Recognition of Money Judgments in France" (1956), 5 *Am J Comp L* 248.
Note that the concept of "fraud" refers in this connection to fraudulent evasion of the law *(fraude à la loi)* rather than fraudulent conduct in the foreign proceedings, which would be a matter to be addressed by reference to public policy, Gilles Cuniberti, "The Liberalization of the French Law of Foreign Judgments" (2007), 56 *ICLQ* 931, 937.

941 Cour de Cassation (1st Civil Chamber 1), 4 October 1967 *(Bashir)*, [1968] *Rev Crit DIP* 98; [1969] Clunet 102, https://www.legifrance.gouv.fr/juri/id/JURITEXT000006976566, holding that the foreign procedure could be reviewed only on the grounds of infringement of international public policy and respect for the rights of the defence.

942 Cour de Cassation (1st Civil Chamber), 20 February 2007 *(Cornelissen)*, [2007], *Recueil Dalloz* 1115, https://www.legifrance.gouv.fr/juri/id/JURITEXT000017636147/.

943 Cour de Cassation (1st Civil Chamber), 6 February 1985 *(Simitch)*, [1985] *Rev Crit DIP* 369; [1985] *Clunet* 460, https://www.legifrance.gouv.fr/juri/id/JURITEXT000007015413.

944 Cour de Cassation (1st Civil Chamber 1), 23 May 2006 *(Prieur)*, [2006] *Rev Crit DIP* 871; [2006] *Clunet* 1365, https://www.legifrance.gouv.fr/juri/id/JURITEXT000007052608/. For a summary of recent case law, see Cuniberti, "Liberalisation" (n. 940).

4. Substantive review (II) – Kingdom of the Netherlands

264. Prior to the imposition of French law in 1811[945], Dutch courts had applied the principle of reciprocity[946]. In 1838, the new Code of Civil Procedure (partly inspired by French law[947]) prohibited the execution of foreign jugments in the Kingdom, save where expressly authorised by law, and provided for the relitigation of disputes before the Dutch courts[948]. Although this provision explicitly referred only to execution, not recognition, and may originally have been designed to protect defendants sued otherwise than in their home court, it came to be viewed as being of more general application in excluding the possibility of according to foreign judgments the formal status of *res judicata*[949].

265. The Hoge Raad nonetheless managed to navigate around this obstacle in the twentieth century by recognising that Dutch courts remain free to assess the authority to be attributed to a foreign judgment and that they may conclude having regard to all the circumstances of the case that it would be contrary to "principles of good faith, equity and equality"[950] if a party were allowed to

945 Text to n. 792.
946 Van de Velden, *Finality* (n. 791), pp. 264-266.
947 Specifically, the Code Michaud (n. 933).
948 Wetboek van Burgerlijke Rechtsvordering (1838), Article 431 (see Foelix, *De l'Effet ou de l'exécution des jugements*, (n. 643), [328], pp. 148-149; Hans Smit, "International *Res Judicata* in the Netherlands: A Comparative Analysis" (1966) 11 *Buffalo L Rev* 165, 168; van de Velden, *Finality* (n. 791), pp. 273-276.
The provision dealing with foreign judgments has the same number (Art. 431) in the amended version of the Code in force today (https://wetten.overheid.nl/BWBR0001827/2024-07-01).
949 Smit (n. 948), esp. 168-169, 171-172, 195-196; van de Velden, *Finality* (n. 791), pp. 277-281, noting the influence in this debate of the jurist Äăron Adolf de Pinto.
950 Goede trouw, billijkheid en rechtsgelijkheid.

relitigate a case after losing[951]. This approach has since been extended to cases where the judgment is relied upon by a judgment creditor, giving rise to what has been described as a "disguised *exequatur*"[952]. The matter remains, however, one in which the court must exercise its evaluative judgment[953].

5. *Evidentiary function – Sweden*

266. Foelix noted that foreign judgments did not have the status of *res judicata* in Sweden, requiring a successful party wishing to secure enforcement against assets in that country to relitigate the matter. In reaching a decision based on the evidence before it, the Swedish court would, however, take into consideration the presentation of facts and the reasons given in the judgment[954]. That remains the position today, except in cases where legislation provides for recognition or enforcement[955].

---

[951] Hoge Raad, 14 November 1924, NJ 1925, 91 *(Bontmantel)*. For more detailed accounts, see Smit (n. 948), 196-207; van de Velden, *Finality* (n. 791), pp. 285-293, 299-306, 349-355.

[952] Hoge Raad, 13 December 1993, NJ 1994, 348 *(Esmil/Enka)*; Hoge Raad [2024] ECLI:NL:HR:2014:2838 *(Gazprombank)*.
In the *Gazprombank* decision, the court laid down the following criteria for reception – (1) that the jurisdiction of the foreign court is generally acceptable according to international standards, (2) the judgment resulted from a procedure that meets the requirements of due process, (3) recognition is not inconsistent with Dutch public order and (4) the absence of any inconsistent decision of a Dutch court or prior decision of a foreign court that is amenable to recognition in the Netherlands.
See also van de Velden, *Finality* (n. 791), pp. 303-306.

[953] Mathijs ten Wolde, "Netherlands", in *Encyclopedia of Private International Law* (n. 300), Vol. 3, at p. 2368.

[954] Foelix, *De l'Effet ou de l'exécution des jugements*, (n. 643), [332], pp. 159-160.

[955] Michael Hellner, "Sweden", in *Encyclopedia of Private International Law* (n. 300), Vol. 3, at p. 2546.

267. In assessing evidential weight to be given to the judgment, Swedish courts take full account of the relevant circumstances. In some instances, the overall effect is tantamount to giving the judgment an effect equivalent to *res judicata*. This is the case, in particular, if no Swedish court would have jurisdiction to determine the underlying claim, for example, because the parties have chosen a foreign court as the exclusive venue for dispute resolution[956].

6. *The common law method – Great Britain and the United States*

268. As noted[957], the position reached in Great Britain and the United States by the middle of the nineteenth century was that a final judgment of a court of competent jurisdiction was not conclusive in enforcement proceedings[958]. A judgment awarding a sum

---

[956] Michael Bogdan, "The Recognition in Sweden of Money Judgments in Civil and Commercial Matters" (1985), 54 *Nordisk Tidsskrift Int'l Ret* 85.

[957] Sections III.D.1 and III.E.2.

[958] There was less certainty as to the reviewability of a foreign judgment when it was relied on defensively for its preclusive effects. Some judges and commentators expressed the view that the judgment was conclusive in these circumstances (see text to nn. 608, 771-772). However, the basis for drawing such a distinction between the two uses was fragile (above, [228]), and the point had never been fully argued and determined in England outside the admiralty context (n. 608). The judicial perception that it was necessary to draw a distinction was, no doubt, fuelled by the belief – later dispelled (below, [269]-[271]) – that the merits of a foreign judgment could be examined *de novo* in enforcement proceedings.
Westlake expressed the opinion that the justice of the judgment could be impeached to the same extent upon its recognition in England as on its enforcement, Westlake, *Treatise* (n. 704), [393], p. 376, and this seems to accord with Story's view and with the approach in *Ricardo* v. *Garcias* (1845) Clark & Finnelly 368. See also *Ostell* v. *Le*

of money could be relied on as a ground of action, being considered *prima facie* to give rise to an obligation to pay, but the justice of the decision could be impeached[959]. The live question, on which authority was divided, was whether this enabled the enforcing court to review the judgment on the ground of a mistake of fact or of law in the reasoning[960].

269. This doubt, as we have seen, had arisen because of a misunderstanding as to the sense in which Lord Mansfield had conceived of a foreign judgment as constituting "*prima facie* evidence of a debt"[961]. Both the English and United States courts had been edging towards the view expressed by Story that the original justice of the judgment could be impeached only in certain circumstances and that a mere mistake (except perhaps one appearing clearly on the record) would not suffice[962].

Page (1852) 2 *De Gex Macnaghten & Gordon* 892; *Rankin* v. *Goddard* (1866) 54 Maine 28. Compare the US cases referred to in *MacDonald* v. *Grand Trunk Ry Co* (n. 772).

959 (England) *Walker* v. *Witter* (n. 603); *Ricardo* v. *Garcias*, above. (Scotland) *Sinclair* v. *Fraser* (n. 598); *Southgate* v. *Montgomerie* (1837) 15 S 507. (United States) *Bissell* v. *Briggs* (n. 615); *Taylor* v. *Briden* (n. 615); Story, *Commentaries* (1834), [608], p. 508. See Foelix, *De l'Effet ou de l'exécution des jugements*, (n. 643), [355], pp. 155-158.

960 Text to nn. 600, and 614-615.

961 See above, [187]; also Westlake, *Treatise* (n. 704), [385], pp. 371-372.

962 (England) *Bank of Australasia* v. *Nias* (1851) 16 QB 717, 735-737 (Lord Campbell CJ); *De Cosse Brissac* v. *Rathbone* (1861) 6 Hurlstone and Norman 301.
(Scotland) *Gladstone* v. *Lindsay* (1868) 6 SLR 71, 73 (Lord Kinloch).
(United States) *Jordan* v. *Robinson* (1838) 15 Maine Reports 167, 168 (Weston CJ); *Silver Lake Bank* v. *Harding* (1832) 5 Ohio 545; *Anderson* v. *Anderson* (1837) 8 Ohio 108 *Cummings* v. *Banks* (1848) 2 Barbour (Sup Ct) 601, 604 (Edmonds J); *Lazier* v. *Westcott* (1862) 26 NY 146; *Rankin* v. *Goddard* (1866) 54 Maine Reports 28, 33 (Appleton

270. The point was settled in England by the judgment of the Court of Queen's Bench in *Godard* v. *Gray*[963] and in the United States by the decision of the Supreme Court in *Hilton* v. *Guyot*[964]. The answer given was the same in both places, but the reasoning was starkly different[965].

271. In *Godard*, Blackburn J *quickly* dispelled the confusion that had arisen following *Walker* v. *Witter*, concluding that the foreign judgment "was considered, not as merely *prima facie* evidence of that cause of action for which the judgment was given, but as in itself giving rise, at least *prima facie*, to a legal obligation to obey that judgment and pay the sum adjudged"[966]. An error of fact

CJ); also *Christmas* v. *Russell* (1866) 72 US 290, 304 (Clifford J); *McMullan* v. *Ritchie* (1890) 41 Fed Rep 502, 504 (Ricks J), affd (1895) 159 US 235; *Dunstan* v. *Higgins* (1893) 138 NY 70. Cf. *Burnham* v. *Webster* (1845) 2 Ware 236, 239, 241 (Ware J) and (1846) 1 Woodbury & Minot 172, 175-178 (Woodbury J), but note the narrow interpretation of that decision in *Hilton* v. *Guyot* (n. 59), 191-193, 194.

963 (1870) 6 QB 139; also *Schibsby* v. *Westenholz* (1870) 6 QB 155.
See Joshua Folkhard and Ian Bergson, "*Godard* v. *Gray* and *Schibsby* v. *Westenholz*", Chap. 4, in William Day and Louise Merrett (eds.), *Landmark Cases in Private International Law*, Oxford: Hart Publishing, 2023.

964 (n. 599); also *Ritchie* v. *McMullan* (1895) 159 US 235.
See further *Johnston* v. *Compagnie Générale Transatlantique* (1926) 242 NY 331. A valuable summary of the case law on this point, in the United States, England and Canada, is provided in the annotation to the report of that case in (1927) 46 ALR 435, 439-566.

965 To borrow Robert Frost's metaphor, this is a case of two diverging roads, with the English courts taking one and United States courts the other, Robert Frost, "The Road Not Taken", in *Mountain Interval*, New York: Henry Holt & Co, 1916, p. 9.

966 *Godard* (n. 963), 150. As the learned judge pointed out *(ibid.)*, this conclusion was supported by a number of recent decisions.

or law, even if appearing on the record[967], did not provide a defence.

272. Unfortunately, in developing this reasoning to address the specific argument that an error of English law had a special status and could be used to impeach a foreign judgment[968], Blackburn J suggested that the proposition that the English courts give effect to a legal obligation arising from the foreign judgment had nothing to do with the notion that foreign judgments are enforced "out of politeness and courtesy to the tribunals of other countries"[969]. Although he did not use the word "comity" in *Godard*, he did use it, with a similarly dismissive air, in *Schibsby* v. *Westenholz*, decided on the same day and on the same theory[970]. He distinguished the principle

---

[967] *Ibid.*, 151.

[968] In *Scott* v. *Pilkington* (1862) 2 Best and Smith 11, 41-42, Cockburn CJ left open the question whether a judgment could be reviewed if the record showed an error of law, disregard of the comity of nations in refusing to apply English law or an erroneous view of English law; in *Simpson* v. *Fogo* (1863) 1 Hemming & Miller 195, 247, Page Wood VC suggested that a foreign judgment *in rem* may be examined, and disregarded, if on its face it appears to have been founded on a perverse disregard of English law in a case properly subject to that law by the comity of nations. See also the cases referred to in *Hilton* v. *Guyot* (n. 599), 197-198, concluding that, in England, a foreign judgment may be impeached for "a manifest and wilful disregard of the law of England".
It is doubtful whether this qualification, if it ever existed, survives today – see Dicey, *Digest* (n. 729), p. 408; *Carl Zeiss Stiftung* v. *Rayner & Keeler Ltd.* [1967] 1 AC 853, 922 (Lord Reid), 928 (Lord Hodson), 978 (Lord Wilberforce); *Air Foyle Ltd.* v. *Center Capital Ltd.* [2002] EWHC 2535, [2004] ILPr 280, [36] (Gross J); *Dicey, Morris & Collins* (n. 5), p. 772, fn. 462 ("only historical interest").

[969] *Ibid.*, 152.

[970] *Schibsby* raised, additionally, a question of adjudicatory jurisdiction. This aspect of the decision will be considered in the following chapter (Sec. IV.D).

"loosely called 'comity'" from the principle that he favoured, the so-called "doctrine of obligation"[971].

273. Doubly unfortunately, in the following passage, Blackburn J rejected a link to principles of natural justice, denying that the opinion of Lord Ellenborough in *Buchanan* v. *Rucker*[972] had been founded on these considerations.

274. These two decisions had the effect of severing the principle that the Court had identified as supporting the enforcement of foreign judgments, the existence of a legal obligation to comply, from both comity and natural justice[973]. This left the supposed principle lacking in principle. Foreign judgments are undoubtedly capable of imposing legal obligations, as constitutive effects, but this does not explain why some but not all of them impose legal obligations that courts in England are willing to recognise and enforce[974]. As the English courts undoubtedly act under a different sovereign authority to that of their foreign counterparts[975], what is the reason, or set of reasons, why in some cases (but not in others) the English court is willing to acknowledge that the foreign court had the authority to bind the parties and is prepared to take steps to secure the effectiveness of its orders?

275. The English courts have not given a convincing answer to this question since 1870[976]. In the first edition

---

[971] *Schibsby* (n. 963), 159. See, more recently, *Adams* v. *Cape Industries* (n. 604), 552-553. Cf. *Agbaje* v. *Agbaje* [2010] UKSC 13, [2010] 1 AC 628, [54] (Lord Collins of Mapesbury: "comity . . . is said to be the basis for the enforcement and recognition of foreign judgments").

[972] Text to n. 668; also below, [330].

[973] Compare the references above, [205].

[974] See *Merck Sharp & Dohme* v. *Merck KGaA* [2021] SGCA 14, [30].

[975] *Gage* v. *Bulkeley* (text to n. 567).

[976] See, for example, *Nouvion* v. *Freeman* (1887) 37 Ch D 244, 256 (Lindley LJ); *Adams* v. *Cape Industries* (n. 504), 518-519, 552-555; *Lucasfilm Ltd.* v. *Ainsworth* [2009] EWCA

of his *Digest on the Conflict of Laws*, published in 1896[977], Albert Venn Dicey (1835-1922)[978] – not by any means an enthusiastic supporter of comity[979] – suggested that[980]:

> "The rights acquired under a foreign judgment stand, in short, in the same position as other rights *duly acquired* under foreign law, and are *entitled to recognition* to, at any rate, the same extent as other rights duly acquired under the law of any civilised country."

Civ 1328, [2010] Ch 503, [191], revd. in part without considering this issue [2011] UKSC 39, [2012] 1 AC 208. In *Rubin* v. *Eurofinance SA* [2012] UKSC 46, [2013] 1 AC 236, [9], Lord Collins of Mapesbury appeared to distance himself from the doctrine of obligation, describing it as "a purely theoretical and historical basis for the enforcement of foreign judgments at common law" which "makes no practical difference to the analysis".
Compare Adrian Briggs, "Recognition of Foreign Judgments: A Matter of Obligation"(2013), 129 *Law Quarterly Review* 87 and *Private International Law in English Courts*, Oxford: Oxford University Press, 2nd ed., 2023, pp. 323-325, applying choice of law reasoning to support the doctrine of obligation; Dickinson, "*Schibsby* v. *Westenholz*" (n. 216) and *Foreign Submission* (n. 197), favouring an approach centred on principles of natural justice.

977 Dicey, *Digest* (n. 729).

978 Lord Collins of Mapesbury, "Dicey, Albert Venn", in *Encyclopedia of Private International Law* (n. 300), Vol. 1, pp. 529-531.

979 Dicey, *Digest* (n. 729), pp. 10-11. Dicey seems to concede, nonetheless, that comity is among "the motives which have led judges or legislators to adopt a particular rule as law", *ibid.*, p. 10.

980 *Ibid.*, p. 413 (emphasis added), referring to the first of his General Principles, *ibid.*, p. 22: "Any right which has been duly acquired under the law of any civilised country is recognised and, in general, enforced by English Courts, and no right which has not been duly acquired is enforced or, in general, recognised by English Courts".

276. The reference to rights having been "duly acquired" raises, in this context, questions as to the legitimacy of exercises of adjudicatory jurisdiction, addressed in the next chapter[981]. At this point in the enquiry, it is of interest to consider Dicey's views as to the considerations that warranted the conclusion that foreign laws, and judgments, are "entitled to recognition" at all. He asserted that this was a matter of logical and practical necessity[982], "the necessary result of the peaceful existence of independent nations combined with the prevalence of commercial intercourse"[983] and essential in order to secure justice for natives and foreigners alike[984]. Dicey considered the principle to be self-evident, decribing it as a maxim or the statement of a fact[985], and universally recognised[986], approving a statement by the then Lord Chancellor, Lord Halsbury, that "[t]he recognition of rights acquired under foreign laws is a leading principle of modern civilisation"[987]. In spirit, if not in method[988], Dicey's approach aligns closely with that of Savigny, whom he had praised as "a man of genius"[989].

277. When first adopted by English judges in the eighteenth century, the deduction that a foreign money judgment gave rise to an enforceable obligation was

---

981 Section IV.D.

982 Dicey, *Digest* (n. 729), pp. 9-10.

983 *Ibid.*, p. 8.

984 *Ibid.*, p. 9.

985 *Ibid.*, p. 23. Among the examples given by Dicey are that of enforcement of a judgment given by the French courts in favour of the victim of a tort committed by a German in Paris.

986 *Ibid.*, p. 23.

987 *Ibid.*, p. 24, referring to *Re Missouri Steamchip Co* (1882) 42 Ch D 321, 335.

988 Dicey, *Digest* above, pp. 15-22, contrasting the "theoretical method" (associated with Savigny) with the "positive method".

989 *Ibid.*, p. 17.

a convenient prop. It offered a partial answer to the constitutional conundrum facing Lord Hardwicke and his successors and addressed the more practical question as to what form the action upon a judgment should take[990].

278. What the judges in *Godard* and *Schibsby* failed to recognise[991], however, was that the doctrine of obligation was itself rooted in ideas of natural justice. To sustain this thesis, there is no need to look beyond *Russell* v. *Smyth*, the first of two cases relied on by Blackburn J to support the existence of a legal obligation to comply with a foreign judgment, and the only one of the two that actually dealt with a claim of that kind[992]. Parke B, on whose dictum the court in *Schibsby* relied[993], expressed his agreement with Lord Abinger, the Chief Baron, that

---

990 Text to nn. 565-566.
Another, odd legacy of the old common law forms of action is the restriction of the entitlement to bring a direct right of action to judgments for a fixed or ascertainable sum of money, *Sadler* v. *Robins* (1808) 1 *Campbell* 253; *Lindsey* v. *Conteh* [2024] ZASCA 13, *Dicey, Morris & Collins* (n. 5), [14R-024] and [14-026]. This is of limited practical significance, as recognition of the *res judicata* status of the matters determined by the foreign court may still provide the basis for the grant of local relief, *Pattni* v. *Ali* [2006] UKPC 51, [2007] 2 AC 85, [27]; *Dicey, Morris & Collins*, above, [14R-024], fn. 95; Hook and Wass, *The Conflict of Laws in New Zealand* (n. 504), [5.190]-[5.194]; Yeo Tiong Min, "The Changing Global Landscape for Foreign Judgments", Yong Pung How Professorship of Law Lecture 2021, https://site.smu.edu.sg/sites/site.smu.edu.sg/files/smu_cebcla/YPH%20Lecture%202021%20Paper.pdf, [66]-[69].
This restriction has been overturned in Canada, *Pro Swing Inc.* v. *Elta Golf Inc.* (n. 8), the Cayman Islands, *Miller* v. *Gianne* [2007] CILR 18 and Jersey, *Brunei Investment Agency* v. *Fidelis Nominees Ltd.* [2008] Jersey LR 337.

991 Or, if they recognised it, failed to account for.

992 *Russell* v. *Smyth* (1842), 9 *Meeson & Welsby* 810. The other case, *Williams* v. *Jones* (1845), 13 *Meeson & Welsby* 628 concerned the judgment of a county court in Wales.

993 *Schibsby* (n. 963), 159.

such an action would lie. Lord Abinger, for his own part, had stated that an action of assumpsit or debt lay for the sum awarded by a court having jurisdiction and that the process and decree must be assumed to have been perfectly regular[994]. He continued[995]:

> "The action may be sustained on the ground of morality and justice. The maxim of the English law is to amplify its remedies and, without usurping jurisdiction, to apply its rules to the advancement of substantial justice. Foreign judgments are enforced in these Courts, because the parties liable are bound in duty to satisfy them."

Both the reasoning, that the English court should apply its remedies to the advancement of substantial justice, and the terminology ("of morality and justice"), reveal a natural law influence[996]. That impression is amplified by Lord Abinger's supporting citation of the judgment of Lord Mansfield in *Robinson* v. *Bland*[997], the decision that introduced Huber's comity to English law[998].

279. In *Hilton* v. *Guyot*, and its companion case *Ritchie* v. *McMullen*[999], the US Supreme Court reached the same general conclusion on the question of substantive review, by a completely different route, and with a significant qualification. The Court subscribed

---

994 *Russell* v. *Smyth* (n. 992), 817,

995 *Ibid.*, 818.

996 Compare the references above, [205]. See also, in different contexts, *Alderson* v. *Temple* (1768) 4 *Burrow* 2235, 2239 (Lord Mansfield); *Howard* v. *Castle* (1796) 6 *Term Rep* 642, 644 (Lord Kenyon); *Wilson* v. *Moore* (1834) 1 *Mylne & Keen* 337, 350-351 (Lord Brougham).
Note also Joseph Story's later formulation of his comity principle in terms of a "moral necessity to do justice" (above, [235]).

997 *Russell* v. *Smyth* (n. 992), 818.

998 See above, [180].

999 (n. 964).

to the view that the effect of the laws of one nation within the dominion of another depended "upon what the greatest jurists have been content to call 'the comity of nations'"[1000]. In a famous and often repeated phrase, they accurately described comity as "neither a matter of absolute obligation, on the one hand, nor of mere courtesy on the other", and as consisting of "the recognition which one nation allows within its territory to the legislative, executive and judicial acts of another nation, having due regard both to international duty and convenience, and to the rights of its own citizens or of other persons who are under the protection of its laws"[1001]. Story's influence here is evident[1002].

280. The Supreme Court turned to consider the effect of foreign judgments *in personam*[1003], focusing on the case of a judgment against a foreigner in proceedings brought by a local citizen or resident of a particular country[1004]. It carried out an extensive review of the English and American authorities regarding the effectiveness of foreign judgments[1005], as well as the

---

1000 *Hilton* v. *Guyot* (n. 599), 163, adding that "[a]lthough the phrase has been often criticised, no satisfactory substitute has been suggested".

1001 *Ibid.*, 163-164. See Cuniberti, "Le fondement" (n. 305), [143]-[168].

1002 *Hilton* v. *Guyot* (n. 599), 164-165, with reference also to the opinion of Taney CJ, in *Bank of Augusta* v. *Earle* (n. 764) and to the writing of Wheaton and Kent.

1003 As to judgments *in rem*, judgments regarding status, other similar judgments and decrees in admiralty proceedings, see *Hilton* v. *Guyot*, above, 167-170.

1004 As to judgments in proceedings between citizens or in favour of a foreigner, see *ibid.*, 170. This led to the supposition that the Court's ruling on the question of reciprocity did not extend to such proceedings in any event (see "Reciprocity and the Recognition of Foreign Judgments" (note) (1927), 36 *Yale LJ* 542, 546-547; Willis L. M. Reese, "The Status in This Country of Judgments Rendered Abroad" (1950, *Columbia Law Review* 783, 791-792).

1005 *Hilton* v. *Guyot* (n. 599), 171-188, 191-193, 194-197.

commentaries of James Kent and Joseph Story[1006]. It then rejected the doctrine of obligation favoured by the English courts, describing it as a remnant of the "ancient fiction" of the "original contract"[1007]. This theory, in the Court's view, was "hardly a sufficient guide at the present day in dealing with questions of international law, public or private, and of the comity of our own country, and of foreign nations"[1008]. Instead, "following the lead of Kent and Story", the Court concluded that the merits of the case should not be retried if the following conditions were met[1009]:

> ". . . there has been opportunity for a full and fair trial abroad before a court of competent jurisdiction, conducting the trial upon regular proceedings, after due citation or voluntary appearance of the defendant and under a system of jurisprudence likely to secure an impartial administration of justice between the citizens of its own country and those of other countries, and there is nothing to show either prejudice in the court or in the system of laws under which it was sitting, or fraud in procuring the judgment, or any other special reason why the comity of this nation should not allow it full effect . . .".

281. A few pages later, the Court reformulated this as a statement of the requirements for a judgment to represent "*prima facie* evidence, at least, of the truth of the matter adjudged; . . . conclusive upon the merits tried in the foreign court, unless some special ground is shown for impeaching the judgment"[1010]. Although it

---

1006 *Ibid.*, 188-191, 193-194, with specific reference to Kent, *Commentaries*, Vol. 2 (n. 615), [120] (6th ed.) and to Story, *Commentaries* (1834) and *Commentaries* (1841), [606]-[608], [618].

1007 *Hilton* v. *Guyot*, above, 201. See Section II.I.2.

1008 *Hilton* v. *Guyot*, above, 201.

1009 *Ibid.*, 202-203.

1010 *Ibid.*, 205-206.

would have been better to avoid the phrase "*prima facie* evidence" that had caused so much difficulty, it was an accurate restatement of the rule established more than a century earlier by the British House of Lords in *Sinclair* v. *Fraser*[1011].

282. A (bare[1012]) majority of the Court nonetheless concluded that the French judgment before it should not be enforced due to a want of reciprocity by France in its treatment of judgments of courts of the United States and other countries[1013]. The Court cited Joseph Story's support for this "very reasonable rule"[1014], concluding that, as he predicted, it had "worked itself firmly into the structure of international jurisprudence"[1015]. This conclusion, the Court emphasised, was not based on "any theory of retaliation upon one person by reason of injustice done to another", but instead[1016] "on the broad ground that international law is founded upon mutuality and reciprocity", "by the principles of international law

---

1011 See above, [183]-[188], [229], [268]-[270]. Unfortunately, the Court blotted its copybook in using a similar formula to describe the effect of a French judgment, which it did not consider to be conclusive on the merits, *Hilton* (n. 599), 228; see below, [282].

1012 5 to 4, Gray J., with whom Field, Brown, Shiras and White J. J. agreed; Fuller C. J. (dissenting), with whom Harlan, Brewer and Jackson J. J. agreed.

1013 *Hilton* v. *Guyot* (n. 599), 210. The same objection did not apply to the judgment of the Canadian court at issue in *Ritchie* v. *McMullen* (n. 964), which was held to be conclusive.

1014 *Hilton* v. *Guyot* (n. 599), referring also to the work of the English barrister, Jabez Henry, on whom Story had relied for the proposition (long since falsified) that the Dutch courts observed reciprocity (above, [229]-[230]), as well as to supportive judicial statements, in England and the United States, *Hilton*, above, 212-214 and to more recent academic writing, *ibid.*, 214-215.

1015 *Hilton*, above, 227.

1016 *Ibid.*, 228.

recognised in most civilized nations, and by the comity of our own country"[1017].

283. The Chief Justice, Melville Fuller, dissented from this conclusion. In his view, the doctrine of *res judicata*, as applied to domestic judgments, should apply also to foreign judgments, "on the same general ground of public policy that there should be an end to litigation"[1018]. This was, he thought, a doctrine of local, not international, law[1019]. Rights acquired under foreign judgments are private rights acquired under foreign laws, and such rights should be given effect under the law of the United States[1020]. Although comity may have been the original source of this rule, "it prevails today by its own strength"[1021]. No requirement of reciprocity should be imposed, as "[t]he application of the doctrine of *res judicata* does not rest in discretion; and it is for the government, and not for its courts, to adopt the principle of retortion", if necessary[1022].

284. The Supreme Court's decision on the reciprocity issue was not generally well received in the United States or elsewhere in the common law world[1023]. The decision was not binding on the courts or legislatures of

1017 *Ibid.*, 228.
1018 *Ibid.*, 229.
1019 *Ibid.*
1020 *Ibid.*
1021 *Ibid.*, 233.
1022 *Ibid.*, 234.
1023 An anonymous note in a respected English law journal called for its swift reversal (1896), 12 *Law Quarterly Review* 302, 303. The journal's editor, Sir Frederick Pollock, Professor of Jurisprudence at the University of Oxford, was a colleague and friend of Dicey and the note adopts Dicey's acquired rights theory (above, [275]-[276]).
See also Louisa B. Childs, "Shaky Foundations: Criticism of Reciprocity and the Distinction between Public and Private International Law" (2006), 38 *Journal of International Law and Politics* 221, 252-253.

the individual States[1024], and this constitutional limitation has resulted in a patchwork of rules throughout the United States[1025]. When, in 1962, the Commissioners on Uniform State Laws approved model legislation in the form of the Uniform Foreign-Money Judgments Act, a deliberate decision was taken to omit any requirement of reciprocity[1026]. Indeed, one of the purposes of this initiative had been to resolve difficulties in the recognition and enforcement of United States' judgments that have been attributed to the decision in *Hilton*[1027]. Nevertheless, ten of the forty States that have adopted legislation on the basis of either this law, or the updated version adopted by

---

1024 As to the early practice of courts exercising federal jurisiction, see Donald J. Zadeck, "Enforcement of Judgments *in Personam*: Reciprocity" (1950), 10 *Louisiana L Rev* 319, 321-323.

1025 The courts of New York refused to impose a reciprocity requirement in *Johnston* v. *Compagnie Générale Transatlantique* (n. 964) and in *Cowens* v. *Ticongeroga Pulp and Paper Co* (1927) 219 NY Supp 284. See also *Coulbourn* v. *Joseph* (1943) 195 Ga 723 (Sup Ct Georgia). The Californian legislature rejected the rule in its Code of Civil Procedure, s. 1915, as amended (1907). A survey of State practice in 1962 added Conneticut, Georgia, Illinois, Louisiana and Puerto Rico to the list of dissenting voices (Ehrenzweig, *Treatise* (n. 777), p. 165).
Further doubts were case on the precedential status of *Hilton* v. *Guyot* following the decision of the US Supreme Court in *Erie Railroad* v. *Tomkins* (1938) 304 US 364 to the effect that, in ruling on matters of substance, a federal court must apply the law of the State in which it sits, absent a controlling federal law. See Reese, "Status" (n. 1004), 786-788, 790; American Law Institute, *Recognition and Enforcement of Foreign Judgments: Analysis and Proposed Federal Statute* (reporters: Andreas Lowenfeld and Linda Silberman) (Philadelphia: American Law Institute, 2006), pp. 2-3.

1026 *Bank of Montreal* v. *Kough* (1980) 612 F 2d 467, 471-472.

1027 "The Uniform Money-Judgments Recognition Act" (note) (1955), 64 *Michigan L Rev* 305, 306.

the Commissioners in 2005 [1028], added a provision either authorising or requiring their courts to deny recognition on the ground of a want of reciprocity [1029]. More recently, the American Law Institute included a reciprocity requirement within its proposal for a federal statute [1030].

285. Although courts in other common law systems did not follow the lead of the United States' Supreme Court on reciprocity [1031], legislation adopted in the United Kingdom in 1933 to facilitate the conclusion of bilateral treaties contains a provision allowing an executive order to restrict the enforcement of judgments in circumstances where the Crown is satified that the treatment by a foreign country of United Kingdom judgments is "substantially less favourable" than that accorded by United Kingdom courts to courts of that country [1032]. This formula has been widely adopted in other parts of the Commonwealth [1033],

---

1028 Uniform Foreign-Country Money Judgments Recognition Act (2005), which also contains no reciprocity provision (National Conference of Commissioners on Uniform State Laws, *Uniform Foreign-Country Money Judgments Recognition Act 2005* (2005), Prefatory Note, p. 1).

1029 American Law Institute, *Recognition and Enforcement* (n. 1025), p. 100.

1030 *Ibid.*, pp. 92-105 (para. 7).

1031 Note, however, that the point was left open by the Singaporean Court of Appeal in *Merck Sharp & Dohme Corp* v. *Merck KGaA* (n. 945), [39]; see Yeo, "The Changing Global Landscape" (n. 990), [43]-[50] and below, [401]-[402]. Cf. text to n. 557.

1032 Foreign Judgments (Reciprocal Enforcement) Act 1933 (UK), s. 9.

1033 See e.g. Reciprocal Enforcement of Judgments Act 1934 (New Zealand), s. 10; Reciprocal Enforcement of Foreign Judgments Act 1935 (Tanzania), s. 11; Foreign Judgments (Reciprocal Enforcement) Law 1935 (Cyprus), s. 11; Foreign Judgments (Reciprocal Enforcement) Act 1935 (Fiji), s. 11; Foreign Judgments (Reciprocal Enforcement) Act 1937 (Zambia), s. 12; Reciprocal Enforcement of Judgments Act 1958 (Malaysia), s. 9; Reciprocal Enforcement of Foreign Judgments Act 1959 (Singapore), s. 12; Foreign Judgments (Reciprocal Enforcement) Act 1960 (Nigeria), s. 12;

but there is no evidence that the power to make such an order has ever been exercised in any of these legal orders[1034].

7. Reciprocity free reception – Italy

286. Under the Civil Code and Code of Civil Procedure of the unified Italian State, adopted in 1865, foreign judgments were received under conditions more favourable than those operating elsewhere in Europe. Judgments meeting certain conditions, concerning adjudicatory jurisdiction, compliance with procedural

---

Foreign Judgments (Reciprocal Enforcement) (Jersey) Law 1960, s. 10; Foreign Judgments (Reciprocal Enforcement) Ordinance 1960, (Hong Kong), s. 11; Foreign Judgments (Reciprocal Enforcement) Act 1961 (Mauritius), s. 12; Foreign Judgments (Reciprocal Enforcement) Ordinance 1961 (St Helena), s. 11; Foreign Judgments (Reciprocal Enforcement) Act 1961 (Seychelles), s. 12; Judgments (Reciprocal Enforcement) (Isle of Man) Act 1968, s. 8; Foreign Judgments (Reciprocal Enforcement) Act 1969 (St Kitts and Nevis), s. 11; Foreign Judgments (Reciprocal Enforcement) Act 1973 (Nauru), s. 10; Reciprocal Enforcement of Judgments Act 1976 (Papua New Guinea), s. 9; Reciprocal Enforcement of Judgments Act 1988 (Tonga), s. 10; Judgments (International Enforcement) Act 1981 (Botswana), s. 11; Foreign Judgments Act 1991 (Australia), s. 13; Courts Act 1993 (Ghana), s. 87; Foreign Judgments Reciprocal Enforcement Law 1996 (Cayman Islands), s. 10; Enforcement of Foreign Judgments Act (St Lucia), s. 11; Foreign and Commonwealth Judgments (Reciprocal Enforcement) Act, Laws of Barbados, cap. 201; s. 17; Reciprocal Enforcement of Foreign Judgments Act (revised 2000) (Brunei), s. 10; Foreign Judgments (Reciprocal Enforcement) Act (revised 2000) (Uganda), s. 10; Reciprocal Enforcement of Judgments Act (Belize), s. 17. No similar provision is to be found in the legislation adopted by Canadian provinces, which followed a different model.

1034 Based on information currently available. In particular, no order has been made under the legislation in force in Australia or the United Kingdom.

requirements and compatibility with Italian public policy[1035], were recognised without formality and enforced following a request by a party or the adjudicating court. No condition of reciprocity was imposed.

Legislative decrees adopted after the First World War imposed significant restrictions upon the free reception of judgments in Italy[1036]. These were not fully relaxed until 1995[1037].

8. *Emerging patterns*

287. At the end of the First World War, the naturalised American, Ernest Lorenzen, conducted a broader survey of State practice, drawing material from over fifty legal orders across five continents[1038]. He was not encouraged, concluding that there are "no principles which have so far met with anything like universal approval"[1039]. He suggested that the lack of uniformity "arises from a deep-

---

1035 Codice Civile (1865), Preliminary Part, Articles 10 and 11; Codice Di Procedura Civile (1865), Title XII (Arts. 941-950). The four matters to be investigated (Codice Di Procedura Civile, Art. 941) were the competence of the adjudicating court, the due summoning of the parties, that they were lawfully represented or held in contempt, compatibility of the judgment with Italian public policy and internal public law.

1036 Gian Paolo Romano, "Italian Rules on Adjudicatory Jurisdiction and Enforcement of Foreign Judgments" (2005), *Annales de la Faculté de droit d'Istanbul* 405, 423-431. See esp. Article 941 of the Codice di Procedura Civile, as amended by the Decree of 30 July 1919, allowing a review of the merits in a range of circumstances, Lorenzen, "Enforcement" (n. 921) (2nd part), 292-293.

1037 Law No. 218, 31 May 1995 (Riforma del sistema italiano di diritto internazionale privato), Title IV, esp. Article 64.

1038 Africa was represented in the survey only by South Africa, and Asia by India and Japan. Although there was no representative from Oceania, many of its legal orders had inherited the English common law.

1039 Lorenzen, "Enforcement" (n. 921) (1st part), 188.

rooted distrust in the administration of justice in other countries, and the fear arising therefrom that irreparable injury may be done to an individual"[1040].

288. Lorenzen classified legal orders both according to the enforcement procedure adopted[1041] and the general attitude towards enforcement. Under the latter heading, he put to one side those legal orders that would not enforce a foreign judgment absent a treaty or convention[1042]. As to the rest, his principal division was between legal orders that imposed a reciprocity requirement and those that did not. The former group formed the majority of those surveyed[1043]. Within the latter group, Lorenzen identified three distinct approaches, which he labelled by reference to their most prominent early proponents, the "Italian system", "French system" and "English system". The first was characterised by its liberal approach to recognition and enforcement[1044], the second by its practice of

---

1040 *Ibid.*

1041 Contrasting the "Anglo-American" approach (followed also in Denmark) of requiring an action on the judgment, with the "Continental" approach of requiring a local act of authorisation *(exequatur)*, *ibid.*, 192-193.

1042 *Ibid.*, 193-194 (Finland, Haiti, the Netherlands, Japan, Russia, Santo Domingo, Serbia, certain Swiss cantons, Sweden, Norway). Additionally, he noted (*ibid.*, 193) that Turkey would not enforce judgments against Turkish subjects.

1043 *Ibid.*, 199-200 (Argentina, Austria, Bosnia-Herzegovina, Bulgaria, Chile, Columbia, Croatia and Slavonia, Cuba, Egypt, Guatemala, Honduras, Hungary, Liechtenstein, Mexico, Monaco, Montenegro, Panama, Paraguay, Peru, Romania, the Baltic States, Spain, certain Swiss cantons, Uruguay, Venezuela).

1044 *Ibid.*, 194-196, noting the post-war restrictions on this approach in Italy (text to n. 1036). Lorenzen placed the following legal orders within this group – Brazil, Portugal, San Marino, certain Swiss cantons and Costa Rica. Greece also applied a liberal policy in proceedings without a Greek party, Lorenzen, "Enforcement" (n. 921) (2nd part), 291.

examining the merits of the foreign decision[1045]: and the third by its intermediate position of not examining the merits while scrutinising the justice of the decision[1046].

289. Lorenzen's survey nonetheless confirmed that there were common elements in the now substantial body of comparative law. The judgment must be final and capable of immediate execution where it was rendered[1047]. The receiving order must be satisfied that the judgment was rendered by a court of competent jurisdiction[1048]. The summons must have been regularly served[1049]. A judgment will not be enforced if it conflicts with the fundamental rules or policies of the receiving order[1050]. Many legal orders imposed additional protections in the case of judgments entered in default of appearance[1051]. A significant number applied rules favouring their own nationals or persons locally resident[1052]. There remained, of course, significant differences of detail, not least on the question whether jurisdictional and procedural requirements were governed by the law of the adjudicating order or the receiving order or a combination of the two[1053].

290. The principal controversies at this time related to the questions of substantive review and reciprocity.

1045 Lorenzen, "Enforcement", above (1st part), 196-198 (France, Belgium, Luxembourg, certain Swiss cantons). Greece applied this approach in proceedings with a Greek party, *ibid.*, 2nd part, 291 and Quebec allowed defences to be relitigated, *ibid.*, 290.

1046 *Ibid.*, 1st part, 198-199 (England; Canada, excluding Quebec; India; South Africa).

1047 *Ibid.*, 2nd part, 268-269.

1048 *Ibid.*, 269-276.

1049 *Ibid.*, 276-277.

1050 *Ibid.*, 279-280.

1051 *Ibid.*, 281.

1052 See the materials, *ibid.*, 283-302 for Argentina, Bosnia Herzegovina, Germany, Greece, Hungary, Italy, Peru, Portugal, Turkey.

1053 *Ibid.*, 269-276. See Section IV.D.

Other nations have since followed France[1054] in moving away from substantive review[1055]. In legal orders willing to recognise foreign judgments, *révision au fond* is becoming an endangered species[1056].

291. By contrast, notwithstanding its detractors[1057], the requirement of reciprocity has endured and has gained arguably its most significant patronage in the People's Republic of China[1058]. Until recently, China

---

1054 See above, [263].

1055 E.g. Belgium: Loi portant le Code de droit international privé, 27 July 2004, Article 25 (2); Luxembourg: Nouveau Code de procédure civile, as amended by the Law of 27 June 2018, Article 1112; Switzerland: Federal Act on Private International Law, 18 December 1987, Article 27 (3).

1056 As to the position in Asia, see Adeline Chong, "Moving Towards Harmonistation in the Recognition and Enforcement of Foreign Judgment Rules in Asia" (2020), 16 *J Priv Int L* 31, 45-46.

1057 A great deal of ink has been spilt on the topic. For generally critical accounts, see von Bar, *Theorie und Praxis* (n. 3), Vol. 2, [415], pp. 420-423 and [455]-[456], pp. 506-513, Gillespie, *Theory and Practice* (n. 3), pp. 900-901, 974-979; "Reciprocity and the Recognition of Foreign Judgments" (note) (n. 1004), 547-549; Joseph Beale, *A Treatise on the Conflict of Laws*, New York: Baker, Voorhis & Co, 1935, Vol. 2, pp. 1381-1389; Lenhoff, "Reciprocity" (n. 929); Michael Martinek, "The Principle of Reciprocity in the Recognition and Enforcement of Foreign Judgments – History, Presence and . . . No Future" (2017), *Journal of South African Law* 36; Béligh Elbalti, "Reciprocity and the Recognition and Enforcement of Foreign Judgments: A Lot of Bark but Not Much Bite" (2017), 13 *J Priv Int L* 184; Anatol Dutta, "Reciprocity", in *Encyclopedia of Private International Law* (n. 300), Vol. 2, pp. 1465-1471.
For more receptive appraisals of the reciprocity requirement, see Childs, "Shaky Foundations" (n. 300); John Coyle, "Rethinking Judgments Reciprocity" (2014), 92 *North Carolina Law Review* 1110, 1119-1125; Cuniberti, "Le fondement" (n. 300), [173]-[235], pp. 201-233.
See Section V.B.5.

1058 The Singaporean Court of Appeal has also recently made overtures in this direction (n. 1031). As to the (varying)

had recognised and enforced judgments only on the basis of a formal treaty relationship[1059], even though its Civil Procedure Law explicitly authorised recognition and enforcement on the principle of reciprocity, absent a treaty[1060]. As early as 1996, the Supreme People's Court had been open to the possibility of reciprocity being established as a matter of fact by reason of the actual practice of foreign States in recognising foreign judgments[1061]. Chinese courts did not act on this principle until much later[1062]. In 2022, the Court signalled its willingness to support a policy of *de jure* reciprocity, requiring neither a treaty nor a judicial precedent concerning the enforcement of Chinese judg-

---

practice elsewhere in Asia, see Chong, "Moving Towards Harmonistation" (n. 1056), 53-57. In Europe, recent codifications have seen a move away from the reciprocity requirement, Tanja Domej, "Recognition and Enforcement of Judgments (Civil Law)", in *Encyclopedia of Private International Law* (n. 300), Vol. 2, p. 1476; also Elbalti, "Reciprocity" (n. 1057), 187-188.

1059 On the grounds for contesting recognition and enforcement under Chinese law, see below, [348].

1060 Civil Procedure Law of the People's Republic of China, adopted 9 April 1991, Article 266. Civil Procedure Law, as amended by the Standing Committee of the China People's Conference, 1 September 2003, Article 298. See Wenliang Zhang, *Recognition and Enforcement of Foreign Judgments in China: Rules, Practice and Strategies*, Alphen aan den Rijn: Kluwer Law International, 2014.

1061 Jeanne Huang, "Developing Chinese Private International Law for Transnational Civil and Commercial Litigation" (2023), 70 *Netherlands Int L Rev* 205, 226, referring to *Gomi Akira* v. *Dalian Fari Seafood Ltd.* (1996) 1 *SPC Gazette* 29; also William S. Dodge and Wenliang Zhang, "Reciprocity in China – US Judgments Recognition" (2020), 53 *Vanderbilt J Transnational L* 1541, 1551-1553.

1062 Jeanne Huang, "Developing Chinese Private International Law for Foreign Judgments: A Substitute or a Preliminary Step to Ratify the Two HCCH Conventions?" (2024), 57 *The International Lawyer* 101, 104.

ments[1063]. In the absence of a formal commitment, the requirement may be satisfied in an individual case by evidence of the law in force in a foreign country or a consensus or understanding between the two nations falling short of a treaty[1064]. The Supreme People's Court exercises oversight through a review mechanism[1065].

292. As this brief account of Chinese law shows, the reciprocity requirement can take many forms, ranging in stringency from formal (treaty) reciprocity[1066] to a factual enquiry as to whether a particular legal order has enforced or is receptive to the enforcement of judgments

---

1063 Huang, "Developing Chinese Private International Law for Transnational Civil and Commercial Litigation" (n. 1061), 226, referring to the Minutes of the National Court's Symposium on Foreign-Related Commercial and Maritime Trials, 24 January 2022.

1064 *Ibid.*, 227-229.
In 2017, representatives of the participating States at the 2nd China-ASEAN Justice forum, held in Nanning, declared that, in the case of mutual recognition of foreign civil or commercial judgments, the existence of reciprocity between their legal orders may be presumed absent contrary practice. For the text of the Nanning Declaration, 8 June 2017, see https://cicc.court.gov.cn/html/1/219/208/209/800.html, [7].

1065 Huang, "Developing Chinese Private International Law for Transnational Civil and Commercial Litigation" (n. 1061), 229.

1066 This remains the position, for example, in Austria (Exekutionsordnung (EO), s. 406; Decree of 8 September 2020 on international legal assistance and other legal relations with foreign countries in civil matters (RHEZiv 2020), s 41; also Helmut Heiss, "Austria", in *Encyclopedia of Private International Law* (n. 300), at p. 1393). See also Chong, "Moving Towards Harmonisation" (n. 1056), 54 (Lao PRD, Cambodia); Cuniberti, "Le fondement" (n. 305), [179], pp. 203-204 (Liechtenstein). Although the Civil Procedural Code of the Russian Federation appears to demand a treaty commitment, this requirement has been softened, Elbalti, "Reciprocity" (n. 1057), 197-199).

of the courts of the nation imposing the requirement[1067]. More complex forms exist. In Germany, for example, the courts investigate whether the adjudicating order recognises German judgments of the relevant class on terms that as a whole are "essentially equivalent or less stringent" than the German rules[1068]. Elsewhere, particularly in the Arab world, reciprocity does not operate as a bar but promotes equal treatment by ensuring that the conditions for reception of a judgment are no less stringent than the adjudicating order would apply to a judgment of the receiving order[1069]. In some legal orders, the rule applies only to judgments granted against nationals of the receiving order[1070]. The burden of proving reciprocity varies, with a rebuttable presumption operating in some legal orders[1071].

G. *Formal co-operation: In search of perfection*

293. The end of the nineteenth century also saw burgeoning international collaboration in this field, seeking to overcome impediments to the effectiveness of judgments and ensure reciprocity through binding treaty commitments.

1067 See the Chinese practice, discussed above, [291]; Cuniberti, above, [180]-[193], pp. 204-212.

1068 Martiny (n. 931), 750-751. A similar approach is taken in Japan and South Korea (see Chong, "Moving Towards Harmonisation" (n. 1056), 54; Elbalti, "Reciprocity" (n. 1057), 192-194; Cuniberti, above, [200]-[207], pp. [204]-[207]).

1069 Elbalti, above, 186, fn. 9 (Egypt, Yemen, Bahrain, United Arab Emirates, Qatar, Kuwait, Mauritania, Libya, Syria and Palestine); Cuniberti, above, [197]-[199], pp. 214-215.

1070 Elbalti, above, 189, fn. 33; Cuniberti, above, [211]-[212], pp. 219-220 (Czech Republic).

1071 Elbalti, above, 189, fn. 35 and 200, fn. 89 (Croatia, Serbia, Slovenia, Ukraine); also Chong, "Moving Towards Harmonisation" (n. 1056), 55; Nanning Declaration (2017) (n. 1064).

294. A few treaties concluded before 1800 had contained provisions dealing with foreign judgments[1072]. During the nineteenth century, bilateral treaties began to be concluded specifically for this purpose. Although many of these were between the thirty-nine members of the German Confederation[1073], the nations concluding such treaties before the end of the century extended across the European continent and into South America[1074]. The common law nations stood aloof. The United Kingdom did not conclude such a treaty until

---

1072 Foelix refers, for example, to treaties between France-Sardinia* (1760) and between France-Switzerland (1778), Foelix, *De l'Effet ou de l'exécution des jugements* (n. 643), [282], pp. 87-88. [*extended to Italy by declaration (1860)]. See also Ralf Michaels, "Recognition and Enforcement of Judgments", in *Max Planck Encyclopedia of Public International Law* (n. 476), [9], referring to a treaty concluded in 1715 between France and certain Swiss cantons.

1073 For further information, see Foelix, above, [206]-[252], pp. 216-261.

1074 France-Switzerland (1828); Austria-Sardinia* (1841) (authentication); Baden-France (1846); Sardinia*-Spain (1851); Denmark-Sweden/Norway (1861); France-Swiss Confederation (1869); Austria/Hungary-Moldavia/Wallachia (1871); Argentine Republic-Italy (1887); Germany-Serbia (1892); Spain-Switzerland (1896); Belgium-France (1899) [sources: Oxford Historical Treaties (https://opil-ouplaw-com.ezproxy-prd.bodleian.ox.ac.uk/home/OHT) and Lorenzen, "Enforcement" (n. 921) (first part), 194, fn. 33] [* extended to Italy].

Provisions concerning foreign judgments were also included within the following consular treaties: Austria/Hungary-Serbia (1881), Italy-Romania (1881) [source: *Actes de la Conférence de la Haye chargée de réglementer diverses matières de droit international privé* (12-27 September 1893) (La Haye, Imprimerie Nationale, 1893), Part 2)].

For later treaty practice, see below, [299].

1934[1075]. In civil matters, the United States has yet do so[1076].

295. The century also saw the first efforts at multilateral co-operation. Early examples of provisions dealing with the enforcement of foreign judgments are to be found in the Rhine navigation conventions concluded in 1830 and 1868[1077]. A notable early example is the Convention on International Civil Procedure concluded by the members of the Congress of South American Private International Law in Montevideo in 1889, which provides for the cross-border reception of judgments[1078] between State parties subject to conditions concerning international jurisdiction, the enforceability or *res judicata* status of the judgment, procedural matters and public policy[1079].

1075 United Kingdom-France (1934); United Kingdom-Belgium (1934).

1076 A draft bilateral treaty with the United Kingdom was signed in 1976 but never concluded (Draft Convention between the United Kingdom and the United States for the Reciprocal Recognition and Enforcement of Judgments in Civil Matters, Cmnd 6771 (1977), 16 *International Legal Materials* 71). The United States is a signatory to the Hague Convention on Choice of Court Agreements (2005) and the Hague Convention on the Recognition and Enforcement of Judgments in Civil and Commercial Matters (2019) but has yet to ratify either (below, [302]).
See also Kurt H. Nadelmann, "The United States of America and Agreements on Reciprocal Enforcement of Judgments" (1953), 1 *Neth Int L Rev* 156.

1077 Ralf Michaels, "Recognition and Enforcement of Judgments" (n. 1072), [14].

1078 The provision applies also to arbitral awards.

1079 Tratado de Derecho Procesal Internacional (Montevideo, 11 November 1889), Article 5. The Convention, ratified by Argentina, Bolivia, Colombia, Paraguay, Peru and Uruguay, was revised in 1940. Brazil is also a party to the revised convention. An earlier convention on conflict of laws issues, concluded in Lima in 1878, did not enter into force. See Alejandro M. Garro, "Unification and Harmonization of Private Law in Latin America" (1992), 40 *Am J Comp L* 587, 589-591.

296. As this example shows, the development of common rules among nations with different traditions could more easily be achieved through institutional efforts. In 1874, the Government of the Netherlands proposed to hold a conference on the enforcement of foreign judgments, inviting governments in Europe as well as the United States to send representatives. Although this initiative did not fly[1080], it was the first of many emanating from the Low Countries, in particular through the individual efforts of Tobias Asser (1836-1913). The Dutchman had been one of the founding members of the Institut de Droit International, which had held its first meeting in Ghent in 1873[1081]. He had long argued that closer international co-operation in the field was essential, advocating the conclusion of treaties supplementing rules on mutual recognition and enforcement with provisions addressing questions of adjudicatory jurisdiction as well as minimum procedural standards[1082]. He carried these ideas forward into his

[1080] Arthur Eyffinger, *TMC Asser – Founder of the Hague Tradition* (The Hague: TMC Asser Press, 2011), pp. 27-28; Gaert de Baere and Alex Mills, "TMC Asser and Public and Private International Law: The Life and Legacy of a Practical Legal Statesman" (2011), 42 *Neth Yb Int L* 3, 20-21.
For the response of the United States' Government, see Kurt J. Nadelmann, "Ignored State Interests: The Federal Government and International Efforts to Unify Rules of Private Law" (1954), 102 *Univ Pennsylvania L Rev* 323, 323-324.

[1081] Eyffinger, *Founder of the Hague Tradition*, above, pp. 24-27.
For Asser's career and achievements, see in addition to the works referred to above (n. 1080), "Tobias Asser – Biographical (Nobel Peace Prize, 1911)", https://www.nobelprize.org/prizes/peace/1911/asser/biographical/.

[1082] Tobias Asser, "De l'effet ou de l'exécution des jugements rendus a l'étranger en matière civile et commercial" (1869), 1 *Revue de droit international et de législation comparée* 82 (Part 1), 408 (Part 2) and 473 (Part 3); de Baere and Mills (n. 1080), 12-13.

role as rapporteur when the Institut considered the topic, culminating in a resolution adopted at its meeting in Paris in 1878[1083]. The text involved a compromise between Asser's strongly held internationalist approach and the decentralised model favoured by Edouard Clunet[1084]. Nevertheless, Asser was able to secure a recommendation that national laws and conventions include uniform rules on adjudicatory jurisdiction as well as minimum guarantees regarding procedural standards[1085].

297. Foreign judgments also found a place in the early work programme of the International Law Association, founded in 1873[1086], in Brussels, as the Association for the Reform and Codification of the Law of Nations. The Association's first resolution on the subject was at its 11th Conference held in Milan (1883)[1087]. Asser's

---

1083 Institut de Droit International "Exécution des jugements" (Resolution), Paris, 5 September 1878.

1084 *Ibid.*, Article 1. See Eyffinger, *Founder of the Hague Tradition* (n. 1080), p. 29.

1085 Institut de Droit International "Exécution des jugements" (n. 1083), Article 2.
In Article 5, Asser was able to include a specific provision governing imprisonment for debt, a topic on which he had written extensively, Arthur Eyffinger, *TMC Asser – In Quest of Liberty, Justice and Peace*, The Hague: Brill Nijhofff, 2019, Vol. 1, [16.3], pp. 485-496. The topic was addressed in early conventions of the Hague Conference (see the Conventions relating to civil procedure, concluded on 14 November 1896 (Art. 17) and 17 July 1905 (Art. 24)).
For later resolutions, see Institut de Droit International, "Vœu en vue d'éviter les conflits en matière de procédure" (Resolution), Geneva, 5 September 1874, [3]; "Autorité et exécution des jugements étrangers" (Resolution), Vienna, 25 August 1924.

1086 As to Asser's links to the Association, see de Baere and Mills (n. 1080), 19-20; Eyffinger, *Founder of the Hague Tradition* (n. 1080), pp. 23-24.

1087 For the diplomatic efforts that followed that resolution, see Nadelmann, "Ignored State Interests" (n. 1080), 327-329. A diplomatic conference planned for Rome in 1885 did

next effort to strengthen international ties was to have a much wider and enduring impact. Using his influence as an advisor to the Dutch Government, he revived the earlier plan for an international conference to discuss private international law issues. On this occasion, the plan bore fruit and representatives of thirteen European nations met under Asser's Presidency in The Hague from 12 to 27 September 1893[1088]. Work continued at later conferences held in 1894[1089], 1900[1090] and 1904[1091]. Before Asser's death, in 1913, shortly before the Great War, his contributions to international relations had been recognised by the award of the Nobel Peace Prize in

not take place due to an outbreak of cholera in the city. The subsequent resignation of Pasquale Mancini as Italy's Minister of Foreign Affairs brought an end to the initiative. See the Report of the Foreign Judgments and Evidence Committee, presented to the Association's 33rd Conference held in Stockholm (1924), which summarises its subsequent work. On that occasion, delegates discussed Proposed Rules for the Enforcement of Foreign Judgments, rejecting any requirement of reciprocity, International Law Association, *Report of the Thirty-Third Conference*, London: Sweet & Maxwell, 1925, pp. 146-151.

At its 49th Conference held in Hamburg (1960), the Association adopted a Model Act respecting the recognition of foreign money judgments. See Kurt H. Nadelmann, "Hamburg Model Act Respecting the Recognition of Foreign Money Judgments" (1960), 9 *Am J Comp L* 518.

1088 Germany, Austria-Hungary, Belgium, Denmark, Spain, France, Italy, Luxembourg, the Netherlands, Portugal, Romania, Russia and Switzerland were represented on that occasion, *Actes de la Conférence de la Haye* (n. 1074), Part 1, pp. 19-21. Great Britain and Sweden-Norway declined the invitation. See Eyffinger, *Founder of the Hague Tradition* (n. 1080), pp. 35-38.

1089 On this occasion, Sweden-Norway also participated. See Eyffinger, above, pp. 39-40.

1090 *Ibid.*, pp. 41-42.

1091 *Ibid.*, pp. 42-43, without the particpation of Denmark but with Japan.

1911[1092]. The Nobel Foundation has described him as the "Hugo Grotius of his time"[1093].

298. The topic of foreign judgments did not appear on the agenda of the Hague Conference until its fifth session in 1925[1094]. On this occasion, twenty-two nations were represented including, for the first time, Great Britain[1095]. Although some delegations, led by Italy and Japan, had been willing to consider a multilateral treaty, the more cautious preference of the majority was to develop a model bilateral convention, based on existing practice and containing core provisions that could be supplemented and modified by negotiation[1096].

1092 Presentation Speech by Jørgen Gunnarsson Løvland, Chairman of the Nobel Committee, 10 December 1911 (https://www.nobelprize.org/prizes/peace/1911/ceremony-speech/).
Asser's role in the Hague Peace Conferences of 1899 and 1907 is described by Eyffinger, *ibid.*, Chaps. 7 and 11.

1093 https://www.nobelprize.org/prizes/peace/1911/asser/speedread/.

1094 Conférence de la Haye de Droit International Privé, *Actes de la Cinquième Session tenue du 12 Octobre au 7 Novembre 1925*, La Haye: Imprimerie Nationale, 1926, pp. 95-193, 332.

1095 Denmark resumed its participation. Austria and Hungary, as well as Sweden and Norway, were separately represented. Other newcomers included Estonia, Serbia-Croatia-Slovenia and Czechoslovakia.

1096 Report prepared by the members of the drafting committee, M. V. Merz, Switzerland; J. Kosters, Netherlands; M. A. C. De Sousa Santos Bandeira, Portugal, *Actes de la Cinquième Session* (n. 1094), pp. 182-192.
In 1928, the text was amended to remove reference to arbitration awards and additional provisions were added to enable the Convention to be formally adopted (see Conférence de la Haye de Droit International Privé, *Actes de la Sixième Session tenue du 5 au 28 Janvier 1928* (La Haye: Imprimerie Nationale, 1928), pp. 389-394, considering also a proposal by the Japanese delegation to modify the condition relating to default judgments (Art. 1 (4)).

Tobias Asser would have been displeased not only at this timidity but also at the decision to make no positive provision for questions of adjudicatory jurisdicition[1097]. The text adopted[1098] set out four pre-conditions to an obligation to recognise and execute judgments from other Contracting States – (1) that the rules of international judicial jurisdiction adopted by the adjudicating State are not excluded by the receiving State, (2) that recognition is not contrary to public policy or principles of public law of the receiving State, (3) that the judgment has the status of *res judicata* and (4) for default judgments, that the defendant has been declared in default according to the laws of the adjudicating State or treaties between the adjudicating States and receiving States[1099].

299. Whether this instrument was directly implicated or not[1100], the following period saw a rapidly growing number of bilateral foreign judgments conventions, extending beyond the States that had participated in the Hague Conference[1101]. A second significant burst of

---

1097 *Actes de la Cinquième Session,* above, pp. 183, 186-188.

1098 *Ibid.*, pp. 193, 332.

1099 Projet d'une Convention relative à la reconnaissance et l'exécution de décisions judiciaires, Article 1 (also Arts. 2-3 regarding the conditions and procedures for requests for execution).
See Georges Droz and Adair Dyer, "The Hague Conference and the Main Issues of Private International Law for the Eighties" (1981), 3 *Northwestern J Int L and Business* 155, 176-178.

1100 See Droz and Dyer, above, pp. 178-179. The United Kingdom's approach to the negotiation of bilateral agreements was the product of *ad hoc* diplomacy rather than negotiations based on the text of any previous international instrument (see the Report of the Foreign Judgments (Reciprocal Enforcement) Committee, December 1932 (Cmd 4213), [14]-[17], pp. 14-17).

1101 E.g. [1926-1945] Italy-Turkey (1926); Czechoslovakia-Switzerland (1926); Czechoslovakia-Portugal (1927); Ger-

activity occurred, after the Second World War, between the late 1950s and early 1970s[1102]. More significantly, in this period of around half a century, several multilateral conventions were concluded at a regional level. The

many-Switzerland (1929); Egypt-Palestine (1929); France-Italy (1930); Austria-Turkey (1930); Italy-Switzerland (1933); France-United Kingdom (1934); Belgium-United Kingdom (1935); Switzerland-Sweden (1936); Germany-Italy (1936); also Belgium-Netherlands (1925) [sources: League of Nations Treaty Series; Council of Europe, *The Practical Guide to the Recognition and Enforcement of Foreign Judicial Decisions in Civil and Commercial Law* (Strasbourg: Council of Europe, 1975), pp. 186-187].

1102 E.g. [1955-1975] Austria-Belgium (1957) (maintenance); France-Morocco (1957); Belgium-Germany (1958); Italy-Netherlands (1959); Austria-Germany (1959); Austria-Belgium (1959); Belgium-Switzerland (1959); Greece-Yugoslavia (1969); Germany-United Kingdom (1960); Austria-Switzerland (1960); Austria-Yugoslavia (1960); Austria-Yugoslavia (1961) (alimony); Norway-United Kingdom (1961); Austria-United Kingdom (1961); Greece-Germany (1961); Belgium-Italy (1962); Germany-Netherlands (1962); Austria-Netherlands (1964); Italy-United Kingdom (1964); Austria-France (1966); Austria-Israel (1966); Netherlands-UK (1967); Liechtenstein-Switzerland (1968); France-Spain (1969); Germany-Tunisia (1969); Israel-United Kingdom (1970); Italy-Lebanon (1970); Austria-Italy (1971); Austria-Luxembourg (1971); France-Yugoslavia (1971); Austria-Liechtenstein (1973); Belgium-Yugoslavia (1973); Austria-Poland (1974); Greece-Romania (1974) [sources: UN Treaty Series; Council of Europe, *The Practical Guide* (n. 1101); Council Regulation (EC) No. 44/2001 of 22 December 2000 on jurisdiction and the recognition and enforcement of judgments in civil and commercial matters (as amended), Article 69; Campbell (ed.), *Enforcement of Foreign Judgments* (n. 921)); Habib Mohammed and Sharif Al Mulla, "Conventions of Enforcement of Judgments in the Arab States" (1999), 14 *Arab Law Quarterly* 33].

regional co-operation extended across Europe[1103], to the Middle East[1104] and the Americas[1105].

1103 Scandinavia: Convention between Denmark, Finland, Iceland, Norway and Sweden regarding the Recognition and Enforcement of Judgments, Copenhagen, 19 March 1932; also Convention between the same nations on the Recognition and Enforcement of Judgments in Civil Matters, Copenhagen, 11 October 1977.
Baltic: Convention between Estonia, Latvia and Lithuania concerning the Reciprocal Recognition and Enforcement of Judgments in Civil Matters, Kaunas, 14 November 1935.
Benelux: Treaty between Belgium, the Netherlands and Luxembourg in Jurisdiction, Bankruptcy, and the Validity and Enforcement of Judgments, Arbitration Awards and Authentic Instruments, Brussels, 24 November 1961.
European Economic Community: 1968 Brussels Convention on Jurisdiction and the Enforcement of Judgments in Civil and Commercial Matters (Belgium, Germany, France, Italy, Luxembourg, the Netherlands), Brussels, 27 September 1968 ("1968 Brussels Convention").
In the following period, see Convention on Jurisdiction and the Enforcement of Judgments in Civil and Commercial Matters (Austria, Belgium, Denmark, Finland, France, Germany, Greece, Iceland, Ireland, Italy, Luxembourg, the Netherlands, Norway, Portugal, Spain, Sweden, Switzerland, United Kingdom) (Lugano, 1988) ("1988 Lugano Convention").

1104 Convention of the Arab League on the Enforcement of Judgments and Arbitral Awards (Jordan, Syria, Iraq, Saudi Arabia, Lebanon, Egypt, Yemen), 14 September 1952.

1105 Convention on Private International Law (Bustamente Code), Title X (Argentina, Bolivia, Brazil, Chile, Colombia, Costa Rica, Cuba, Dominican Republic, Ecuador, El Salvador, Guatemala, Haiti, Honduras, Mexico, Nicaragua, Panama, Paraguay, Peru, Uruguay, Venezuela), Havana, 20 February 1928. In addition, the Montivideo Convention (above, [295]) was amended in 1940.
In the following period, see Inter-American Convention on Extraterritorial Validity of Foreign Judgments and Arbitral Awards, Montevideo, 8 May 1979; Inter-American Convention on Jurisdiction in the International Sphere for the Extraterritorial Validity of Foreign Judgments, La Paz, 24 May 1984.

300. Meanwhile, the Hague Conference on Private International Law – established as a permanent intergovernmental organisation in 1955 [1106] – had continued to plough the furrow but with little reward. A Convention on the Recognition and Enforcement of Judgments, concluded in 1971 after much effort, limped into force with only three ratifications by the end of the twentieth century [1107]. The reasons offered for its failure included its complexity and its failure to regulate questions of jurisdiction directly [1108]. It is, however, also notable that of the twenty-three States that were members of the Hague Conference in 1971, all but five [1109] were European and six were the Member States of the European Economic Community that had successfully concluded the 1968 Brussels Convention [1110]. The success of the latter Convention in the following years [1111], and its extension

1106 Statute of the Hague Conference on Private International Law, The Hague, 31 October 1951, entering into force on 15 July 1955.

1107 Convention on the Recognition and Enforcement of Foreign Judgments in Civil and Commercial Matters, The Hague, 1 February 1971. Today, the Convention has 5 State parties (Albania, Cyprus, Kuwait, the Netherlands, Portugal).

1108 Hague Conference on Private International Law, *International Jurisdiction and Foreign Judgments in Civil and Commercial Matters*, Preliminary Document No. 7 of 7 April 1997 (rapporteur: Catherine Kessedjian), [7]-[9].

1109 Japan, Egypt, Israel, United States, Canada.

1110 (n. 1103).

1111 Denmark, Ireland and the United Kingdom acceded in 1978; Greece in 1982; Spain and Porgugal in 1989; Austria, Finland and Sweden in 1996. From 2001, the Convention was superseded by Council Regulation (EC) No. 44/2001 of 22 December 2000 on jurisdiction and the recognition and enforcement of judgments in civil and commercial matters ("Brussels I Regulation"), which in turn was superseded by Regulation (EU) No. 1215/2012 of the European Parliament and of the Council of 12 December 2012 on jurisdiction and the recognition and enforcement of judgments in civil and commercial matters (recast) ("Recast Brussels I Regulation").

through the 1988 Lugano Convention[1112], undoubtedly drew oxygen away from the Hague instrument.

301. Not easily discouraged, the organisation launched a new initiative in 1992[1113], taking an early decision to pursue a double convention covering rules on adjudicatory jurisdiction *and* the reception of foreign judgments[1114]. At this time, there was renewed cause for optimism. By the end of 1993, the organisation's membership had grown to more than forty nations, with new members from six continents, including China and several, newly independent former Eastern Bloc nations[1115]. A Special Commission painstakingly put together a preliminary draft convention[1116], which was presented to a Diplomatic Conference in 2001. Although some progress was made[1117], the project hit the rocks over disagreements – most significantly, between the United

---

1112 (n. 1103). This Convention was superseded by the Convention on Jurisdiction and the Recognition and Enforcement of Judgments in Civil and Commercial Matters between the European Community, Denmark, Iceland, Norway and Switzerland (Lugano, 30 October 2007) ("2007 Lugano Convention").

1113 Hague Conference on Private International Law, "Some Reflections of the Permanent Bureau on a General Convention on Enforcement of Judgments" (Preliminary Document No. 17 of May 1992).

1114 Hague Conference on Private International Law, "Final Act of the Seventeenth Session", point B.2 (*Proceedings of the Seventeenth Session*, Vol. 1, p. 43).

1115 The new, non-European members were (in order of accession) Argentina, Australia, Suriname, Venezuela, Uruguay, China, Mexico, Chile, Morocco. The new European members were Poland, Cyprus, Hungary, Romania, Slovenia, Latvia, Czechoslovakia.

1116 Hague Conference on Private International Law, "Report on the Preliminary draft Convention on Jurisdiction and Foreign Judgments in Civil and Commercial Matters" (Preliminary Document No. 11, August 2000) (rapporteurs: Peter Nygh, Fausto Pocar), pp. 4-18.

1117 Hague Conference on Private International Law, "Interim Text – Summary of the Outcome of the Discussion in

States and the members of the European Community[1118] – about the draft convention's form and scope and the content of its jurisdictional rules[1119]. In 2002, while reaffirming the great importance that they attached to the harmonisation of rules concerning jurisdiction and foreign judgments on a global basis, the members of the Conference charged the Permanent Bureau and a working group with the task of seeing what could be salvaged[1120].

302. This proved to be an inspired decision, leading to the conclusion of two new treaties[1121].

– The Convention on Choice of Court Agreements, concluded on 30 June 2005, combines rules of juris-

---

Commission II of the First Part of the Diplomatic Conference" (6-20 June 2001).

1118 The European Community had acquired external competence in civil justice matters following the entry into force of the Treaty of Amsterdam on 1 May 1999, and the European Commission was acting to co-ordinate its members' approach to the negotiations. The European Union became a member of the Hague Conference in its own right in 2007.

1119 Hague Conference on Private International Law, "Some Reflections on the Present State of Negotiations on the Judgments Project in the Context of the Future Work Programme of the Conference" (Prel. Doc. No 16 of February 2002); Linda Silberman, "Comparative Jurisdiction in the International Context: Will the Proposed Hague Judgements Convention Be Stalled?" (2002), 52 *De Paul L Rev* 319; Eva Jueptner, *A Hague Convention on Jurisdiction and Judgments, Why Did the Judgments Project (1992-2001) Fail?*, Cambridge: Intersentia, 2024.

1120 Hague Conference on Private International Law, "Commission I on General Affairs and Policy held on 22-24 April 2002", [3], https://assets.hcch.net/docs/e0fe16d4-e078-4ec0-bf3f-23c33b5848cf.pdf and "Final Act of the Nineteenth Session", point C.2, *Proceedings of the Nineteenth Session*, Vol. 1, p. 45.

1121 See Louise Ellen Teitz, "Another Hague Judgments Convention Bucking the Past to Provide for the Future" (2019), 29 *Duke Journal of Comparative and International Law* 491.

diction with a requirement to recognise and enforce judgments in situations where parties to a commercial relationship have agreed to confer exclusive jurisdiction on a court or the courts of a Contracting State[1122]. This Convention currently has thirty-five State parties, predominantly current or former members of the European Union[1123]. China and the United States are among the nations that have signed the Convention and are yet to ratify it[1124].

- The Convention on the Recognition and Enforcement of Foreign Judgments in Civil or Commercial Matters, concluded on 2 July 2019, sets out a framework for the

1122 The key concept of an "exclusive choice of court agreement" is defined in Article 3, rules of jurisdiction for the chosen and non-chosen courts in Articles 5-6 and the rules governing recognition and enforcement in Chapter III (Arts. 8-15).
See the *Explanatory Report* by Trevor Hartley and Masauro Dogauchi, *Proceedings of the Twentieth Session*, Vol. 3, pp. 784-863, https://assets.hcch.net/docs/0de60e2f-e002-408e-98a7-5638e1ebac65.pdf.

1123 In addition to the twenty-seven current members of the EU, the State parties are (in order of accession) Mexico, United Kingdom, Singapore, Montenegro, Ukraine, Moldova, Albania and Switzerland. The EU concluded the treaty on behalf of its Member States.

1124 The other signatories are North Macedonia, Israel and Costa Rica. See New York City Bar, Working Group on Three Private International Law Treaties, Report (March 2024), https://www.nycbar.org/wp-content/uploads/2024/03/20221065-ThreePrivateInternationalLawTreaties.pdf; John Coyle, "Recent US Developments concerning the Hague Judgments Convention and COCA", Conflicto flaws.net, https://conflictoflaws.net/2024/recent-u-s-developments-concerning-the-hague-judgments-convention-and-coca/; Wei Cai and Jonathan Kolied, "Between National Interests and Global Business: China's Possible Reservations to the Hague Convention on Choice of Court Agreements" (2020), 11 *J Int Disp Settlement* 295; Brooke Marshall and Mary Keyes, "Australia's Accession to the Hague Convention on Choice of Court Agreements" (2017), 41 *Melb Uni L Rev* 246.

recognition and enforcement of judgments between Contracting States in matters falling within its scope where the adjudicating court has exercised jurisdiction on one or more of the bases provided for[1125]. Within its first six years, this Convention has gained thirty-one State parties, with Albania, Ukraine, Uruguay and the United Kingdom joining the Member States of the European Union[1126]. Again, the United States is among the other nations to have signed the Convention, without ratifying it[1127].

303. The Hague Conference has identified the wider project, which continues to explore avenues for closer collaboration in the field of civil justice[1128], as being one

---

1125 These jurisdictional bases are set out in Hague Judgments Convention (2019), Articles 5-6 (below, Sec. V.B.3), with grounds for refusal set out in Article 7 (below, Sec. IV.B.1 and 4).
See Francisco Garcimartin and Geneviève Saumier, *Convention of 2 July 2019 on the Recognition and Enforcement of Foreign Judgments in Civil or Commercial Matters – Explanatory Report*, The Hague: HCCH, 2020, https://assets.hcch.net/docs/a1b0b0fc-95b1-4544-935b-b842534a120f.pdf.

1126 Currently, the UK has declared its intention to apply the Convention only to England and Wales, although this will likely change in the future.
As to the UK's decision to accede, UK Ministry of Justice, *The Hague Convention of 2 July 2019 on the Recognition and Enforcement of Foreign Judgments in Civil or Commercial Matters (Hague 2019) – Response to Consultation*, 23 November 2023. For the UK implementing legislation, see Recognition and Enforcement of Judgments (2019 Hague Convention etc.) Regulations (SI 2024/713).

1127 The other signatories are Israel, Kosovo, Montenegro, North Macedonia and the Russian Federation. As regards the United States' possible ratification of the Hague Judgments Convention, see New York City Bar Working Group Report (n. 1124); Coyle, "Recent US Developments" (n. 1124).

1128 See the summary and further materials at https://www.hcch.net/en/projects/legislative-projects/jurisdiction.

of the reasons why its membership now numbers ninety nations with a broad geographical distribution[1129]. In this sphere at least, the future seems bright.

H. Global governance and human rights

304. The horrifying global and regional conflicts and unimaginable atrocities in the first half of the twentieth century catalysed a new global legal order centred on the promotion of peace and the protection of human rights. The League of Nations, established at the Paris Peace Conference in 1920, was unable to prevent a second World War or the Holocaust. Its Covenant nonetheless offered a vision of a global community founded on co-operation, rather than self-interest, and with the object of securing peace and security by pursuing, among other goals, "the maintenance of justice . . . in the dealings of organised peoples with each other"[1130]. Building on this model, the United Nations, established in 1946, set out among its purposes "to develop friendly relations among nations based on respect for the principle of equal rights and self-determination of peoples, and to take other appropriate measures to strengthen universal peace", "to achieve international co-operation in solving international problems of an economic, social, cultural or humanitarian character" and "to be a centre for harmonising the actions of nations in the attainment of these common ends"[1131].

[1129] Hague Conference on Private International Law, "Some Reflections" (n. 1119), [4], p. 5.
The geographical make up of the Conference's membership is currently as follows (as at 1 July 2024): Africa 8, Asia and Middle East 17, Australasia 2, Europe 45, North and Central America 9, South America 9.

[1130] Covenant of the League of Nations (Versailles, 28 June 1919), Preamble.

[1131] UN Charter (n. 18), Article 1.

305. The members of this new organisation committed themselves to promoting and encouraging respect for human rights and fundamental freedoms for all, without discrimination[1132]. To this end, in December 1948, the General Assembly adopted the Universal Declaration of Human Rights. This instrument is notable in its focus on the individual alongside the organs of political society as sharing responsibility for affirming and securing the universal and effective recognition and observance of the entitlements set out[1133]. Its first article is a remarkable distillation of the central tenets of natural law reasoning[1134]:

> "All human beings are born free and equal in dignity and rights. They are endowed with reason and conscience and should act towards one another in a spirit of brotherhood."

306. The human rights recognised in this instrument included the entitlement "*in full equality* to a fair and public hearing by an independent and impartial tribunal" in the determination of a person's rights and obligations[1135].

1132 *Ibid.*, Article 1 (3); also Article 55 *(c)*.

1133 Universal Declaration of Human Rights (General Assembly Resolution 217A, 10 December 1948), Preamble. See A. H. (Arthur) Robertson, *Human Rights in the World*, Manchester: University of Manchester Press, 1972, pp. 25-28.

1134 Universal Declaration of Human Rights, above, Article 1. See Hersch Lauterpacht, "The Universal Declaration of Human Rights" (1948), 25 *British Yb Int L* 354. For a critical reaction, see Hannah Arendt, "The Rights of Man: What Are They?" (1949), 3 *Modern Review* 24 and *The Origins of Totalitarianism*, New York: Harcourt Brace & Co, 1951, Chap. 9. See further Ralf Michaels, "The Right to Have Private Rights" (2024), 74 *Univ Toronto LJ* (supplement) 128.

1135 Universal Declaration of Human Rights, above, Article 10 (emphasis added). See also International Covenant on Civil

307. The Univeral Declaration is, on any measure, "a milestone document in the history of human rights"[1136]. It has inspired more than seventy human rights treaties[1137]. The first of these was the European Convention on Human Rights, drafted by the Council of Europe and approved by its Member States in November 1950. In doing so, the signatories reaffirmed their belief in the fundamental freedoms that are "the foundation of the justice and peace in the world"[1138].

308. The European Convention guarantees to every person in the determination of their civil rights and obligations "a fair and public hearing within a reasonable time by an independent and impartial tribunal established by law"[1139]. Although the focus of attention in the application of this provision is on "the rights of the defence"[1140], its protection is double-edged, securing access to justice also for those who pursue claims[1141].

---

and Political Rights (1966), Article 14 (1). The significance of the reference to equality is explored below (Secs. IV.C and V.B.4).

1136 United Nations, "Universal Declaration of Human Rights", https://www.un.org/en/about-us/universal-declaration-of-human-rights.

1137 *Ibid.*

1138 Convention for the Protection of Human Rights and Fundamental Freedoms, Rome, 4 November 1950, Preamble. See Robertson (n. 1133), Chap. 3.

1139 *Ibid.*, Article 6. See Francis G. Jacobs, The European Convention on Human Rights, Oxford: Clarendon Press, 1975, pp. 76-111.
For the corresponding provisions in other regional instruments, see the Inter-American Convention on Human Rights (1969), Article 8 (1); African Charter on Human and Peoples' Rights (1981), Article 7 (1); Charter of Fundamental Rights of the European Union (2000), Article 47.

1140 E.g. *Avotiņš* v. *Latvia* (Application No. 17502/07) (2017) 64 EHRR 76.

1141 With respect to questions of adjudicatory jurisdiction, see *Arlewin* v. *Sweden* (Application No. 22302/10) (2016)

The European Court of Human Rights has recognised that the right of access to a court guaranteed by Article 6 (1) of the ECHR extends to the effectiveness of a judicial decision[1142] and has a cross-border dimension[1143]. The underlying premise is that the right to a fair trial would be "illusory" if a judicial decision were to remain inoperative[1144]. Although this line of case law is immature,

41 BHRC 571; *Naït-Liman* v. *Switzerland* (Application No. 51357/07) (2018) 45 BHRC 639.

1142 *Hornsby* v. *Greece* (Application No. 18357/91) (1997) 24 EHRR 250; *Négrépontis-Giannisis* v. *Greece* (Application No. 56759/08), 3 May 2011.

1143 *McDonald* v. *France* (Application No. 18648/04), 29 April 2008; *Shokolov* v. *Armenia and Moldova* (Application No. 40358/05), 31 July 2012, [66].
See Patrick Kinsch, "Enforcement as a Fundamental Right" (2014), *Nederlands Internationaal Privaatrecht* 540, 541-543; Louwrens R. Kiestra, *The Impact of the European Convention on Human Rights on Private International Law*, The Hague: TMC Asser Press, 2014, Chap. 7; James J. Fawcett, Máire Ní Shúilleabháin and Sangeeta Shah, *Human Rights and Private International Law*, Oxford: Oxford University Press, 2016, [5.07]-[5.28], [7.91]-[7.92]; Cuniberti, "Le fondement" (n. 305), [63]-[72]. Separately, the right to a family life under Article 8 has been held to demand recognition of foreign judgments involving questions of personal status, see Kinsch, above, 540-541.

1144 *Hornsby* (n. 1142), [40], followed in the case of foreign judgments in *McDonald* (n. 1143) and *Négrépontis-Giannisis* (n. 1143). In the latter two cases, the foreign judgment did not meet the conditions for its recognition in the receiving legal order. In *McDonald*, the application was held inadmissible on the ground of the applicant's procedural misconduct. In *Négrépontis-Giannisis*, the European Court of Human Rights found a violation of Article 6 on the ground that a public policy exception had been applied in a disproportionate manner. In other cases, the alleged breach has concerned the machinery for execution of a decision that did meet the conditions for its recognition and enforcement (see the references in Kinsch, above, 545, fn. 25; Fawcett, Ní Shúilleabháin and Shah, above, [5.11]-[5.19]).

and its precise limits unclear[1145], it has the potential to evolve into a *prima facie* duty on the part of Contracting States to support the administration of justice in other nations, a treaty-based duty of humanity[1146].

I. Summary and conclusions

309. The law of foreign judgments developed, like sedimentary rock, in layers. First, frameworks were developed by continental European scholars with a deep understanding and appreciation of natural law ideas. These frameworks influenced the early development of the law in both common law and civilian systems. In the nineteenth century, distinct national frameworks evolved. In some cases, these built upon the pre-existing frameworks, with some acknowledgement of their natural law heritage. In others, they departed from them, with the resulting rules displaying varying degrees of receptiveness to foreign judgments. In some legal orders, judges were left to grapple with the constitutional, theoretical and practical questions arising from the existence of a multiplicity of legal orders engaging in a common endeavour to resolve disputes affecting the political societies that they serve.

310. In a parallel development, nations increasingly recognised the importance of collaborating with respect to the administration of civil justice and identified the

---

1145 Kinsch, above 542-543; Fawcett, Ní Shúilleabháin and Shah, above, [5.23]-[5.27]; Cuniberti, "Le fondement" (n. 305), [69]-[72].

1146 Similarly, in Spain, the constitutional right to effective judicial protection (Constitution, Art. 24) is considered to support the recognition and enforcement of foreign judgments on the basis that there is a right to an *internationally* effective protection (see Miguel Virgós Soriano and Francisco J. Garcimartín Alférez, *Derecho procesal civil internacional*, Madrid: Editorial Civitas, 2007, pp. 37-42).

recognition and enforcement of judgments as being central to this aspiration. The collaboration was pursued through bilateral and regional treaties. More recently, after significant institutional efforts thoughout the past century, the Hague Conference of Private International Law appears to have secured a breakthrough in global collaboration in this domain with the entry into force of its Choice of Court (2005) and Judgments Conventions (2019).

311. Over time, the world has become more and more receptive to the recognition and enforcement of foreign judgments. This is consistent with wider developments in the global legal order, promoting peace, justice and the protection of individual human rights.

CHAPTER IV

NATURAL LAW'S LEGACY: "NATURAL JUSTICE" AS A GROUND OF IMPEACHMENT

A. Justice and injustice

312. That courts dispense justice is often taken for granted. That is true of governments, of all political colours, who cut funding to court services and raise fees for litigants on the basis of an aspiration that the justice system should be self-funding. This shortsighted policy overlooks the public good attached to the resolution of disputes. A functioning justice system is not a necessary criterion for Statehood in international law, but it is a vital function of government of any political society, ancient or modern[1147]. Consider the alternatives – at best, private and non-transparent consensual methods of dispute resolution open to those willing and able to pay or a slide towards what Grotius termed "private war"[1148] in which each contestant judges their own entitlement and violence or the threat of violence serve as the tools of enforcement.

313. Flick through a newspaper and you likely will read of gang violence, road rage incidents or acts of vengeance by organised criminal networks. These are manifestations of private war. In the words of Thomas Hobbes, life in a world in which disputes are settled by these methods would be "solitary, poore, nasty, brutish and short"[1149]. The thought should lead us to treasure

[1147] Section II.I.1; also *R (UNISON)* v. *Lord Chancellor* [2017] UKSC 51, [2020] AC 869, [71].

[1148] See above, [60].

[1149] Hobbes, *Leviathan*, Chap. 13, [62], p. 89.

what we still have, whatever we may perceive to be the shortcomings of our own justice systems.

314. Courts around the world seek to resolve disputes not only between the members of the political societies that they represent but also between those members and others and between parties who do not belong to the political society before whose courts they litigate. Indeed, courts in a select few legal orders have so great a reputation for dispensing justice that parties with few or no ties to the societies served by these courts actively choose to have their disputes resolved by them, by the device of a choice of court agreement.

315. There is, however, no denying that courts sometimes dispense injustice, in domestic as well as in cross-border cases. This is something that we should take seriously. Instances of public outrage at miscarriages of justice in the criminal or civil courts are timely reminders of the fact that injustice is an inherent risk in any system of human decision-making.

316. All legal systems need mechanisms to address this risk, both structurally (for example, by the careful selection and training of judges and the design of civil procedure rules) and in individual cases (for example, by encouraging active case management and allowing judgments to be reviewed on appeal). There is, however, a trade off in allowing for the possibility of reopening a judicial decision. As the well-worn Latin maxim[1150] reminds us, it is in the public interest that litigation should be at an end, as disputes will otherwise fester. If the losing party were only bound when a state of perfect justice has been attained, the advantages that we seek from our civil justice systems would be illusory. Litigation would never be at an end. It is also in the interests of individual litigants that the adjudication should be effective in resolving the dispute, addressing the disequilibrium

[1150] *Interest reipublicae ut sit finis litium.*

in the parties' relationship and avoiding the burden of continued contention between them[1151]. As Vattel and Savigny acknowledged[1152], there has to be a compromise between finality and fine-tuned justice[1153].

317. An extra dimension exists when the effectiveness of a judgment depends on its recognition or enforcement in legal orders other than the adjudicating order[1154]. Every political society has its own conception as to what is just or unjust, substantively and procedurally, reflecting its own history, culture and values[1155]. If all were to insist that no dispute could be resolved except in accordance with their own individual conceptions of justice, there would be an archipelago of judicial islands, in a Hobbesian contest of self-interest[1156]. The proposition that political societies, and their members, should strive to promote the just and peaceful settlement of disputes calls for a different mindset and framework in addressing and resolving questions of justice in cross-border disputes. This demands what Alex Mills has labelled "justice pluralism". As he explains[1157]:

> "If a foreign judgment is to be recognised through a procedure which does not involve rehearing the dispute, a different conception of justice is involved. Recognising a foreign judgment involves recognising

1151 Reflected in the maxim, *nemo debet bis vexari pro una et eadem causa*. As to the relationship between the two maxims, see *Arthur J. S. Hall And Co* v. *Simons* [2000] UKHL 38, [2002] 1 AC 615, 701 (Lord Hoffmann).

1152 See above, [78] and [249].

1153 Von Mehren, "Recognition and Enforcement" (n. 493), 21-24; Leah Brilmayer, *Conflict of Laws*, New York: Aspen Law & Business, 2nd ed., 1995, pp. 298-299.

1154 Von Mehren, above, 32-33.

1155 Brilmayer (n. 1153), pp. 300-301.

1156 See above, [48], [53].

1157 Mills, *Confluence* (n. 222), p. 8; also Paul Schiff Berman, *Global Legal Pluralism*, Cambridge: Cambridge University Press, 2012, esp. Chap. 9.

that a foreign decision is no less just because it resolves a dispute in a way which might not be identical to standards of justice for local disputes."

318. The specific scenario that concerns us in this chapter is one in which a party dissatisfied with the outcome of litigation seeks to challenge recognition or enforcement of the judgment in another legal order on the basis of an argument that the judgment is in some sense "unjust". This may be because the rules of law applied to determine the dispute do not conform to the receiving order's own view of a just allocation of entitlements and responsibilities. Or it may be because of structural failings in the adjudicating order's judicial system, such as endemic corruption or procedures that the receiving order considers to be unsound. Or something may have gone wrong in the course of the proceedings, through the fault of judges or litigants. In these cases, the conflict of laws rules of the receiving order must balance the injustice that will be perpetuated if the foreign judgment is treated as authoritative in resolving the dispute, against the unhappy consequences of a continuing contest between the parties, in which the receiving order is now engaged, if it is not. Which is the lesser of two evils?

319. Every legal order must face up to this dilemma in defining and circumscribing the right to appeal against decisions of its own courts. Although it is inapt to describe a court asked to recognise or enforce a judgment emanating from a separate legal order as a "court of appeal"[1158], a similar quandary presents itself in this dimension as well. It differs in one important respect – the court whose judgment is being considered is not part

1158 *Tarleton* v. *Tarleton* (1815) 4 *Maule and Selwyn* 20, 22 (Lord Ellenborough). Cf. *Houlditch* v. *Marquess of Donegal* (n. 609), 479 (Lord Brougham LC).
The opinion of Lord Brougham was not followed by the Court of Queen's Bench in *Godard* v. *Gray* (n. 963) (Sec. III.F.6).

of the receiving order, with constitutional responsibility for the administration of justice within that order. The framework of rules for the recognition and enforcement of foreign judgments, however framed, must uphold the receiving order's fundamental values.

B. Tools, techniques and terminology for addressing injustice in foreign judgments

1. Classifying the grounds of opposition

320. The objects of our enquiry are the tools, techniques and terminology used to deal with the situation in which one party claims to have been the victim of injustice in a foreign court and resists recognition and enforcement on that ground. We will consider the grounds for refusal of recognition and enforcement set out in the following national and international instruments: (1) Articles 7 and 10 of the 2019 Hague Judgments Convention, (2) Article 45 (1) of the European Union's Recast Brussels I Regulation[1159], (3) Section 4 of the United States' Uniform Foreign-Country Money Judgments Recognition Act (2005), (4) Article 300 of the Civil Procedure Law of China, as amended[1160] and (5) Clauses 6 and 14 of the Commonwealth Model Law on the Recognition and

---

1159 Regulation (EU) No. 1215/2012 (n. 1111).

1160 Most recently, by the 5th Amendment adopted by the Standing Committee of the National People's Congress and following closely the wording of Article 46 of Conference Summary of the Symposium on Foreign-Related Commercial and Maritime Trials of Courts Nation-wide issued by the China's Supreme People's Court on 31 December 2021 (see Jeanne Huang, "Developing Chinese Private International Law for Transnational Civil and Commercial Litigation" (n. 1061) and "Developing Chinese Private International Law for Foreign Judgments" (n. 1062)).

Enforcement of Judgments (2018)[1161], alongside (6) the equivalent grounds recognised by three common law systems, Australia, Canada and England[1162].

321. The grounds can be divided into three groups. First, grounds of opposition that are linked to pre-conditions for recognition and enforcement, including the finality of the judgment and the foreign court's adjudicatory jurisdiction. Second, those concerned with the substantive content of the adjudication. Third, those concerned with the mechanisms by which the adjudication was brought about. Our focus here is on the last group, although this overlaps with the second. We will consider questions of adjudicatory jurisdiction separately[1163].

322. The second and third groups are represented in the table reproduced in the Annex with the former (Group A) numbered A.1 to A.5 and the latter (Group C) numbered C.1. to C.13. Public policy grounds (Group B), straddling these two groups, sit in between.

323. In overview, there are some grounds of opposition that are common to all the regimes surveyed. Each regime has a provision giving primacy to the fundamental principles of the recognising legal order, typically expressed as a "public policy" exception[1164]. Each gives

---

[1161] The Commonwealth Office of Civil and Criminal Justice Reform, *Model Law on the Recognition and Enforcement of Foreign Judgments*, considered and endorsed by Commonwealth Law Ministers at their meeting of 16-19 October 2017, held in Nassau, https://thecommonwealth.org/commonwealth-model-laws.

[1162] Excluding for this purpose any statutory regime, for example, the Foreign Judgments (Reciprocal Enforcement) Act 1933 (UK) and the Foreign Judgments Act 1991 (Cth), but taking into account statutory modifications of the common law such as those contained in ss. 32-33 of the Civil Jurisdiction and Judgments Act 1982 (UK).

[1163] Section IV.D.

[1164] Annex, B.1. This exception is kept within narrow bounds, and often accompanied by a general prohibition on reviewing the substance of the decision, for errors of fact or law

priority, albeit in varying ways, to conflicting judgments of courts of the recognising legal order and other legal orders[1165].

324. There are also some striking differences in approach. For example, breach of a dispute resolution agreement is a ground for opposing recognition and enforcement under the Hague Judgments Convention, the US model legislation, the Chinese Civil Procedure Law and in the United Kingdom[1166], but not under the Recast Brussels I Regulation[1167] or the common law of Australia or Canada. The Brussels I regime, unlike the others, does not have a specific fraud exception, although its public policy exception offers some protection where such allegations are advanced[1168]. The Hague Judgments Convention, the Commonwealth Model Law and the UK have specific grounds relating to awards of damages that go beyond the award of simple compensation[1169],

(see Hague Judgments Convention, Article 4 (2); Recast Brussels I Regulation (n. 1111), Article 52; Commonwealth Model Law (n. 1161), cl. 6 (2); *Godard* v. *Gray* (n. 963)).

1165 Annex, A.1, A.2. Where there are conflicting judgments, a completely harmonious resolution of the dispute may no longer be possible. The recognising legal order must select a suitable rule to choose between the competing judgments. A judgment of the receiving order will often be favoured irrespective of timing (see e.g. Hague Judgments Convention, Article 7 (1) *(e)*; Recast Brussels I Regulation, above, Article 45 (1) *(c)*. Cf. Civil Procedure Law (China), Article 300 (4)). For judgments from outside the receiving order, the judgment first in time will generally be preferred (see e.g. Hague Judgments Convention, Art. 7 (1) *(f)*; Recast Brussels I Regulation, above, Art. 45 (1) *(c)*).

1166 Annex, C.2. For the UK legislation, see Civil Jurisdiction and Judgments Act 1982, s. 32.

1167 Recast Brussels I Regulation (n. 1111), Article 45 (3).

1168 *Interdesco SA* v. *Nullifire Ltd.* [1992] 1 Lloyd's Rep 180 (EWHC). See Annex, C.1.

1169 Hague Judgments Convention, Article 10 (1); Protection of Trading Interests Act 1980 (UK), s. 5 (Annex, A.4, A.5).

whereas other regimes address such questions through the prism of public policy[1170].

2. Breach of agreement and fraud: Perspective matters

325. The breach of agreement and fraud grounds are instructive examples of the multidimensional nature of questions of natural justice[1171]. If the enquiry focuses on the relationship of the individual parties, the arguments for denying effectiveness to a foreign judgment when the successful party has either promised not to bring proceedings in the adjudicating court, or has lied or engaged in some other form of deliberate misconduct to procure the judgment, seem compelling. Abiding by seriously intended agreements and avoiding deceptive conduct are commonly cited examples in natural law accounts of (perfect) obligations upon all human beings[1172].

326. If, however, one takes a broader, systemic perspective, two counterarguments present themselves. First, the institutions that administer justice within a legal order have duties to protect the persons who are

---

1170 Case C-633/22 *Real Madrid Club de Fútbol* v. *Société Editrice du Monde SA* [2024] ECLI:EU:C:2024:843, [57]-[74] (CJEU) and ECLI:EU:C:2024:127, [138]-[158] (Opinion of Adv Gen Szpunar).
See also Cedric Vanleenhove, *Punitive Damages in Private International Law* (Cambridge: Cambridge University Press, 2017), esp. Chaps. 4 and 6.

1171 Section V.B.2.

1172 As to the binding force of agreements under precepts of natural law, see above, [80].
As to fraud, see Grotius, *Prize*, Chap. 2 (Prolegomena), [10], p. 34; Hobbes, *Leviathan*, Chap. 30, [179], pp. 235-236; Pufendorf, *Nature and Nations*, Book 3, Chap. 6, [8], p. 411 and Book 4, Chap. 1, [8]-[10], pp. 470-475; Pufendorf, *Whole Duty*, Book 1, Chap. 9, [13], pp. 114-115 and Chap. 10, [1], pp. 119-120; Vattel, *Nations*, Book 3, Chap. 10, [177], pp. 577-578.

members of, or otherwise participate in, a political society, and those persons have a *prima facie* entitlement to seek that protection. On this view, the adjudicating order has a stronger interest than the receiving order in determining *(a)* whether the constitutional right of access to its courts can be waived by agreement and *(b)* the appropriate mechanisms for addressing allegations of misconduct in the course of civil proceedings before its courts. Second, the wider interests of the political societies involved and of their members, in particular in the just and peaceful settlement of disputes, are engaged. The interests of the parties, although important, are not paramount. It is perfectly proper, and indeed desirable in terms of justice pluralism, for the receiving legal order to have these considerations in mind when it frames its rules, and this explains the (legitimate) differences in the degree of receptiveness towards foreign judgments[1173].

3. "Natural justice": The common law's natural law artefact

327. We turn to the remaining grounds, beginning with the ground of opposition, recognised in England and other common law systems, for non-compliance with the requirements of "natural justice". The terminology is striking, but what does it signify?

328. Despite differences of emphasis and detail in the "natural justice" ground across the common law world, there is significant common ground[1174]. Their rules share five key features.

[1173] As to the relationship between the common law's fraud defence and principles of natural justice, see Andrew Dickinson, "*Abouloff* v. *Oppenheimer* Revisited", Chap. 9, in J. Harris and C. McLachlan, *Essays in International Litigation for Lord Collins* (Oxford: Oxford University Press, 2022).

[1174] Annex, C.3. A valuable summary is to be found in the judgment of majority of the Supreme Court of Canada in

(1) The requirements of natural justice relate to the mechanisms by which the judgment was produced, not the outcome of the dispute[1175].

---

the leading case in that jurisdiction, *Beals* v. *Saldahna* (n. 504), [61]-[62], [64].
As to the law of England and Wales, see *Jacobson* v. *Frachon* (1928) 138 LT 386, esp. at 392 (Atkin L. J.); *Adams* v. *Cape Industries* (n. 504), 563-572; Francis Taylor Piggott, *Foreign Judgments and Jurisdiction*, London: Butterworth & Co, 1908, pp. 400-411; *Dicey, Morris & Collins* (n. 5), [14R-158]-[14-167] (Rule 55). In *Jacobson*, Atkin L. J. preferred the term "substantial justice" and this term is sometimes still used today, although interchangeably with the language of natural justice (see *Jacobson* v. *Frachon*, above, 392 (Atkin L. J.); *Dicey, Morris & Collins*, above, [14-160], fn. 644).
As to the law of Australia, see *Boele* v. *Norsemeter* [2002] NSWCA 363, [24] (Giles J. A. with whom Handley and Beazley J. J. A. agreed); *Spirits International BV* v. *Federal Treasury Enterprise (FKP) Sojuzplodoimport* [2011] FCAFC 69, [50] (Rares J.); Martin Davies, Andrew Bell, Paul Le Gay Brereton and Michael Douglas, *Nygh's Conflict of Laws in Australia*, Chatswood: LexisNexis Australia, 10th ed., 2019, [40.82]-[40.88]; Reid Mortensen, Richard Garnett, Mary Keyes, *Private International Law in Australia*, Chatswood: LexisNexis Australia, 5th ed., 2023, [5.29]-[5.32].
As to the law of Commonwealth African nations, see Oppong, *Private International Law in Commonwealth Africa* (n. 504), pp. 340-347.
As to the law of New Zealand, see Hook and Wass, *The Conflict of Laws in New Zealand* (n. 504), [5.268]-[5.283].
As to the law of Singapore, see Adeline Chong and Man Yip, *Singapore Private International Law*, Oxford: Oxford University Press, 2023, [5.76]-[5.79].

1175 The terms of the judgment may nonetheless evidence a serious procedural irregularity (see *Federal Treasury Enterprise (FKP) Sojuzplodoimport* v. *Spirits International BV (No. 2)* [2012] FCA 23, [46] (Edmonds J.); *Maximov* v. *Open Joint Stock Company Novolipetsky Metallurgichesky Kombinat* [2017] EWHC 1911 (Comm), [2017] 2 CLC 121, [15]).

(2) The burden of proving a violation of those requirements lies on the party who asserts it[1176].
(3) That the adjudicating order adopts procedures that differ, even significantly, from those followed by the receiving order does not of itself establish nonconformity with the requirements of natural justice[1177].
(4) Equally, however, a court's compliance with its own procedural rules will not satisfy the requirements of natural justice, if the mechanism does not conform to the receiving order's essential standards[1178].
(5) The core requirements of natural justice include, in addition to notice and an adequate opportunity to be heard, a requirement that the tribunal be impartial[1179].

As to the substantive aspect of the denial of natural justice, consisting in the entitlement to legal protection without discrimination, see text to n. 627 and below, [354] and [397].

1176 *Jamieson* v. *Robb* (1881) 7 VLR 170, 176 (Stephen J.); *Beals* v. *Saldanha* (n. 504), [61] (Major J.). For earlier English cases establishing this presumption of compliance by the foreign court, see e.g. *Cowan* v. *Braidwood* (1840) 1 Manning & Granger 882, esp. at 893 (Maule J., in the course of argument); *Henderson* v. *Henderson* (1844), 6 *Queen's Bench Reports* 288, 298 (Lord Denman C. J.); *Reynolds* v. *Fenton* (1846), 3 *Common Bench Reports* 187; *Barber* v. *Lamb* (1860), 8 *Common Bench Reports* (New Series) 95, 100 (Erle C. J.).

1177 *Jacobson* v. *Frachon* (n. 1174), 392; *Nygh's Conflict of Laws* (n. 1174), [40.84].

1178 *Yin* v. *Wu* [2023] VSCA 130, [86]-[87].

1179 For a notable early example, see *Price* v. *Dewhurst* (1837), 8 *Simons* 279. As the editors of *Dicey, Morris & Collins* (n. 5) note, at [14-141], if the foreign court has been bribed, the natural justice plea tends to merge with one of fraud. See also *Boele* v. *Norsemeter* (n. 1174), [24] (Giles J. A.); *Beals* v. *Saldanha* (n. 504), [62] (Major J.); *SHN Grundstuecksverwaltungsgesellschaft MBH & Co* v. *Hanne*, 2014 ABCA 168, [19]-[21]. Cf. *Beals*, above, [72] and *Oakwell Engineering Ltd.* v. *Enernorth Industries Inc.*

329. From the seventeenth to the nineteenth centuries, the specific term "natural justice" was widely used in a variety of contexts to signal that a rule or principle being applied by a court in England had been inspired or influenced by insights that the judges had gained, directly or indirectly, from commentaries on the law of nature. The presence of this influence can be seen in the writing of Bracton, Coke and Blackstone [1180]. The common law was infused with natural law ideas, which themselves evolved over time [1181]. A famous example from the eighteenth century is provided by the judgment of Lord Mansfield in *Moses* v. *Macferlan*, a case well known to students of the English law of unjust enrichment. There, he invoked "natural justice" to justify the existence of a duty to repay the amount of an improperly obtained judgment [1182].

(2006) 81 OR (3d) 288, where the question of judicial bias was consider principally under the heading of public policy.

1180 Richard H. Helmholz, "Natural Law and Human Rights in English Law: From Bracton to Blackstone" (2005), 3 *Ave Maria Law Review* 1 and *Natural Law in Court* (n. 24), Chap. 4.

1181 As one author puts it, "[t]he 'law of nature' to which Blackstone referred was not the natural law of Aquinas or even of Bracton and Coke in England. It was more akin to the natural law of Grotius". John Underwood Lewis, "Blackstone's Definition of Law and Doctrine of Legal Obligation as a Link between Early Modern and Contemporary Theories of Law" (1968), 3 *Irish Jurist* 336, 340; see also Paul Lucas, "*Ex Parte* Sir William Blackstone, 'Plagiarist': A Note on Blackstone and the Natural Law" (1963), 7 *The American Journal of Legal History* 142.

1182 (1760) 2 Burrow 1005, 1009, 1012 ("the gist of this kind of action is, that the defendant, upon the circumstances of the case, is obliged by the ties of natural justice and equity to refund the money"). See *Sempra Metals Ltd.* v. *Inland Revenue Commissioners* [2007] UKHL 34, [2008] 1 AC 561, [105] (Lord Nicholls), [174] (Lord Walker), [209] (Lord Mance).

330. With respect to foreign judgments, the roots of the natural justice ground can be traced to observations made by the Lord Chancellor, Lord Ellenborough, in the landmark case of *Buchanan* v. *Rucker*, in which the writ issued against a non-resident defendant had been nailed to the court house door in Tobago[1183]. Faced with the submission from the renowned advocate William Garrow (for the judgment creditor) that a foreign judgment should be treated with the same respect as an English judgment, his Lordship replied[1184]:

> "That may be so if the judgment appears on the face of it consistent with reason and justice; but it is contrary to the first principles of justice that either in civil or criminal proceedings, a man should be condemned before he is heard."

331. The specific term "natural justice" was first used in a foreign judgments case in England in 1826, to support the case for enforcement[1185]. It was used to describe a ground for refusal five years later[1186].

332. Its survival into the twenty-first century is triply puzzling. First, with the passage of time, the direct influence of natural law reasoning on the common law has faded, and the remaining visible traces of its influence are few and far between. The language of natural justice is now in active service only in the conflict of laws, and also in public law[1187], to describe minimum procedural

---

1183 See further text to n. 1288.

1184 (1807) 1 Campbell 62, 66. See also the report of the subsequent hearing *en banc* (1808) 9 East 192 and Lord Ellenborough's decision in the later case of *Cavan* v. *Stewart* (1816) 1 Starkie 525.

1185 *Arnott* v. *Redfern* (text to n. 672).

1186 *Becquet* v. *MacCarthy* (1831) 2 *Barnewall and Adolphus* 951, 958-959.

1187 See e.g. *Al Rawi* v. *Security Service* [2010] EWCA Civ 482, [13] (Lord Neuberger MR); *Kioa* v. *West* (1985) 159 CLR 550, 582 (Mason J.); *Canadian Cable Television Assn.* v.

standards for adjudication[1188]. Second, the terminology may seem at best cryptic and at worst specious. If it is humankind's nature to be selfish (Hobbes), or sociable (Pufendorf), or to aspire to be virtuous (Aristotle), what (one may ask) does this tell us about the requirements of justice in a decision-making context or otherwise? If, as Hobbes asserts, the administration of justice in the natural order leaves every human to decide in his or her own interest, neither impartiality nor the entitlement to a fair hearing would be inherent in that decision-making process[1189].

333. Third, the use of this terminology in the conflict of laws appears to be confined to the common law world outside the United States. It has not taken hold elsewhere[1190].

American College Sports Collective of Canada, Inc. (CA) [1991] 3 FC 626, 639 (McGuigan J. A.).

1188 See generally Hedley H. Marshall, *Natural Justice*, London: Sweet & Maxwell, 1959, esp. Chaps. 1-2.

1189 According to Locke, "[i]n the state of nature there wants a known and indifferent judge with authority, to determine all difference according to the established law. For every one in that stage being both judge and executioner of the law of nature, men being partial to themselves, passion and revenge is very apt to carry them too far, and with too much heat in their own cases", Locke, *Two Treatises,* 2nd treatise, Chap. 9, [125], p. 351.

1190 Unsurprisingly, given its heritage, the Commonwealth Model Law (n. 1161) does refer, in cl. 6 (3) *(c)*, to "natural justice" in tandem with "procedural fairness". On the relationship between these two concepts, see James Edelman, "Why Do We Have Rules of Procedural Fairness?", speech, 4 September 2015, https://www.fedcourt.gov.au/digital-law-library/judges-speeches/speeches-former-judges/justice-edelman/edelman-j-20150904, "A convenient language to adopt in this area is to think of the procedural fairness as a description of the relevant rules and natural justice as the basic underlying principle of procedural fairness. On this understanding, natural justice is not a rule which is capable of direct application. It involves principles which inform the contours of the rules".

4. *"Natural justice": By any other name*[1191]*?*

334. The United States stands aside from its common law cousins. In *Hilton* v. *Guyot*, the members of the Supreme Court used the term "natural justice" only once, in quoting an English writer[1192]. The rule that they espoused listed the requirements for a "fair and impartial trial"[1193] – regular proceedings, due citation or voluntary appearance of the defendant, a system of jurisprudence likely to secure an impartial administration of justice between citizens and others and the absence of prejudice in the court or in the system of laws under which it was sitting[1194].

335. The United States' uniform legislation, in its original (1962) and revised (2005) versions[1195], draws inspiration from *Hilton*[1196]. Both versions use the terms "impartial tribunal" and "due process of law" to describe flaws in the judicial system of the adjudicating legal order[1197]. They contain separate, specific provisions

---

1191 William Shakespeare, *Romeo and Juliet*, Act 2, Scene 2 ("A rose by any other name would smell as sweet").

1192 *Hilton* v. *Guyot* (n. 599), 197, citing Francis Taylor Piggott, *The Law and Practice of the Courts of the United Kingdom relating to Foreign Judgments and Parties out of the Jurisdiction*, London: W. Clowes and Sons, 2nd ed., 1884, pp. 380-381. There are several other references in the pleadings and in the argument, mostly referring to English decisions.

1193 *Hilton* v. *Guyot*, above, 206.

1194 *Ibid.*, 202 (see n. 1009).

1195 Uniform Foreign Money Judgments Recognition Act 1962 ("UFMJR 1962"); Uniform Foreign-Country Money Judgments Recognition Act 2005 ("UFCMJR 2005"), https://www.uniformlaws.org/committees/community-home?CommunityKey=ae280c30-094a-4d8f-b722-8dcd614a8f3e.

1196 National Conference of Commissioners on Uniform State Laws, *Uniform Foreign-Country Money Judgments Recognition Act 2005* (n. 1028), Comments to s. 4, [5].

1197 UFMJR 1962 (n. 1195), s. 4 *(a)* (1); UFCMJR 2005 (n. 1195), s. 4 *(b)* (1). See Annex, C.10, C.11.

requiring that the defendant be given sufficient notice of the proceeding[1198]. The 2005 Act, but not its predecessor, uses the terms "integrity" and "due process of law" to describe shortcomings in the proceedings leading to judgment[1199]. The "due process" requirements track the wording of the fifth and fourteenth amendments to the United States Constitution, with impressive legal ancestry dating back to 1354[1200]. The US courts, and the authors of the uniform legislation, have nonetheless made clear that what is required in this context is "fairness in an international sense" rather than strict compliance with the intricacies of the constitutional due process requirement[1201].

336. There are inevitably differences of detail between legal orders – the US model legislation hives off the question of notice of the existence of proceedings into a discrete provision[1202] and expressly authorises a

---

1198 UFMJR 1962, above, s. 4 *(b)* (1); UFCMJR 2005, above, s. 4 *(c)* (1). See Annex, C.4.

1199 UFCMJR 2005, above, s. 4 *(c)* (7)-(8). See also American Law Institute, *Recognition and Enforcement* (n. 1025), draft Act, para. 5 *(a) (i)*, *(ii)*, *(iv)*, with commentary at pp. 58-60, 68-72. See Annex, C.12, C.13.

1200 Library of Congress, "Magna Carta: Muse and Mentor Due Process of Law", https://www.loc.gov/exhibits/magna-carta-muse-and-mentor/due-process-of-law; Congress, "Historical Background on Due Process", https://constitution.congress.gov/browse/essay/amdt5-5-2/ALDE_00013722/.
See John V. Orth, *Due Process of Law – A Brief History*, Lawrence KS: Kansas University Press, 2003, Chaps. 1 and 2.

1201 National Conference of Commissioners on Uniform State Laws, *Uniform Foreign-Country Money Judgments Recognition Act 2005* (n. 1028), Comments to s. 4, [5], with reference to *Society of Lloyd's* v. *Ashenden* (2000) 233 F3d 473 (7th Circuit). For a recent example, highlighting differences between the 1962 and 2005 model legislation, see *Dejoria* v. *Maghreb Petroleum Exploration, SA* (2019) 935 F 3d 381 (5th Circuit).

1202 This is also the practice of other common law systems in their legislation on the subject and in bilateral treaties

system-wide[1203] review for compliance with impartiality and due process requirements[1204]. There is, however, no reason to think that a significant rupture has opened up in the common law world in these matters. After all, the Supreme Court in *Hilton* had considered "all the authorities upon the subject and of the trend of judicial opinion in this country and in England"[1205] and the formulation of the rule in that case anchors the provisions in the United States' uniform legislation[1206].

337. Other instruments find different ways to cover the same ground. The Hague Judgments Convention

---

to which that legislation gives effect (see e.g. Foreign Judgments (Reciprocal Enforcement) Act 1933 (UK), s. 4 (1) *(a) (iii)*; Foreign Judgments Act 1991 (Australia), s. 7 (2) *(a) (iv)*).

1203 Text to n. 1197. In *Society of Lloyd's* v. *Ashenden* (n. 1201), the Court held that legislation adopted on the 1962 model did not authorise a case specific review of compliance with due process. As noted (text to n. 1199), the 2005 model legislation adds additional case specific grounds.

1204 This ground of opposition is very cautiously guarded and rarely successful (see American Law Institute, *Restatement (4th) – The Foreign Relations Law of the United States*, para. 483, Reporters' Notes, [2]); also William S. Dodge, "Against Systemic Review of Foreign Judgments" (2022), 28 *Southwestern J Int L* 368).
It is doubtful whether an Australian court would be willing to undertake a review of this kind – see *Voth* v. *Manildra Flour Mills Pty Ltd.* (1990) 171 CLR 538, 559, Mason C. J., Deane, Dawson and Gaudron J. J., but cf. *Maduro Board of the Central Bank of Venezuela* v. *Guaido Board of the Central Bank of Venezuela* [2021] UKSC 57, [2023] AC 156, [157]-[159].
As to English law, the editors of *Dicey, Morris & Collins* (n. 5) express the view (at [14-159]) that "questions of natural justice should at least ordinarily be addressed to the specific circumstances under which the foreign judgment was obtained, rather than the features of the foreign legal system as a whole". See also *Hebei Huaneng Industrial Development Co Limited* v. *Shi* [2020] NZHC 2992, [32].

1205 *Hilton* v. *Guyot* (n. 599), 202.

1206 See above, [334]-[335].

combines specific provisions governing the adequacy and form of notification of the document governing the claim and fraud [1207], with a discrete reference within the public policy exception to "fundamental principles of procedural fairness" of the recognising State [1208]. Again, conformity lies just below the surface. In their Explanatory Report, Professors Garcimartin and Saumier explain that "in some States, fundamental principles of procedural fairness (also known as due process of law, natural justice or the right to a fair trial) are constitutionally mandated" [1209]. They note that the reference in Article 7 (1) *(c)* of the Convention to "fundamental principles of procedural fairness" overlaps with the specific provisions governing notification of the claim and fraud in sub-paragraphs *(a)* and *(b)* and express the view that:

> "This overlap should ensure that adequate procedural protection is provided to parties facing recognition and enforcement proceedings regardless of the particular way in which those issues are dealt with in the requested State."

338. Accordingly, the "fundamental principles of procedural fairness" to which the Convention refers have a chameleon-like quality, conforming with the common law's "natural justice" and "due process" requirements and also with specific, constitutionally protected rights to a fair trial in other legal orders.

339. Long embedded as principles of the common law [1210], the past century has seen nominate fair trial rights

---

1207 Article 7 (1) *(a) (i)* and *(ii)* (notification) and Article 7 (1) *(b)* (fraud). See Annex, C.1, C.4, C.7.

1208 Article 7 (1) *(c)*. See Annex, C.8.

1209 Garcimartín and Saumier, *Explanatory Report* (n. 1125), [261].

1210 See e.g. *Al Rawi* v. *The Security Service* [2011] UKSC 34, [2012] AC 531, [10]-[17]; *Traditional Rights and Freedoms – Encroachments by Commonwealth Laws* (ALRC Report 129), Chap. 8.

given prominence in global and regional human rights instruments [1211] and in national written constitutions [1212]. In the recognition and enforcement of judgments, the obligation of the receiving order's courts to conform to these international and constitutional standards may require them to investigate the course of proceedings giving rise to the judgment, even though the foreign court is constitutionally independent and the originating legal order may not be party to any relevant international instrument [1213]. In a sense, this gives an "indirect effect" to the instruments in question [1214], although that language is misleading as the right to a fair trial is directly engaged in the proceeding in which recognition or enforcement is sought. Vigilance in securing fair and equal access to justice does not stop when a judgment is delivered [1215].

340. Within the EU's Brussels I regime, and the parallel Lugano Convention [1216], the right to a fair trial is protected by combining a specific ground of refusal for

---

1211 Section III.H.

1212 See Ana Koprivica, "Right to a Fair Trial in Civil Law Cases", in Rainer Grote, Frauke Lachenmann and Rüdiger Wolfrum (eds.), *Max Planck Encyclopedia of Comparative Constitutional Law*, Oxford: Oxford University Press, 2018, https://oxcon.ouplaw.com/home/MPECCOL, [14]-[28].

1213 *Pellegrini* v. *Italy* (Application no 30882/96) (2001) 35 EHRR 44; *Dolenc* v. *Slovenia* (Application No. 20256/20), (2023) 76 EHRR 3 (ECtHR). As to the differing approaches required according to whether the adjudicating court is itself required to comply with the ECHR, and the nature of the breach, see Mills, *Confluence* (n. 222), pp. 286-287; *Merchant International Company Ltd.* v. *Natsionalna Aktsionerna Kompaniia Naftogaz* [2012] EWCA Civ 196, [69]-[71]. As to the standard of proof, see *Popoviciu* v. *Curtea De Apel Bucharest* [2023] UKSC 39, [2023] 1 WLR 4256, [58]-[58] (extradition proceedings).

1214 *Government of The United States of America* v. *Montgomery (No. 2)* [2004] UKHL 37, [2004] 1 WLR 2241, [22].

1215 See above, [308]

1216 Text to n. 1112.

default judgments given without sufficient notification to the defendant of the initiation of proceedings[1217] with a narrowly formulated public policy *(ordre public)* ground[1218]. In its case law, the European Court of Justice has consistently declared that the public policy exception encompasses the non-conformity of the proceedings giving rise to the judgment with the right to a fair trial recognised in Article 6 of the European Convention on Human Rights (to which all Member States are party) and Article 47 of the EU's Charter of Fundamental Rights, modelled on ECHR, Article 6[1219]. The ECHR's fair trial right has also underpinned the European Court's interpretation of the specific protection provided in the case of default judgments[1220].

341. As noted[1221], Article 6 of the European Convention, tracked in Article 47 of the Charter, requires "a fair and public hearing within a reasonable time by an independent and impartial tribunal established by law". On their face, the first and last elements (a fair hearing by an independent and impartial tribunal) substantially overlap with the two principal limbs of the common law's natural justice requirement[1222]. The requirement for a "public hearing" and the demand for a hearing "within a reasonable time" go beyond this, although neither

---

1217 Recast Brussels I Regulation (n. 1111), Article 45 (1) *(b)*: Lugano Convention 2007 (n. 1112), Article 34 (1). See Annex, C.4.

1218 Recast Brussels I Regulation, above, Article 45 (1) *(a)*; 2007 Lugano Convention, above, Article 34 (2). See Annex, B.1.

1219 Case C-7/98, *Krombach* v. *Bamberski* [2000] ECR I-1935, [44]; Case C-559/14, *Meroni* v. *Recoletos Limited* [2016] ECLI:EU:C:2016:349, [44]-[45].

1220 Case C-283/05, *ASML Netherlands BV* v. *Semiconductor Industry Services GmbH* [2006] ECR I-12041, [24]-[28]; Case C-70/15, *Lebek* v. *Domino* [2016] ECLI:EU:C:2016:524, [34]-[36].

1221 Text to n. 1139.

1222 Text to n. 1179.

would cause a common lawyer to lose sleep[1223]. The scope of Article 6 has, however, been extended by the jurisprudence of the Court of Human Rights to include, for example, a principle of equality of arms and protection against self-incrimination, as well as requirements that the court or tribunal examine the arguments and evidence presented by the parties and give appropriate reasons for its decision[1224]. In common law systems that are party to the European Convention, the concept of natural justice will, to some extent at least, be shaped by the Strasbourg jurisprudence[1225].

342. Importantly, as the European Court of Justice has emphasised, the right to a fair trial, like other fundamental rights, is not unfettered and may be subject to restrictions that are proportionate and in the public interest[1226]. In applying the public policy ground in the Brussels I regime, the European Court has limited the role of the recognising or enforcing Member State to considering whether there was a "manifest and disproportionate infringement of the right to be heard", having regard to all of the circumstances of the case and, in particular, the remedies available to the party

---

1223 As to the former, see *Al Rawi* v. *The Security Service* (n. 1210), [10]-[11], [22] (Lord Dyson), referring in the latter passage to "the common law principles of natural justice and open justice". As to the latter, see *Paal Wilson & Co A/s* v. *Partenreederei Hannah Blumenthal* [1983] AC 854, 891 (Kerr L. J.); *Natwest Markets Plc* v. *Bilta (UK) Ltd.* [2021], *EWCA Civ* 680, [43]-[45].

1224 William A. Schabas, *The European Convention on Human Rights: A Commentary*, Oxford: Oxford University Press, 2015, pp. 287-298.

1225 See e.g. *Merchant International* v. *Naftogaz* (n. 1213), esp. at [68] (requirement of finality); also *Dicey, Morris & Collins* (n. 5), [14-166].

1226 Case C-394/07, *Gambazzi* v. *DaimlerChrysler Canada Inc.* [2009] ECLI:EU:C:2009:219, [29]; Case C-619/10, *Trade Agency Ltd.* v. *Seramico Investments Ltd.*[2012] ECLI:EU:C:2012:531, [55]; *Lebek* (n. 1220), [37].

alleging the infringement[1227]. More recently, the Court has specifically required that party to avail itself of the remedies available in the Member State of origin, unless circumstances make it too difficult or impossible to use them[1228].

343. Similarly, the notification ground in Article 45 (1) *(b)* of the Recast Brussels I Regulation[1229] demands that the defendant bring proceedings to set aside a default judgment in the adjudicating order if it is possible to do so. As the European Court has affirmed, the purpose of this qualification is to strike a fair balance between the need to ensure the effectiveness of judgments within the European Union, on the one hand, and respect for the rights of the defence, on the other[1230].

344. A common lawyer, in particular one who has never been a citizen of the European Union, might be tempted to set its rules and case law to one side, as the products of a regime that depends on the close constitutional ties that exist between the Member States of the European Union, or the close trade and treaty relations between the parties to the Lugano Convention. The EU's human rights based approach nevertheless offers at least two valuable insights for all legal orders.

345. First, in emphasising that injustice has many potential causes and that the jurisprudential tools needed to avoid it cannot be kept within fixed categories. The principles gathered by common law systems under the banner of "natural justice" should be open to incremental development, and not confined to notice, the opportunity to be heard and impartiality of the tribunal.

346. Second, in supporting an approach that is sensitive both to the procedural landscape in the adjudicating

[1227] *Gambazzi*, above, [46]-[47]; *Trade Agency*, above, [59]-[62].
[1228] *Meroni* (n. 1219), [49].
[1229] See also 2007 Lugano Convention (n. 1112), Article 34 (2).
[1230] *Lebek* (n. 1220), [48].

order and to the particular facts of the case and acknowledging that the parties as well as the court have a responsibility to prevent and remedy injustice at its source.

347. In this spirit, the English Court of Appeal has acknowledged that "it would . . . be anomalous if our courts were obliged wholly to disregard the existence of a perfectly good remedy under a foreign system of procedure in considering whether the defective operation of that procedure has led to a breach of natural justice"[1231]. The Court doubted whether this more nuanced approach would extend to a breach of the "traditional" requirements of due notice and an adequate opportunity to be heard[1232], and courts in England, Australia and Canada have since accepted that qualification[1233]. The reservation was unnecessary[1234]. A party that deliberately chooses not to take an opportunity provided by the adjudicating order to challenge a judicial decision on particular grounds, with awareness of the underlying facts, should not be allowed to invoke those grounds when opposing the recognition or enforcement of the "tainted judgment" if a reasonable person with the same knowledge would likely have acted differently[1235].

1231 *Adams* v. *Cape Industries* (n. 504), 569. Cf. *Nygh's Conflict of Laws* (n. 1174), [40.88]; *Nyunt* v. *First Property Holdings Pte Ltd.* [2022] NSWCA 249, [125] (Bell C. J.).

1232 *Adams* v. *Cape Industries*, above, 568-569.

1233 *Agbara* v. *The Shell Petroleum Development Company of Nigeria Ltd.* [2019] EWHC 3340 (QB), [41] (Jason Coppel QC); *Cortés* v. *Yorkton Securities Inc.* [2007] BCSC 282, 278 DLR (4th) 740, [118]-[130] (Myers J.); *Zhou* v. *Jing* [2023] NSWSC 214, [52]-[54] (Elkhaim A. J.).

1234 The Court of Appeal was influenced by its understanding of the English case law relating to challenges on the ground of fraud, but this case law is itself in need of review (see Dickinson, "*Abouloff* v. *Oppenheimer* Revisited" (n. 1173)).

1235 Dickinson, "*Abouloff* v. *Oppenheimer* Revisited", above, 224. This formulation builds on the approach favoured by one member of the UK Supreme Court (Lord Sumption) in

The mechanism provided by the adjudicating order must, however, be both reasonably available and adequate to redress the injustice complained of. For example, the mechanism for addressing a complaint that the foreign court of tribunal was biased must provide an adequate opportunity for the issue of impartiality to be heard by a differently constituted (and itself unbiased) court and, if held to be well-founded, result in a full rehearing of the merits by an impartial adjudicator.

348. In Article 300 of its recently amended Civil Procedure Law [1236], China combines a ground specifically requiring a lawful summons and a reasonable opportunity to be heard, with a more general provision demanding that a Chinese court refuse recognition and enforcement if the judgment "violates the basic principles of the Chinese law or is detrimental to the state sovereignty, security and public interest" [1237]. On its face, the latter provision allows significant latitude to the Chinese courts, and it will be interesting to see whether the Supreme People's Court provides further guidance as the new set of rules beds down. This ground seems, in any event, broad enough to cover (for example) a case in which there was evidence demonstrating an actual or apparent lack of impartiality on the part of the foreign court.

---

a domestic fraud case, *Takhar* v. *Gracefield Developments Ltd.* [2019] UKSC 13, [2020] AC 450, [63]. See also *Mengiste* v. *Endowment Fund for the Rehabilitation of Tigray* [2017] *EWCA Civ* 1326, [57] (Arden L. J.), [74] (Davis L. J.); Mortensen, Garnett and Keyes, *Private International Law in Australia* (n. 1174), [5.33].

1236 Article 300 (2), referring also to the lack of representation for parties with legal capacity. See Annex, B.1, C.4, C.5 and C.6.

1237 For more detailed account of the Chinese rules, see Huang, "Developing Chinese Private International Law for Foreign Judgments" (n. 1062); also Zheng Sophia Tang, Yongping Xiao and Zhengxin Huo, *Conflict of Laws in the People's Republic of China*, Cheltenham: Edward Elgar, 2018, Chap. 6.

C. Levelling up

349. This survey suggests that values transcend terminology. Whether judges speak in terms of "natural justice" or "due process" or "procedural fairness" or the "right to be heard" or "basic principles of law" or other similar formulation[1238], they share a core conception of the basic conditions for a just adjudication – all parties must have sufficient knowledge of the proceedings to enable them to present their case, they must be given a reasonable opportunity to present that case and to address that of their opponent and the adjudicating body must be independent. Although there are, of course, differences in the definition and practical application of these ideas, the shared vision nonetheless projects itself strongly.

350. The continued use in common law systems of the language of "natural justice" to capture their own vision of the essential standards that judges and the legal orders that they represent must attain if their decisions are to be given any credit may seem outdated and in some respects unhelpful[1239]. The law would be more accessible if, in future, judges were to refer to "fundamental principles of procedural fairness" or other similar descriptive term[1240]. However, a willingness to update linguistic conventions and to shape the underlying principles to meet the needs and demands of modern society should not allow us to slip the anchor provided by judges and writers of the past.

351. This common law usage reminds us that human attitudes to the administration of justice have been shaped for centuries by values that transcend particular legal

---

[1238] E.g. in Spain, Article 46 (1) *(b)* of Law 29/2015 (30 July 2015) on international judicial co-operation in civil matters refers to the "rights of the defence of any of the parties" ("los derechos de defensa de cualquiera de las partes").

[1239] See above, [332].

[1240] See above, [337]; also Edelman, "Why Do We Have Rules of Procedural Fairness?" (n. 1190).

traditions. Equality before the law[1241] is arguably the most important of these ubiquitous values[1242], inherent in any system for the settlement of disputes, whether within a single political society or between the members of different political societies[1243].

352. Whatever substantive distribution of rights and responsibilities a civil society may consider to be appropriate, justice is not attainable if the law is not administered impartially, whether because the decision-maker does not exercise independent judgment or because only one side of the dispute is adequately heard. The procedural standards gathered by the common law under the banner of natural justice are, as H. L. A. Hart explained[1244]:

> "... guarantees of impartiality or objectivity, designed to secure that the law is applied to all those and only to those who are alike in the relevant respect marked out by the law itself".

353. This idea is perfectly captured in the Universal Declaration of Human Rights, proclaiming the universal entitlement *in full equality* to a fair and public hearing by an independent and impartial tribunal[1245].

354. The principle of equality before the law has a more complex substantive aspect, the right to equal protection of the law without discrimination[1246]. The

1241 Section II.D.

1242 Universal Declaration of Human Rights (1948), Article 7.

1243 Hart, *The Concept of Law* (n. 168), pp. 158-160. See above, [67].

1244 Hart, *The Concept of Law*, above, 160.

1245 Universal Declaration of Human Rights (1948), Article 10 (above, [306]). See further Charles T. Kotuby Jr and Luke A. Sobota, *General Principles of Law and International Due Process*, Oxford: Oxford University Press, 2017, pp. 165-183.

1246 *Ibid.*, Article 7.

principle of equal protection requires that a legal order treats like cases alike, and different cases differently, in regulating legal entitlement[1247], but this formulation leaves a gap to be filled in specifying the standards by reference to which differences in treatment are to be judged as just or unjust[1248]. Hart points out that among political societies, as well as among individuals, "[f] undamental differences, in general moral and political outlook, may lead to irreconcilable differences and disagreement as to what characteristics of human beings are to be taken as relevant for the criticism of law as unjust"[1249]. There is, nonetheless, a broad measure of consensus in human rights instruments as to the core protected characteristics – race, skin colour, sex, language, religion, political or religious belief, national or social origin[1250]. More recently, measures have been adopted to dismantle barriers to equality linked to physical or mental impairments, age or sexual orientation[1251]. In the recognition and enforcement of judgments, the substantive aspect of the principle of equality is best considered as a discrete, homogenised aspect of public policy, emphasising our common humanity and natural equality.

1247 Hart, *The Concept of Law* (n. 168), p. 159. See further Finnis, *Natural Law and Natural Rights* (n. 22), pp. 173-177.

1248 Hart, The Concept of Law, above, pp. 161-163.

1249 *Ibid.*, p. 161.

1250 Universal Declaration of Human Rights (1948), Article 2; European Convention on Human Rights (1950), Article 14; Inter-American Convention on Human Rights (1969), Article 1; African Charter of Human and Peoples' Rights (1981), Article 2; Charter of Fundamental Rights of the European Union (2000), Article 21; also Asian Human Rights Charter (1998), [6.2], [8]-[11].

1251 Charter of Fundamental Rights of the European Union (2000), Article 21.

D. Adjudicatory jurisdiction: A question of natural justice?

355. All modern systems for the recognition and enforcement of judgments, whether local or treaty based, have requirements pertaining to the foreign court's authority to adjudicate upon the parties' dispute[1252]. As with other aspects of the law in this field, these vary greatly. The European Union, having adopted a common set of rules allocating jurisdiction among the courts of its Member States and demanding mutual trust in the application of those rules, strictly regulates the circumstances in which the adjudicating court's jurisdiction can be reviewed[1253]. Many legal orders, including, for example, those of Germany, Japan and South Korea[1254], adopt a "mirror image principle" in which they use the same standards in assessing the competence of the foreign court as they apply to their own courts[1255]. Italian courts examine whether the foreign court had authority according to the principles applied within the Italian legal order[1256]. Elsewhere, for example, in the Philippines[1257], the focus is on the question whether the adjudicating court was competent under its own rules of jurisdiction. Other legal orders, including (for example) those of France[1258],

---

1252 See generally von Mehren, "Recognition and Enforcement" (n. 493), esp. at 51-74.

1253 Recast Brussels I Regulation, Recital (26) and Article 45 (1) *(e)*, (2) and (3).

1254 Martiny, (n. 931), 734; Sawaki, (n. 930), 31-32; Chong, "Moving towards harmonisation" (n. 1056), 43.

1255 Martiny, above, 734; Sawaki, above, 31-32; Chong, "Moving Towards Harmonisation", above, 43.

1256 Law No. 218, 31 May 1995, Article 64 (1) *(a)*.

1257 Chong, "Moving Towards Harmonisation" (n. 1056), 42.

1258 Cour de Cassation (1st Civil Chamber), 6 February 1985 *(Simitch)* (n. 943). The French court must satisfy itself that there is an actual connection between the dispute and the

Spain[1259] and Switzerland[1260], apply discrete standards, operating independently of the rules governing the adjudicatory jurisdiction of their own courts.

356. Most common law systems belong to the last group, applying autonomous rules to determine the adjudicating court's competence "in an international sense"[1261]. In *Schibsby* v. *Westenholz*, the Court of Queen's Bench rejected the submission that the mirror image principle formed part of English law[1262]. Although there was renewed interest in this principle in the middle of the twentieth century[1263], the revival was short lived[1264]. The

---

country of the foreign court ("si le litige se rattache d'une manière caracterisée au pays dont le juge a été saisi").

1259 Law 29/2015 (30 July 2015), Article 46 (1) *(c)*, requiring a reasonable connection ("una conexión razonable"), which is presumed when the foreign court has based its international jurisdiction on criteria similar to those provided for in Spanish law.

1260 Federal Act on Private International Law, 18 December 1987, Article 26, predominantly applying the jurisdictional standards laid down elsewhere in the Act.

1261 *Pemberton* v. *Hughes* [1899] 1 Ch 781. In this case, the Court of Appeal held that it was immaterial whether the court had jurisdiction under its own rules (*ibid.*, 790-794 (Lindley L. J.)). See *Dicey, Morris & Collins* (n. 5), [14-129]-[14-132]; Dickinson, "*Schibsby* v. *Westenholz*" (n. 216), 437-439.
In the United States, authority is divided as to whether it is necessary to establish the adjudicating court's jurisdiction under its own law as well as under the autonomous local US standard (see e.g. *Evans Cabinet Corp* v. *Kitchen Intern, Inc.* (2010) 593 F 3d 135, 140).

1262 *Schibsby* v. *Westenholz* (n. 963), 159.

1263 Prompted by the decision in a matrimonial case, *Travers* v. *Holley* [1953] P 246, and by observations made by Denning L. J. in *Re Dulles Settlement* (n. 197), 851.

1264 *Re Trepca Mines Ltd.* [1960] 1 WLR 1273, 1281-1282 (Hodson L. J.); *Rubin* v. *Eurofinance* (n. 976), [127] (Lord Collins of Mapesbury); *Dicey, Morris & Collins* (n. 5), [14-094]. As the editors of *Dicey, Morris & Collins* point out (at [14-094]), "there is no obvious need for there to be symmetry between the jurisdiction which is exercised by an

modern English rule, followed in many other common law systems, takes a "closed list" approach[1265] to the question of the foreign court's adjudicatory jurisdiction. Over time, the list of possible grounds canvassed in *Schibsby*, drawing on earlier authority[1266], has been pruned. The defendant's status as a subject of the foreign legal order, the defendant's presence at the time the cause of action arose and the presence of property locally situated in the possession of the defendant are no longer recognised bases of jurisdiction under the current English rules[1267]. Only presence within its territory at the time the proceedings were served[1268], submission to the jurisdiction by bringing a claim, voluntary appearance of the defendant other than for a protected purpose[1269] and agreement are firmly established as grounds of jurisdiction[1270]. Even residence, not accompanied by

---

English court which is asked to adjudicate (but which does not do so with any concern for whether its judgment may be enforced outside the jurisdiction), and that 'jurisdiction' of a foreign court which means that, as far as the common law is concerned, its judgment may be recognised as *res judicata* in England".

1265 Dickinson, "*Schibsby* v. *Westenholz*" (n. 216), 429-437.

1266 *Schibsby* v. *Westenholz* (n. 963), 161-163.

1267 *Dicey, Morris & Collins* (n. 5), [14-088]-[14-090]; Kutner, "Recognition and Enforcement" (n. 503), 27-33, 38-41. Australian case law offers some support for "active citizenship" as a ground of adjudicatory jurisdiction (*Independent Trustee Services Ltd.* v. *Morris* [2010] NSWSC 1218; *Liu* v. *Ma* [2017] VSC 810). See below, [392].

1268 The Court of Appeal in *Adams* left open the question whether presence at the time that the proceedings were issued would suffice (*Adams* v. *Cape Industries* (n. 504), 518).

1269 Civil Jurisdiction and Judgments Act 1982 (UK), s. 33.

1270 *Dicey, Morris & Collins* (n. 5), [14R-058]-[14-086] (Rule 47); Kutner, "Recognition and Enforcement" (n. 503). The defendant's presence, as opposed to residence, at the time proceedings were instituted was not one of the grounds suggested by the Court in *Schibsby*. It was first

presence at the time proceedings were instituted, falls within a grey area[1271].

357. Adrian Briggs, a staunch defender of the way in which the rules are currently framed, argues that the court's authority emanates either from its physical power over the litigant or the litigant's consent to be bound by the judgment[1272]. A similar rationale was offered by A. V. Dicey, arguing that the power of adjudication rested either on the ability of the sovereign of a country to give an effective judgment (the principle of effectiveness) or on a person's voluntary submission (the principle of submission)[1273]. The English Court of Appeal has

---

recognised in *Carrick* v. *Hancock* (n. 504), on the basis that "all persons within any territorial dominion owe their allegiance to its sovereign power and obedience to all its laws and not the lawful jurisdiction of its Courts" (*ibid.*, 60 (Lord Russell L. C.J.)). Although much criticised, the rule was endorsed by the Court of Appeal in *Adams* v. *Cape Industries* (n. 504), 517-519, and applied in that case to a corporate defendant (see *Dicey, Morris & Collins*, above, [14-069]-[14-071]).

For the position in other common law systems, see above, [153].

1271 Although the earlier authorities, including *Schibsby*, referred specifically to residence (*Dicey, Morris & Collins*, above, [14-064]), the point was left open in *Adams*, above, 518. Although later authority suggests that residence, without presence, will suffice (*State Bank of India* v. *Murjani Marketing*, unreported, 27 April 1991), this point is still contested (Briggs, *Private International Law in English Courts*, Oxford: Oxford University Press, 2nd ed., 2023, p. 327; Kutner, "Recognition and Enforcement" (n. 503), 25-27).

Absent presence or residence, carrying on local business is not enough, however substantial it may be and whatever its relationship to the dispute (*Emanuel* v. *Symon* [1908] 1 KB 302; *Lucasfilm Ltd.* v. *Ainsworth* (n. 976), [192]-[194]).

1272 Briggs, "Recognition of Foreign Judgments: A Matter of Obligation" (n. 976), 90-94; Briggs, *Private International Law in English Courts*, above, pp. 323-325.

1273 Dicey, *Digest* (n. 968), pp. 38-43, 369-379.

suggested that the court's authority over a person present when served with process is itself rooted in the individual's tacit consent to abide by local laws for the duration of the visit[1274].

358. The proposition that the authority to adjudicate may arise from the consent of the parties is attractive from a natural law perspective, as the nomination by the parties of a "common judge" to adjudicate their dispute was identified as a means of promoting the peaceful settlement of disputes, avoiding a scenario in which each acted as judge of their own cause[1275]. This works well in a case in which there is a choice of court agreement, to which the parties have unquestionably consented, and also in a case where a party, as claimant or counterclaiming defendant, has willingly submitted a claim for adjudication by a particular court. It is, however, less well equipped to deal with the case of a defendant who, while protesting that the court has no authority, participates in the proceedings in order to protect local interests, such as assets under threat of seizure or business continuity or reputation[1276]. Moreover, as we have seen, it is stretched beyond credulity when used to explain why the members of a political society are bound by exercises of legislative or adjudicatory authority by those who govern it[1277]. Incredulity stretches to disbelief if we are to understand that a person temporarily present in a particular place is to be taken to consent to *any conceivable* exercise of adjudicatory authority by its courts, whether or not the dispute has any connection to the purpose of the visit,

---

1274 *Adams* v. *Cape Industries* (n. 504), 555-556. See Dickinson, "*Schibsby* v. *Westenholz*" (n. 216), 434-437.

1275 Section II.G.

1276 Andrew Dickinson, "Foreign Submission" (n. 197). See also Johannes Voet, *Commentarius*, Book 2, Title 1, [20], Vol. 1, pp. 220-221.

1277 Section II.I.2.

while a person born and residing in that place cannot be bound while remaining abroad[1278].

359. Theories based on the court's ability to deliver an effective judgment (Dicey) or its power over the defendant's person (Briggs) are also unconvincing[1279]. In Dicey's view, an "effective judgment" is "a decree which the sovereign, under whose authority it is delivered, has in fact the power to enforce against the person bound by it"[1280]. But a nation does not have the power to secure the effectiveness of decisions of its courts by taking action beyond its borders[1281], and the act of seeking recognition or enforcement elsewhere is an admission of the limitations on its authority (liberty). Moreover, although the defendant's physical presence no doubt places them under a legal obligation to attend court when summoned, as they would be obliged to comply with a lawful direction from a police constable, and non-compliance with the summons may legitimately attract an official sanction – including by denying the opportunity to defend the case and issuing judgment in default[1282] – the combination of temporary presence and sovereign command does not provide a convincing reason why an independent legal order should respect any resulting adjudication as being conclusive regardless of its subject matter or should enforce the judgment imposed as a sanction for non-compliance with another

[1278] Hook and Wass, *The Conflict of Laws in New Zealand* (n. 504), [5.108].

[1279] Attempts to rely on Huber's account to support jurisdiction based on the defendant's presence are wide of the mark for the reasons given above (Sec. III.C.5). For Huber, the presence of the defendant is a *further* pre-requisite to the exercise of adjudicatory authority in cases in which jurisdiction is founded on the act giving rise to proceedings in order to ensure a fair process (see above, [157]).

[1280] Dicey, *Digest* (n. 968), p. 39.

[1281] See above, [110].

[1282] See *Gambazzi* v. *DaimlerChrysler Canada* (n. 1226).

legal order's commands[1283]. Nor does it explain why under these theories adjudicatory authority comes to an end when the defendant departs before proceedings can be served, without regard to the defendant's conduct during their stay or the degree of connection that the dispute or the parties may have with the political society that the adjudicating court represents.

360. Before *Schibsby*, courts in the British Isles had taken a different approach to the question whether the foreign court was one of competent jurisdiction[1284]. They asked themselves whether the circumstances in which the court had asserted and exercised adjudicatory jurisdiction were demonstrably contrary to principles of natural justice applied in England or, to use Lord Ellenborough's terminology in *Buchanan* v. *Rucker*, the "first principles of justice"[1285]. This approach demanded an assessment not only of the manner in which the defendant had been notified of proceedings, and given an opportunity to answer the claim, but also of the defendant's connection to the adjudicating legal order. The assessment was informed by the practices adopted by the enforcing legal order in dealing with absent defendants in proceedings before its courts[1286]. The justice of the foreign decision was presumed, placing the burden on the defendant to set out the reasons for impugning it and to prove its case[1287]. In *Buchanan* v. *Rucker*, in which enforcement was refused, it appeared that the defendant had never

[1283] As to the need to segregate prescriptive and adjudicatory jurisdiction in considering this issue, see Dickinson, "Keeping Up Appearances" (n. 218), 9-10.

[1284] Dickinson, "*Schibsby* v. *Westenholz*" (n. 216), 440-447.

[1285] *Buchanan* v. *Rucker* (n. 1184), 66 (above, [330]).

[1286] *Douglas* v. *Forrest* (n. 767), 700-701; *Maubourquet* v. *Wyse* (1867) 1 *Irish Rep CL* 471, 497-498.

[1287] *Molony* v. *Gibbons* (1810) 2 Campbell 502; *Cowan* v. *Braidwood* (n. 1176); *Reynolds* v. *Fenton* (n. 1176); *Maubourquet* v. *Wyse*, above.

been resident or even present in Tobago[1288]. In *Douglas* v. *Forrest*, the defendant, although absent, was a native of Scotland possessed of land there[1289]. Although the Scots court followed a similar procedure to that used by the Tobagan court in *Buchanan*[1290], the judgment creditor prevailed in that case[1291]. In *Becquet* v. *MacCarthy*, the defendant was alleged to have committed a tort on the island of Mauritius and, although he had departed, continued to hold a Crown office there[1292]. Again, the justice of the judgment was upheld[1293]. By contrast, in *Don* v. *Lippmann*, the defendant had been a prisoner in France during the Napoleonic Wars when he signed two bills of exchange. He had already returned to England, being unable as an alien enemy to re-enter France, when proceedings were brought against him[1294]. In refusing to give effect to the French judgment, Lord Brougham observed that *Douglas* "shows how much the application of the rule is affected by the circumstances", adding that *Becquet* "has been supposed to go to the verge of the law, but the defendant . . . held a public office in the very colony in which he was originally sued"[1295]. Presence at the time proceedings were commenced did not suffice

---

[1288] *Buchanan* v. *Rucker* (n. 1184), 67; also (1808) 9 East 192, 194. Cf. *Cavan* v. *Stewart* (n. 1194), 529-530.
The Rucker family owned plantations in Tobago and elsewhere, although the role of the defendant, Sigismund Rucker, in the business is unclear. See the report of the will of Sigismund's uncle, John Anthony Rucker at the website of the Centre for the Study of the Legacies of British Slavery, https://www.ucl.ac.uk/lbs/person/view/2146649779.

[1289] *Douglas* v. *Forrest* (n. 767), 693.

[1290] The summons had been nailed to the market cross of Edinburgh and the pier and shore of Leith *(ibid.)*.

[1291] *Ibid.*, 702-703.

[1292] *Becquet* v. *MacCarthy* (n. 1186), 955.

[1293] *Ibid.*, 958-959.

[1294] *Don* v. *Lippmann* (1837) 5 Clark & Finnelly 1, 1-2, 6-7, 20.

[1295] *Ibid.*, 20-21.

to demonstrate the validity of the proceedings, just as absence did not serve to demonstrate their invalidity[1296].

361. The subtlety of this approach was lost when the tie to natural justice was severed in *Godard* and *Schibsby*[1297]. One hundred and fifty years later, the mechanical rules applied in these common law jurisdictions have become increasingly hard to defend[1298].

362. The United States and Canada, by contrast, follow the mirror image principle, assessing the competence of foreign courts using rules aligned with those that they apply to determine the limits of jurisdiction of their own courts[1299]. In both nations, the "traditional" (i.e. late

---

1296 *Cowan* v. *Braidwood* (n. 1176), 895 (Maule J.).

1297 See above, [272]-[278].

1298 Dickinson, "*Schibsby* v. *Westenholz*" (n. 216), 466, arguing that the decision "led the English common law along a narrow stream into the stagnant waters that it occupies today"; also Ardavan Arzandeh, "Reformulating the Common Law Rules on the Recognition and Enforcement of Foreign Judgments" [2019], *Legal Studies* 39; Alexander Layton, "English Common Law on the Recognition and Enforcement of Judgments: Time for a Review?" (2023), 56 *International Law and Politics* 249, 253-256.

1299 In the United States, the "due process" requirement was developed to resolve questions of adjudicatory jurisdiction within the local constitutional order (*International Shoe Co* v. *Washington* (n. 197)) and later applied to non-US judgments (see e.g. *Cherun* v. *Frishman* (1964) 236 *F Supp* 292 (DC); *Somportex Ltd.* v. *Philadelphia Chewing Gum Corp* (1971) 453 *F 2d* 435 (3rd Circuit); *Davidson Company* v. *Allen* (1973) 508 *P 2d* 6 (Nevada); *Bank of Montreal* v. *Kough* (1977) 430, *F Supp* 1243 (ND Cal) and (1980) 612 *F 2d* 467 (9th Circuit); *Royal Bank of Canada* v. *Trentham* Corp (1980) 492 *F Supp* 885 (SD Texas); *Hunt* v. *BP Exploration Company* (Libya) *Ltd.* (1980) 492 *F Supp* 885 (ND Texas); *Koster* v. *Automark Industries Inc.* (n. 288); *Ackerman* v. *Levine* (1985) 610 *F Supp* 633 (SDNY) and (1986) 788 *F 2d* 830 (2nd Circuit); *Oman International Finance Ltd.* v. *Hoiyong Gems Corp* (1985) 616 *F Supp* 351 (Rhode Island); *De la Mata* v. *American Life Insurance* (1991) 771 *F Supp* 1375 (Delaware).

nineteenth century) bases of jurisdiction – presence and submission/consent[1300] – have been supplemented[1301] by broader and more flexible tests attuned to the interests of justice.

363. In Canada, the test laid down by the Supreme Court is whether the adjudicating order "had a real and substantial connection with either the subject matter of

---

As each US State applies its own law within the framework of the Constitution, a variety of approaches have been taken, with some examining whether the adjudicating court had jurisdiction under its own rules and others considering their "long arm" statutes alongside the "due process" requirement (see James P. George, "Facilitating Money Judgment Enforcement between Canada and the United States" (2020), 72 *Hastings LJ* 99, 131-135; Tanja J. Monestier, "Whose Law of Personal Jurisdiction? The Choice of Law Problem in the Recognition of Foreign Judgments" (2016), 96 *Boston Univ L Rev* 1729, 1739-1743).

In Canada, the "real and substantial" connection test was first developed with respect to the recognition and enforcement of judgments within Canada, *Morguard Investments Ltd.* v. *De Savoye* [1990] 3 SCR 1077, then extended to foreign judgments, *Beals* v. *Saldanha* (n. 504) and later applied to questions of the adjudicatory jurisdiction of Canadian courts, *Club Resorts Ltd.* v. *Van Breda* (n. 504).

1300 United States: *Pennoyer* v. *Neff* (n. 216); *Burnham* v. *Superior Court of California* (n. 2); *Pennsylvania Fire Insurance Co of Philadelphia* v. *Gold Issue Mining & Milling Co* (1917) 243 US 93; *Mallory* v. *Norfolk Southern Railway Co* (2023) 600 US 122; UFMJR 1962 (n. 1195), s. 5 *(a)* (1)-(3); UFCMJR 2005 (n. 1195), s. 5 *(a)* (1)-(3).

Canada: see, in addition to the authorities referred to in the preceding footnote, *Morgan* v. *Guimond Boats Ltd.*, 2006 FCA 401, [25]-[27]; *Litecubes LLC* v. *Northern Light Products*, 2009 BCSC 181, [45]-[59]; *Mehralian* v. *Dunmore*, 2023 ONSC 1044, [29].

1301 It is, however, no easy task to reconcile the principles described below, [363]-[365], with the proposition that jurisdiction can be based on the defendant's fleeting presence at the time of service, regardless of the subject matter of the dispute (see above, [358]-[359]). See the Canadian authorities referred to in n. 504.

the action or the defendant"[1302]. The Court explained that[1303]:

> ". . . the test requires that a significant connection exist between the cause of action and the foreign court. Furthermore, a defendant can reasonably be brought within the embrace of a foreign jurisdiction's law where he or she has participated in something of significance or was actively involved in that foreign jurisdiction. A fleeting or relatively unimportant connection will not be enough to give a foreign court jurisdiction. The connection to the foreign jurisdiction must be a substantial one".

364. The rationale for this approach is that "[m]odern ideas of order and fairness require that a court must have reasonable grounds for assuming jurisdiction where the participants to the litigation are connected to multiple jurisdictions"[1304].

365. In the United States, beyond the grounds specifically listed in the uniform legislation (where applicable)[1305], the central question has been formulated as one of "due process", demanding an enquiry as to the "quality and nature"[1306] of the defendant's contacts or ties with the adjudicating legal order so as to make it "reasonable and just, according to [the United States'] traditional conception of fair play and substantial justice" to recognise the court's authority to adjudicate[1307]. Defendants must be given a "fair warning" that a particular activity may subject them to the jurisdiction of a foreign

1302 *Beals* v. *Saldanha* (n. 504), [23], [28].
1303 *Ibid.*, [32].
1304 *Ibid.*, [22].
1305 UFMJR 1962 (n. 1195), ss. 4 *(a)* (2) and 5 *(a)*; UFCMJR 2005 (n. 1195), ss. 4 *(b)* (2) and 5 *(a)*.
1306 *International Shoe Co* v. *Washington* (n. 197), 319.
1307 *Ibid.*, 320.

court[1308]. That requirement will be satisfied if a non-resident[1309] defendant "purposefully avails itself of the privilege of conducting activities within the forum state thus invoking the benefits and protections of its laws"[1310], if the obligation in dispute arises out of or relates to those activities[1311] and if the assertion of jurisdiction is fair and reasonable in all the circumstances[1312]. In assessing the question of "reasonableness", the primary concern, particularly in international litigation[1313], is the burden that the proceedings will impose on the defendant, although other factors are taken into account – the interests of the claimant and of the forum, the interest of securing the efficient judicial resolution of the dispute and the procedural and substantive interests of other nations[1314].

1308 *Shaffer* v. *Heitner* (1977) 433 US 186, 218 (Stevens J.); *Burger King* v. *Rudzewicz* (1985) 471 US 462, 472 (Brennan J.).

1309 By contrast, if the defendant is "essentially at home" in the foreign forum, general jurisdiction extends to any and all claims brought against the defendant (*Goodyear Dunlop Tires Operations, SA* v. *Brown* (2011) 564 US 915, 919; *Daimler AG* v. *Bauman* (2014) 571 US 117).

1310 *Hanson* v. *Denckla* (1958) 357 US 235, 253; *International Shoe Co* v. *Washington* (n. 197), 319; *Shaffer* v. *Heitner* (n. 1308), 216; *Burger King* v. *Rudzewicz* (n. 1308), 472-476; *Asahi Metal Industry Co Ltd.* v. *Superior Court of California* (1986) 480 US 102, 108-109 (O'Connor J.); *Ford Motor Co* v. *Montana Eighth Judicial District Court* (2021) 592 US 351, 5-7 (Kagan J.).

1311 *International Shoe Co* v. *Washington,* above, 319; *Helicopteros Nacionales* v. *Hall* (1984) 466 US 408, 414 (Blackmun J.); *Burger King* v. *Rudzewicz* above, 472; *Ford Motor Co* v. *Montana,* above, 7-15.

1312 *World-Wide Volkswagen Corp* v. *Woodson* (1980) US 286, 292-294 (White J.), 299-301, 307-313 (Brennan J., dissenting).

1313 *Asahi Metal Industry* v. *California* (n. 1313), 114-116.

1314 *World-Wide Volkswagen* v. *Woodson* (n. 1312), 292; *Asahi Metal Industry* v. *California* (n. 1310), 114-116.

366. It is no accident that these approaches have been developed within legal orders that embrace the doctrine of comity[1315]. The courts in these two legal orders, alive to changing patterns of trade and commerce and to advances in communication and travel[1316], sought to strike a balance between the parties' interests as well as between those of adjudicating and receiving orders. The central idea in each approach is that, by engaging in activities in a particular locality, the defendant enlivens the adjudicatory jurisdiction of its courts in respect of disputes that are sufficiently connected to that activity. As the United States Supreme Court explained[1317]:

> "[T]o the extent that a corporation exercises the privilege of conducting activities within a state, it enjoys the benefits and protection of the laws of that state. The exercise of that privilege may give rise to obligations, and, so far as those obligations arise out of or are connected with the activities within the state, a procedure which requires the corporation to respond to a suit brought to enforce them can, in most instances, hardly be said to be undue."

Grotius' principle of natural equity[1318] lives on.

1315 United States: *Hilton* v. *Guyot* (n. 599) and *Ritchie* v. *McMullen* (n. 964) [279]; *Somportex Ltd.* v. *Philadelphia Chewing Gum* (n. 1299), 440; *Cunard Steamship Co* v. *Salen Reefer Services AB* (1985) 775 F 2d 452, 457 (2nd Circuit); *Turner Entertainment Co* v. *Degeto Film GmbH* (1994) 25 F 3d 1512, 1519 (11th Circuit).
Canada: *Morguard Investments* v. *De Savoye* (n. 1299), 1095-1096; *Pro-Swing* v. *Elta* (n. 8), [26]-[27]; *Beals* v. *Saldanha* (n. 504), [20], [27]-[28] (Major J.), [166]-[168] (Le Bel J.).

1316 United States: *World-Wide Volkswagen* v. *Woodson* (n. 1312), 292-293; *Burnham* v. *Superior Court of California* (n. 2), 617-618 (Scalia J.); *Honda Motor Co Ltd.* v. *Oberg* (1994) 512 US 415, 431 (Stevens J.).
Canada: *Morguard Investments*, above, 1098; *Beals* v. *Saldanha,* above, [21], [26].

1317 *International Shoe Co* v. *Washington* (n. 197), 320.

1318 See above, [82].

CHAPTER V

RENATURALISATION?

A. Introduction

367. This special course recounts a history of ideas, in considering the influence of texts on the law of nature and nations on the rules applied today to regulate the recognition and enforcement of judgments between legal orders. By the nature of the enterprise, this account is selective. The works that we have studied in depth were written in a different period and in political, societal and economic conditions very different from those that prevail today. Their authors were European or North American men practising the Christian faith. The determined pursuit of a human-centred approach to this topic, or any other aspect of the conflict of laws, calls for wider and more diverse examination and discussion of theory and practice than that undertaken in this forum, enriching the analysis and conclusions with insights gained from scholars of different genders, faiths, ethnic and geographic origins, legal traditions, social backgrounds and lived experiences. The course offers, therefore, only an exploratory survey of part of the terrain.

368. The following examples illustrate the abundant resources that may inform future work on this, and related, topics [1319].

1. Mutual aid

369. Non-legal scholarship may offer valuable insights. Writing in 1967, the international lawyer, Wilfred

---

[1319] For further reflection, see Henri Batiffol, *Aspects philosophiques du droit international privé*, Paris: Dalloz, 1956, [64]-[78], pp. 144-171.

Jenks (1909-1973), drew upon anthropological accounts of social co-operation, and in particular on the work of the Russian naturalist and anarchist philosopher, Peter Kropotkin [1320], to advance the argument that "[m]utual aid is among the most civilising influences of any human society" [1321]. This idea is, Jenks submits [1322]:

> ". . . no new-fangled nostrum of rootless radicals; it is part of the imperishable tradition of western and eastern civilisation alike; all that is new is the need to extend the range and scope of the concept to correspond to a scale and content of human relationships which now encompass the world and embrace an ever more complex pattern of activities".

2. *Peaceful resolution of disputes by means other than adjudication*

370. We should likewise be conscious of, and sensitive to, varying approaches to the peaceful settlement of disputes and attitudes to adjudication in other legal and philosophical traditions. In *The Great Equal Society*, Korean scholars, Young-oak Kim and Jung-kyu Kim, draw attention to the Confucian virtue, *ren*, commonly translated as benevolence but embracing ideas of empathy, compassion and humanity [1323]. For Confucius, the ideal society, observing this virtue, was one in which

---

1320 Peter Kropotkin, *Mutual Aid*, New York: McLure Phillips & Co, 1902.

1321 C. Wilfred Jenks, "Mutual Aid in International Law", Ch. 6, in *Law in the World Community*, London: Longmans, 1967, pp. 66-82 (at p. 66).

1322 *Ibid.*, p. 67. Jenks addresses mutual aid in law enforcement, with reference to the enforcement of foreign judgments, at pp. 71-74.

1323 Young-oak Kim and Jung-kyu Kim, *The Great Equal Society: Confucianism, China and the 21st Century*, Singapore: World Scientific Publishing, 2013, p. 4.

contentious proceedings would be unnecessary[1324]. As the Chinese jurist, Albert H. Y. Chen, explains, "[l]itigation is considered to be a negative social phenomenon because it is a deviation from and a disruption of harmonious social relationships"[1325]. Disputes are to be avoided or peacefully resolved, if at all possible, and when they do arise, "[t]he dominant Confucian philosophy requires officials – instead of judging the dispute and imposing a binding judgment on the parties – to mediate the dispute and search for a solution which is agreeable to and voluntarily accepted by the disputants"[1326]. Although litigation is on the increase, the Confucian ideal remains influential in Chinese and Japanese society[1327]. These insights are valuable, suggesting that the Singapore Mediation Convention[1328] should take its place alongside

1324 Confucius, *Analects*, Book 12, Chap. 13 ("At hearing lawsuits I am no better than others. What is needed is to stop lawsuits"), trans. Leonard A. Lyall, *The Sayings of Confucius*, London: Longmans, Green & Co, 1909), https://www.gutenberg.org/files/24055/24055-h/24055-h.htm.

1325 Albert H. Y. Chen, "Mediation, Litigation and Justice", Chap. 11, in Daniel A. Bell and Hahm Chaibong (eds.), *Confucianism for the Modern World*, Cambridge: Cambridge University Press, 2003, at p. 260.

1326 *Ibid.*, p. 262, with illustrations (pp. 263-266); also Dong Jiang and Xioahong Ma, "The Analects and Sense of Justice: The Spirit of Law and Historical Practice" (2020), 46 *Modern China* 281, 296-299. For criticisms of the traditional approach, see Chen, above, pp. 270-274.
Pufendorf and Vattel contrast the role of mediators of peace with that of arbitrators, Pufendorf, *Nature and Nations*, Book 5, Chap. 13, [7], pp. 830-831; Vattel, *Nations*, Book 2, Chap. 18, [328], p. 450.

1327 Dana Zartner, *Courts, Codes, and Custom: Legal Tradition and State Policy Toward International Human Rights and Environmental Law*, Oxford: Oxford University Press, 2014, pp. 219-220, 236.

1328 United Nations Convention on International Settlement Agreements Resulting from Mediation, New York, 20 December 2018, opened for signature in Singapore, 7 August 2019. The Convention currently has eighteen State parties.

the two Hague Conventions[1329] as a landmark in international relations in this field.

3. Citizens of the world

371. Since antiquity, philosophers have declared human beings to be citizens of the world[1330]. Cosmopolitan[1331] accounts build on this beguiling idea[1332]. Immanuel Kant conceived of a cosmopolitan right, operating alongside civil or political right *(ius civitatis)* and international right *(ius gentium)* as constituent elements of public right, that is to say, "the sum total of those laws which require to be made universally public in order to produce a state of right"[1333]. Giving the example of hospitality to a visiting stranger, Kant describes the cosmopolitan right as a "right of resort", explaining that "all men are entitled to present themselves in the society of others by virtue of their right to communal possession of the earth's surface"[1334]. This "natural right", distinguished from philanthropy[1335], extended no further than was necessary to enable individuals to

---

1329 See above, [302].

1330 Sententiae Antiquae, "'Citizens of the World' from Diogenes to Marcus Aurelius", https://sententiaeantiquae.com/2016/06/04/citizens-of-the-world-from-diogenes-to-marcus-aurelius/, with reference to Diogenes Laertius, *Lives of the Philosophers*, [6.63] (on Diogenes the Cynic), Cicero, *Tusculan Disputations* [I.108] (on Socrates); Seneca, *De vita beata*, [20.5]; Epictetus, *Dissertationes*, [1.9.1]; Marcus Aurelius, *Meditations* [3.11] and [4.1].

1331 From the Greek "kosmopolitēs" ("citizen of the world").

1332 Pauline Kleingeld and Eric Brown, "Cosmopolitanism", in Edward N. Zalta (ed.), *The Stanford Encyclopedia of Philosophy*, Winter 2019 ed., https://plato.stanford.edu/archives/win2019/entries/cosmopolitanism/.

1333 Kant, "The Metaphysics of Morals" (n. 50), [43]; also *ibid.*, [53]-[62], pp. 136-137, 172-173; Kant, "Perpetual Peace" (n. 50), pp. 99-108.

1334 Kant, "Perpetual Peace", above, p. 106. See above, [38].

1335 *Ibid.*, p. 105.

seek to enter into relations with one another[1336]. That, in Kant's view, was sufficient for distant continents to "enter into peaceful mutual relations which may eventually be regulated by public laws, thus bringing the human race nearer and nearer to a cosmopolitan constitution"[1337].

372. More recently, Karen Knop (1960-2022) fleshed out two conceptions of world citizenship. The first, "citizens of humanity" visualises the individual as "a member of humanity under universal natural law", benefiting from internationally recognised human rights[1338]. The second, "private citizens of the world" consists of "an amalgam of national private law relations"[1339], reflecting the choices made by individuals as to their own spheres of existence and action[1340], which bring them within the legislative (and adjudicatory) authority of municipal legal systems[1341]. Whereas Knop's stated purpose was to augment the public international lawyer's toolbox[1342], the principal challenge for conflict of laws scholars is to elucidate the relationship between these two concepts[1343].

1336 *Ibid.*, p. 106.

1337 *Ibid.*

1338 Karen Knop, "Lorimer's Private Citizens of the World" (2016), 27 *Eur J Int L* 447, 450. They are likewise subject to obligations imposed on individual actors by international humanitarian and criminal law (*ibid.*, 453-455).

1339 *Ibid.*, 450.

1340 *Ibid.*, 451, 459.

1341 *Ibid.*, 455.

1342 *Ibid.*, 475.

1343 Roxana Banu, "Private International Law's Ambivalent Humanism" (2024), 74 *University of Toronto LJ* (Supplement) 28.
It might, for example, be possible to seek to unify the two conceptions of world citizen by conceiving of a "right to have private rights" as the private side of human rights law, see Ralf Michaels, "The Right to Have Private Rights" (n. 1134).

B. Exposition

373. With the foregoing comments in mind, we can try to draw the threads within the preceding chapters together.

1. The pursuit of natural justice

374. Natural justice concerns itself with the administration of justice and, in particular, with mechanisms for the resolution of disputes between natural or legal[1344] persons as to their relative entitlement.

375. The interests of natural justice are served by the *peaceful* and *just* resolution of disputes, by adjudication if other means prove ineffective[1345].

376. To maintain peaceful relations and for the protection of its members, a political society's legal order must establish mechanisms for the adjudication of disputes. In doing so, it must strike a balance between accuracy and finality in determining questions of relative entitlement[1346]. Accuracy is promoted, for example, by the careful design of civil procedure rules, by measures designed to select and retain the most able judges and by

---

1344 The natural law accounts studied here understandably focus on the position of human beings rather than the artificial legal personhood conceived to further haman collaboration. Pufendorf refers to them as private societies, being "composite moral persons", Pufendorf, *Nature and Nations*, Book 1, Chap. 1, [13]. For further discussion, see Hobbes, *Leviathan*, Chap. 22; Maximilian Koessler, "The Person in Imagination or *Persona Ficta* of the Corporation" (1949), 9 *Louisiana L Rev* 435; Roger Scruton and John Finnis, "Corporate Persons" (1989), 63 *Proceedings of the Aristotelian Society* 239.

1345 See above, [66], [76]-[78], [106].

1346 Von Mehren, "Recognition and Enforcement" (n. 493), 21-24, referring to principles of "correctness" and "repose" and acknowledging (*ibid.*, 22) that "embracing one to the complete exclusion of the other would be intolerable". See above, [78], [249], [316].

allowing an unsuccessful party to raise grounds of appeal against a decision at first instance. Finality is achieved through the principle of *res judicata* and related rules [1347]. The *res judicata* principle is aptly described as a general principle of international due process [1348]. It serves the interests of the parties, by promoting the stability of legal relations, and of the wider society, by providing an effective means to manage conflict [1349]. By seeking to promote accuracy of decision-making, a political society seeks perfection in the administration of justice within its own society [1350]. By seeking to promote finality, a political society pursues the goal of securing peace within its society [1351]. Natural justice seeks to promote both objects at the same time. Each legal order must decide how best to strike the balance between them.

377. To secure the just and peaceful resolution of a dispute, a legal order must also have the means to ensure that its decisions are effective [1352]. If a litigant is at liberty to ignore the determination of its relative entitlement, and to act in effect as the judge in its own cause, the

---

1347 *Virgin Atlantic Airways Ltd.* v. *Zodiac Seats UK Ltd.* [2013] UKSC 46, [2014] AC 160, [17] (Lord Sumption). See above, [249].

1348 Kotuby Jr and Sobota, *General Principles of Law and International Due Process* (n. 1245), pp. 197-202; van de Velden, *Finality* (n. 491), pp. 1-2; Case C-116/20, *SC Avio Lucos SRL* v. *Agenţia de Plăţi şi Intervenţie pentru Agricultură* [2022] ECLI:EU:C:2022:273.

1349 See above, [316]; also Digest 5.1.75 (Julian, *Digest*, Book 36) and 44.2.6 (Paul, *On the Edict*, Book 70).

1350 By setting an example for others, and enhancing its ability to aid the perfection of other nations in the administration of justice, this may be seen as serving the offices of humanity, see Vattel, *Nations*, Book 2, Chap. 1, [13], p. 267.

1351 See above, [75]-[77]; also [101].

1352 See Vattel, *Nations*, Book 1, Chap. 13, [160], p. 186 ("The best laws are useless if they be not observed"). See also above, [68]. A legal order may take provisional or protective measures before a final decision with a view to securing its effectiveness, see text to n. 1363.

administration of justice is liable to be frustrated and the peaceful resolution of the dispute obstructed.

378. Among the many impediments to the effectiveness of a judgment are limitations on the liberty of a legal order to take steps outside its domain, most obviously by seizing assets located beyond its territory or by controlling court proceedings in another, independent legal order. In these circumstances, securing the effectiveness of the judgment in accordance with the dictates of natural justice, i.e. in a peaceful and just manner, will require the assistance of another legal order.

379. In exercising its liberty to determine how it will administer justice within its own society, every legal order may decide for itself whether it is willing to offer such assistance and, if so, on what terms. It may decide, for example, the forms of assistance it is willing to provide, the types of judgment that it will accommodate, whether it requires a request from the adjudicating order or from one of the parties, the conditions imposed to establish the authority of the adjudicating court to determine the dispute[1353] and whether to insist on reciprocity from the adjudicating order[1354].

380. In taking those decisions, the legal order ought to have regard to two imperfect (that is to say, unenforceable) obligations that are integral to the natural law toolbox and can equally be supported on pragmatic grounds[1355]. The first is the duty to take steps to maintain peaceful relations among human beings, and in particular to maintain peaceful relations between the members of one's own political society and the members of another political society[1356]. The second is the duty, whether expressed in terms of comity or as a duty of humanity, to provide assistance to secure the perfection of other

1353 Section V.B.3
1354 See below, [401].
1355 See above, [109].
1356 See above, [107]-[108], [304]-[307].

nations, in this case in the administration of justice[1357]. The legal order must exercise judgment in deciding how to accommodate and, where necessary, to balance these two obligations. A political society may choose to prioritise its own perfection over the imperatives of securing peace and promoting the perfection of others, without committing an internationally wrongful act[1358]. In this sphere, this means that it can refuse to provide assistance to secure the effectiveness of a foreign judgment when that would come into conflict with its own fundamental rules or values. What is described here as the duty of humanity with respect to the administration of justice is also, obviously, subject to the limitation that it does not require a legal order to provide assistance to secure the effectiveness of what it considers to be an unjust decision[1359].

381. If every legal order were willing only to recognise or enforce a foreign judgment resulting from a procedure that conformed in all respects to its own, or on the condition that the foreign court reached the same conclusion that a court of the receiving order would have reached if it had decided the dispute, its offer of assistance would be illusory. "Justice pluralism"[1360], and common sense, favour rules that build in a degree of tolerance to differences in substantive or procedural rules and that place the burden on the party alleging injustice to assert and prove it in an appropriate forum, whether in the adjudicating order or in the receiving order[1361]. The exclusive liberty of each nation to administer justice within its own domain[1362], in combination with

1357 See above, [98]-[100], [148], [160]-[161], [191]-[195].
1358 See above, [101].
1359 See above, [194].
1360 See above, [317].
1361 See above, [328], point 2 and [342]-[347].
1362 See above, [191]-[195].

the principle of equality between nations[1363], support a robust presumption that justice has been served in the adjudicating order[1364], demanding that the complainant prove on the basis of cogent evidence[1365] the matters said to render the judgment unjust and ordinarily requiring that the complainant use remedies available locally in the adjudicating order, unless the circumstances make this impossible or excessively difficult[1366].

382. Although the objectives of securing peace and perfection in justice are aligned in the pursuit of natural justice, they have different profiles and may demand a different emphasis in the formulation of rules, as well as in their application. To give two illustrations:

- Prioritising the peaceful settlement of disputes would emphasise the importance of judgments that are final and conclusive, having the status of *res judicata*, whereas the cause of advancing the administration of justice has a wider focus and could quite easily accommodate, for example, provisional or protective measures aimed at preserving the status quo[1367].
- The mutual nature of the duty of humanity[1368] calls for reciprocity, whereas the endeavour to secure peace may be valuable for human society even if unreciprocated[1369].

1363 See above, [103], [224].

1364 See above, [119] (Johannes Voet), [182]-[183] (reception in Scotland), [191]-[194] (Vattel), [360] (early English practice).

1365 In relation to Article 6 of the ECHR, see *Popoviciu* v. *Curtea De Apel Bucharest* (n. 1213), [58]-[78] (Lord Lloyd-Jones), contrasting the approach when a denial of justice has occurred in the past with a case in which there is a risk that justice will be denied in the future.

1366 See above, [342]-[347].

1367 Case C-391/95, *Van Uden Maritime* v. *Kommandit-gesellschaft in Firma Deco-Line* [1998] ECR I-7091.

1368 See above, [65], [100]-[102].

1369 See above, [59], [106].

2. *Multidimensional justice*

383. When designing or developing rules for the recognition and enforcement of foreign judgments, there is an understandable tendency for legislators and judges to take an approach in which the interests of the parties to the dispute, or those of the public (State) interest, predominate[1370]. At least in theory, the "doctrine of obligation" favoured by the English common law[1371] treats the matter as one of corrective justice between litigants, in which the interests of the adjudicating order are put to one side and those of the receiving order operate only at the margins. By contrast, Story's formulation of maxims and his comity principle draw particular attention to the need to reconcile competition between those exercising sovereign authority[1372]. Whether a legal order chooses to impose a requirement of reciprocity or not is often expressed in terms of a preference for the interests of the State or the interests of the parties[1373].

384. Natural law accounts encourage us to recognise that the analysis can be conducted on many levels, all of which deserve our attention. In relations between the parties, there may exist a perfect obligation to abide by the adjudication (most obviously, arising from a choice of court agreement[1374]); alternatively, the successful party may have violated a perfect, natural obligation in securing the judgment (through fraud or breach of an agreement[1375]). At the same time, the parties may have a collective relationship with each other through

---

1370 See more generally Banu, *Nineteenth-Century Perspectives* (n. 655), esp. Chaps. 2, 3, 5 and 7-9.

1371 Section III.F.6.

1372 This is largely a matter of packaging – Story did not overlook the individual perspective, see Banu, *Nineteenth-Century Perspectives* (n. 655), pp. 29-35, 184-189.

1373 See the materials referred to at n. 1057.

1374 See above, [358].

1375 Section IV.B.2.

their membership of, or association with, a political society[1376]. Moreover, as human beings, they remain in any event subject to imperfect obligations, grounded in principles of natural law, to secure peace and to come to the aid of others. The nations that are the embodiment of political societies may be subject to perfect obligations themselves, through a treaty or established customary practice[1377], in addition to the imperfect obligations that have been highlighted[1378]. Nor must "human rights", generating obligations of nations towards individuals, belonging to their own or another society, be overlooked. Accordingly, for individual relationships, we can identify three relational perspectives (private/corrective justice; political association; duties of humanity), which fall to be considered alongside the relations involving the nations whose legal orders exercise adjudicatory authority with respect to invidual relationships.

385. Although her account takes a different and more wide-ranging approach to the subject, Roxana Banu's description of the "relational internationalist perspective", exemplified by the work[1379] of the Dutch scholar and diplomat, Josephus Jitta (1854-1925), captures the complex web of relationships involved:

> "[T]he relational internationalist perspective [is] a theory that places individuals at the center of a range

---

[1376] Section II.I.3.

[1377] See text to n. 322 and below, [400].

[1378] See above, [380].

[1379] Notably, D. Josephus Jitta, *La méthode du droit international privé*, The Hague: Belifante Frères, 1890 and *The Renovation of International Law on the Basis of a Juridical Community of Mankind / La rénovation du droit international sur la base d'un communauté juridique du genre humain*, The Hague: Martinus Nijhoff, 1919. See Banu, *Nineteenth-Century Perspectives* (n. 655), pp. 59-68, 282-288 and Chap. 9 (the quote below is from p. 292); Roxana Banu, "The Pragmatic Idealism of Josephus Jitta" [2020] *Rev Crit DIP* 5.

of concentric circles representing different dimensions of relationality. Relational internationalists placed the individual in relationship to the other party(ies) of the private law relationships, emphasized the relationships that individuals have with various communities and groups apart from their private law relationships, . . . and finally integrated all of these relationships into a broader notion of humanity."

386. Jitta identified a tripartite order of relationships, between the State and individuals, between the State and mankind and between State and State[1380]. Although a legal order may legitimately choose to favour one or more of these relational perspectives in the design of its rules, it should not put blinkers on so as to overlook others entirely[1381].

3. *Adjudicatory jurisdiction: Seeking a "common judge"*

387. Questions of adjudicatory jurisdiction are among the most important to be addressed in designing and applying rules that regulate foreign judgments[1382]. The world's legal orders offer divergent accounts of the set of circumstances in which a foreign court will be considered to have authority to determine a dispute[1383].

388. John Locke's vision of a "common judge" with authority to adjudicate the parties' dispute[1384] has the potential to serve as a valuable organising idea, enabling us to identify four different routes by which a court or

1380 Jitta, *The Renovation*, above, pp. 9-11.
1381 See above, [379]-[382].
1382 Jitta, *The Renovation* (n. 1379), pp. 77, 174-175, describing the existence of jurisdiction as the main condition for enforcement and requiring a "reasonably founded jurisdiction". See also American Law Institute, *Recognition and Enforcement* (n. 1025), para. 6, with commentary, pp. 85-92.
1383 Section IV.D.
1384 See above, [108], point 2.

the courts of a particular legal order may be considered to have gained authority to adjudicate a given dispute between two or more parties by reason of the parties' relationship with each other or with the adjudicating order – (1) consent, (2) natural equity, (3) membership of a political society and (4) participation in a political society. The rules of adjudicatory jurisdiction to be found in the Hague Choice of Court and Hague Judgments Conventions will be used to illustrate these routes.

389. The first of these routes, highlighted in the discussion of arbitration as a peaceful means of resolving disputes[1385], is the parties' agreement upon a common judge[1386]. The receiving legal order may lay down conditions for recognising the existence and validity of such an agreement, to demand an element of formality or to account (for example) for a relative inequality in the parties' bargaining power or their conduct towards each other in negotiating the agreement[1387].

390. Next, the parties' conduct as litigants may identify a common judge. This is obviously true of the claimant[1388], who chooses to submit a particular dispute for determination, and who may without difficulty be said to consent to adjudication of its subject matter, including any closely related counterclaim[1389]. The same

---

[1385] Section II.G. See, in particular, Hobbes, *Citizen*, Chap. 3, [20]-[21], pp. 51-52.

[1386] Hague Choice of Court Convention, Article 8 (1); Hague Judgments Convention, Article 5 *(1) (m)*.

[1387] See Hague Choice of Court Convention, Article 2 (1); Hague Judgments Convention, Article 5 (2) *(b)*; also Recast Brussels I Regulation (n. 1111), Articles 15, 19, 23 and 45 (1) *(c)*.

[1388] Hague Judgments Convention, Article 5 (1) *(c)*. As to the position of a counter-claiming defendant, see Hague Judgments Convention, Article 5 (1) (l); *Desarrollo Immobiliario y Negocios Industriales de Alta* [2014] EWHC 1460 (QB), [82]-[89].

[1389] See *Murthy* v. *Sivajothi* [1999] 1 WLR 467 (EWCA).

cannot straightforwardly[1390] be said of a defendant who participates in proceedings, who may outwardly deny that the court has authority to adjudicate and assert that their participation was under legal compulsion, without any realistic alternative, to protect its locally situated assets or other interests[1391]. However, by seeking a favourable decision and engaging the resources of both the court and their opponent, participating defendants expose themselves to the argument based on natural equity[1392], that having actively sought an advantage, i.e. a favourable determination of their entitlement, it is not unjust to impose on them the concomitant disadvantage of being bound by an unfavourable judgment[1393].

1390 Contrast the position of a defendant who expressly consents to jurisdiction in the course of the proceedings giving rise to the judgment (see Hague Judgments Convention, Article 5 (1) *(e)*, requiring that consent be express and Article 5 (2) *(a)*, imposing additional requirements for consumers and employees).

1391 Text to n. 1276; also *AES Ust-Kamenogorsk Hydropower Plant LLP* v. *Ust-Kamenogorsk Hydropower* JSC [2011] EWCA Civ 647, [2012] 1 WLR 920, [14], [170] [183], [187] (Rix L. J.), [200] (Stanley Burnton L. J.); Dickinson, "Foreign Submission" (n. 197), 310-313.

1392 See above, [82].

1393 *Re Dulles Settlement (No. 2)* (n. 197), 847 (Evershed M. R.: "[A] man cannot both have his cake and eat it. He cannot fight the issue on the merits, and at the same time preserve the right to say, if the worst comes to the worst, that the court has no jurisdiction to decide against him"); also Dickinson, "Foreign Submission" (n. 197), 317-319. Cf. Civil Jurisdiction and Judgments Act 1982 (UK), s. 33 (on which, see Dickinson, above, 308-313).

Article 5 (1) *(f)* of the Hague Judgments Convention is framed more narrowly. In particular, a defendant who contest jurisdiction on plausible grounds may advance merits-based arguments without engaging this basis for recognition and enforcement under the Convention.

Note also Johannes Voet, *Commentarius*, Book 2, Title 1, [20], Vol. 1, pp. 220-221, acknowledging the need to distinguish the position of claimant and defendant.

391. The third route relies on a party's[1394] relationship with the adjudicating order, recognising relationships of different kinds, with the extent of adjudicatory authority varying according to the degree of connection. In this connection, Josephus Jitta helpfully distinguishes between claims to exercise adjudicatory jurisdiction based on citizenship, domicile, mere residence and participation in local business life without presence[1395]. In his view, adjudicatory jurisdiction, involving a power to find and to establish the decisive rule in a legal dispute, "is justified when the real elements of a juridical contest are so closely attached to a State that the reasonable order of international social life requires the decisive rule for the solution of the said contest to be found and fixed by the judiciary of the said State"[1396].

392. At the upper end of the scale in terms of the strength of the connection, an individual who is a member in the fullest sense of a political society, as a citizen or subject, or who has their home within its domain, may be assumed to participate to such a degree in the affairs of the society that it would not be unjust to subject them to the authority of those that the political society appoints to act as judges. The receiving order may define these concepts. In particular, it may choose how to combine objective and subjective factors in determining whether an individual is at home in a particular place[1397]. Although nationality has faded as a connecting factor for the

---

1394 With a particular focus on the position of defendants. As to the position of claimants, see text to n. 1388.

1395 Jitta, *The Renovation* (n. 1379), pp. 9, 102-105.

1396 *Ibid.*, pp. 76-77.

1397 The common law's concept of domicile gives greater weight to a person's subjective intention in comparison with the concept of habitual residence used in Article 5 (1) *(a)* of the Hague Judgments Convention (see Garcimartín and Saumier, *Explanatory Report* (n. 1125), [142]; *Dicey, Morris & Collins* (n. 5), [6R-037], Rule 12 (domicile of choice); also Jitta, *The Renovation*, above, pp. 103-104.

recognition and enforcement of foreign judgments[1398], and more generally in private international law[1399], the practical objections to its use (that it is unpredictable, that its application is unclear when the nation comprises several legal orders, that it is ill-equipped to deal with cases of multiple nationality or Stateless persons[1400]) can be satisfactorily addressed by using a concept of "active citizenship" that identifies and locates a person's exercise of privileges conferred by citizenship, such as voting or using a passport to leave or enter a nation's territory, in order to identify the legal order with which the citizenship is most closely connected[1401]. For corporations, membership of a political society may be signified by the place of incorporation or real seat and the concept of "home" by the principal place of business[1402].

393. With respect to a person residing or visiting the territory associated with a political society without being at home there, or a person who while not being present actively participates in the day-to-day life of a political society, the question of adjudicatory jurisdiction should be tackled by having regard to the particular nature, quality and purpose of the individual's connection to the society and by recognising adjudicatory jurisdiction on a proportionate basis having regard to that assessment and the nature of the dispute[1403]. This accords with

---

1398 Text to n. 1267.

1399 Heinz-Peter Mansel, "Nationality", in *Encyclopedia of Private International Law* (n. 300), Vol. 2, pp. 1289-1301.

1400 Mansel, above, pp. 1299-1300; *Dicey, Morris & Collins* (n. 5), [14-090].

1401 See *Nygh's Conflict of Laws* (n. 1174), [40.24]-[40.25].

1402 See Recast Brussels I Regulation, Article 63; *Daimler AG* v. *Bauman* (n. 1309), 18-19; Hague Judgments Convention, Article 5 (1) *(b)*.

1403 For the principle of proportionality, see Jitta, *The Renovation* (n. 1379), p. 104 ("a *subjectus temporarius* . . . is subjected to the local law in the proportion to his penetration in the local social life").

the principle of natural equity and is exemplified by the decision of the United States Supreme Court in *International Shoe Co* and the decisions following it[1404]. If a person exercises the privilege of conducting activities in a particular place, it is not unjust to subject them to the authority of its judges provided that the dispute is one that arises out of or has a sufficient connection with those activities and that requiring them to litigate in that forum does not impose an undue burden on them[1405]. The receiving order may specify the nature of the connection required, having regard to contemporary social and business practices. For example, in a contractual dispute, a person's presence in a particular place at the moment that a contract was executed would have had much greater significance in the seventeenth century[1406] than it does today given that a contract may be concluded across the ocean by a single mouse click or swipe on a portable device[1407]. Moreover, if the dispute concerns the performance, rather than the formation, of the contract, the connection to the place of formation seems more remote and a stronger case can be made for recognising the exercise of adjudicatory jurisdiction by a court in the actual or agreed place of performance[1408]. For torts,

---

1404 See above, [365]-[366].

1405 *International Shoe Co* v. *Washington* (n. 197), 319-320. See, with respect to the activities of a branch, agency or other establishment, Hague Judgments Convention, Article 5 (1) *(c)*. See also above, [156] (Huber).

1406 See above, [87], [150]-[152], [154].

1407 See *FS Cairo (Nile Plaza)* v. *Brownlie* [2021] UKSC 45, [2022] AC 995, [213] (Lord Leggatt); also, with respect to the role played by the place of contracting in determining the law applicable to a contract, *Amin Rasheed Corp* v. *Kuwait Insurance Co* [1984] AC 50, 62 (Lord Diplock, UKHC); *Fleming* v. *Marshall* [2011] NSWCA 86, [62]-[66] (Macfarlan J. A.).

1408 Hague Judgments Convention, Article 5 *(1) (g)*. The Hague Judgments Convention attaches no significance to the place of formation of a contract.

this approach suggests that the primary focus for rules of adjudicatory jurisdiction should be on the defendant's conduct, rather than its consequences[1409].

394. Finally, the approach suggested here has no place for adjudicatory jurisdiction based on the defendant's temporary presence if the dispute otherwise had no connection to the adjudicating order[1410].

4. Equal justice

395. The principle of natural equality is central to the pursuit of natural justice. Applied to relations between independent nations, it demands respect for the way in which other legal orders administer justice[1411] and underpins the principle of reciprocity[1412]. Applied to the relationship between individual litigants and the adjudicating order, it establishes the basic conditions for a just adjudication, that the tribunal be impartial *(nemo iudex in sua causa)*, that the defendant be notified of the proceedings and that the parties have a fair opportunity to present their case *(audi alteram partem)*[1413].

1409 See Hague Judgments Convention, Article 5 *(1) (j)*, requiring that "the act or omission directly causing such harm occurred in the State of origin, irrespective of where that harm occurred". The ground is, however, limited to non-contractual obligations arising from death, physical injury, damage to or loss of tangible property. A focus on bodily injury would reflect the natural entitlement to such protection (Section II.C). The extension to damage to tangible property, but not injury to economic or other intangible rights, cannot easily be rationalised in this way. The limits may be explicable on the basis that acts or omissions giving rise to "physical" injury were considered jurisdictionally more significant or on the practical ground that a rule formulated in these terms is more certain in its scope.

1410 See above, [153]-[159], [356]-[359]. The Hague Judgments Convention does not recognise this basis of jurisdiction.

1411 See above, [381].

1412 See above, [65] and below, [399].

1413 Section IV.C.

396. In considering whether to apply the principle of equality beyond these core requirements, a legal order may need to have regard to pre-existing inequalities between the parties as a matter of fact, in particular in the faculties and resources that they have to assert their entitlement, and to consider measures to ensure that those inequalities do not substantially impair access to justice. Especially in complex cases, natural equality arguably demands an approximate "equality of arms", extending at least to access to independent and expert legal advice and the means of presenting evidence[1414].

397. The principle of natural equality also has a substantive aspect, the entitlement to equal protection of the law without discrimination. In the recognition and enforcement of judgments, this is appropriately safeguarded through each legal order's conception of public policy, reflecting differences in political and moral outlook that still exist while upholding the ideal of a common humanity[1415].

5. *A common enterprise*

398. Advancing the interests of natural justice requires a collaborative effort[1416]. The receiving order declares its preparedness to support an adjudicating legal order in resolving a dispute, while remaining vigilant against becoming an accessory to injustice or compromising its own core values. For its own part, in cross-border situations, the adjudicating order must be mindful that

---

1414 *Steel and Morris* v. *United Kingdom* (Application No. 68416/01), [59]-[72]. See, in a different context, *Vedanta Resources plc* v. *Lungowe* [2019] UKSC 20, [2020] AC 1045, [89], [93], [95], [98]; *Limbu* v. *Dyson Technology Ltd* [2024] EWCA Civ 1564, [2025] ICR 560, esp. at [59]-[60].

1415 See above, [354].

1416 *Wikely* v. *Kea Investments Ltd.* [2024] NZCA 609, [165] ("without collaboration between legal systems litigation would in many cases prove fruitless").

it may lack the means to secure the effectiveness of its judgments and do everything in its power to ensure that its procedures are fair and transparent and that its judgments will travel well.

399. As with many human endeavours, the interests of natural justice are more likely to be advanced if this relationship is reciprocal and less likely to be advanced if it is not. Pufendorf's argument that a want of mutuality of obligation was "repugnant to the natural equality of men"[1417] applies with equal force to the relations between nations and their legal orders[1418].

400. The surest route to this reciprocity is through a treaty or other arrangement[1419]. The network of bilateral and multilateral connections between the world's legal orders is ever growing. The two Hague Conventions, on choice of court agreements and judgments, promise to carry this collaboration to new heights. The Conventions score highly in terms of promoting the values of natural justice[1420]. They adopt prudent rules of adjudicatory jurisdiction[1421], promote the effectiveness of judgments by specifying that recognition and enforcement may be

---

1417 Pufendorf, *Nature and Nations*, Book 3, Chap. 4, [8], p. 388, discussed above, [65].

1418 See above, [103].

1419 Text to n. 322 (Johannes Voet).

1420 For a critical appraisal of the Hague Choice of Court Convention, see Gary Born, "The Hague Convention on Choice of Court Agreements: A Critical Assessment" (2021), 169 *U Penn L Rev* 2019. Cf. in response to criticisms of the Convention advanced by the aforementioned author, Trevor Hartley, "Is the Hague Choice of Court Convention Really a Threat to Justice and Fair Play? A Reply to Gary Born", https://eapil.org/2021/06/30/is-the-2005-hague-choice-of-court-convention-really-a-threat-to-justice-and-fair-play-a-reply-to-gary-born/.

1421 See the references in footnotes within Section V.3; also Pietro Franzina, "The Jurisdictional Filters", in Matthias Weller, João Ribeiro-Bidaoui, Moritz Brinkmann and Nina Dethlof (eds.), *The HCCH 2019 Judgments Convention – Cornerstones, Prospects, Outlook*, Oxford: Hart, 2023.

refused only on specified grounds[1422] and precluding any review of the merits[1423], while at the same time allowing the requested Contracting State to deny recognition or enforcement, if among other cases, this would be manifestly incompatible with its public policy, including its fundamental principles of procedural fairness[1424].

401. Absent a formal treaty relationship, every legal order must judge for itself whether to adopt a reciprocity requirement and, if so, the form that requirement should take[1425]. In doing so, and in the implementation of a reciprocity requirement in individual cases, lawmakers should be mindful of constitutional arrangements for taking what are, in essence, foreign affairs decisions[1426], as well as the injustice that individuals (even if they belong to the non-reciprocating legal order) may suffer if left without a means to secure the effectiveness of their judgments[1427]. They should also consider the practical consequences of imposing such a requirement, including the potential impact on litigation and litigants before their own courts[1428] and the prospect of stand-off situations in which two legal orders refuse to assist one another in the administration of justice until the other makes the first move[1429]. The economic and other consequences of leaving disputes unresolved must also be calculated.

1422 Hague Choice of Court Convention, Article 8 (1); Hague Judgments Convention, Article 4 (1).
1423 Hague Choice of Court Convention, Article 8 (2); Hague Judgments Convention, Article 4 (2).
1424 See above, [337]-[338].
1425 See above, [291]-[292].
1426 For this reason, the matter may be considered more suitable for determination by the executive or legislature rather than by the courts.
1427 Cuniberti, "Le fondement" (n. 305), [235].
1428 Coyle, "Rethinking Judgments Reciprocity" (n. 1057), 1119-1125; Cuniberti, "Le fondement", above, [232]-[234].
1429 If the object of the measure is to encourage other legal orders to make that move, it becomes necessary to consider

402. If a legal order decides to impose such a requirement[1430], a presumption that reciprocity is assured in the adjudicating order[1431], coupled with a proportionate mechanism for responding to situations in which there is concrete evidence that another legal order is withholding assistance (i.e. targeted retorsion rather than disengagement), may offer a path though the thicket.

C. *Summing up*

403. In 1872, the editor of the seventh edition of Joseph Story's renowned work on the conflict of laws began his observations on foreign judgments with the following statement[1432]:

> "There is no title connected with the general subject of the conflict of laws more embarrassing than that which we are now considering."

404. Edward Hatch Bennett's assessment was wrong at the time of writing, and its accuracy has not improved with age. No topic within the conflict of laws is more fascinating or offers greater insights as to the workings of the subject than the rules governing the reception of foreign judgments. Whether one agrees with that assessment, or the conclusions offered here, the endeavour will not have been in vain if readers of this work

---

whether it is likely to achieve that end, see Coyle, above, 1148-1165; Cuniberti, above, [210]-[230].

1430 See American Law Institute, *Recognition and Enforcement* (n. 1025), pp. 92-105 (para. 7).

1431 Text to n. 1071. See Chong, "Moving Towards Harmonisation" (n. 1056), 55, referring to the Nanning Declaration approved at the 2nd China-ASEAN Justice Forum (8 June 2017) (n. 1064), [7].

1432 Joseph Story and Edward Hatch Bennett (eds.), *Commentaries on the Conflict of Laws, Foreign and Domestic*, Boston: Little, Brown and Co, 7th ed., 1872, [618a] (p. 763).

have discovered here something that inspires them to deepen their understanding of the topic or of the conflict of laws more generally.

405. The guiding principle is clear. The rules of the conflict of laws should promote the just and peaceful resolution of disputes, whenever that can be done without jeopardising other fundamental and essential objectives of a particular society; at the same time, injustice should be identified and rooted out wherever it may fester.

406. In this endeavour, the natural law toolbox has much to offer. The accounts studied here remind us that human relationships transcend legal orders: that those relationships are founded on the principle of equality before the law; that nations, their rulers, officials and judges are servants not masters; and that the administration of justice performs a vital function in securing peaceful relations between the inhabitants of this planet. The toolbox is not a panacea, or a universal or unshakeable source of truth, but we should carry it with us whenever we think about the subject.

ANNEX (CHAPTER IV)

Grounds for Opposing Recognition and Enforcement of Judgments

	Description of ground for opposing recognition or enforcement	*Hague Judgments Convention (2019)* *Article 7 (1) (unless stated)*	*Recast Brussels I Regulation (2012) (EU)* *Article 45 (1)*	*Uniform Foreign Country Money Judgments Recognition Act (US)* *s. 7 (b) and (c)*	*Civil Procedure Law (China) (revised 2024)* *Article 300*	*Commonwealth Model Law (2018)* *Clause 6 (3) (unless stated)*	*Common law (as modified by statute) (Aus) (Can) (UK)*
A.1	Inconsistency with local judgment	*(e)*	*(c)*	*(c)* (4)	(4)	*(b)*	All
A.2	Inconsistency with recognised foreign judgment	*(f)*	*(d)*				All
A.3	Local *lis pendens*					*(a)*	
A.4	Non-compensatory damages	Article 10 (1)				Article 14 (1)	
A.5	Multiple damages						UK
B.1	Public policy	*(c)* [Main part, including (in second sub-part) infringements of security or sovereignty. See also first sub-part below]	*(a) (ordre public)*	*(c)* (3)	*(5)* (violation of basic principles of PRC law or harm to national sovereignty, security or public interest of PRC)	*(d)*	All

	Description of ground for opposing recognition or enforcement	*Hague Judgments Convention (2019)* *Article 7 (1) (unless stated)*	*Recast Brussels I Regulation (2012) (EU)* *Article 45 (1)*	*Uniform Foreign Country Money Judgments Recognition Act (US)* *s. 7 (b) and (c)*	*Civil Procedure Law (China) (revised 2024)* *Article 300*	*Commonwealth Model Law (2018)* *Clause 6 (3) (unless stated)*	*Common law (as modified by statute) (Aus) (Can) (UK)*
C.1	Fraud	*(b)*		*(c)* (2)	(3)	*(e)*	All
C.2	Breach of dispute resolution agreement	*(d)*		*(c)* (5)	(1) *(c)*	Article 14 (1)	UK
C.3	Natural justice					*(c)* ("procedural fairness and natural justice")	All
C.4	Inadequate notice of originating process	*(a) (i)*	*(b)*	*(c)* (1)	(2) [1st part] (not lawfully summoned)		
C.5	No reasonable opportunity to present case				(2) [2nd part]		
C.6	Party lacking capacity not properly represented				(2) [3rd part]		
C.7	Mode of service of originating process	*(a) (ii)*					

	Description of ground for opposing recognition or enforcement	*Hague Judgments Convention (2019)* *Article 7 (1) (unless stated)*	*Recast Brussels I Regulation (2012) (EU)* *Article 45 (1)*	*Uniform Foreign Country Money Judgments Recognition Act (US)* *s. 7 (b) and (c)*	*Civil Procedure Law (China) (revised 2024)* *Article 300*	*Commonwealth Model Law (2018)* *Clause 6 (3) (unless stated)*	*Common law (as modified by statute) (Aus) (Can) (UK)*
C.8	Incompatibility with fundamental principles of procedural fairness	*(c)* [First sub-part]				*(c)* ("procedural fairness and natural justice")	
C.9	Breach of protective rules of jurisdiction		*(e)*				
C.10	Systemic impartiality			*(b)* (1)			
C.11	Systemic lack of due process			*(b)* (1)			
C.12	Want of integrity of the court giving judgment			*(c)* (7)			
C.13	Incompatibility with due process in the specific proceeding			*(c)* (8)			

BIBLIOGRAPHY

For other references to source material, and pinpoints within individual sources, readers are referred to the footnotes within Chaps. I to V

The Law of Nature – Introductory and General Materials

Austin, J., *The Province of Jurisprudence Determined*, London: John Murray, 1832, Lectures V and VI.

Banner, S., *The Decline of Natural Law—How American Lawyers Once Used Natural Law and Why They Stopped*, Oxford: Oxford University Press, 2021.

Bentham, *A Fragment of Government*, London: T. Payne, 1776, in the edition edited by J. H. (James) Burns and H. L. A. (Herbert) Hart, Cambridge: Cambridge University Press, 1988, Chap. 1.

Finnis, J., *Natural Law and Natural Rights*, Oxford: Clarendon Press, 1980, Chaps. 1-2, 7 and 12.

Hart, H. L. A., *The Concept of Law*, Oxford: Oxford University Press, 3rd ed., 2012, Chaps. 8-10.

Helmholz, R. H., "Natural Law and Human Rights in English Law: From Bracton to Blackstone" (2005), 3 *Ave Maria Law Review* 1.

–, *Natural Law in Court*, Cambridge: Harvard University Press, 2015.

Le Fur, L., "La théorie du droit naturel depuis le XVIIe siècle et la doctrine moderne" (1928), 18 *Recueil des cours* 259.

Rommen, H. A., *Die ewige Wiederkehr des Naturrechts*, Leipzig: Jacob Hedner, 1936, trans. Thomas R. Hanley, *The Natural Law – A Study in Legal and Social History and Philosophy*, St Louis, B. Herder, 1947.

Story, J., "Nature, Law of", in F. Lieber (ed.), *Encyclopedia Americana* (Philadelphia: Lea & Blanchard, Vol. 9, 1835), p. 150 *et seq*.

The Law of Nations – Introductory and General Materials

Koskenniemi, *From Apology to Utopia – The Structure of International Legal Argument*, Helsinki: Lakimiesliiton Kustannus, 1989, Chap. 2.

Neff, S. C., *Justice among Nations*, Harvard: Harvard University Press, 2014, Chaps. 4-8.

Nussbaum, A., *A Concise History of the Law of Nations*, New York: Macmillan Co, 1953, Chaps. 4 and 5.

O'Connell, M. E., "The Role of Natural Law in the Rise and Decline of European International Law", Chap. 15 in A. van Aaken, P. d'Argent, L. Mälksoo and J. J. Vasel (eds.), *The Oxford Handbook of International Law in Europe*, Oxford: Oxford University Press.

Ryan, S., "Fundamental Legal Conceptions and the International Law of (Civil) Jurisdiction" (2025), 42 *Australian Yearbook Int L* 130.

Story, J., "Nations, Law of", in F. Lieber (ed.), *Encyclopedia Americana*, Philadelphia: Lea & Blanchard, Vol. 9, 1835, p. 141 *et seq.*

Seventeenth and Eighteenth Century Accounts of the Law of Nature and Nations – Principal Works

Blackstone, W., *Commentaries on the Laws of England*, Oxford, Clarendon Press, 4 volumes, 1765-1769 in the edition edited by Wilfried Prest, Oxford: Oxford University Press, 2016, Book 1, Introduction, Section 2.

Boullenois, L., *Traité de la personnalité et de la réalité des lois, coutumes ou statuts, par formes d'observations*, Paris: Guillaume Desprez, 1766, Vol. 1, Observation XXV.

Grotius, H., *De Iure Bellis Ac Pacis Libri Tres*, Paris: Apud Nicholas Buon, 1625, trans. anon., *The Rights of War and Peace*, London: W. Innys, 1738, using the 1724 French edition by Jean Barbeyrac.

–, *De Iure Praedae*, manuscript completed in 1606 and published posthumously, H. G. Hamaker (ed.), Den Haag: Martinus Nijhoff 1868), trans. G. L. Williams, *Commentary on the Law of Prize and Booty*, Oxford: Clarendon Press, 1950.

Hobbes, T., *Elementa Philosophica de Cive*, Amsterdam: Elzevir, 1647, trans. and ed. R. Tuck and M. Silverthorne, *On the Citizen*, Cambridge: Cambridge University Press, 1998.

–, *Leviathan*, London: Andrew Crooke at the Green Dragon in St Paul's Churchyard, 1651, ed. R. Tuck, Cambridge: Cambridge University Press, 1991.

Kant, I., *Zum ewigen Frieden – Ein philosophischer Entwurf*, Königsberg, Friedrich Nicovius, 1795, trans. H. B. Nisbet, "Perpetual Peace", in H. Reiss (ed.), *Kant – Political Writings* (Cambridge: Cambridge University Press, 2nd ed., 1991, pp. 93- 130.

Locke, J., *Two Treatises of Government*, London: printed for

Awnsham and John Churchill, revd. 1698, ed. P. Laslett, Cambridge: Cambridge University Press, 1988, 2nd treatise.

Pufendorf, S., *De Jure Naturae et Gentium, Libro Octo*, Lund: Adam Junghans, 1672, in the revised edition, Amsterdam: Apud Andeream de Hoogenhuysen, 1688, trans. C. H. Oldfather and W. A. Oldfather, *Of the Law of Nature and Nations*, Vol. 17, in J. B. Scott (ed.), *The Classics of International Law*, Oxford: Clarendon Press, 1934.

–, *De Officio Hominis et Civis Juxta Legem Naturalem Libri Duo*, Lund: Adam Junghans, 1673, trans. A. Tooke, *The Whole Duty of Man according to the Law of Nature*, London: R. Gosling, J. Pemberton and B. Motte, 5th ed., 1735.

Vattel, E., de *Le droit des gens*, London, 1758, in the posthumous, revised edition of 1773 (Neuchâtel: La Société Typographique) trans. anon., *The Law of Nations*, London: G. G. and J. Robinson, 1797.

Wolff, C., *Jus Gentium Methodo Scientifica Pertrachtatum* (Halle, 1749) in the revised edition, Frankfurt: Aere Societatis Venetae, 1764, trans. Joseph H. Drake, *The Law of Nations Treated according to the Scientific Method*, Vol. 13 in James Brown Scott (ed.), *The Classics of International Law*, Oxford: Clarendon Press, 1934.

Seventeenth and Eighteenth Century Accounts of the Law of Nature – Other Materials

Stephen Darwall, *Modern Moral Philosophy – From Grotius to Kant*, Cambridge: Cambridge University Press, 2023, Chaps. 1, 2 and 8.

Dutch Jurists of the Late Eighteenth and Early Nineteenth Century – Principal Works

Huber, U., *De Jure Civitatis libri tres*, Franeker: Johannes Gyselaar, 1684; Franeker: Apud Henricum Amama and Zachariam Taedema, 3rd ed., 1694.

–, *Digressiones Justinianae, In Partes Duas*, Franeker: Apud Johannem Gysellar, Henricum Amama and Zachariam Taedama, 1688.

–, *Heedendaegse Rechts-geleertheyt, soo elders als in Frieslandt gebruikelijk*, Leeuwarden: Hero Nauta, 1686, trans. P. Gane, *The Jurisprudence of My Time*, Durban: Butterworth & Co Africa Ltd., 1939.

–, *Positiones Juris secundum Institutiones et Pandecta*, Franeker: Apud Johannem Gyselaar, 4th ed., 1685.

–, *Praelectionum Juris Civilis, Pars Prior, Quae est secundum Institutines Justinaeas*, Franeker: Apud Henricum Amama and Zachariah Tedama, 1687.
–, *Praelectionum Juris Romani et Hodierni, Pars II, Quae est ad Libros undeviginti priores Pandectarum*, Franeker: Apud Henricum Amama and Zachariam Taedema, 1689.
–, *Praelectionum Juris Romani, Pars III*, Franeker: Apud Henricum Amama and Zachariam Taedema, 1690.
Thomasius, C. (comp.), Christian Thomasius (compiler), *Praelectionum Juris Civilis Tomis Tres, Secundundum Institiones et Digesta Justiniani, Editio Nova*, Leipzig: Jo. Friderici Gledischii, 1707.
–, *Ulrici Huberi Positiones sive lectiones juris contractae secundum et Institutiones et Pandectas*, Leipzig and Frankfurt: Mauritii Georgii Weidmanni, 1685?.
Voet, J., *Commentarius ad Pandectas*, Leiden: Johannes Verbessel, Vol. 1, 1698, trans. Gane, P., *The Selective Voet, Being the Commentary on the Pandects (Paris edition of 1829)*, Durban: Butterworth & Co (Africa) Ltd., Vol. 1, 1955.
Voet, P., *De Statutis Eorumque Concursu*, Amsterdam: Johannes van Waesberge, 1661, trans. A. B. Edwards and D. M. Kriel, "The Selective Paulus Voet", reproduced in (2007), 13 *Fundamina: A Journal of Legal History* 1, 55-309.

Dutch Jurists of the Late Eighteenth and Early Nineteenth Century – Other Materials

Decock, W., and J. Oosterhuis (eds.), *Great Christian Jurists in the Low Countries*, Cambridge: Cambridge University Press, 2021, Chaps. 7 and 8.
Hatzimihail, N. E., *Preclassical Conflict of Laws*, Cambridge: Cambridge University Press, 2021, Chaps. 11-14.
Llewelyn Davies, D. J., "The Influence of Huber's *De conflictu legum* on English Private International Law" (1937), 18 *British Yb Int L* 49.
Lorenzen, E. G., *"Huber's De Conflictu Legum"* (1919), 23 *Illinois L Rev* 376.
Weinstein, J., "The Dutch Influence on the Conception of Judicial Jurisdiction in Nineteenth Century America" (1990), 38 *Am J Comp L* 73.

Common Law Reception

Anton, A. E., "The Introduction into English Practice of Continental Theories on the Conflict of Laws"

(1956), 5 *International and Comparative Law Quarterly* 534.

Cairns, J., "Importing Our Lawyers from Holland: Netherlands Influences on Scots Law and Lawyers in the Eighteenth Century", Chap. 8 in *Law, Lawyers and Humanism*, Edinburgh: Edinburgh University Press, Vol. 1, 2015.

Feenstra, R., "Scottish-Dutch Legal Relations in the Seventeenth and Eighteenth Centuries", in T. C. Smout (ed.), *Scotland and Europe 1200-1850*, Edinburgh: John Donald, 1986.

Henry, J., *A Treatise on the Difference between Personal and Real Statutes and Its Effect on Foreign Judgments, Contracts, Marriages and Wills*, London: S. Sweet, 1823.

Home, H. (Lord Kames), *Principles of Equity*, Edinburgh: A. Kincaid, 1760; Edinburgh: A. Kincaid and J. Bell, 2nd ed., 1767; Edinburgh: J. Bell and W. Creech, 3rd ed., 1778, Book 3, Chap. 8, Section VI.

Livermore, *Dissertation on the Questions Which arise from the Contrariety of the Positive Law of Different States and Nations*, New Orleans: Benjamin Levy, 1828, Dissertation I.

Mijers, E., "Scottish Students in the Netherlands 1680-1730", Chap. 10, in A. Grosjean and S. Murdoch (eds.), *Scottish Communities Abroad in the Early Modern Period*, Boston: Brill, 2005.

Watson., A., "The Failure of Scottish Legal Education in the Seventeenth Century, and the American Civil War", in *Authority of Law; and Law*, Stockholm: Distribueras av Rönnells Antiqvariat, 203, Lecture 7.

Evolution of Law and Practice – Nineteenth and Twentieth Century

Asser, T., "De l'effet ou de l'exécution des jugements rendus a l'étranger en matière civile et commercial" (1869), 1 *Revue de droit international et de législation comparée* 82, 402 and 473.

Bar, L. von, *Theorie und Praxis des Internationalen Privatrechts*, Hannover: Hahn'sche Buchhandlung, 1889, Vol. 2, Book 11, [411] *et seq.*

Banu, R., *Nineteenth-Century Perspectives on Private International Law*, Oxford: Oxford University Press, 2018.

–, "The Pragmatic Idealism of Josephus Jitta" [2020] *Rev Crit DIP* 5.

Dicey, A. V., *A Digest on the Law of England with Reference to the Conflict of Laws*, London: Stephens and Sons, 1896, Introduction and Chap. 16.

Kegel, G., "Story and Savigny" (1989), 37 *Am J Comp L* 39.

Jitta, D. J., *La méthode du droit international privé*, The Hague: Belifante Frères, 1890.

–, *The Renovation of International Law on the Basis of a Juridical Community of Mankind / La rénovation du droit international sur la base d'un communauté juridique du genre humain*, The Hague: Martinus Nijhoff, 1919.

Lorenzen, E. G., "Story's Commentaries on the Conflict of Laws – One Hundred Years After" (1934), 48 *Harvard L Rev* 15.

Michaels, R., "Globalising Savigny? The State in Savigny's Private International Law and the Challenge from Europeanisation and Globalization", pp. 119-144 in M. Stolleis and W. Streeck (eds.), *Aktuelle Fragen zu politischer und rechtlicher Steuerung im Kontext der Globalisierung*, Baden-Baden: Nomos, 2007.

Nadelmann, K. H., "Bicentennial Observations on the Second Edition of Joseph Story's *Commentaries on the Conflict of Laws*" (1988), 28 *Am J Comp L* 67.

–, "Joseph Story's Contribution to American Conflicts Law: A Comment" (1961), 5 *Am J Legal History* 23.

–, "Wächter's Essay on the Collision of Private Laws of Different States" (1964), 13 *Am J Comp L* 414.

Piggott, F. T., *Foreign Judgments and Jurisdiction*, London: Butterworth & Co, 1908, Chaps. 1-3.

Savigny, F. C. von, *System des heutigen Römischen Rechts*, Berlin: Veit, 1840-1849 [Vol. 1, 1840, Vol. 5, 1841 and Vol. 8, 1849]. [Vol. 1 trans in part William Holloway, *System of the Modern Roman Law*, Madras, J. Higginbotham, 1867. Vol. 8 trans. William Guthrie, *Private International Law, A Treatise on the Conflict of Laws and the Limits of Their Operation in respect of Place and Time*, Edinburgh, T & T Clark, 1869.]

Story, J., *Commentaries on the Conflict of Laws, Foreign and Domestic*, Boston: Hilliard, Gray and Co, 1834; Boston, Charles C. Little and James Brown, 2nd ed., 1841; Boston: Charles C. Little and James Brown, 3rd ed., 1846.

Velden, J. B. van de, *Finality of Litigation*, Groningen: Ulrich Huber Institute, 2014, Part II.

Wächter, K. G. von, "Über die Kollision der Privatgesetze verschiedener Staaten" (1841), 24 *Archiv fur die Civilis-*

tische Praxis 230; (1842) 25 *Archiv fur die Civilistische Praxis* 1, 161 and 361.

Westlake, J., *A Treatise on Private International Law, or the Conflict of Laws*, London: W. Maxwell, 1858, Chaps. 6 and 12.

Evolution of Law and Practice – Comparative Surveys

Campbell, D. (ed.), *Enforcement of Foreign Judgments*, London: LLP Limited, 1997.

Chong., A., "Moving Towards Harmonisation in the Recognition and Enforcement of Foreign Judgment Rules in Asi" (2020), 16 *J Priv Int L* 31.

Council of Europe, *The practical guide to the recognition and enforcement of foreign judicial decisions in civil and commercial law*, Strasbourg: Council of Europe, 1975.

Foelix, J. G. G., *De l'Effet ou de l'exécution des jugements dans les pays étrangers*, Paris: Joubert, 1843.

Lorenzen, E. G., "The Enforcement of American Judgments Abroad" (1919), 29 *Yale LJ* 188 and (1920) 29 *Yale LJ* 268.

Mohammed, H., and S. Al Mulla, "Conventions of Enforcement of Judgments in the Arab States" (1999), 14 *Arab Law Quarterly* 33.

Standing International Forum of Commercial Courts, *Multilateral Memorandum on Enforcement of Commercial Judgments for Money*, 2nd ed., 2021, https://sifocc.org/sifocc_documents/sifocc-memorandum-on-enforcement-2nd-with-international-working-group-commentary/.

Evolution of Law and Practice – Modern Accounts

American Law Institute, *Recognition and Enforcement of Foreign Judgments: Analysis and Proposed Federal Statute* (reporters: Andreas Lowenfeld and Linda Silberman), Philadelphia: American Law Institute, 2006.

Berman, *Global Legal Pluralism*, Cambridge: Cambridge University Press, 2012, Chap. 9.

Brilmayer, *Conflict of Laws*, New York: Aspen Law & Business, 2nd ed., 1995, Chap. 7.

Briggs, A., *Private International Law in English Courts*, Oxford: Oxford University Press, 2nd ed., 2023, Chap. 5.

–, "Recognition of Foreign Judgments: A Matter of Obligation" (2013), 129 *Law Quarterly Review* 87.

Chong, A., and M. Yip, *Singapore Private International Law*, Oxford: Oxford University Press, 2023, Chap. 5.

Collins, L. (Lord Collins of Mapesbury), and J. Harris (eds.),

Dicey, Morris & Collins – The Conflict of Laws, London: Sweet & Maxwell, 16th ed., 2022, Vol. 1, Chap. 14.

Cuniberti, "Le fondement de l'effet des jugements étrangers" (2018), 394 *Recueil des cours* 93.

–, "The Liberalization of the French Law of Foreign Judgments" (2007), 56 *ICLQ* 931.

Davies, M., A. Bell, P. L. G. Brereton and M. Douglas, *Nygh's Conflict of Laws in Australia*, Chatswood: LexisNexis Australia, 10th ed., 2019, Chap. 40.

Dickinson, A., "Foreign Submission" (2019), 135 *Law Quarterly Review* 294.

–, "Keeping Up Appearances: The Development of Adjudicatory Jurisdiction in the English Courts" (2016), 86 *British Yb Int L* 6.

–, "*Schibsby* v. *Westenholz* and the Recognition and Enforcement of Judgments in England" (2018), 134 *Law Quarterly Review* 426.

Folkhard, J., and I. Bergson, "*Godard* v. *Gray* and *Schibsby* v. *Westenholz*", Chap. 4, in W. Day and L. Merrett (eds.), *Landmark Cases in Private International Law*, Oxford: Hart Publishing, 2023.

George, J. P., "Facilitating Money Judgment Enforcement between Canada and the United States" (2020), 72 *Hastings LJ* 99.

Hook, M., and J. Wass, *The Conflict of Laws in New Zealand*, Wellington: LexisNexis NZ, 2020, Chap. 5.

Huang, J., "Developing Chinese Private International Law for Foreign Judgments: A Substitute or a Preliminary Step to Ratify the Two HCCH Conventions?" (2024), 57 *The International Lawyer* 101.

–, "Developing Chinese Private International Law for Transnational Civil and Commercial Litigation" (2023), 70 *Netherlands Int L Rev* 205.

Kutner, P., "Recognition and Enforcement of Foreign Judgments – The Common Law's Jurisdictional Requirements" (2019) 83 *RabelsZ* 1.

Mehren, A. T. von, "Recognition and Enforcement of Foreign Judgments – General Theory and the Role of Jurisdictional Requirements" (1980), 167 *Recueil des cours* 13.

Michaels, R., "Recognition and Enforcement of Judgments", in A. Peters and R. Wolfrum (eds.), *Max Planck Encyclopedia of Public International Law*, Oxford: Oxford University Press, 2008-), https://opil.ouplaw.com/home/mpil.

Mills, A., *The Confluence of Public and Private International Law*, Cambridge: Cambridge University Press, 2009, Chaps. 1, 2 and 5.

Monestier, T. J., "Whose Law of Personal Jurisdiction? The Choice of Law Problem in the Recognition of Foreign Judgments" (2016), 96 *Boston Univ L Rev* 1729.

Mortensen, R., R. Garnett and M. Keyes, *Private International Law in Australia*, Chatswood: LexisNexis Australia, 5th ed., 2023, [5.29]-[5.32].

Oppong, R. F., *Private International Law in Commonwealth Africa*, Cambridge: Cambridge University Press, 2013, Chap. 17.

Rutherglen, G., and J. Y. Stern, "Sovereignty, Territoriality and the Enforcement of Judgments", Chap. 1, in P. B. Stephen (ed.), *Foreign Court Judgments and the United States Legal System*, Leiden: Brill Nijhoff, 2014.

Sawaki, T., "Recognition and Enforcement of Foreign Judgments in Japan" (1989), 23 *International Lawyer* 29.

Yeo, T. M., "The Changing Global Landscape for Foreign Judgments", Yong Pung How Professorship of Law Lecture 2021, https://site.smu.edu.sg/sites/site.smu.edu.sg/files/smu_cebcla/YPH%20Lecture%202021%20Paper.pdf.

International Co-operation

Born, G., "The Hague Convention on Choice of Court Agreements: A Critical Assessment" (2021), 169 *U Penn L Rev* 2019.

Garcimartin, F., and G. Saumier, *Convention of 2 July 2019 on the Recognition and Enforcement of Foreign Judgments in Civil or Commercial Matters – Explanatory Report*, The Hague: HCCH, 2020, https://assets.hcch.net/docs/a1b0b0fc-95b1-4544-935b-b842534a120f.pdf.

Hartley, T., "Is the Hague Choice of Court Convention Really a Threat to Justice and Fair Play? A Reply to Gary Born", EAPIL, https://eapil.org/2021/06/30/is-the-2005-hague-choice-of-court-convention-really-a-threat-to-justice-and-fair-play-a-reply-to-gary-born/.

Hartley, T., and M. Dogauchi, *Convention of 20 June 2005 on Choice of Court Agreements – Explanatory Report, Proceedings of the Twentieth Session*, Vol. 3, pp. 784-863.

Jueptner, E., *A Hague Convention on Jurisdiction and Judgments, Why Did the Judgments Project (1992-2021) Fail?*, Cambridge: Intersentia, 2024.

Nadelmann, K. H., "Hamburg Model Act Respecting the

Recognition of Foreign Money Judgments" (1960), 9 *Am J Comp L* 518.
Silberman, L. "Comparative Jurisdiction in the International Context: Will the Proposed Hague Judgements Convention be Stalled?" (2002), 52 *De Paul L Rev* 319.
Teitz, L. E., "Another Hague Judgments Convention Bucking the Past to Provide for the Future" (2019), 29 *Duke Journal of Comparative and International Law* 491.
Weller, M., J. Ribeiro-Bidaoui, M. Brinkmann and N. Dethlof (eds.), *The HCCH 2019 Judgments Convention – Cornerstones, Prospects, Outlook*, Oxford: Hart, 2023.

Comity

Briggs, A., "The Principle of Comity in Private International Law" (2012), 354 *Recueil des cours* 65.
Endicott, T., "Comity among Authorities" (2015), 68 *Current Legal Problems* 1.
Getman-Pavlova, I., "The Concept of 'Comity' in Ulrik Huber's Conflict Doctrine", Higher School of Economics Research Paper WP BRP/LAW.2023, https://papers.ssrn.com/sol3/papers.cfm?abstract_id=2240233.
Nadelmann, K. H., "The Comity Doctrine: Introduction" (1966), 65 *Michigan L Rev* 1.
Paul, J. R., "Comity in International Law" (1991), 32 *Harvard Int L J* 1.
Schultz, T., and J. Mitchenson, "The History of Comity" (2019), 4 Jus Gentium – *Journal of Legal History* 383.
Watson, A., *Joseph Story and the Comity of Errors*, Athens: University of Georgia Press, 1992.
Yntema, H. E., "The Comity Doctrine" (1966), 65 *Michigan L Rev* 9.

Reciprocity

Anon., "Reciprocity and the Recognition of Foreign Judgments" (note) (1927), 36 *Yale LJ* 542.
Childs, L. B., "Shaky Foundations: Criticism of Reciprocity and the Distinction between Public and Private International Law" (2006), 38 *Journal of International Law and Politics* 221.
Coyle, J., "Rethinking Judgments Reciprocity" (2014), 92 *North Carolina Law Review* 1110.
Lenhoff, A., "Reciprocity and the Law of Foreign Judgments: A Historical-Critical Analysis" (1956), 3 *Louisiana L Rev* 465.
Martinek, M., "The Principle of Reciprocity in the

Recognition and Enforcement of Foreign Judgments – History, Presence and . . . No Future" (2017), *Journal of South African Law* 36.

Elbalti, B., "Reciprocity and the Recognition and Enforcement of Foreign Judgments: A Lot of Bark but Not Much Bite" (2017), 13 *J Priv Int L* 184.

Global Governance and Human Rights

Arendt, H., "The Rights of Man: What Are They?" (1949), 3 *Modern Review* 24.

Lauterpacht, H., "The Universal Declaration of Human Rights" (1948), 25 *British Yb Int L* 354.

Michaels, R., "The Right to Have Private Rights" (2024), 74 *Univ Toronto LJ* (supplement) 128.

Robertson, *Human Rights in the World*, Manchester: University of Manchester Press, 1972, Chaps. 2 and 3.

Natural Justice, Due Process and Fair Trial Rights

Dickinson, "*Abouloff* v. *Oppenheimer* Revisited", Chap. 9, in J. Harris and C. McLachlan, *Essays in International Litigation for Lord Collins*, Oxford: Oxford University Press, 2022.

Edelman, "Why Do We Have Rules of Procedural Fairness?", speech, 4 September 2015, https://www.fedcourt.gov.au/digital-law-library/judges-speeches/speeches-former-judges/justice-edelman/edelman-j-20150904.

Fawcett, J. J., M. Ní Shúilleabháin, and S. Shah, *Human Rights and Private International Law*, Oxford: Oxford University Press, 2016, Chaps. 5 and 7.

Kiestra, L. R., *The Impact of the European Convention on Human Rights on Private International Law*, The Hague: TMC Asser Press, 2014, Chaps. 7 and 8.

Kinsch, P., "Enforcement as a Fundamental Right" (2014), *Nederlands Internationaal Privaatrecht* 540.

Kotuby Jr, C. T., and L. A. Sobota, *General Principles of Law and International Due Process*, Oxford: Oxford University Press, 2017, Chap. 3.

Marshall, H. H., *Natural Justice*, London: Sweet & Maxwell, 1959, Chaps. 1-2 and 5.

Orth, J. V., *Due Process of Law – A Brief History*, Lawrence KS: Kansas University Press, 2003, Chaps. 1 and 2.

Other Reference Materials

Banu, R., "Private International Law's Ambivalent Humanism" (2024), 74 *University of Toronto LJ* (Supplement) 28.

Basedow, J., G. Rühl, F. Ferrari and P. De Miguel Asensio, *Encyclopedia of Private International Law*, Cheltenham: Edward Elgar, 2017.
–, Briggs, A., "Recognition and Enforcement of Judgments (common law)", Vol. 2, p. 1479 *et seq.*
–, Dornis, T., "Comity", Vol. 1, p. 382 *et seq.*
–, Domej, T., "Recognition and Enforcement of Judgments (Civil Law)", Vol. 2, p. 1471 *et seq.*
–, Dutta, A., "Reciprocity", Vol. 2, p. 1466 *et seq.*
–, Michaels, R., "Story, Joseph", Vol. 2, p. 1659 *et seq.*
–, "Wächter, Carl Georg von", Vol. 2, p. 1824 *et seq.*
–, Sonnentag, "Savigny, Friedrich Carl von", Vol. 2, p. 1609 *et seq.*
–, Wolde, M., "Huber, Ulrik", Vol. 1, p. 875 *et seq.*
–, "Voet, Paulus and Johannes", Vol. 2, p. 1820 *et seq.*
–, Chen, A. H. Y., "Mediation, Litigation and Justice", Chap. 11, in Daniel A. Bell and Hahm Chaibong (eds.), *Confucianism for the Modern World*, Cambridge: Cambridge University Press, 2003.
De Nova, R., "Historical and Comparative Introduction to Conflict of Laws" (1966), 118 *Recueil des cours* 435.
Jenks, C. W., "Mutual Aid in International Law", Chap. 6, in *Law in the World Community*, London: Longmans, 1967.
Kim, Y-O., and J.-K. Kim, *The Great Equal Society: Confucianism, China and the 21st Century*, Singapore: World Scientific Publishing, 2013, Chap. 1.
Knop, K., "Lorimer's Private Citizens of the World" (2016), 27 *Eur J Int L* 447.
Pagden, A., *The Englightenment and Why It Still Matters*, Oxford: Oxford University Press, 2015.

ABOUT THE AUTHOR

Biographical Note

Andrew Dickinson, born 1971 in Southport, United Kingdom. Educated at Dane Court Grammar School, Broadstairs.

Studied Law at St Edmund Hall, University of Oxford, BA Jurisprudence (1993); Bachelor of Civil Law (1994) (Vinerian Scholar).

Completed Legal Practice Course at the College of Law, Chester (1995). Qualified as a Solicitor, England and Wales (1997). Granted Higher Rights of Audience (2002).

Clifford Chance LLP (Solicitor, 1997-2003; Consultant Solicitor, 2003-2019). British Institute of International and Comparative Law (Visiting Fellow, 2003-2021; Honorary Senior Fellow, from 2021). University of Sydney (Visiting Professor 2010; Professor in Private International Law, 2011-2013). Max Planck Institute Luxembourg (External Scientific Fellow, 2013-2014). University of Oxford (Professor of Law, 2013-2023; Professor of the Conflict of Laws, from 2023). St Catherine's College, University of Oxford (Tutorial Fellow in Law, from 2013; Senior Tutor, from 2025). Notre Dame Law School (Global Distinguished Visiting Professor, 2024). New York University School of Law (Scholar in Residence, 2024).

One of the Specialist Editors of *Dicey, Morris & Collins – The Conflict of Laws*, Lord Collins of Mapesbury and Jonathan Harris KC (gen. eds.), 15th and 16th eds. Member, UK Ministry of Justice Steering Committee on Private International Law (North, then Mance Committee), from 2006. Joint Series Editor, OUP Private International Law Series, from 2017. Founding Member of the editorial board of the Journal of Private International Law. Associate Member, International Academy of Comparative Law.

Principal Publications

A. Books

The Rome II Regulation: The Law Applicable to Non-Contractual Obligations, Oxford: Oxford University Press, 2008.

State Immunity: Selected Materials and Commentary, Oxford:

Oxford University Press 2004, with Rae Lindsay and James P. Loonam.

B. Edited Works

Dicey + 100 Albert Venn Dicey: A Centennial Commemoration, Cambridge: Intersentia, 2024, with Timothy Endicott and Wolfgang Ernst.

Dicey, Morris and Collins – The Conflict of Laws, Lord Collins of Mapesbury and Jonathan Harris (gen. eds.), London: Sweet & Maxwell, 15th ed., 2012 and 16th ed., 2022, with responsibility for Chaps. 32-35 in 16th ed.

A Conflict of Laws Companion – Essays in Honour of Adrian Briggs, Oxford: Oxford University Press 2021, with Edwin Peel.

Commercial Issues in Private International Law, Oxford: Hart Publishing 2019, with Michael Douglas, Vivienne Bath and Mary Keyes.

The Brussels I Regulation Recast, Oxford: Oxford University Press 2015, with Eva Lein.

Australian Private International Law for the 21st Century: Facing Outwards, Oxford, Hart Publishing 2014, with Mary Keyes and Thomas John.

C. Journal Articles

"Beyond Comity" [2024], 20 *Journal of Private International Law* 586.

"Electronic Trade Documents and the Conflict of Laws in the United Kingdom" [2024], *Lloyd's Maritime and Commercial Law Quarterly* 55.

"Reframing Jurisdiction: A New Scheme?" (2022), 41 *Civil Justice Quarterly* 317, with Adrian Briggs.

"Realignment of the Planets – Brexit and European Private International Law" (2021), 41 *IPRax* 213.

"Foreign Submission" (2019), 135 *Law Quarterly Review* 294.

"Tough Assignments: The European Commission's Proposal on the Law Applicable to the Third-Party Effects of Assignments of Claims" (2018), 38 *IPRax* 337.

"*Schibsby* v. *Westenholz* and the Recognition and Enforcement of Judgments in England" (2018), 134 *Law Quarterly Review* 426.

"Acts of State and the Frontiers of Private (International) Law" (2018), 14 *Journal of Private International Law* 1.

"Close the Door on Your Way Out: Free Movement of Judgments in Civil Matters – A 'Brexit' Case Study" (2017), *Zeitschrift für Europäisches Privatrecht* 540.

T. Endicott and W. Ernst (eds.), *Dicey + 100 Albert Venn Dicey: A Centennial Commemoration*, Cambridge: Intersentia 2024.

"Future Landmarks: Scanning the Horizon", Chap. 19, in W. Day and L. Merrett (eds.), *Landmark Cases in Private International Law*, Oxford: Hart Publishing, 2023.

"*Abouloff* v. *Oppenheimer* Revisited", Chap. 9, in J. Harris and C. McLachlan (eds.), *Essays in International Litigation for Lord Collins*, Oxford: Oxford University Press, 2022.

"Taming Anti-Suit Injunctions", Chap. 4, in A. Dickinson and E. Peel (eds.), *A Conflict of Laws Companion – Essays in Honour of Adrian Briggs*, Oxford: Oxford University Press, 2021.

"United Kingdom", Chap. 51, in D. Girsberger, T. Kadner Graziano and J. Neels (eds.), *Choice of Law in International Commercial Contracts*, Oxford: Oxford University Press, 2021.

"Virtual Currencies and the Conflict of Laws", Chap. 5, in D. Fox and S. Green (eds.), *Private Law Implications of Crypto-Currencies*, Oxford: Oxford University Press, 2019.

"*In Absentia*: The Evolution and Reform of Australian Rules of Adjudicatory Jurisdiction", Chap. 2, in M. Douglas, V. Bath, M. Keyes and A. Dickinson (eds.), *Commercial Issues in Private International Law*, Oxford: Hart Publishing 2019.

"Rome II Regulation: Tort/Delict" and "United Kingdom", in J. Basedow, G. Rühl, F. Ferrari and P. De Miguel Ascesio (eds.), *Encyclopaedia of Private International Law*, Cheltenham: Edward Elgar, 2017.

Chaps. 1 (background and Introduction), 16 (transitional provisions) and 18 (final provisions), in A. Dickinson and E. Lein (eds.) *The Brussels I Regulation Recast*, Oxford: Oxford University Press, 2015.

"Article 15", in C. Tams and R. O'Keefe (eds.), *The United Nations Convention on Jurisdictional Immunities of States and Their Property*, Oxford: Oxford University Press, 2013.

"Free Movement of Judgments in the EU: Knock Down the Walls But Mind the Ceiling", in E. Lein (ed.), *The Brussels I Proposal Uncovered*, London: British Institute of International and Comparative Law, 2012.

"Legal Certainty – Too Much of a Good Thing?", in P. de Vareilles-Sommières (ed.), *Forum Shopping in the European Judicial Area*, Oxford: Hart Publishing, 2007.

LIST OF PRINCIPAL ABBREVIATIONS

Grotius, *Prize*	Hugo Grotius, *De Iure Praedae*, manuscript completed in 1606 and published posthumously (H. G. Hamaker (ed.), Den Haag: Martinus Nijhoff 1868), trans. Gwladys L. Williams, *Commentary on the Law of Prize and Booty*, Oxford: Clarendon Press, 1950 and reproduced in the edition edited by Martine Julia van Ittersum for the *Natural Law and Enlightenment Classics* series, Indianapolis: Liberty Fund, 1998, https://oll.libertyfund.org/title/ittersum-commentary-on-the-law-of-prize-and-booty.
Grotius, *War and Peace*	Hugo Grotius, *De Iure Bellis Ac Pacis Libri Tres*, Paris: Apud Nicholas Buon, 1625, trans. anon., *The Rights of War and Peace*, London: W. Innys, 1738, using the 1724 French edition by Jean Barbeyrac, reproduced in the edition edited by Richard Tuck for the *Natural Law and Enlightenment Classics* series, Indianapolis: Liberty Fund, 2005, https://oll.libertyfund.org/title/grotius-the-rights-of-war-and-peace-2005-ed-3-vols.
Hague Choice of Court Convention	Convention on Choice of Court Agreements, The Hague, 30 June 2005, https://www.hcch.net/en/instruments/conventions/full-text/?cid=98.
Hague Judgments Convention	Convention on the Recognition and Enforcement of Foreign Judgments in Civil or Commercial Matters, The Hague, 2 July 2019, https://www.hcch.net/en/instruments/conventions/full-text/?cid=137.

Hobbes, *Citizen*	Thomas Hobbes, *Elementa Philosophica de Cive*, Amsterdam: Elzevir, 1647, trans. and edited Richard Tuck and Michael Silverthorne, *On the Citizen*, Cambridge: Cambridge University Press, 1998.
Hobbes, *Leviathan*	Thomas Hobbes, *Leviathan*, London: Andrew Crooke at the Green Dragon in St Paul's Churchyard, 1651, in the edition edited by Richard Tuck, Cambridge: Cambridge University Press, 1991.
Huber, *De Conflictu Legum*	*Praelectionum Juris Romani et Hodierni, Pars II, Quae est ad Libros undeviginti priores Pandectarum,* Franeker: Apud Henricum Amama and Zachariam Taedema, 1689, Book 1, Title 3, Appendix (entitled *"De Conflictu Legum Diversarum in Diversiis Imperiis"*), trans. D. J. Llewelyn Davies, "The Influence of Huber's *De conflictu legum* on English Private International Law" (1937), 18 *British Yb Int L* 49, 64-78 using the Latin text of the later 1707 edition, Leipzig: Johann Friedrich Gleditsch.
Johannes Voet, *Commentarius*	Johannes Voet, *Commentarius ad Pandectas*, Leiden: Johannes Verbessel, Vol. 1, 1698, trans. Percival Gane, *The Selective Voet, Being the Commentary on the Pandects (Paris edition of 1829)*, Durban: Butterworth & Co (Africa) Ltd., Vol. 1, 1955.
Locke, *Two Treatises*	John Locke, *Two Treatises of Government*, London: printed for Awnsham and John Churchill, revised ed. 1698, in the edition edited by Peter Laslett, Cambridge: Cambridge University Press, 1988.
Paulus Voet, *De Statutis*	Paulus Voet, *De Statutis Eorumque Concursu*, Amsterdam: Johannes van Waesberge, 1661, trans. A. B. (Basil)

Edwards and D. M. (David) Kriel, "The Selective Paulus Voet", reproduced in (2007), 13 *Fundamina: A Journal of Legal History* 1, 55-309, https://journals.co.za/toc/funda/13/1.

Pufendorf, *Nature and Nations* — Samuel Pufendorf, *De Jure Naturae et Gentium, Libro Octo*, Lund: Adam Junghans, 1672, in the revised edition, Amsterdam: Apud Andeream de Hoogenhuysen, 1688, trans. Charles Henry Oldfather and William Abbott Oldfather, *Of the Law of Nature and Nations*, Vol. 17 in James Brown Scott (ed.), *The Classics of International Law*, Oxford: Clarendon Press, 1934.

Pufendorff, *Whole Duty* — Samuel Pufendorf, *De Officio Hominis et Civis Juxta Legem Naturalem Libri Duo*, Lund: Adam Junghans, 1673, trans. Andrew Tooke, *The Whole Duty of Man according to the Law of Nature*, London: R. Gosling, J. Pemberton and B. Motte, 5th ed., 1735, reproduced in the edition edited by Ian Hunter and David Saunders for the *Natural Law and Enlightenment Classics* series (Indianapolis: Liberty Fund, 2002), https://oll.libertyfund.org/title/tooke-the-whole-duty-of-man-according-to-the-law-of-nature-1673-2003.

Savigny, *System* — Friedrich Carl von Savigny, *System des heutigen Römischen Rechts*, Berlin: Veit, 1840-1849 [Vol. 1, 1840; Vol. 5, 1841; Vol.6, 1847 and Vol. 8, 1849], https://www.deutschestextarchiv.de/book/show/savigny_system08_1849.

Vol. 1 trans. in part William Holloway, *System of the Modern Roman Law*, Madras: J. Higginbotham, 1867. Vol. 8 trans. William Guthrie, *Private International Law, A Treatise on the Conflict of Laws and the Limits of Their Operation in respect of Place and Time*, Edinburgh: T & T Clark, 1869.

Story, *Commentaries* (1834)	Joseph Story, *Commentaries on the Commentaries Conflict of Laws, Foreign and Domestic*, Boston: Hilliard, Gray and Co, 1834.
Story, *Commentaries* (1841)	*Commentaries on the Conflict of Laws, Foreign and Domestic*, Boston: Charles C. Little and James Brown, 2nd ed., 1841.
Story, *Commentaries* (1846)	*Commentaries on the Conflict of Laws, Foreign and Domestic*, Boston: Charles C. Little and James Brown, 3rd ed., 1846.
Vattel, *Nations*	Emer de Vattel, *Le droit des gens*, London, 1758, in the posthumous, revised edition of 1773, Neuchâtel: La Société Typographique, trans. anon., *The Law of Nations*, London: G. G. and J. Robinson, 1797, reproduced in the edition edited by Béla Kapossi and Richard Whatmore for the *Natural Law and Enlightenment Classics* series, Indianapolis: Liberty Fund, 2008, https://oll.libertyfund.org/title/whatmore-the-law-of-nations-lf-ed.
Wolff, *Nations*	Christian Wolff, *Jus Gentium Methodo Scientifica Pertrachtatum*, Halle, 1749 in the revised edition, Frankfurt: Aere Societatis Venetae, 1764 trans. Joseph H. Drake, *The Law of Nations Treated according to the Scientific Method*, Vol. 13 in James Brown Scott (ed.), *The Classics of International Law*, Oxford: Clarendon Press, 1934, reproduced with a revised translation in the edition edited by Thomas Ahnert for the *Natural Law and Enlightenment Classics* series, Indianapolis: Liberty Fund, 2017.

**PUBLICATIONS
OF THE HAGUE ACADEMY
OF INTERNATIONAL LAW**

COLLECTED COURSES

Since 1923 the top names in international law have taught at The Hague Academy of International Law. All the volumes of the *Collected Courses* which have been published since 1923 are available, as, since the very first volume, they are reprinted regularly in their original format.
Since 2008, certain courses have been the subject of a pocketbook edition.
In addition, the total collection now exists in electronic form. All works already published have been put "on line" and can be consulted under one of the proposed subscription methods, which offer a range of tariffs and possibilities.

WORKSHOPS

The Academy publishes the discussions from the Workshops which it organizes. The latest title of the Workshops already published is as follows: *Topicality of the 1907 Hague Conference, the Second Peace Conference* (2007).

CENTRE FOR STUDIES AND RESEARCH

The scientific works of the Centre for Studies and Research in International Law and International Relations of The Hague Academy of International Law, the subjects of which are chosen by the Curatorium of the Academy, have been published, since the Centre's 1985 session, in a publication in which the Directors of Studies reported on the state of research of the Centre under their direction. This series has been discontinued and the title of the latest booklet published is as follows: *Rules and Institutions of International Humanitarian Law Put to the Test of Recent Armed Conflicts.* Nevertheless, when the work of the Centre has been of particular interest and originality, the reports of the Directors of Studies together with the articles by the researchers form the subject of a collection published in the series The Law Books of the Academy.

Requests for information, catalogues and orders for publications must be addressed to

MARTINUS NIJHOFF PUBLISHERS

P.O. Box 9000, 2300 PA Leiden The Netherlands **http://www.brill.nl**

POCKETBOOKS OF THE ACADEMY

(By chronological order of publication)

1
Gaillard, E.: Aspects philosophiques du droit de l'arbitrage international, 2008, 252 pages.
(ISBN 978-90-04-17148-0)

2
Schrijver, N.: The Evolution of Sustainable Development in International Law: Inception, Meaning and Status, 2008, 276 pages. (ISBN 978-90-04-17407-8)

3
Moura Vicente, D.: La propriété intellectuelle en droit international privé, 2009, 516 pages.
(ISBN 978-90-04-17907-3)

4
Decaux, E.: Les formes contemporaines de l'esclavage, 2009, 272 pages. (ISBN 978-90-04-17908-0)

5
McLachlan, C.: Lis Pendens in International Litigation, 2009, 492 pages.
(ISBN 978-90-04-17909-7)

6
Carbone, S. M.: Conflits de lois en droit maritime, 2010, 312 pages. (ISBN 978-90-04-18688-0)

7
Boele-Woelki, K.: Unifying and Harmonizing Substantive Law and the Role of Conflict of Laws, 2010, 288 pages.
(ISBN 978-90-04-18683-5)

8
Onuma, Y.: A Transcivilizational Perspective in International Law, 2010, 492 pages.
(ISBN 978-90-04-18689-7)

9
Bucher, A.: La dimension sociale du droit international privé. Cours général, 2011, 552 pages.
(ISBN 978-90-04-20917-6)

10

Thürer, D. : International Humanitarian Law : Theory, Practice, Context, 2011, 504 pages. (ISBN 978-90-04-17910-3)

11

Alvarez, J. E. : The Public International Law Regime Governing International Investment, 2011, 504 pages. (ISBN 978-90-04-18682-8)

12

Wang, G. : Radiating Impact of WTO on Its Members' Legal System : The Chinese Perspective, 2011, 384 pages. (ISBN 978-90-04-21854-3)

13

Bogdan, M. : Private International Law as Component of the Law of the Forum, 2012, 360 pages. (ISBN 978-90-04-22634-0)

14

Davey, W. J. : Non-discrimination in the World Trade Organization : The Rules and Exceptions, 2012, 360 pages. (ISBN 978-90-04-23314-0)

15

Xue Hanqin : Chinese Contemporary Perspectives on International Law — History, Culture and International Law, 2012, 288 pages. (ISBN 978-90-04-23613-4)

16

Reisman, W. M. : The Quest for World Order and Human Dignity in the Twenty-first Century : Constitutive Process and Individual Commitment. General Course on Public International Law, 2012, 504 pages. (ISBN 978-90-04-23615-8)

17

Dugard, J. : The Secession of States and Their Recognition in the Wake of Kosovo, 2013, 312 pages. (ISBN 978-90-04-25748-1)

18

Gannagé, L. : Les méthodes du droit international privé à l'épreuve des conflits de cultures, 2013, 372 pages. (ISBN 978-90-04-25750-4)

19

Kohler, Ch. : L'autonomie de la volonté en droit international privé : un principe universel entre libéralisme et étatisme, 2013, 288 pages.

(ISBN 978-90-04-25752-8)

20

Kreindler, R. : Competence-Competence in the Face of Illegality in Contracts and Arbitration Agreements, 2013, 504 pages.

(ISBN 978-90-04-25754-2)

21

Crawford, J. : Chance, Order, Change : The Course of International Law. General Course on Public International Law, 2014, 540 pages.

(ISBN 978-90-04-26808-1)

22

Brand, R. A. : Transaction Planning Using Rules on Jurisdiction and the Recognition and Enforcement of Judgments, 2014, 360 pages.

(ISBN 978-90-04-26810-4)

23

Kolb, R. : L'article 103 de la Charte des Nations Unies, 2014, 416 pages.

(ISBN 978-90-04-27836-3)

24

Benvenisti, E. : The Law of Global Governance, 2014, 336 pages. (ISBN 978-90-04-27911-7)

25

Yusuf, A. A. : Pan-Africanism and International Law, 2014, 288 pages.

(ISBN 978-90-04-28504-0)

26

Kono, T. : Efficiency in Private International Law, 2014, 216 pages.

(ISBN 978-90-04-28506-4)

27

Cachard, O., Le transport international aérien de passagers, 2015, 292 pages. (ISBN 978-90-04-29773-9)

28
Corten, O. : La rébellion et le droit international, 2015, 376 pages.
(ISBN 978-90-04-29775-3)

29
Frigo, M., Circulation des biens culturels, détermination de la loi applicable et méthodes de règlement des litiges, 2016, 552 pages.
(ISBN 978-90-04-32129-8)

30
Bermann, G. A., International Arbitration and Private International Law, 2017, 648 pages.
(ISBN 978-90-04-34825-7)

31
Bennouna, M., Le droit international entre la lettre et l'esprit, 2017, 304 pages.
(ISBN 978-90-04-34846-2)

32
Murphy, S., International Law relating to Islands, 376 pages.
(ISBN 978-90-04-36154-6)

33
Hess, B., The Private-Public Law Divide in International Dispute Resolution, 328 pages.
(ISBN 978-90-04-38490-3)

34
Rau, A. : The Allocation of Power between Arbitral Tribunals and State Courts, 2018, 608 pages.
(ISBN 978-90-04-38891-8)

35
Muir Watt, H. : Discours sur les méthodes du droit international privé (des formes juridiques de l'inter-altérité, 2019, 608 pages.
(ISBN 978-90-04-39558-9)

36
Nolte, G. : Treaties and Their Practice – Symptoms of Their Rise or Decline, 2018, 288 pages.
(ISBN 978-90-04-39456-8)

37

Cuniberti, G. : Le fondement de l'effet des jugements étrangers, 2019, 288 pages.

(ISBN 978-90-04-41180-7)

38

D'Avout, L. : L'entreprise et les conflits internationaux de lois, 875 pages.

(ISBN 978-90-04-41668-0)

39

Brown Weiss, E. : Establishing Norms in a Kaleidoscopic World, 528 pages.

(ISBN 978-90-04-42200-1)

40

Brunnée, J. : Procedure and Substance in International Environmental Law, 2020, 240 pages.

(ISBN 978-90-04-44437-9)

41

Rajamani, L. : Innovation and Experimentation in the International Climate Change Regime, 2020, 336 pages.

(ISBN 978-90-04-44439-3)

42

Kessedjian, C. : Le tiers impartial et indépendant en droit international, juge, arbitre, médiateur, conciliateur, 2020, 832 pages.

(ISBN 978-90-04-44880-3)

43

Maljean-Dubois, S. : Le droit international de la biodiversité, 2021, 590 pages.

(ISBN 978-90-04-46287-8)

44

Dasser, F. : "Soft Law" in International Commercial Arbitration, 2021, 300 pages.

(ISBN 978-90-04-46289-2)

45

Peters, A. : Animals in International Law, 2021, 641 pages.

(ISBN 978-90-04-46624-1)

46

Besson, S.: La *due diligence* en droit international, 2021, 363 pages.

(ISBN 978-90-04-46626-5)

47

Ferrari, F.: Forum Shopping Despite Unification of Law, 2021, 446 pages.

(ISBN 978-90-04-50291-8)

48

Wolfrum, R.: Solidarity and Community Interests: Driving Forces for the Interpretation and Development of International Law, 2021, 663 pages.

(ISBN 978-90-04-50832-3)

49

Kolb, R.: Le droit international comme corps de « droit privé » et de « droit public », 2022, 967 pages.

(ISBN 978-90-04-51836-0)

50

Tladi, D.: The Extraterritorial Use of Force against Non-State Actors, 2022, 193 pages.

(ISBN 978-90-04-52147-6)

51

Schabas, W. A.: Relationships between International Criminal Law and Other Branches of International Law, 2022, 272 pages.

(ISBN 978-90-04-52149-0)

52

Bollée, S.: Les pouvoirs inhérents des arbitres internationaux, 2023, 306 pages.

(ISBN 978-90-04-67848-4)

53

Laghmani, S.: Islam et droit international, 2023, 168 pages.

(ISBN 978-90-04-67850-7)

54

Kovács, P.: L’indidividu et sa position devant la Cour pénale internationale, 528 pages.

(ISBN 978-90-04-69428-6)

55

Moollan, S.: Parallel Proceedings in International Arbitration. Theoretical Analysis and the Search for Practical Solutions, 134 pages.
(ISBN 978-90-04-69430-9)

56

Stephan, P. B.: Applying Municipal Law in International Disputes, 320 pages.
(ISBN 978-90-04-69609-9)

57

Lim, C. L.: The Aims and Methods of Postcolonial International Law, 288 pages.
(ISBN 978-90-04-69615-0)

58

Corten, O.: Le champ juridique international, 528 pages.
(ISBN 978-90-04-69613-6)

59

Blokker, N.: Legal Facets of the Practice of International Organizations, 368 pages.
(ISBN 978-90-04-69611-2)

60

Gómez Robledo, J. M.: Le droit international du désarmement : entre idéalisme et réalisme, 160 pages.
(ISBN 978-90-04-73561-3)

61

D'Avout, L.: La cohérence mondiale du droit, 1032 pages.
(ISBN 978-90-04-73567-5)

62

Sicilianos, L.-A.: La dimension humaine du droit international, 1054 pages.
(ISBN 978-90-04-73565-1)

63

Reinisch, A.: The Settlement of Disputes Involving International Organizations, 404 pages.
(ISBN 978-90-04-73563-7)

64

Tigroudja, H.: Conflits armés et droit international des droits de l'homme, 422 pages.

(ISBN 978-90-04-73569-9)

65

McLachlan, C.: On the Interface between Public and Private International Law, 403 pages.

(ISBN 978-90-04-73571-2)

66

Dickinson, A.: Natural Justice in Recognition and Enforcement of Foreign Judgments, 346 pages.

HORS COLLECTION

SPECIAL EDITIONS

1998 Dupuy, R.-J. (dir. publ./ed.).
Manuel sur les organisations internationales/A Handbook on International Organizations.
(714 pages)
(ISBN 978-90-247-3658-4)
2e édition publiée en 2008,
(1008 pages)
(ISBN 978-90-411-1119-7)

1991 Dupuy, R.-J., and D. Vignes (eds.).
A Handbook on the New Law of the Sea.
(2 volumes)
(Volume 1, 900 pages, ISBN 978-0-7923-0924-3)
(Volume 2, 882 pages, ISBN 978-0-7923-1063-1)

2012 Hommage du Curatorium à son Président/Tribute of the Curatorium to its President.
Le 90e anniversaire de Boutros Boutros-Ghali/The 90th Birthday of Boutros Boutros-Ghali.
(288 pages)
(ISBN 978-90-04-24618-8)

2015 Crawford, J.
Hasard, ordre et changement: le cours du droit international.
(448 pages)
(Broché, ISBN 978-90-04-29921-4)
(Relié, ISBN 978-90-04-29922-1)

2017 Yusuf, A. A.
Panafricanisme et droit international.
(219 pages)
(Broché, ISBN 978-90-04-34138-8)

2018 Bennouna, M.
International Law: Between the Letter and the Spirit.
(240 pages)
(Broché, ISBN 978-90-04-40143-3)

2022 Reisman, W. M.
The Quest for World Order and Human Dignity in the Twenty-First Century. Constitutive Process and Individual Commitment.
(352 pages)
(Broché, ISBN 978-90-04-52898-7)

2022 Nascimbene, B.
Nationality Law and the Law of Regional Integration Organisation. Towards New Residence Status?
(216 pages)
(Broché, ISBN 978-90-04-53636-4)

2023 Besson, S.
Due diligence in International Law
(256 pages)
(Broché, ISBN 978-90-04-53865-8)

2024 Casella, P. B.
International Law, History and Culture
(592 pages)
(Broché, ISBN 978-90-04-69450-7)

RECUEIL DES COURS

COLLECTED COURSES

Tome/Volume 400 (2018)

Chedly, L. : L'efficacité de l'arbitrage commercial international, 9-624.

(ISBN 978-90-04-42388-6)

Tome/Volume 401 (2019)

Wood, D. P. : Extraterritorial Enforcement of Regulatory Laws, 9-126.

Nishitani, Y. : Identité culturelle en droit international privé de la famille, 127-450.

(ISBN 978-90-04-42389-3)

Tome/Volume 402 (2019)

Kinsch, P. : Le rôle du politique en droit international privé. Cours général de droit international privé, 9-384.

Dasser, F. : "Soft Law" in International Commercial Arbitration, 385-596.

(ISBN 978-90-04-42392-3)

Tome/Volume 403 (2019)

Daudet, Y. : 1919-2019, le flux du multilatéralisme, 9-48.

Kessedjian, C. : Le tiers impartial et indépendant en droit international, juge, arbitre, médiateur, conciliateur, 49-643.

(ISBN 978-90-04-42468-5)

Tome/Volume 404 (2019)

Rajamani, L. : Innovation and Experimentation in the International Climate Change Regime, 9-234.

Sorel, J.-M. : Quelle normativité pour le droit des relations monétaires et financières internationales ?, 235-403.

(ISBN 978-90-04-43142-3)

Tome/Volume 405 (2019)

Paulsson, J.: Issues arising from Findings of Denial of Justice, 9-74.

Brunnée, J.: Procedure and Substance in International Environmental Law, 75-240. (ISBN 978-90-04-43300-7)

Tome/Volume 406 (2019)

Bundy, R.: The Practice of International Law, Inaugural Lecture, 9-26.

Gama, L.: Les principes d'UNIDROIT et la loi régissant les contrats de commerce, 27-343.

(ISBN 978-90-04-43611-4)

Tome/Volume 407 (2020)

Wouters, J.: Le statut juridique des standards publics et privés dans les relations économiques internationales, 9-122.

Maljean-Dubois, S.: Le droit international de la biodiversité, 123-538. (ISBN 978-90-04-43643-5)

Tome/Volume 408 (2020)

Cançado Trindade, A. A.: Reflections on the Realization of Justice in the Era of Contemporary International Tribunals, 9-88.

González Beilfuss, C.: Party Autonomy in International Family Law, 89-361.

(ISBN 978-90-04-44504-8)

Tome/Volume 409 (2020)

Shany, Y.: The Extraterritorial Application of International Human Rights Law, 9-152.

Besson, S.: La *due diligence* en droit international, 153-398.

(ISBN 978-90-04-44505-5)

Tome/Volume 410 (2020)

Koh, H. H.: American Schools of International Law, 9-93.

Peters, A.: Animals in International Law, 95-544.

(ISBN 978-90-04-44897-1)

Tome/Volume 411 (2020)

Cahin, G.: Reconstrution et construction de l'Etat en droit international, 9-573.

(ISBN 978-90-04-44898-8)

Tome/Volume 412 (2020)

Momtaz, D.: La hiérarchisation de l'ordre juridique international. Cours général de droit international public, 9-252.

Grammaticaki-Alexiou, A.: Best Interests of the Child in Private International Law, 253-434.

(ISBN 978-90-04-44899-5)

Tome/Volume 413 (2021)

Ferrari, F.: Forum Shopping Despite Unification of Law, 9-290.

(ISBN 978-90-04-46100-0)

Tome/Volume 414 (2021)

Pellet, A.: Le droit international à la lumière de la pratique: l'introuvable théorie de la réalité. Cours général de droit international public, 9-547.

(ISBN 978-90-04-46547-3)

Tome/Volume 415 (2021)

Trooboff, P. D.: Globalization, Personal Jurisdiction and the Internet. Responding to the Challenge of adapting settled Principles and Precedents. General Course on Private International Law, 9-321.

(ISBN 978-90-04-46730-9)

Tome/Volume 416 (2021)

Wolfrum, R.: Solidarity and Community Interests: Driving Forces for the Interpre-tation and Development of International Law. General Course on Public International Law, 9-479.

(ISBN 978-90-04-46827-6)

Tome/Volume 417 (2021)

D'Argent, P.: Les obligations internationales, 9-210.

Schabas, W. A.: Relationships Between International Criminal Law and Other Branches of International Law, 211-392.

(ISBN 978-90-04-47239-6)

Tome/Volume 418 (2021)

Bollée, S.: Les pouvoirs inhérents des arbitres internationaux, 9-224.

Tladi, D.: The Extraterritorial Use of Force against Non-State Actors, 225-360.

(ISBN 978-90-04-50380-9)

Tome/Volume 419 (2021)

Kolb, R.: Le droit international comme corps de « droit privé » et de « droit public ». Cours général de droit international public, 9-668.

(ISBN 978-90-04-50381-6)

Tome/Volume 420 (2021)

Perrakis, S.: La protection internationale au profit des personnes vulnérables en droit international des droits de l'homme, 9-497.

(ISBN 978-90-04-50382-3)

Tome/Volume 421 (2021)

Estrella Faria, J. A.: La protection des biens culturels d'intérêt religieux en droit international public et en droit international privé, 9-333.

(ISBN 978-90-04-50829-3)

Tome/Volume 422 (2021)

Karayanni, M.: The Private International Law of Class Actions: A Functional approach, 9-248.

Mahmoudi, S.: Self-Defence and "Unwilling or Unable" States, 249-399.

(ISBN 978-90-04-50830-9)

Tome/Volume 423 (2022)

Kinnear, M.: The Growth, Challenges and Future Prospects for Investment Dispute Settlement, 9-36.

Weller, M.: "Mutual Trust": A Suitable Foundation for Private International Law in Regional Integration Communities and Beyond?, 37-378.

(ISBN 978-90-04-51411-9)

Tome/Volume 424 (2022)

Asada, M.: International Law of Nuclear Non-proliferation and Disarmament, 9-726.

(ISBN 978-90-04-51769-1)

Tome/Volume 425 (2022)

Metou, B. M.: Le contrôle international des dérogations aux droits de l'homme, 9-294.

Silva Romero, E.: Legal Fictions in the Language of International Arbitration, 295-423.

(ISBN 978-90-04-51770-7)

Tome/Volume 426 (2022)

Kuijper, P. J.: Delegation and International Organizations, 9-240.

McCaffrey, S. C.: The Evolution of the Law of International Watercourses, 241-384.

(ISBN 978-90-04-51771-4)

Tome/Volume 427 (2022)

Kaufmann-Kohler, G.: Indépendance et impartialité du juge et de l'arbitre dans le règlement des différends entre investisseurs et Etats (leçon inaugurale), 9-50.

Boyle, A.: International Lawmaking in an Environmental Context, 51-108.

Weller, M.-P.: La méthode tripartite du droit international privé: désignation, reconnaissance, considération, 109-210.

Mourre, A.: La légitimité de l'arbitrage, 211-288.

(ISBN 978-90-04-52770-6)

Tome/Volume 428 (2023)

Laghmani, S.: Islam et droit international, 9-128.

Oyarzábal, M. J. A.: The Influence of Public International Law upon Private International Law in History and Theory and in the Formation and Application of the Law, 129-525.

(ISBN 978-90-04-54440-6)

Tome/Volume 429 (2023)

Moreno Rodríguez, J. A.: Private (And Public) International Law In Investment Arbitration, 9-702.

(ISBN 978-90-04-54462-8)

Tome/Volume 430 (2023)

Casella, P. B.: Droit international, histoire et culture, 9-610.

(ISBN 978-90-04-54463-5)

Tome/Volume 431 (2023)

Yeo, T. M.: Common Law, Equity and Statute. The Effect of Juridical Sources on Choice-of-Law Methodology, 9-88.

Frigessi di Rattalma, M.: New Trends in Private International Law of Insurance Contracts, 89-200.

Roosevelt III, K.: The Third Restatement of Conflict of Laws, 201-284.

Sands, P.: Colonialism: A Short History of International Law in Five Acts, 285-410.

(ISBN 978-90-04-54464-2)

Tome/Volume 432 (2023)

Ruiz Fabri, H.: La justice procédurale en droit international, 9-44.

Shaw, M.: A House of Many Rooms: The Rise, Fall and Rise Again of Territorial Sovereignty?, 45-78.

Kovács, P.: L'individu et sa position devant la Cour pénale internationale, 79-421.

(ISBN 978-90-04-54465-9)

Tome/Volume 433 (2023)

(ISBN 978-90-04-54469-7)

Tome/Volume 434 (2023)

(ISBN 978-90-04-69182-7)

Tome/Volume 435 (2023)

(ISBN 978-90-04-69432-3)

Tome/Volume 436 (2024)

 (ISBN 978-90-04-69912-0)

Tome/Volume 437 (2024)

(ISBN 978-90-04-69913-7)

Tome/Volume 438 (2024)

Lehmann, M.: Crypto-économie et droit international, 9-384.

(ISBN 978-90-04-70670-5)

Tome/Volume 439 (2024)

Hey, E.: Making Sense of Soft Law, 9-114.

Galindo, G. R. B.: The Inviolabilities of the Diplomatic Mission, 115-288.

Gomez-Robledo, J. M.: Le droit international du désarmement: entre idéalisme et réalisme, 289-3974.

(ISBN 978-90-04-70671-2)

Tome/Volume 440 (2024)

Sicilianos, L.-A.: La dimension humaine du droit international, Cours général de droit international public, 9-768.

(ISBN 978-90-04-72244-6)

Tome/Volume 441 (2024)

Stanivuković, M.: Property Rights of Individuals after Changes of Territorial Sovereignty, 9-351.

Reyes, A.: The Use of Domestic Law to regulate the Conduct of Individuals, Corporations and Governments Extraterritorially, 353-495.

(ISBN 978-90-04-72245-3)

Tome/Volume 442 (2024)

Kamto, M.: Le droit international et la décolonisation inachevée, 9-78.

Reinisch, A.: The Settlement of Disputes Involving International Organizations, 79-342.

(ISBN 978-90-04-72246-0)

Tome/Volume 443 (2024)

D'Avout, L.: La cohérence mondiale du droit. Cours général de droit international privé, 9-724.

(ISBN 978-90-04-72247-7)

Printed in October 2025
by Triangle Bleu,
59600 Maubeuge (France)

Setting : R. Mirland,
59870 Warlaing (France)

66/10-25.